WESTMAR COLLEGE LIBRARY

The Anthem in England and America

The Anthem in England and America

ELWYN A. WIENANDT and ROBERT H. YOUNG

The Free Press, New York · Collier-Macmillan Limited, London

M783.4
W647

ML
3265
.W53

Copyright ©1970 by The Free Press
A Division of The Macmillan Company
Printed in the United States of America
All rights reserved. No part of this book may be
reproduced or transmitted in any form or by any means,
electronic or mechanical, including photocopying, recording,
or by any information storage and retrieval system,
without permission in writing from the Publisher.
The Free Press
A Division of The Macmillan Company
866 Third Avenue, New York, N. Y. 10022
Collier-Macmillan Canada Ltd., Toronto, Canada
Library of Congress Catalog Card Number: 76-76225

printing number
1 2 3 4 5 6 7 8 9 10

83804

For Patricia and Betty

Preface

Serious research in church music has, for the most part, been confined to
scholars who have made significant studies of certain small areas, have surveyed the entire field in a single study, or have attempted to write from a national or denominational viewpoint. In the case of anthems, such studies have been too much limited by the veneration of English cathedral style, a fact that has left much valuable material untouched. We have brought together here the various features of anthem history in a continuous narrative, using the term "anthem" in its broad sense of religious music that is sung chorally and, except for some of its American beginnings, in connection with a regular church service. That much of this literature has lately found its way into educational choral groups is naturally significant as well.

It has been our purpose to show that the English had an important field of choral activity outside the usually discussed cathedral tradition, and that it is from this parochial and Nonconformist practice that the American anthem first derived its patterns. Much music hitherto unmentioned in studies of this kind has been discussed here. Practically none of it appears in modern editions. Since an overview of the entire period of the anthem's history is impossible because of the absence of complete musical examples in chronological order, the authors have prepared two volumes of representative music that can be used with this text, either to illustrate the anthem style of each country and period as it is reached in class work, or to use as performance material with existing choral groups of educational institutions and churches. The advantages of examining complete compositions as well as the examples contained in the text can be magnified if the works are performed either in or out of the classroom. The volumes, *Fifteen Anthems from England* and *Fifteen Anthems from America*, are published by J. Fischer & Bro. Church musicians will find them interesting for service music since they provide materials not presently published elsewhere.

No book of this nature can be better than is permitted by the availability of the music to be studied. It has been our good fortune to have access to the music libraries of Baylor University and Southwestern Baptist Theological Seminary, the combination of which provides one of America's richest collections of English and American printed church music from before the twentieth century. In addition, the Readex Microprints of early American materials produced by the American Antiquarian Society (comprising the Evans bibliography up to 1800 and the Shaw-Shoemaker bibliography, 1801-1819) in the Baylor University Library has made possible the study of American collections and tune-books previously unavailable. The generosity of music publishers in England and America who supplied lists and samples of their choral materials was of substantial assistance in our study.

Specifically, we are happy to express our thanks to the Graduate Research Committee of Baylor University for a grant that assisted us in our research. Among the numerous librarians who gave freely of time and assistance are Bessie Hess Smith and Jean F. Tolbert of Baylor University, and Phillip W. Sims and Sara Thompson of Southwestern Baptist Theological Seminary. Keith MacMillan, Executive Secretary of the Canadian Music Centre, deserves our special thanks for his assistance.

E. A. W.
R. H. Y.

Acknowledgments

Materials that are owned or copyrighted by various organizations and business firms have been of great importance in the preparation of this book. Our grateful acknowledgment is made to those listed below. Their contributions are fully identified at those points in the book where they are put to use.

Abingdon Press, Nashville; Augsburg Publishing House, Minneapolis; Baylor University Library, Waco, Texas; The Bettmann Archive, New York; Boston Music Co., Boston; Canadian Music Centre, Toronto; The Cathedral of St. John the Divine, New York; The Clarendon Press, Oxford; Concordia Publishing House, St. Louis; J. Curwen & Sons Ltd., London; Carl Fischer, Inc., New York; J. Fischer & Bro., Glen Rock, N. J.; H. T. FitzSimons Company, Inc., Chicago; Galaxy Music Corporation, New York; The H. W. Gray Company, New York; Hollywood First Presbyterian Church, Hollywood, California; Lorenz Publishing Company, Dayton, Ohio; Novello & Company Ltd., London; Oxford University Press, London; Oxford University Press, New York; Theodore Presser Company, Bryn Mawr, Pennsylvania; G. Schirmer, Inc., New York; The Society for Promoting Christian Knowledge, London; Stainer & Bell, Reigate, Surrey; and Washington Cathedral, Washington, D. C.

Contents

Preface   vi

Abbreviations of Works Commonly Cited   x

List of Tables   xii

List of Plates   xiii

1 *From the Reformation to the Commonwealth*   1

2 *The Restoration and the St. James Group*   36

3 *A Century of Adjustment*   91

4 *The Anthem in Nonconformist Chapels and Parish Churches, 1700-1825*   126

5 *The Beginnings of the American Anthem*   169

6 *American Compilers and Borrowers*   206

7 *The English Anthem to about 1920*   243

8 *The Rise of an American Market for Choral Music*   300

9 *England in the Twentieth Century—The Emergence of Canadian Anthems*   346

10 *Twentieth-Century America—A Melting Pot of Tastes*   403

Bibliography   460

Index   471

Abbreviations of Works Commonly Cited

Arnold CM   Samuel Arnold (ed.), *Cathedral Music*. 4 volumes. London: For the editor, 1790.

Boyce CM   William Boyce (ed.), *Cathedral Music*. 3 volumes. London: By the editor, 1760–1778.

CMC   Elwyn A. Wienandt, *Choral Music of the Church*. New York: The Free Press, 1965.

DNB   *The Dictionary of National Biography*. 22 volumes and 6 supplements. London: Oxford University Press, 1885–1901; 1927–1959.

EECM   *Early English Church Music*. Edited by Frank Ll. Harrison *et al*. London: Stainer and Bell Ltd. for The British Academy. 9 volumes to 1969.

Grove's   *Grove's Dictionary of Music and Musicians*. Edited by Eric Blom (5th edition). New York: St. Martin's Press, 1954. 9 volumes. Supplement (Volume X), 1961.

HAM   Archibald T. Davison and Willi Apel (eds.), *Historical Anthology of Music*. Cambridge: Harvard University Press, 1959. Two volumes with examples numbered consecutively through both volumes. The numbering of this printing varies at times from that of earlier ones.

Harley   Thomas Tudway, "A Collection of the Most Celebrated Services and Anthems . . . ". British Museum MSS Harley 7337–7342.

HS   John Page, *Harmonia Sacra*. 3 volumes. London: Printed and published for the editor, 1800.

MGG   *Die Musik in Geschichte und Gegenwart*. Edited by Friedrich Blume. Kassel: Bärenreiter-Verlag, 1949–1968. 14 volumes.

OCB   *The Old Cheque-Book: or Book of Remembrance of the Chapel Royal from 1561 to 1744*. Edited by Edward F. Rimbault. [London]: Printed for the Camden Society, 1872; reprinted, New York: Da Capo Press, 1966.

PRMA   *Proceedings of the Royal Musical Association*. London: 1874– . Papers read before the Association; each paper with a different author and title.

TCM   P. C. Buck *et al.*, (eds.), *Tudor Church Music*. 10 volumes. London: Oxford University Press, 1922–1929.

TCMO   Single anthems in octavo format, all from the Tudor period. Published by Oxford University Press, each with a different number.

TECM   *The Treasury of English Church Music*. Edited by Gerald H. Knight and William L. Reed. 5 volumes. London: Blandford Press, 1965.

List of Tables

TABLE 1 Structure of Locke's verse anthem, *Sing unto the Lord, O ye saints of his* 49

TABLE 2 Structure of Locke's full anthem with verses, *When the Son of man* 53

TABLE 3 Structure of Creyghton's full anthem with verses, *Praise the Lord, O my soul* 58

TABLE 4 Structure of Turner's verse anthem, *Behold now, praise the Lord* 77

TABLE 5 Structure of Croft's verse anthem, *The Lord is my strength* 98

TABLE 6 Anthem excised from Handel's *Messiah* 159

TABLE 7 Form of *Hymn for Easter* 162

TABLE 8 The anthems in Lyon's *Urania* 179

TABLE 9 Clef and signature patterns in pre-*Urania* volumes 188

TABLE 10 Anthems by English composers in several important American collections before and after the Revolution 207

TABLE 11 Billings' tempo instructions translated into metronomic equivalents 210

TABLE 12 Form of Horatio Parker's anthem, *The Lord is my light* 343

List of Plates

FIGURE 1   *Choir of the Cathedral of Saint John the Divine, Boys' Section*   6

FIGURE 2   *Charles II at worship in the Chapel Royal*   48

FIGURE 3   *A page from* Urania *showing an anthem by James Lyon*   187

FIGURE 4   *A singing school in eighteenth-century America*   195

FIGURE 5   *Two versions of "Denmark," showing modifications of the voice placement and of notational practice*   220–221

FIGURE 6   *The Index to the Boston Handel and Haydn Society volume of* 1821   233

FIGURE 7   *The cover page of an issue of Lorenz's* The Choir Leader   316

FIGURE 8   *The assembled choirs of Hollywood First Presbyterian Church*   404

FIGURE 9   *The choir boys of Washington Cathedral in procession*   442–443

CHAPTER ONE

From the Reformation to the Commonwealth

The etymology of the term *anthem* can be traced to a date far earlier than we need for this study, since we are concerned with music that begins with the English Reformation. It is necessary, however, to examine the source of this word to see if there is a continuous musical practice, modified only by the requirements of a new religious situation, that parallels the acceptance of the term in the English Church. The word may be followed back to various forms of *antiphon*, a term denoting the category of plainsong sung before and after psalms and canticles. It was the function of antiphons to amplify the text of scriptural material to which they were attached. They were numerous because such scriptural sections were used several times each day.

References to the antiphon have been traced from as early as the beginning of the Christian era,[1] but the various spellings, forms, and meanings in English begin much later, perhaps not until around the eleventh century.[2] Their variety is of some interest, but their bearing upon the study of English-language religious music is slight; therefore, a pair of examples will suffice to show the use of the term before the establishment of England's own religious practice. At the end of the fourteenth century we can find the term *anthem* in Chaucer's *Canterbury Tales*, simply as one of the variant spellings for antiphon. Near the end of "The Prioress's Tale," we read:

---

[1] Bruno Stäblein, "Antiphon(e)," in *MGG*, I, 523–45.
[2] *The Oxford English Dictionary* (1933), I, 358–59.

> To me she cam, and bad me for to singe,
> This antem verraily in my deyinge,
> As ye han herd, and, whan that I had songe,
> Me thoughte, she leyde a greyn up-on my tonge.[3]

Variant spellings produce *anteme*, *antime*, *antym*, *antheme*, and *anthephen*. Chaucer's reference is to one of the four antiphons B.M.V. (*Beatae Mariae Virginis*), the *Alma redemptoris mater*, which is clearly mentioned shortly before the passage quoted here. The appearance of the word is significant in pointing the way to post-Reformation use. As we shall see shortly, the importance lies more in its association with the Marian antiphon than in the variety of spellings encountered.

Another example, from about the year 1520, illustrates two spellings as well as defines the position of these pieces within the religious service. "After the Hympne cometh Antempnes and psalmes. Antem ys as moche to saye as a sownyng before, for yt ys begonne before the Psalmes; yt is as moche to say as a sownynge ageynste."[4] Here is further evidence that the reference is to the antiphon, for the historic place of the antiphon is at the opening of the psalm or canticle, and at its close as well. It is not this general type of antiphon that is most significant in the ancestry of the anthem, but the Marian antiphons that are of greatest importance, for it is those that were replaced when the English Church made its break with Latin texts. The four antiphons B.M.V.[5] were in common use throughout Europe as plainsong pieces from the Middle Ages onward. While these antiphons apparently had originally been attached to psalms, they were later set aside as a group of votive antiphons to be performed at the end of Compline.[6] Each of the four pieces was assigned to a different season of the year on the Continent, but in England this was often not the case. The English adaptation of the pieces to polyphonic style preceded similar attempts by Continental composers, taking place about the middle of the fourteenth century.[7]

In a general sense, any antiphon that appears in polyphonic form is a motet; that is, a choral piece set to text other than that of the Ordinary of the Mass. Motet is a more suitable designation for these pieces because the four texts involved are not true antiphons, inasmuch as they have been removed from the traditional function of preceding and following psalms and canticles. Still, to prevent their being lost in the vast literature of motets, reference here will be made to them in the usual way. It must be borne in mind, however, that as motets they form another link in a chain of continuity from motet to anthem.

[3] *The Complete Works of Geoffrey Chaucer*, ed. Walter A. Skeat (2nd ed.; Oxford: Clarendon Press, 1900), IV, 187.

[4] *The Oxford English Dictionary*, I, 358.

[5] *Alma redemptoris mater, Ave regina caelorum, Regina caeli laetare*, and *Salve, regina*.

[6] Votive antiphons are discussed in detail by Frank Ll. Harrison, *Music in Medieval Britain* (*Studies in the History of Music*, ed. Egon Wellesz) (2nd ed.; London: Routledge and Kegan Paul, 1963), 81–88 *et passim*.

[7] *Ibid.*, 295–98.

As has been observed, the traditional place for the antiphons B.M.V. was at the close of Compline, the last of the Canonical Hours. In the English practice, our sole concern here, two distinct differences arose: (1) The votive antiphons were not restricted to the Office of Compline, but were transferred to another devotional service that followed it. (2) The number of votive antiphons was not limited to four as in the Roman practice, but increased greatly in number because of England's greater freedom from the strict Gregorian usage. The principal liturgical pattern at that time is found in the Sarum Use, which eventually encompassed most of England, remaining the ruling practice until it was prohibited by specific injunction in the first *Booke of the Common Praier* in 1549.[8]

With the emergence of English religious autonomy, still Catholic but no longer Roman, changes became necessary in the musical and liturgical practices. One of these changes, divesting the antiphons B.M.V. of their place in the religious observance, is found in the Royal Injunction of 1548, directed to the officials of Lincoln Minster. specifying that

> they shall from hensforthe synge or say no Anthemes off our lady or other saynts but onely of our lorde And them not in laten but choseyng owte the best and moste soundyng to cristen religion they shall turne the same into Englishe settynge therunto a playn and distincte note, for euery sillable one, they shall singe them and none other,

.   .   .

> they shall euery Sonday Wensday and Fryday and festiuall day in this Cathedrall churche afore the high masse in the myddyll of the chore singe thenglishe Letanye and Suffrages the same beyng begunne of hym that executeth the high masse or by too of the olde vicars, and so done in order as yt is appoynted in the preface before the sayd Englishe letanye.

> And also they shall haue the Epistle and gospell of the high masse redde every day in Englishe and not in laten. And the same to be redde euery day in the same place where they were accustomed to be redde on Sonedayes with such distincte audible playn voice as the chore and the standers by shall well vnderstande the reader.[9]

The emphasis is not simply on the change from Latin to English, but makes special and repeated reference to clarity and distinct rendition of the texts.

The Anglican Church had no place for the antiphon as such. Its interest in choral musical utterance was confined to the Service and to the nonliturgical motet which came to be known by the still current term, *anthem*. The anthem was, at the outset, simply a replacement for one or another kind of motet—a substitution, perhaps only a translation—in which the essential features were (1) the English language, (2) syllabic

---

[8] Harrison, "Sarum, Use of," in *MGG*, XI, 1422–26.

[9] *Statutes of Lincoln Cathedral*, eds. Henry Bradshaw and Chr. Wordsworth (Cambridge: University Press, 1897), II, 592–93. This Injunction was issued early in the reign of Edward VI (1537–1553), who ruled from 1547 to 1553. Since the Injunction can hardly be attributed to a child of ten, it was probably instigated by Thomas Cranmer or some other leading religious figure of the time.

setting of the text, and (3) restriction of text subjects to avoid the formerly popular Marian poems and pieces in praise of saints. This, of course, ruled out the continuation of the Marian antiphons.

That was the situation when matters came to a head sufficiently for the English religious and political leaders to separate publicly from Roman domination. By the middle of the sixteenth century the path was plain. While there were severe problems for the clergy and the public, those of the church musicians were most obvious, for they existed in the audible portions of the religious observance. These men were suddenly expected to provide suitable music for a religious practice differing so much from the old one that either wholesale revision of existing music or the preparation of completely new compositions had to be undertaken. The Mass and motet of the Roman Catholic practice had to be abandoned in both fact and name. In their places came the Service and the anthem. While the former was a daily observance, restricted as to text by its liturgical function, the latter was less limited and, in general, was an optional feature of worship. The anthem's great variety, popularity, and superior musical qualities may be attributed in part to the freedom with which it could be developed, and in part to the fact that it was not tied in any way to Anglican Chant, which was itself a compromise with Catholicism that suffered by comparison with its precursors, Gregorian and Sarum plainsong.

We may be certain that the anthem was accepted into the Anglican practice without much hesitation. Many such pieces existed before any mention was made of how they were to be used in the daily Services. They must have fallen into the existing pattern of activities in such a way that no disturbance was caused by their presence. They must, therefore, have continued in place of some earlier musical observance, or they were used in a manner that caused them to be accepted without question.

Important as the votive antiphon was to the English Catholic tradition, there is no visible direct link between the antiphon and its successor in name, the anthem; that is, we find no cases where antiphons have been adapted to English texts, thus becoming anthems. To some extent, the function of the anthem is not at all clear. The fact that its text is often based on Scripture indicates only the limits imposed on it by ecclesiastical propriety; the fact that its position in the religious observance was not carefully specified indicates also that the liturgical restrictions so carefully laid on the Service did not extend to the anthem. We commonly find references to the performance of an anthem after the Third Collect or after the sermon, but this is hardly illuminating. Early Services ended with the Third Collect, and the performance of an anthem after that point indicates only that an impressive ornament to worship was gladly tolerated so long as it remained in the shadow of liturgical practice. There is a thin, flexible line of demarcation between religious functional music and concert performance. As an unauthorized but acceptable intruder into the religious observance, the anthem was in a position to take on importance as a kind of entertainment. Its performance after the Third Collect put it outside liturgical boundaries, but connected it with the worship activity, since those gathered for that purpose had not dispersed. Since it was present, a safeguard of appropriate text would have been advisable to insure the anthem a continuing position of dignity. The Church failed to make clear what the limitations of text might be, and a rather loosely interpreted practice may be seen from the very beginnings of anthem composition.

The motet had also held an unstable place in the Roman rite, for it was generally a polyphonic substitute for plainsong segments from the Proper of the Mass. Anthems could not take over any position held within the service by motets, inasmuch as anthem texts were not so clearly prescribed. However, text restrictions did exist. Words for anthems usually came from Scripture, from metrical psalms, from Collects, and a few from unspecified non-scriptural sources.[10] These will all be considered in greater detail in connection with some of the composers who used them. At this point it may be noted, however, that the range of texts is considerably larger than it was for the motet. The fact that some of the earliest anthem composers simply made adaptations of motets to fit the circumstances might indicate an immediate need of something for the choirs to sing, and that translation of texts not open to doctrinal dispute provided a simple means of satisfying that need.

Not all churches had choirs that could deal with part-singing, even when it was simplified in the manner specified by the Royal Injunction of 1548. Any discussion of anthems, then, is bound to be limited to the "Quires and Places where they sing," for small parish churches and larger churches with diminished forces could not be expected to participate regularly in this kind of music. The number of fully staffed establishments is larger than we often suppose. No less than forty-one cathedrals, chapels, and churches where daily Services were sung before the Restoration can be identified.[11]

Before proceeding to a study of the development of the English anthem, it is necessary that we understand the position, organization, and responsibilities of the choir in the Anglican churches where daily Services were sung.

The first choirs after the English Reformation were, of course, simply the choirs that had been in existence during the centuries of Catholic rule. They were made up of boy choristers, who sang the uppermost part—variously called the *treble, meane,* or *medius*—and of men, known as vicars-choral or Gentlemen of the Chapel, who sang the other parts. The highest of the adult parts, corresponding roughly to the modern alto part, was called the *contratenor,* and the singers on that part were also known as *countertenors.*[12] These singers were disposed on both sides of the area in the east end of the church (Figure 1). The sanctuary, which was reserved for the altar and the liturgical

[10] The statement in Manfred F. Bukofzer, *Music in the Baroque Era* (New York: W. W. Norton & Company, Inc., 1947), 199, that "the words of the anthems were restricted to the psalms" must not, of course, be credited as accurate.

[11] Peter le Huray, "Towards a Definitive Study of Pre-Restoration Anglican Service Music," *Musica Disciplina,* XIV (1960), 169, gives a list of place names with the number of men and boys in each choir.

[12] Not to be confused with *castrati.* While the *castrato* voice was highly acclaimed by English opera audiences of the Baroque period, there was no place for such singers in the English Church. Countertenors, whose voices were natural (and who did not employ falsetto, as implied by some sources) apparently abounded in England. Seventeenth-century choirs contained about as many of them as of tenors and basses combined.

acts of the priest and his assistants, stood usually at the extreme east end. Next came the large area of the choir, now often called *chancel*, on each side of which were rows of seats or stalls in which the singers sat along with other officials of the Church. Those on the south, or Dean's, side were known as *decani*, and they ranked highest because of their association with the greater prestige of the Dean. Those on the north, or Precentor's, side were called the *cantoris*. This distinction was known long before the break with Roman Catholicism, but it is essentially an English arrangement. A good description of the disposition of personnel is given in the fourteenth-century *Ordinale Exon.* of 1337:

> In front sat the 14 choristers, viz. 7 boys "in prima forma" on each side of the quire. Behind them the "secundarii," the *annivellarii*, 12 vicars-choral, in deacon's or subdeacon's order, six a side, "in secundis formis." The four "custores ecclesie" stood likewise in the second form, two of their number being annivelars. So also was the clerk of St Mary, who had charge of her chapel and attended her offices. The succentor at Exeter was appointed from the choir. Likewise the subtreasurer was chosen "de ministris chori." In the middle of the choir *in superiori gradu* twenty-four priest-vicars were placed according to the use of Exeter, twelve on either side. The twenty-four canons, their "domini," sat, in sixes, right and left of them. The four principal dignitaries were placed as at Lincoln, Salisbury, and elsewhere, after the Bayeux fashion, in the terminal stalls: the Dean by the south of the choir door with the Archdeacon of Exon. next him, and the Subdean (who at Exeter held also the office of *poenitentiarius episcopi*) in the third stall. To the north of the entrance was the Precentor, with the Archdeacon of Cornwall to his left. Then at the other extremity of the *Decani* side was the Chancellor (next the Bishop's throne), and to his left the Archdeacon of Totnes.[13]

It is evident from this single description that the use of divided choirs was widespread, if only from the references to seating arrangements in other cathedrals. No comprehensive studies of the history of English choirs has been made, but several sources may be examined with profit.[14]

In the Middle Ages, the responsibilities of these choirs had been spread over the Mass and the Canonical Hours, a constant and rigorous discipline by modern standards. No undue hardships were involved, however, since the adult members were usually in religious orders and the children were also in residence as trainees of the *scholae*. When the old fraternal foundations were dissolved at the break between English authority and the Papacy, the responsibilities of singers became somewhat

---

[13] *Statutes of Lincoln Cathedral*, II (1), cxcvi–cxcvii, which goes on to explain that the *annivellarii* (also called *annivelars* or *annueleeres*) "were priests employed for singing anniversary masses of the dead."

[14] Harrison, *Music in Medieval Britain*, 50–52; Harrison, "English Polyphony (ca. 1470–1540)," *Ars Nova and the Renaissance: 1300–1450*, eds. Dom Anselm Hughes and Gerald Abraham, Vol. III: *The New Oxford History of Music* (London: Oxford University Press, 1960), 305–6; article, "Cathedral Music (Anglican)," in *Grove's*, II, 123–24, and X, 65–67; *MGG*, II, 1090–91.

FIGURE I (opposite). *Choir of the Cathedral of Saint John the Divine, Boys' Section. (Photo courtesy of the Cathedral School of Saint John the Divine, New York.)*

fewer. The performance of chants and polyphony connected with the Services, and the singing of anthems became the principal activities. The employment of men, and the recruitment and training of boys continued to be important to the perpetuation of the choral tradition, but the men had to be paid and not merely supported as heretofore. As mercenaries with outside interests, their loyalties were divided. Only those in the wealthiest places, the chapels royal, came to develop a new tradition.

The earliest composers to achieve prominence were organists, choir members, or officials of the various chapels. The most highly respected, and incidentally the most remunerative, of these positions were naturally to be had at the Chapel Royal at St. James's Palace and St. George's Chapel in Windsor Castle, the former being far more prestigious than the latter. There was some exchange of materials between these two leading chapels and the lesser places where Services were sung.

> Clearly there must have been ways in which the music of the Chapels Royal passed into general circulation. No doubt the choirmasters of the two royal chapels were asked for copies of the latest services and anthems when they visited provincial cathedrals in search of choristers. The Gentlemen of the Chapel Royal probably helped to spread the Chapel music abroad, too, for many of them held part-time appointments in other choirs.[15]

The holding of simultaneous appointments was no longer permitted after the Restoration. The documents of the Chapel are clear in prohibiting joint positions, announcing such restrictions in a document dated December 19, 1663:

> No man shalbe admitted a Gentleman of his Majesties Chappell Royall but shall first quit all interest in other quires, and those that relate at present to other churches besides the Chappell, shall declare their choice either to fix at their churches, or to the Chappell, by the first day of March, his Majestie not permitting them to belong to both. And all the Gentlemen of his Majesties Chappell shall have their habitations within or neer the City of London, to be ready to attend at all times when the Deane or Sub Deane shall summon them.[16]

Since the chapels royal were in the forefront, we shall find their composers are the most prominent, but it should not be supposed that their influence was completely ingrown, or that they were oblivious to the development of talent outside, talent that could be requisitioned and put to use at the chapels themselves. Naturally, the first composers to emerge in this area were the same ones who had established firm reputations in pre-Reformation music. Some of them remained true to the Roman Church, while others identified themselves with the new English practices from the outset.

Christopher Tye (ca. 1500–1573), John Shepherd (ca. 1521–1563), Robert White (ca. 1530–1574), Thomas Tallis (ca. 1505–1585), and to a considerable extent also John Mundy (ca. 1529–1591) and Thomas Causton (?–1569) were active as the earliest group of composers to produce works specifically for the English practice. These are not all the composers who made the earliest efforts, but they have emerged as the consistent

---

[15] Peter le Huray, "The English Anthem, 1580–1640," in *PRMA*, LXXXVI (1959–1960), 3–4.
[16] *OCB*, 81.

producers with representative pieces extant. Certainly not every composer of a half-dozen pieces with English text can be brought into a brief review of the early period of anthem composition, but the first attempts deserve more than cursory consideration.

Christopher Tye made early use in his anthems of a feature already common in motets, the division of a lengthy text into two *partes*, the second of which served to complement the first both in satisfactory rounding out of the text and in balancing the music through contrast. His *I will exalt thee*[17] illustrates the flexibility of such a piece: Either half may be performed independently of the other, or the two parts may form a consecutive whole. It also shows the alternation of sections between the *decani* and *cantoris* sides of the choir as a means of achieving variety.

Well in the forefront of those early composers was Thomas Tallis, whose works were naturally intended for the Catholic Church in his early years.[18] Unfortunately, only a few of his works with English text have been published, and none of those in a critical edition. Contrary to information supplied by both Burney and Hawkins,[19] and repeated in other sources, we are able to trace a number of his anthems to motets. These are probably his renditions of his own earlier works into English. There are apparently eighteen anthems written originally for the Anglican practice, and another nine that are adaptations of Latin motets.[20] All the motet adaptations save one are from Tallis' *Cantiones Sacrae*, which he and William Byrd published jointly in 1575.

Tallis wrote at least three anthems prior to 1550.[21] It is evident in those works that he was making a conscious effort to abide by the restrictions imposed by Archbishop Cranmer to the effect that texts should be set with just one note to a syllable.[22] *If ye love me*[23] is almost entirely syllabic, having only an occasional neumatic passage of two or three notes to a syllable. While a lesser composer might have found such restrictions disastrous, Tallis was able to create a work of striking beauty and simplicity. In anthems, probably of later origin, such as *O Lord, give thy Holy Spirit*,[24] and *This is my commandment*,[25] Tallis continued to observe the syllabic principle, with neumatic or melismatic passages occurring, for the most part, at cadential points.

In the anthems adapted from his Latin motets, Tallis again bent every effort to hold to syllabic writing. *I call and cry to thee*,[26] adapted from *O sacrum convivium*,[27] is virtually as syllabic as his anthems originally set in English. However, in its original

---

[17] Boyce, *CM*, II, 10–18; *TCMO* 59; excerpt printed in *CMC*, 144. *TCMO* omits *decani* and *cantoris* indications, thereby losing an important feature of the piece.

[18] Other composers, most of whom produced little for the new religious establishment, are mentioned by earlier writers. See, for example, Myles Birket Foster, *Anthems and Anthem Composers* (London: Novello and Company, 1901), 17–18, 21–23.

[19] *TCM*, VI, xvii–xviii.

[20] Listed in *Grove's*, VIII, 398–99; see also Denis Stevens, *Tudor Church Music* (New York: W. W. Norton & Co., 1961), 61, where only seventeen anthems are mentioned.

[21] *Grove's*, VIII, 297, lists three with dates before 1550. *TCM*, VI, xviii, shows six.

[22] *CMC*, 458–59, prints the complete text of Cranmer's letter to King Henry VIII, in which modifications of text and music are suggested.

[23] *TCMO* 69. [24] *TCMO* 68; Harley 7337, 63–64. [25] *TCMO* 70.

[26] Boyce, *CM*, II, 5–9; Harley 7337, 41–46. [27] *TCM*, VI, 210–13.

Latin setting, this motet was quite syllabic also; in fact, quasi-syllabic settings are not at all uncommon in the Latin motets of Tallis.[28] It is possible that too much emphasis might be laid on the power of Anglican opinion as a force in this style development. Simplicity may well have been seen as a desirable feature prior to Cranmer's letter.

The place of William Byrd (1543–1623) as the leading composer of Tudor England is undisputed; his works, while not always masterpieces, were of consistently high quality, and often carried the stamp of genius. Biographical data concerning him are well known; a student of Thomas Tallis, organist at Lincoln Cathedral, and a Gentleman of the Chapel Royal, he was a leading musician of his day. Although he was closely associated with the Anglican Church and was favored at court, he remained a Roman Catholic throughout his life; hence, he composed motets and anthems, Masses and Services with equal facility.

It is in the works of Byrd that we first encounter a new type of anthem which employs one or more solo voices alternating with full choir. The solo passages are accompanied by organ or viols, and since these solo passages often carried the designation *versus*, the new type became known as the *verse anthem* in contrast to the older motetlike setting now termed *full anthem*. One is hesitant about setting exact dates, especially in an area of study such as this where so many questions remain unanswered; nevertheless, it is quite possible that Byrd's verse anthem, *Christ rising again*,[29] which appeared in *Songs of Sundrie Natures*, 1589, was the first of its kind.

The work abounds in interest. It is an early example of *concertato*-like writing, involving three distinct performing groups: two solo voices, a four-part choir, and viols. Word-painting is seen, first in the instrumental parts, where "rising" is suggested by ascending lines in successive voices, then in the opening solo passages where the initial melodic interval enlarges with each statement of the text, "Christ rising"— first a major third, then a perfect fourth, and finally a perfect fifth (Example 1*a*). Again, word-painting is suggested by a succession of quick-note ascending passages on the text, "he liveth unto God" (Example 1*b*), and a striking contrast between the *partes* is achieved where triple time replaces duple, and the passage from I Cor. 15 springs to life.

Of particular interest is *Sing we merrily unto God | Blow up the trumpet*, a double-anthem setting of Ps. 81:1–4, SSATB.[30] Vivid word-painting is found in *pars II* where, in connection with the text, "Blow up the trumpet in the new moon," the melodic material in the upper voices imitates a trumpet call while the bass part sustains the root of the chord (Example 2). This anthem appeared in *Psalmes, Songs, and Sonnets*, 1611, and another setting of the same psalm, *Sing joyfully unto God our strength*,[31] was composed by Byrd, probably at an earlier date. Fellowes lists the latter as a two-part

[28] See *O Nata Lux de Lumine*, TCM, VI, 209–10, and *In Manus Tuas Domine*, ibid.. 202–3.
[29] *HAM* 151, where *pars I* only is given. Both *partes* are printed in *The Collected Works of William Byrd*, ed. Edmund H. Fellowes (London: Stainer and Bell, 1937–1950), XIII, 280–301.
[30] *The Collected Works of William Byrd*, XIV, 106–24.
[31] Boyce, *CM*, II, 34–40.

Example 1a.   *Christ rising again*, William Byrd (*The Collected Works of William Byrd*, XIII, 281).

Example 1b.   *Ibid.*, 286–87.

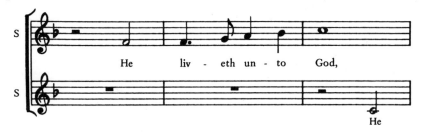

Used with permission of Stainer & Bell Ltd., Reigate, Surrey.

Example 2. *Sing we merrily unto God (Pars II)*, William Byrd (*The Collected Works of William Byrd*, XIV, 116).

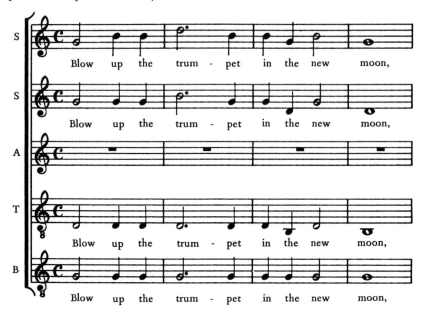

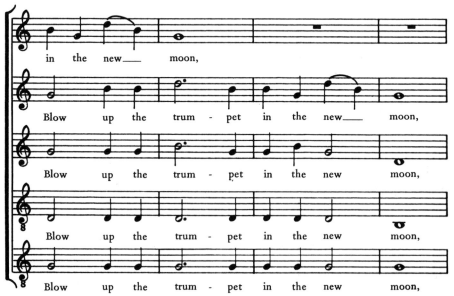

Used with permission of Stainer & Bell Ltd., Reigate, Surrey.

Example 3. *Sing joyfully unto God our strength*, William Byrd (Boyce, *CM*, II, 37).

anthem when, in reality, it is a single setting.[32] The elided cadence at "Blow the trumpet" (Example 3) is evidence of Byrd's intention to avoid a break at this point. As in the other setting, he outlined the tones of a major triad in the fashion of a trumpet call. This is one of the anthems that kept Byrd's name alive in the seventeenth and eighteenth centuries by its inclusion in the influential Barnard and Boyce collections.

The fact that Byrd set Psalm 81:1–4 twice is of interest from two standpoints: the possible functions that could be served by different texts, and the sources of the texts themselves. Concerning the use of these pieces, Peter le Huray points out that *Sing joyfully unto God our strength* is to be found in choir part-books, while the double anthem, *Sing we merrily*, is not. Then, too, the voice distribution, SSAATB, of the former anthem is quite normally found in choirs, while the distribution of the latter, SSSAT, is not. He comes to the conclusion that *Sing joyfully unto God our strength* was intended as an anthem, while *Sing we merrily* had the function of a sacred madrigal.[33]

An investigation of the two texts reveals that they are drawn from different sources. *Sing we merrily unto God | Blow up the trumpet* was taken from the Great Bible of 1539, the leading English translation of the sixteenth century. While this is a source one would expect to find in use, that of *Sing joyfully unto God our strength* is not, for it is drawn from the Geneva Bible of 1660, a translation made by the Marian exiles in Geneva and brought back to England in the early years of Elizabeth's reign. Although not authorized by the Queen, it seemed to carry her silent assent and was popular among Protestants.[34]

The entire matter of Byrd's use of anthem texts might be considered at this point. Of some fifty-six anthems, thirty-seven draw from the Book of Psalms for text. Twenty of these are in versified form, although only two are from the Sternhold and Hopkins *Whole Booke of Psalmes*, 1562. The rest seem to be drawn from various Elizabethan poets. The seven Penitential Psalms found in *Songs of Sundrie Natures* are a part of this group. Of the seventeen psalm settings in prose form, five are from the Great Bible, two are from the Geneva Bible, and the balance are from other sixteenth-century versions. The only other biblical text used by Byrd is found in the previously mentioned *Christ rising again*.

Another source of anthem texts was Collects or Collect-like prayers. Byrd set four of these, one of which (*Prevent us, O Lord*) is found in the *Book of Common Prayer*. It would be quite difficult to account for an anthem setting of a Proper Collect, or one that is mandatory in any one of the Services; however, the one in question falls into a group of optional Collects, found at the end of Communion, which may be said "as often as the occasion shall serve, after the Collects either of Morning or Evening Prayer,

---

[32] *Grove's*, I, 1064, and Edmund H. Fellowes, *William Byrd* (2nd ed.; London: Oxford University Press, 1948), 137.

[33] *PRMA*, LXXXVI (1959–1960), 9.

[34] Ira Maurice Price, *The Ancestry of Our English Bible* (2nd ed. rev., William A. Irving and Allen P. Wikgren; New York: Harper and Brothers, 1907), 263.

Communion, or Litany, by the discretion of the Minister."[35] Since this Collect may be used after the three prescribed Collects of Morning and Evening Prayer, and since this is also the traditional place where the anthem is to be sung, it is quite logical that Byrd should have given this text a musical setting, thus combining two functions in one.

Carols provide yet another source of texts for Byrd, who set three for Christmas and one for New Year's Day. The term *carol* provides, in itself, something of a problem when it is included in a study of the anthem since, as a type, the carol is nonliturgical. However, it would be well to recall that the anthem is only quasi-liturgical (see p. 4), and it is not surprising that Byrd would set these texts, which he clearly labeled *carowle* or *caroll*, in his usual anthem style.

We are next faced with the question concerning Byrd's intentions for these pieces—were they actually conceived as anthems? Peter le Huray believes that the verse anthems with viol accompaniment were not generally used in cathedral or chapel services since they are found only in what he calls *secular sources*.[36] In this case, two of Byrd's three Christmas carols, from *Songs of Sundrie Natures*, 1589, *From Virgin pure this day did spring*, and *An earthly tree, a heavenly fruit*, are eliminated since they belong to this category. On the other hand, Erik Routley, in dealing with what he terms *motet carols*, speaks of Byrd's settings as "church anthems, designed for a trained choir."[37] Likewise, Fellowes classifies these compositions as anthems.[38] Since definite proof is lacking for either point of view, the question of when they were sung, and by whom, must remain unsettled, although we may continue to regard these works as anthems in the broadest sense. It must be borne in mind that le Huray's argument is a strong one, supported by the absence of viol parts in cathedral manuscripts.

The remaining source from which Byrd drew anthem texts was non-biblical religious poetry. Of nearly ten such texts, only two are identified as to author; *From Virgin's womb* is by Francis Kindlemarsh (fl. 1570), and *Alack, when I look back* is from the pen of William Hunnis, an Elizabethan poet.

Taken as a whole, Byrd's contribution to anthem literature is impressive; among pre-Restoration composers, the quantity of his output is exceeded only by that of Thomas Tomkins. He appears to be the pioneer composer of verse anthems, and the quality of his composition contributed substantially to the high standards of Tudor church music.

Another Tudor composer of some importance to this study is Thomas Weelkes (ca. 1575–1623), organist at Chichester Cathedral. Although considerably younger than William Byrd, Weelkes outlived him by only four months, and it is interesting to note that his output of forty-eight anthems is only slightly less than that of Byrd. Since the majority of those anthems exist only in manuscript, it is not possible to make

---

[35] Rubric at the close of Communion, *Book of Common Prayer*.
[36] *PRMA*, LXXXVI (1959–1960), 9, 10.
[37] Erik Routley, *The English Carol* (London: Herbert Jenkins, 1958), 126.
[38] Fellowes, *op. cit.*, 144.

Example 4. *O how amiable are thy dwellings,* Thomas Weelkes (*TCMO* 90 [revised], 9–10).

Used with permission of Oxford University Press.

a conclusive evaluation of them; nevertheless, some impression of his work in that form may be had from the few anthems in print.

Let thy merciful ears, O Lord[39] is a setting of the Proper Collect for the Tenth Sunday after Trinity. Moving in its simplicity, it befits the plaintive spirit of the prayer. Again we are faced with the question of how such a setting was used in the Service. Was it sung in place of recitation at the appointed time in the liturgy, or was it a mere repetition of what had already been spoken? In the case of Morning and Evening Prayer, the repetition of this prayer by the choir would be separated only by two Ordinary Collects; in the Communion, there was no customary place for the anthem. Repetition of this sort might well have been offensive to the liturgical sensibilities of the clergy, and it is quite possible that such Collects were sung instead of recited, but it is also possible that they could have been sung immediately after their recitation.

Another anthem of unusual beauty is O how amiable are thy dwellings, SAATB.[40] The extensive "Amen" ending (Example 4), while found in the anthems of other composers of the time, seems to be a hallmark with Weelkes, for it is used often by him, and it provides opportunity for melismatic writing, creating a sense of soaring freedom after the limitations of the quasi-syllabic treatment used in the main body of the text.

Most widely known is Weelkes's setting of the popular text, Hosanna to the Son of David.[41] Scored for SSATBB, it is characterized by a weaving of polyphonic parts and interesting rhythmic patterns. A feature that is uncommon, and perhaps unique to Weelkes, is a final statement of part of the text in Latin in the last seven measures. The fact that "Hosanna" is the same in both languages, plus the general familiarity of worshipers with this text, probably prompted Weelkes to this unusual treatment. In another anthem, Gloria in excelsis Deo, a 6,[42] Weelkes carried the Latin-English combination even further. The anthem is in three distinct sections, each of which closes with an authentic cadence; the form of both music and text is ABA. Again, Weelkes incorporated a very familiar Latin text, for in the first and third sections the words "Gloria in excelsis Deo" are used. Section B, "Sing, my soul, to God thy Lord, all in glory's highest key," might be considered a free paraphrase on the Latin text. The temporary division, at this point, of the parts into alternating high and low voice choirs (see Example 5) is not unlike Venetian motet practice, although the element of spatial separation is not involved here. Again, Weelkes closes the anthem with an extended "Amen" section.

Although his anthem writing is not all on the same high level as the examples cited, it appears that as his church works become more widely known, Weelkes may yet be regarded as one of the leading Tudor composers of church music.

That interest in the verse anthem did not diminish after Byrd's initial efforts is apparent in the works of Orlando Gibbons (1583–1625). Of his forty anthems, only

---

39 TCMO 35.   40 TCMO 90.
41 TCMO 9.   42 TECM, II, 154–65.

Example 5. *Gloria in excelsis Deo*, Thomas Weelkes (*TECM*, II, 157).

Used with permission of The Royal Musical Association, c/o Stainer & Bell Ltd., Reigate, Surrey, England.

Example 6. *O clap your hands/God is gone up*, Orlando Gibbons (Boyce, *CM*, II, 70–71).

fifteen are of the full variety, while twenty-five are verse anthems. This slight im-
balance is not attributable to any feeling he may have had that a superior expression
was possible in the newer form, at least so far as we can judge from the pieces themselves. The full anthems are, on the whole, the better of the two varieties. A number of
interesting features may be found in the double anthem, *O clap your hands | God is
gone up*.[43] The two parts are settings of unequal portions of Psalm 48, a Proper psalm
for Evening Prayer for Ascension Day. Set throughout for eight voices, i.e., SATB
decani and *cantoris*, the work is an excellently wrought piece of counterpoint that
follows, at the same time, the restrictions of writing for the Anglican practice. It is
syllabic, except for a few deliberate deviations into melismatic passages. That the few
runs are placed deliberately is evident from the fact that they intensify such words as
"all" and "great." The contrapuntal device employed is that popular Renaissance one
using points of imitation, wherein each phrase of text is set in as many parts as practical
with a single melodic-rhythmic pattern, and in which a new musical idea is introduced
with each subsequent text segment. The process makes possible a modified kind of text-
painting, as is shown in Example 6, where all the clearly audible voices make vigorous
leaps on the words "which is highly exalted," and the interior parts, which are unable
to move so freely, flesh out the harmony in less vigorous fashion. Gibbons' high position in the final outpouring of contrapuntal art in England is emphasized by a number
of other pieces, especially his *Hosanna to the Son of David, a 6*.[44]

To return to the verse anthem, we have noted that most of Gibbons' pieces fell
into that category. Sixteen of these are conveniently gathered into a single volume[45]
where they may be considered as a group. Some of the anthems are for a solo voice and
chorus; others are for two, three, and even four soloists in alternation with chorus. In
very few instances does Gibbons call for the full eight-part chorus that is available. The
full sections more often employ the common SAATB texture that was standard in
large choirs. A representative piece for solo and chorus is the verse anthem *Behold,
Thou hast made my days*,[46] in three verses for contratenor and three full sections
SAATB. Dated 1618, it is a mature work that shows Gibbons' continuing interest in
polyphonic texture, even in the verse sections where the solo voice is surrounded by
imitative instrumental writing, phrases often being forecast by the instruments, and the
voice making the final polyphonic entry. At each full section, the chorus material is
drawn from the end of the preceding verse, both text and music having been stated
earlier by the soloist. The choral repetition has the same melodic outline, but covers a
broader range, thus intensifying the utterance through both change of texture and
melodic contours. The second verse section employs some of the declamatory style
that Gibbons introduced into anthems, giving less emphasis to contrapuntal relation-

[43] *TCM*, IV, 236–49; Boyce, *CM*, II, 59–74; *TCMO* 40.

[44] *TCM*, IV, 208–14; *TCMO* 39; Harley 7339, 273–77; Boyce, *CM*, 41–47; Add. Ms. 30087, 139v–142.

[45] *Orlando Gibbons; Verse Anthems*, ed. David Wulstan (Vol. III of *EECM*, ed. Frank Ll. Harrison;
London: Stainer and Bell, 1964).

[46] *EECM*, III, 24–37; *TCM*, 147–57; Harley 7337, 264–68; Add. Ms. 30087, 167v–172.

ships between voice and instruments, and repeatedly employing delayed accents, a device derived from the Italian style. Generally, the Italian declamatory passages placed strong syllables of text on weak beats at the opening of a phrase; Gibbons appears less concerned with accent of text here than with the delaying feature. Text-painting is also present, especially in the phrase "He heapeth up riches" (Example 7). The closing section also takes on a pathetic character by quoting from the "Lachry-mae" tunes of Dowland and Gibbons, as well as showing a close relationship to Tomkins' *Hear my prayer*.[47] The accompaniment is independent of the voice parts in

Example 7. *Behold, Thou hast made my days*, Orlando Gibbons (Harley 7337, 265).

the verse sections, but duplicates the choral lines in the full sections. In many ways, this work parallels the pattern of the better-known verse anthem *This is the record of John*.[48]

Those verse anthems that are set for two or more soloists show similar arrangements of polyphonic interest in the verse, and a greater emphasis on homophonic writing in the full sections. No such division of emphasis prevails in the full anthems, for they are polyphonic throughout. The absence of instrumental support, as well as the full texture of the complete choir, makes this possible. It is not to be viewed as a remnant of Renaissance practice when a composer clings to polyphonic style, but more likely the recognition that no satisfactory long piece could at that time be written in block-chord style. Gibbons did not turn his back on the possibility of syllabic chordal writing, but he used it only moderately. In the double anthem *a 4, Deliver us, O Lord our God | Blessed be the Lord God*,[49] this contrast between contrapuntal and chordal organization is easily noted. *Pars I* is contrapuntal until the final cadence. There are three points of imitation and, since the first is repeated, a total of four canonic entries. Variety is achieved within these, in addition to the thematic difference created by the

47 *EECM*, III, 216.   48 *HAM* 172; *EECM*, III, 179–92; *TCM*, IV, 297–304.
49 *TCM*, 170–72; Add. Ms. 30087, 57v–59v.

new points of imitation, by varying the order in which the voices enter, as follows: BTAS, TBAS, STBA, and TBSA. *Pars II* is essentially chordal, but closes with an extended "Amen" section that is again polyphonic. The piece is quite short for a double anthem, but it displays a careful organization of materials that is even more apparent in Gibbons' larger full anthems. Despite its brevity, the piece deserves careful study, including consideration of the possible connection between textual content and the choice of chordal or contrapuntal material.

Text sources have already been examined in connection with Byrd, and it is worth noting that Gibbons was not an exception (nor were his successors) to the general pattern that developed from Byrd's practice so far as scriptural sources and functions of text were concerned. The Geneva Bible and the Great Bible still played a large part in providing materials—*Hosanna to the Son of David*, for example, derived its text from a number of places in the Geneva Bible of 1557. The days, liturgical or occasional, for which the pieces were destined are a mixed lot. The possibility that some of the pieces are what le Huray called secular anthems cannot be completely discounted, although most of them are unmistakably pointed toward church services. There are anthems that use Collects as their texts; some that draw upon psalms, both Proper and general, some that are specific as to the day upon which they should be performed, and a number are occasional pieces, intended for weddings, composed at the request of some friend or official, or are in connection with the health or whereabouts of the King. All in all, the pieces we have generally classed together under the name of anthem show a great variety of types and functions, even this early in their history.

If any evidence were needed that the music of this period can greatly reward continued research, one need only consider the case of Thomas Tomkins (1572–1656), the most important member of a large and important musical family. As recently as the fifth edition of *Grove's*, the list of works was confined to a few titles of pieces still in manuscript.[50] A brief tercentenary appreciation of the composer's significance appeared after the dictionary was undoubtedly already in press,[51] and a full-scale study of the composer was published shortly thereafter.[52] The importance of these new studies, especially the latter, resulted in a complete revision and extensive listing of materials in the supplementary volume to *Grove's*.[53] Most important to the study of Tomkins' church music is the complete listing of the contents of his *Musica Deo Sacra*, published after his death, most probably under the editorial supervision of his son, Nathaniel. *Musica Deo Sacra* is the largest source of Tomkins' anthems, containing ninety-four;[54]

[50] *Grove's*, VIII, 497. However, an extensive and apparently complete list is supplied in Peter le Huray, *Music and the Reformation in England, 1549–1660 (Studies in Church Music*, ed. Erik Routley) (New York: Oxford University Press, 1967).

[51] Bernard Rose, "Thomas Tomkins, 1575?–1656," in *PRMA*, LXXXII (1955–1956), 89–105.

[52] Denis Stevens, *Thomas Tomkins; 1572–1656* (London: Macmillan & Co., 1957).

[53] *Grove's*, X, 440–42.

[54] Stevens, *Thomas Tomkins*, 74, n. 1. Comments following that do not refer directly to individual compositions are indebted to Stevens and to *Grove's*.

eighteen that are found in other places bring the total to 112, the largest number written by any composer of the period. Most of the anthems are built on psalm texts, and such a preponderance is not surprising, for the Psalter formed an important part of daily worship. This was evident in our examination of text sources for Byrd, Gibbons, and, to a lesser extent, the other composers considered up to this point. In order to see what place the psalms had in the daily life of the English Church, and whether that place demanded musical emphasis, it is necessary to consider the use of the Psalter before continuing with the music of Tomkins.

Just as the Book of Psalms had played an important daily part in the worship of the Catholic Church, where its contents were sung in plainsong, the same kind of practice was retained in the Anglican liturgy, except that the reading of the Psalter was called for rather than singing. The pertinent rubric from the English *Book of Common Prayer* follows:[55]

THE ORDER HOW THE PSALTER IS APPOINTED TO BE READ

The Psalter shall be read through once every Month, as it is there appointed, both for Morning and Evening Prayer. But in February it shall be read only to the twenty-eighth, or twenty-ninth day of the month.

And, whereas January, March, May, July, August, October, and December have one-and-thirty days apiece; It is ordered, that the same Psalms shall be read the last day of the said months, which were read the day before: so that the Psalter may begin again the first day of the next month ensuing.

And whereas the 119th Psalm is divided into twenty-two portions, and is over-long to be read at one time; It is so ordered, that at one time shall not be read above four or five of the said portions.

And at the end of every Psalm, and of every such part of the 119th Psalm, shall be repeated this Hymn,

Glory be to the Father, and to the Son: and to the Holy Ghost;
As it was in the beginning, is now, and ever shall be; world without end.
Amen.

Note, that the Psalter followeth the division of the Hebrews, and the translation of the great English Bible, set forth and used in the time of King Henry the Eighth, and Edward the Sixth.

With such an Order of Psalms in effect, a question arises over the use of an anthem based on a psalm or portion thereof. Performance of a psalm-text anthem on the day

[55] As that book was adapted to the use of the Protestant Episcopal Church in the United States, the monthly reading of the Psalter was dropped from general worship as a consequence of the "alterations and amendments" to the English Prayer Book. The new book adopted in October, 1789, states: "The Psalms and Lessons to be read every day are to be found in the following Table of Psalms and Lessons for the Christian Year; except only those for the Immovable Holy Days, the Proper Psalms and Lessons for all which days are to be found in the Table for the Fixed Holy Days." The development of the Prayer Book in the United States is discussed by Francis Procter and Walter Howard Frere, *A New History of The Book of Common Prayer* (London: Macmillan and Co., 1951), 234–52.

in which the psalm falls according to the monthly order seems more restrictive than a composer would have cared to endure; performance of such texts on a random basis would have robbed many of them of their special meaning. The Prayer Book, on the other hand, did allow for Proper psalms on six days, thus adding a specific use for thirty-three of the psalms. Strangely, it may seem, there is no great number of settings of these Proper psalms. The reason may lie in the strength of the scriptural accounts associated with these days, for at least four of them are among the most widely known Gospel readings of Christian literature. The Table of Proper Psalms, which follows, is given as it stands in the English Prayer Book; American usage incorporates only a few of them into its table for the same days.

PROPER PSALMS ON CERTAIN DAYS

	Mattins	Evensong
Christmas Day	Psalm 19	Psalm 89
	45	110
	85	132
Ash Wednesday	Psalm 6	Psalm 102
	32	130
	39	143
Good Friday	Psalm 22	Psalm 69
	40	88
	54	
Easter Day	Psalm 2	Psalm 113
	57	114
	111	118
Ascension Day	Psalm 8	Psalm 24
	15	47
	21	108
Whitsunday	Psalm 48	Psalm 104
	68	145

The Anglican composer had available the entire Psalter, as well as versified versions of it, from which to choose anthem texts. Both of these sources were used, but the number and assortment of psalm segments indicate that there was an attempt neither to concentrate on the Proper psalms nor to set even a significant section of the entire Psalter. Since congregational singing, where it was practiced with any regularity, was confined to the metrical psalms, there was no need for composers of choral music to duplicate those texts, in either their original English or versified forms. Small wonder, then, that Collects, topical scriptural passages, and occasional poems of a religious nature played such a large part in anthems. When psalm texts were used, it was common practice to select a few verses, not necessarily consecutive, that would serve the occasion for which the anthem was written. Such procedures neither intruded upon the Order of Psalms as it was read monthly, nor bound the composer to the Proper psalms unless he chose to ally himself with such a text occasionally.

Tomkins' selection of psalm texts for about two thirds of the contents of *Musica Deo Sacra* does not comprise any major deviation from normal practice, for these are not complete psalms, but usually selected portions of text. Among the settings are a great variety of voice distributions, those for more than six-part chorus mostly dating from early in his life. As one expects, the anthems *a 5* are especially well written, probably because Tomkins was willing to lavish his best efforts on this standard arrangement of the choir.[56] There are also nineteen anthems *a 3* for unaccompanied voices, including settings of the seven Penitential Psalms. Tomkins' teacher, William Byrd, had set those seven psalms for three voices, but his versions were to versified texts. There is not sufficient evidence for projecting a direct relationship between the two sets, but the existence of one by each man cannot pass unremarked.

The usual assortment of Collects for special days appears among Tomkins' works (Christmas, Ash Wednesday, Easter, Whitsunday, etc.), as well as three coronation anthems. One of the latter, *Be strong and of good courage*, was composed for the Coronation of James I; two others, *Sadock the priest*,[57] for the Coronation of Charles I, and the verse anthem *O Lord, grant the King a long life*,[58] written for the crowning of one or the other of those monarchs, are also known. These compositions illustrate a number of Tomkins' competencies worthy of mention. He is the first English choral composer to show a clear understanding of the melodic sequence. What we tend to take for granted was a clear innovation in his time,[59] and Tomkins was not content to make the obvious gesture in the solo voice with the organ engaging equally in sequential accompaniment. Generally the repetition phrase is supported by an organ part of greater interest than the first statement for organ. Tomkins' sequences are more than simple canonic entries in a single voice or in settings *a 2*. They take place at various pitch levels and deal with brief phrases of text and music (Example 8).

Another notable feature of Tomkins' pieces, although he cannot be credited with innovation here, is his wide variety of voice distributions in both full and verse anthems. He employs the standard SAATB choir with good effect, but this combination does not predominate. In fact, full anthems *a 5* are a distinct minority, and shifting textures are used in the chorus sections of verse anthems with excellent effect.

[56] The usual large choir of the seventeenth-century English cathedral had divided altos in both the *decani* and *cantoris* groups: SAATB. By combining the alto parts or dividing the others, groupings from *a 4* to *a 10* were readily available.

[57] Known only through its text, attributed to Tomkins in the British Museum collection of words, Harley 6346, and printed in *OCB*, 158.

[58] Printed in *EECM*, V, 73–80. The words do not appear in *OCB* or in other works describing the ceremonies of either coronation. The piece was probably performed in connection with one of the events, but not at the actual ceremony.

[59] The melodic sequence can be found in plainsong and early secular music, but its use in polyphony was replaced by imitative technique, which accomplishes the same thing—repetition at a different pitch—in several voices rather than in one. Sequential treatment in a single voice, or in several voices that do not overlap melodic patterns, had to await the development of accompanied solo writing.

Example 8. *O Lord, grant the King a long life,* Thomas Tomkins (*EECM,* V, 73–74).

the King a long
life, that his years may en - dure,
that his years may en - dure

Used with permission of The British Academy, c/o Stainer & Bell Ltd., Reigate, Surrey.

Example 9. *Great and marvellous*, Thomas Tomkins (*TCMO* 98).

Used with permission of Oxford University Press.

The organ parts supporting solo lines are less laden with the busy activity found in several of his Services. As is evident in the foregoing example, the organ supports the solo voice and sometimes duplicates it with a *basso seguente*, especially when the solo voice is a bass. The device of choral repetition of both text and music in a verse anthem becomes less customary with Tomkins than it was with his predecessors. He breaks away from the normal pattern by repeating only text and supplying modified or new musical material. On occasion, he supplies both new text and music for the chorus.

The full anthems are not yet widely available in practical editions, but a sufficient number may be found to suit most performing groups. *O pray for the peace of Jerusalem*, SSTB,[60] is a simple contrapuntal setting that is syllabic throughout except at cadence points where some mild motion occurs on a single syllable. *Great and marvellous*, SAATB,[61] alternates homophonic and polyphonic sections, and has a brief passage in which the second alto serves as a partner, first to the upper pair of voices and then to the lower pair (Example 9). The same device is used with striking effect in *Then David mourned*, SSATB,[62] where the soprano voices are withheld until the lower voices have set the mood in closely spaced chords, after which the sopranos repeat the text in the upper register.

---

[60] *TCMO* 11. Voice distributions are as shown in modern editions. Music of this period is generally transposed up a third, or even a fourth, to bring it into modern pitch levels.

[61] *TCMO* 98.   [62] Peters Edition No. 6069.

O praise the Lord, all ye heathen, a 12,[63] is not representative of Tomkins' general style, but it is not a unique work, for it shares, understandably, some features of his *Glory be to God, a 10*.[64] The twelve-part piece divides each section of the standard four-part choir into three; *Glory be to God* doubles each part of the available five-part chorus. In each piece, all the voices begin with a single thematic segment and text fragment, but no two at the same time. Subsequent entries are somewhat more varied, each new text section featuring a different theme as in the points of imitation in a Renaissance motet. An especially obvious approach to text-painting appears in *Arise, O Lord, into thy resting place, a 5*,[65] and the device of block chords is used to separate the contrapuntal sections.

Tomkins' skill in counterpoint is considerable. He probably felt it to be one of his strong points, for he based the entire anthem *Turn thou us, good Lord*[66] on a single melodic utterance as a canon four-in-one. The thematic material is presented at two pitch levels, with the second pair of voices entering after the delay of half a measure (Example 10). Canonic writing is rare in the English Church, but it does find its way into settings of the Service where the greater length of each section, and of the total composition, probably joined with a need for variety as a stimulus to some composers.[67]

Tomkins served as organist of Worcester Cathedral until 1646 when, at age seventy-three, he retired to the home of his son, Nathaniel. He was still apparently a vigorous man, capable of continuing in his work, but the revolutionary troops had laid siege to the city, the organs were removed from the cathedral, and services were suspended, not to be resumed until after the Restoration, fourteen years later.[68]

What happened to Tomkins was repeated in one way or another across England. Choral Services were suppressed, choirs were dissolved, and the clergy disenfranchised. This was not the result of a single prohibition, nor of intermittent directives, but a matter of constant harassment by the Republican forces. On June 8, 1647, an ordinance was promulgated abolishing the observance of religious festivals. Other directives were also issued at various times, such as the one of December 24, 1652, specifically forbidding the celebration of Christmas in London.[69] A few passages from John Evelyn's diary will illustrate the effects this program of suppression had on Anglicans who still wished to worship, and they will point up, at the same time, the fact that musicians were completely dispossessed of their former positions in churches as a result of the restrictions.

---

[63] *TCMO* 100 (rev.).

[64] Harley 7339, 34–38. This is the second part of the verse anthem *Behold, I bring you glad tidings*. The entire anthem is printed in Thomas Tomkins, *Thirteen Anthems*, ed. Robert W. Cavanaugh, Vol. IV: *Recent Researches in the Music of the Renaissance* (New Haven: A-R Editions, Inc., 1968), 59–70.

[65] *TECM*, II, 143–53.

[66] Harley 7339, 48–50.

[67] Canonic writing in Services by Tomkins, Gibbons, Blow, Purcell, and Croft is discussed in *CMC*, 179–85.

[68] Stevens, *Thomas Tomkins*, 58.

[69] *The Diary of John Evelyn*, ed. E. S. de Beer (6 vols.; Oxford: Clarendon Press, 1955), III, 145.

Example 10. *Turn thou us,* canon four-in-one, Thomas Tomkins (Harley 7339, 48).

Since public worship was either forbidden or greatly restricted, depending on the occasion and the degree of solemnity one wished to preserve, some Anglicans undertook to hold private services in their homes. Evelyn reports on such a meeting at his home in Deptford, Kent, a few miles downstream from London on the Thames:

> *December* 3 [1654] *Advent* Sonday, there being no Office at the *Church* but extemporie prayers after the *Presbyterian* Way, for now all formes were prohibited, & most of the Preachers Usurpers, I seldome went to *Church* upon solemn *Feasts;* but either went to *Lond:* where privately some of the orthodox sequestered Divines did use the Common Prayer, administer Sacraments &c: or else procured one to officiate in my house: Where fore on the 10th Dr. Rich: Owen (the sequesterd Minister of Eltham) preached to my Family in my Library: on 1: St. *John:* 10. concerning Christs *Advent,* in an excellent discourse & then gave the H. Communion to me & my family:[70]

There is no reference to music, nor does there seem to have been opportunity for its performance in these circumstances. Evelyn's entire attention is devoted to the limitations of freedom for religious practice, here as in the following extract:

[70] *Ibid.,* III, 144–45.

[December] 30 [1655] I went to *Lond:* where Dr. *Wild* (at St. *Greg*) preached the funeral Sermon of Preaching, this being the last day, after which *Cromwells* Proclamation was to take place, that none of the Ch: of England should dare either to Preach, administer Sacraments, Teach Schoole &c. on paine of Imprisonment or Exile; so this was the mournfullest day that in my life I had seene, or the Church of *Eng:* her selfe, since the *Reformation*: to the greate rejoicing of both *Papist* & *Presbyter*:[71]

One of the most offensive of these acts of oppression took place two years later, when planned raids were made on several assembled groups of worshipers. Again, no reference is made to music, a fact that renders quite conclusive what is generally understood about its absence in those years. Evelyn was sincerely interested in music, both in and out of church, and he reported on it so often that its absence in these entries must be regarded as significant:

[December] 25 [1657], I went with my Wife &c: to *Lond:* to celebrate *Christmas day.* Mr. *Gunning* preaching in *Excester* Chapell on 7: *Micha* 2. Sermon Ended, as he was giving us the holy Sacrament, The Chapell was surrounded with Souldiers: All the Communicants and Assembly surpriz'd & kept Prisoners by them, some in the house, others carried away: It fell to my share to be confined to a roome in the house, where yet were permitted to Dine with the master of it, the Countesse of *Dorset, Lady Hatton* & some others of quality who invited me: In the afternoone came *Collonel Whaly, Goffe* & others from *Whitehall* to examine us one by one, & some they committed to the *Martial*, some to Prison, some Committed: When I came before them they tooke my name & aboad, examind me, why contrarie to an Ordinance made that none should any longer observe the superstitious time of the *Nativity* (so esteem'd by them) I durst offend, & particularly be at *Common prayers,* which they told me was but the *Masse* in *English,* & particularly pray for *Charles stuard,* for which we had no Scripture: I told them we did not pray for *Cha: Steward* but for all *Christian Kings, Princes* & *Governors:* The⟨y⟩ replied, in so doing we praied for the K. of *Spaine* too, who was their Enemie, & a *Papist,* with other frivolous & insnaring questions, with much threatning, & finding no colour to detaine me longer, with much pitty of my Ignorance, they dismiss'd me: These were men of high flight, and above Ordinances: & spake spitefull things of our B: Lords nativity: so I got home late the next day blessed be God: These wretched miscreants, held their muskets against us as we came up to receive the Sacred Elements, as if they would have shot us at the Altar, but yet suffering us to finish the Office of Communion, as perhaps not in their Instructions what they should do in case they found us in that Action:[72]

A newspaper account of the raid is interesting as a comparison, for it reports the day's activities from the viewpoint of the party in power:

Decemb. 25

This being the day commonly called *Christmas,* and divers of the old Clergy-men being assembled with people of their own congregating in private to uphold a superstitious observation of the day, contrary to Ordinances of Parliament abolishing the observation of

[71] *Ibid.,* III, 164.   [72] *Ibid.,* III, 203–4.

that and other the like Festivals, and against an express Order of his Highness and his Privy-Council, made this last week; for this cause, as also in regard of the ill Consequences that may extend to the Publick by the Assemblings of ill-affected persons at this season of the year wherein disorderly people are wont to assume unto themselves too great a liberty, it was judged necessary to supppress the said meetings, and it was accordingly performed by some of the Soldiery employed to that end; who at Westminster apprehended one Mr *Thiss cross* [Timothy Thurscross], he being with divers people met together in private; In *Fleet street* they found another meeting of the same nature, where one Dr *Wilde* was Preacher; And at Exeter-house in the Strand they found the grand Assembly, which some (for the magnitude of it) have been pleased to term *the Church of England*; it being (as they say) to be found no where else in so great and so compact a Body, of which Congregation one Mr *Gunning* was the principal Preacher, who together with Dr *Wilde*, and divers other persons, were secured, to give an account of their doings: Some have since been released, the rest remain in custody at the White-Hart in the Strand, til it shall be known who they are: *Publick intelligencer*, 28 Dec. 1657, p. [206]; the notice is reprinted in *Mercurius politicus*, 31 Dec., pp. [199]-200.[73]

These reports comprise only an infinitesimal fraction of those that bear on the subject of suppression of religious activities and, with them, the termination of choral activity in England for upward of a dozen years. The first period of anthem composition was brought to an abrupt halt by such acts, for there were no choirs to sing anthems, and no churches where they were permitted to pursue their accustomed activities. While the normal procedures were disrupted completely, the possibility of further progress was not completely shut off. Among the mature musicians who were affected by the suppression were William Child and Benjamin Rogers, both of whom figure in the music of the Restoration, and who will therefore be considered in the next chapter. Henry Cooke, hardly of an age to achieve musical eminence, improved his skills in secular music and, upon his return to church music at the Restoration, quickly brought the Chapel Royal to a position of importance by strict training and vigorous recruitment of choirboys. Henry Aldrich and Pelham Humfrey were born in 1647; John Blow, two years later. The last two were choristers under Cooke in those early years of the restored Chapel, and all three exerted considerable influence on the future course of English church music.

Whatever the immediate effects of the Commonwealth upon the musical scene in England, the Restoration found a small group of men who, by their earlier experience, would be able to reorganize music at the Chapel Royal until a new generation should introduce a taste for Continental style to enliven the anthem, scandalize the survivors of the old system, and widen the gulf between cathedral and parish church music.

[73] *Ibid.*, III, 205.

CHAPTER TWO

The Restoration and the St. James Group

This day [May 29, 1660] came in his Majestie *Charles* the 2d to London after a sad, & long Exile, and Calamitous Suffering both of the King & Church: being 17 yeares: This was also his Birthday, and with a Triumph of above 20000 horse & foote, brandishing their swords and shouting with unexpressable joy: The wayes straw'd with flowers, the bells ringing, the streetes hung with Tapissry, fountaines running with wine: The Major, Aldermen, all the Companies in their liver⟨ie⟩s, Chaines of Gold, banners; Lords & nobles, Cloth of Silver, gold & vellvet every body clad in, the windos & balconies all set with Ladys, Trumpets, Musick, & ⟨myriads⟩ of people flocking the streetes & was as far as *Rochester*, so as they were 7 houres in passing the Citty, even from 2 in the afternoone 'til nine at night: I stood in the strand, & beheld it, & blessed God: And all this without one drop of bloud, & by that very army, which rebell'd against him: but it was the Lords doing, *et mirabile in oculis nostris*: for such a Restauration was never seene in the mention of any history, antient or modern, since the returne of the *Babylonian* Captivity, nor so joyfull a day, & so bright, ever seene in this nation: this hapning when to expect or effect it, was past all humane policy.[1]

So wrote John Evelyn concerning the return of Charles II to London, an event that marked the end of the Commonwealth and the beginning of the Restoration. After almost two decades of Puritan austerity, which profoundly affected the religious, political, and cultural life of the country, most of the English people were enthusiastic

[1] *The Diary of John Evelyn*, III, 246.

in welcoming the return of monarchic government. With this return came the re-establishment of the Anglican Church, and music once again flourished in the Chapel Royal and the cathedrals.

The Coronation itself, on April 23, 1661, was well supplied with music, both ceremonial and religious. On the day before the event, the King moved through London to the accompaniment of music by cornetts and sackbuts, the procession into Westminster Abbey on the following day was interspersed with trumpeters, and the choir was prominent during the religious observance and the ceremony it dignified. At several points in his description of the ceremony, Evelyn refers specifically to anthems.[2] Samuel Pepys, usually an enthusiastic reporter of all things musical, says with obvious disappointment, "But so great a noise that I could make but little of the musique; and indeed, it was lost to every body."[3] Whatever the success of the choral and instrumental music at that moment of great excitement, we know that musical activity had been on the increase for the eleven months since Charles's entry into London, supported and encouraged by royalty, and appreciated by many others.

However, the resumption of church music at the level attained during the reigns of James I and Charles I was not possible at the outset of the Restoration. Sir John Hawkins gives an account of the problems faced by those whose duty it was to re-establish the old tradition of church music. The primary problem, he relates, was the rebuilding of organs removed or destroyed during the Commonwealth, after which

> The next step towards the revival of cathedral service, was the appointment of skilful persons for organists and teachers of music in the several choirs of the kingdom; a few musicians of eminence, who had served in the former capacity under the patronage of Charles I. namely Child, Christopher Gibbons, Rogers, Wilson, Low, and others, though advanced in years, were yet living; these were sought out and promoted; the four first named were created doctors, and Child, Gibbons, and Low were appointed organists of the royal chapel; Gibbons was also made master of the children there, and organist of Westminster Abbey. Rogers, who had formerly been organist of Magdalen college at Oxford, was preferred to Eton; Wilson had a place both in the chapel and in Westminster choir; and Albertus Bryne was made organist of St. Paul's.
>
> By this method of appointment the choirs were provided with able masters; but great difficulties, arising from the late confusion of the times, and the long intermission of choral service, lay behind. Cathedral churches, from the time of the suppression of monasteries, had been the only seminaries for the instruction of youth in the principles of music; and as not only the revenues appropriated for this purpose were sequestered, but the very institution itself was declared to be superstitious, parents were deprived both of the means and the motives to qualify their children for choral duty, so that boys were wanting to perform those parts of the service which required treble voices. Nay, to such streights were they driven, that for a twelvemonth after the restoration the clergy were forced to supply the want of boys by cornets, and men who had feigned voices. Besides this, those of riper years, whose

[2] *Ibid.*, III, 278–84.
[3] *The Diary of Samuel Pepys*, ed. Henry B. Wheatley (London: G. Bell & Sons, 1893; reprinted, New York: Random House, n.d.), I, 262.

duty it had been to perform choir service, namely, the minor canons and lay-clerks of the several cathedrals, had upon their ejection betaken themselves to other employments; some went into the king's army, others taught the lute and virginals; and others psalmody, to those whose principles restrained them from the use of any other music in religious worship.

In consequence hereof, and of that inaptitude which follows the disuse of any faculty, when the church-service was revived, there were very few to be found who could perform it.[4]

Concerning those named by Hawkins as leading musicians in the early Restoration years, a reliable source confirms the names of William Child, Christopher Gibbons, and Edward Lowe as organists "at the tyme of the Coronation of King Charles the Second, Aprill 23, being St. George's Day, 1661."[5] Also named are Henry Cooke, Master of the Children, and Henry Lawes, Clarke of the Checke. John Wilson was sworn in as Gentleman, October 22, 1662, upon the death of Lawes.[6]

Although he was a prominent and highly respected musician in his time, Henry Lawes (1596–1662) was not a significant contributor to anthem literature. If *Zadock the priest*,[7] an anthem he composed for the Coronation of Charles II, represents the results of his careful attention, it is possible that the fragments of other pieces reported to have existed[8] were actually complete works of similar brevity and general inconsequence.

The problem of reviving cathedral music and bringing it to an effective level was recognized by Edward Lowe (ca. 1610–1682), an organist of the Chapel Royal, who, in 1661, published *A Short Direction for the Performance of Cathedrall Service*.[9] One of his anthems, *O give thanks unto the Lord*,[10] is unusual in several respects. It is a setting of Ps. 136:1–3, 23–24, for STB soli and SATB chorus, in the course of which the choir sings only short responsive settings of "and his glory endureth forever," and a closing Gloria Patri. This use of the Lesser Doxology at the end of an anthem, even when it is part of a psalm text, is not found often.[11] Another feature that identifies Lowe with the traditions of an earlier generation is his consistent practice of stating the opening material of the verse section in the organ before it is heard in the voice, thereby subordinating the vocal entry by permitting it no new material. Men of Lowe's type caused no new surge of interest in composition, but they provide evidence of stability in their perpetuation of an older style.

---

[4] Sir John Hawkins, *A General History of the Science and Practice of Music* (2 vols.; New York: Dover Publications, 1963), II, 689.

[5] *OCB*, 128.   [6] *Ibid.*, 13.

[7] Ms.Ch.Ch.Mus.437; Ch.Ch.Mus.1220–24.   [8] *Grove's*, V, 93.

[9] E[dward]. L[owe]., *A Short Direction for the Performance of Cathedrall Service* (Oxford: William Hall, 1661).

[10] Harley 7339, 80–82.

[11] It was noted on p. 25 above that the Prayer Book required the reading of this Lesser Doxology at the close of every psalm. Its general absence in anthem literature may be attributed to (1) avoidance of deadly repetition since so many psalm texts were used, (2) in appropriateness in connection with incomplete psalms, and (3) its common use in settings of the *Benedictus*, *Magnificat*, and *Nunc dimittis*, as well as the occasionally used optional sections, *Benedictus Dominus*, *Jubilate Deo*, *Cantate Domino*, and *Deus misereatur*.

The prime mover in the preparation and execution of music in the Chapel Royal seems to have been Henry Cooke (1616–1672), who had been a captain in the Royalist forces during the Civil War. He was Master of the Children and, in that capacity, gained an enviable reputation as a choir trainer. Among the children he recruited and developed were Pelham Humfrey, Michael Wise, John Blow, Thomas Tudway, and William Turner, all of whom became leading figures in the development of the anthem. Cooke's success in procuring children for the Chapel was due, in great part, to his use of press-gang tactics, requisitioning and appropriating the best young voices from other churches. The difficulties faced by the Chapel in finding boys were multiplied many times in other cathedrals as a result of these raids. The following notice, dated July 4, 1661, is not unique among surviving documents. "Warrant for the payment of £23 16s. 9d. to Henry Cooke, master of the children of the Chappell, for fetching five boys from Newarke and Lincolnie for his Majesty's service."[12]

Samuel Pepys makes frequent references to Captain Cooke and the music he produced in the Chapel Royal. Evidently even that best endowed of all English choirs had an occasional bad day, for on Sunday, October 14, 1660, Pepys observed that "one Dr. Crofts made an indifferent sermon, and after it an anthem, ill sung, which made the King laugh."[13] On the whole, however, Pepys is lavish in his praise of Cooke. Just one Sunday earlier, he had written of hearing "Dr. Spurstow preach before the King a poor dry sermon; but a very good anthem of Captn. Cooke's afterwards."[14] Several months later, Pepys mentioned going "after dinner to Whitehall Chappell with Mr. Child, and there did hear Captain Cooke and his boy make a trial of an Anthem against to-morrow, which was brave musique."[15] Although Cooke wrote some thirty anthems, none are to be found in Tudway, Boyce, or later collections, suggesting that his talent in composition was limited or, at least, that the taste of another generation found little to cherish in what he had written.

The Mr. Child to whom Pepys alluded was probably William Child (1606–1697), a composer of church music whose life most completely spans the dramatic events of seventeenth-century England. In 1632, he was appointed organist at St. George's Chapel, Windsor, and also at the Chapel Royal in London; he appears to have lived on a small farm during the Commonwealth, and was reinstated as organist for the Chapel Royal at the Restoration. As the composer of a number of Services and forty-five anthems, his contribution to church music was large. Five of the anthems are found in the Tudway collection, three in Boyce, and two in Arnold; several are also available in modern editions.

Since Child composed both before and after the Commonwealth, it is difficult in many cases to determine the period from which a piece derives; however, one of the anthems can be attributed to the Restoration period with certainty, and another probably dates from that time. *O praise the Lord*,[16] *a 6* (listed as *a 5* in *Grove's*), was "com-

---

[12] Henry Cart De Lafontaine, *The King's Musick* (London: Novello and Company, 1909), 134.
[13] *The Diary of Samuel Pepys*, I, 176.   [14] *Ibid.*, I, 173.   [15] *Ibid.*, I, 237.   [16] Harley 7338, 49–52.

Example 11. *O Lord, grant the King a long life*, William Child (Boyce, *CM*, II, 89).

posed by Dr. William Child upon the Restauration of the Church and Royal Family in 1660."[17] A prayer for the King, *O Lord, grant the King a long life*,[18] *a 4*, may also have been composed for the Restoration, but the possibility exists that it is the version mentioned by Scholes, who says that during the Commonwealth Child "occupied a small farm and busied himself with composition—including that of his anthem, *O Lord, grant the King a long life* (which He did not)."[19] There are two anthems, one a verse anthem that cannot be dated; the other, the full anthem in Tudway's collection. The dates and situations mentioned by Tudway are sometimes in error, and full confidence cannot be placed on his statement that the work was performed "at the Restauration."

Although Child's style is in a conservative vein, his use of an extended "hallelujah" at the close of many of his anthems appears to have initiated a feature which would become a chief characteristic of anthem composition in the late seventeenth century, continuing through the first half of the eighteenth century (Example 11).

Two other names belong to the first group of Restoration anthem composers—Christopher Gibbons (1615–1676), second son of the illustrious Orlando Gibbons, and Benjamin Rogers (1614–1698). Gibbons was appointed one of the three organists at the Chapel Royal in 1660, and was private organist to Charles II, as well as organist at Westminster Abbey. His anthems are still in manuscript, including a verse anthem in Tudway's collection, *How long wilt thou forget me, O Lord*.[20]

Rogers is the only composer in this group not associated with the Chapel Royal. After serving as organist at Eton College from 1660, he became lay-clerk and deputy organist at St. George's, Windsor, in 1662, and, two years later, was appointed organist at Magdalen College, Oxford, a position he held for many years.[21] Although he wrote a considerable amount of church music, most of his anthems are still in manuscript; two, however, were published by Boyce and one by Page. These works, uncomplicated and short, have an admirable quality of directness. Of particular beauty is the quiet simplicity of *Teach me, O Lord, the way of thy statutes, a 4*.[22]

The general style of the first generation Restoration composers reflected that of the Tudor period. Italian taste had, however, begun to make itself felt in pre-Commonwealth England in such works as Child's *First set of Psalms*, which first appeared in 1639,[23] and in some of the works of Walter Porter (ca. 1595–1659), a pupil of Monteverdi's who incorporated some of the florid vocal devices of that master into his own works for the English Church and court. Porter's *Praise the Lord*,[24] an extended

   [17] *Ibid.*, 49.   [18] *Ibid.*, 164–65; Boyce, *CM*, II, 87–89.

   [19] Percy A. Scholes, *The Puritans and Music in England and New England* (London: Oxford University Press, 1934), 287.

   [20] Harley 7340, 175–78.

   [21] Rogers may have held several positions simultaneously, after the fashion of Tudor musicians. If he did, he was in an unusual position for a Restoration church musician, for those appointed to the Chapel Royal were subject, after December 19, 1663, to the rule that prohibited the holding of several positions at the same time (see p. 8). This prohibition would have affected a number of the men mentioned by Hawkins.

   [22] Boyce, *CM*, II, 105–7.   [23] *Grove's*, II, 209.   [24] *TECM*, II, 232–47.

verse anthem, has figured bass, some extremely demanding solo lines that require dexterity in both speed and performance of the *trillo*, an ornament that at that period may have been either a rapid tremolo or a trill. Porter's piece is even earlier than the Child collection, for it was included in his *Madrigales and Ayres* of 1632. Neither of these works established a strong enough interest to result in imitation by other composers. Perhaps it was the emphasis on vocal gymnastics that made the Monteverdi ideal unacceptable as English religious music. Italian taste was certainly no stranger to courtly life, and the ready acceptance of instrumental ingredients stemming from Italy, possibly from the tradition of the Venetian school, is evident in the anthems of Matthew Locke (ca. 1630–1677).

Locke's familiarity with Italian instrumental style may already be seen in the fact that he composed the music for cornetts and sackbuts played during the movement of the royal cavalcade from the Tower of London to Whitehall. This is not a "team of brass instruments," as we are led to believe,[25] for only the sackbuts were metallic. The cornetts were undoubtedly the wooden instruments with cup mouthpiece and finger holes that were widely used during the Renaissance and into the Baroque period. The use of these instruments in combination could indicate that Locke understood and cultivated the exciting instrumental ensembles that Giovanni Gabrieli used and that, incidentally, Monteverdi knew as well, although his impact upon English music appears to have been more strongly felt in the area of elaborate vocal style. Locke's distinctive contribution to anthem literature lies in his use of instruments with the voices, as well as in his dramatic declamatory solo and choral lines mentioned elsewhere.[26] Whether Locke was the first, or only one of the first, to write in this style cannot be determined, but it is certain that he was at the Chapel Royal during the years concerned, was one of the few people old enough to have contributed music of this nature, and was one of the very few composers who could handle the instrumental idiom successfully. These facts, coupled with his already mentioned exposure to Italian ideas, make a strong case for his close association with the first works of this type, some of them far more elaborate than we often suspect, forecasting the cantata-anthems that came to full flower under Blow and Purcell.

There is no doubt that musical events developed rapidly after Charles returned to England: Anthems were again heard at religious services, the absence of trebles being compensated by cornetts and falsettists; composers were again producing music for the Anglican observance; and Charles imitated the taste of the French court—where he had been captivated by Louis XIV's band of *vingt-quatre violons*, and possibly by *les petits violons* under the brilliant leadership of Lully—in establishing his own string orchestra that would supply music at both secular and religious functions.[27] The

---

[25] *Grove's*, V, 353.   [26] *CMC*, 149–50.

[27] Charles was not responsible for introducing violins into the band of household musicians, but only for the aping of the French organization. Violins were present as early as 1581, and continued to assume a greater importance from that time onward. See *Grove's*, IV, 756; De Lafontaine, *op. cit.*, *passim*; J. A. Westrup, *Purcell* (London: J. M. Dent and Sons, 1937), 27–33.

problem connected with bringing this music into the Chapel was partly that of producing new music, and here the record becomes confused. We cannot tell exactly who composed the first pieces, nor do we know how complex those first verse anthems with "symphonies" were. Still, we do know quite accurately when the first one was performed, as we shall see in the following account.

The first dated reference to instrumentally supported verse anthems comes from Pepys, who reports his activities for Sunday, September 14, 1662, including a visit

> to White Hall chapel, where sermon almost done, . . . I heard Captain Cooke's new musique. This the first day of having vialls and other instruments to play a symphony between every verse of the anthem; but the musique more full than it was the last Sunday, and very fine it is. But yet I could discern Captain Cooke to overdo his part at singing, which I never did before.[28]

The reference to "Captain Cooke's new musique" may be read to mean either his performers or his own composition. More important is the reference to the preceding Sunday, upon which date Pepys had commented, "I heard a good sermon of the Dean of Ely's, upon returning to the old ways, and a most excellent anthem, with symphonys between, sung by Captain Cooke."[29] We must assume that the instrumental interludes were for organ, since Pepys is emphatic about the use of other instruments for the first time on the following Sunday. Evelyn did not attend services at the Royal Chapel on either occasion. When he finally heard the new type of anthem on December 21, a full three months later than Pepys, he thought he was present at the first performance of such a piece. He says that

> instead of the antient grave and solemn wind musique accompanying the *Organ* was introduced a Consort of 24 Violins betweene every pause, after the *French* fantastical light way, better suiting a Tavern or Play-house than a Church: This was the first time of change, & now we heard no more the *Cornet*, which gave life to the organ, that instrument quite left off in which the English were so skilfull.[30]

Aside from the discrepancy in dates—easily seen as an error on Evelyn's part since he often made the short trip home to Deptford on weekends—there is the question of whether the new group appeared because there was no adequate organ, or whether it was simply more desirable than organ accompaniment.

The Chapel was not without an organ at any time, for it was within weeks of the Restoration (June 17, 1660) that Pepys wrote: "This day the organs did begin to play at White Hall before the King,"[31] and three weeks later he again visited the Chapel, where he "heard very good music, the first time that ever I remember to have heard the organs and singing-men in surplices in my life."[32] Organ music was available and

[28] *The Diary of Samuel Pepys*, I, 475–76.

[29] *Ibid.*, I, 471.

[30] *The Diary of John Evelyn*, III, 347–48.

[31] *The Diary of Samuel Pepys*, I, 120.   [32] *Ibid.*, I, 132.

used during the two years prior to the addition of the King's private music, but there is some question about the quality of the music and the state of the instrument, since in that same year, 1660, Bernard Schmidt, commonly known in England as Father Smith, came from Germany with two nephews and, as a first assignment, began construction of an organ for the Chapel. It was a hurried job, and Burney, who had a high opinion of Smith's work in general, wrote that the instrument "did not quite fulfil the expectations of those who were able to judge its excellence."[33] Thomas Tudway (1650–1726) was living at the time, and, if we may rely on his evidence in this matter, we can supply a date when the instrument was finished, and learn, as well, something of the King's reasons for adding other instruments:

> In the beginning of the year 1662, the first Organ was Erected in his Majestys Chappell in White-Hall . . .
>
> .   .   .   .
>
> His Majesty who was a brisk, & Airy Prince, comeing to the Crown in the Flow'r & vigour of his Age, was soon, if I may so say, tyr'd with the Grave and Solemn way, And Order'd the Composers of this Chappell to add Symphonys &c with Instruments to their Anthems; and therupon Establish'd a Select number of his private Music to play the Symphonys and Retornellos which he had appointed.
>
> The King did not intend by this innovation to alter any thing of the Establish'd way; He only appointed this to be done, when he came himself to the Chappell, which was only upon Sundays in the Morning, on the great festivals, and days of Offering.[34]

The entire character of the English anthem underwent a change to satisfy a whim of Charles II's. The taste of the court and, to a considerable extent, of the Chapel Royal, became seasoned with French musical ideas, especially as to instrumental features. Pepys's comment, "I perceived that the King is a little musicall, and kept good time with his hand all along the anthem,"[35] has often been quoted, but it takes on new meaning when it is read in the light of Roger North's statement about French music. "It was, and is yet a mode among the *Monseurs*, always to act the musick, which habit the King had got, and never in his life could endure any that he could not act by keeping the time."[36] And again, "He could not bear any musick to which he could not keep the time, and that he constantly did to all that was presented to him, and for the most part heard it standing."[37]

It was inevitable that the King's taste should bring about a great change in the style of music which had heretofore been confined to full anthems with *colla parte* organ accompaniment, and verse anthems with organ-accompanied solo sections,

---

[33] Charles Burney, *A General History of Music* (2 vols.; New York: Dover Publications, 1957), II, 343. A strong case for English ancestry of Smith is made in Cecil Clutton and Austin Niland, *The British Organ* (London: B. T. Batsford, Ltd., 1963), 68–70.

[34] Harley 7338, 2ᵛ.

[35] *The Diary of Samuel Pepys*, I, 781.

[36] *Roger North on Music*, ed. John Wilson (London: Novello and Company, 1959), 299.

[37] *Ibid.*, 350.

brief introductory and bridge passages for organ, and chorus settings *colla parte*. His organization of a string orchestra, after the French fashion, for entertainment, and the expansion of its function as part of his churchgoing entertainment was simply a reflection of what he had experienced in France, where the *vingt-quatre violons* served also as instrumental support for the grand motets in the Chapelle Royale.[38] The old style of writing continued at the same time, of course, since the King was not present daily.

Let us return to the question of who may have written those early verse anthems with symphonies. Cooke is a possibility, although we are without any proof of his activity in that vein. If he wrote any, they were of small consequence, since his name is mentioned principally in other connections. The composer would not have been one of the old men who returned to the Chapel at the Restoration, for they were not skilled in instrumental technique, and they had insufficient background in Italian and French styles, both of which are apparent in the resulting pieces. John Jenkins (1592–1678), who could have qualified on the basis of experience in instrumental composition, did not assimilate enough of the Continental style to please the King, nor was his skill in vocal music great. North says "his vein was less happy in the vocall part, for tho' he took pleasure in putting musick to poems, he reteined his instrumentall style so much, that few of them were greatly approved."[39] No significant anthems of his have survived.

The only other strong candidate is Matthew Locke. We have already seen him as an active composer for cornetts and sackbuts; there is evidence of his constant interest in anthem composition for some years after the Restoration; and he was a composer for the King's select group of instrumentalists until his death. Locke was appointed "composer in the private musick in the place of John Coperario," on June 16, 1660,[40] and remained a member of the King's special band until his death. His reported conversion to Catholicism, and his subsequent appointment to the Queen's Chapel at Somerset House, did not diminish his activities at court, although his usefulness as a composer to the Anglican Chapel Royal must have ceased. We must assume that his anthems date from before that event, which was probably soon after the middle of 1666.[41] Whatever positive evidence there is must come from the music itself. If Locke was, indeed, the first composer of anthems with orchestral accompaniment by the King's band, we must have evidence that he was exposed to, and skilled in, the Continental idiom that appears in those anthems.

English composers were writing instrumental music in the last half of the sixteenth century, especially for the virginal. The end of the century saw the appearance

---

[38] The structure of the grand motet is discussed in *CMC*, 334–40.

[39] *Roger North on Music*, 345.   [40] De Lafontaine, *op. cit.*, 114.

[41] *Grove's*, V, 353; *Roger North on Music*, 348. There is no evidence of any anthem composition by Locke after his conversion but, he was not cast out from the company of Chapel musicians. One of his anthems, *Not unto us, O Lord*, was transcribed "into the books of his Majesty's Chappell Royall since anno 1670 to Midsummer 1676." De Lafontaine, *op. cit.*, 305–7.

of the first suites for viols. In both these areas we can find a strong interest in dance forms and, consequently, in stylistic features that were borrowed from the Continent. We need look only to a representative volume of keyboard music,[42] or to a collection of consort pieces,[43] both of which represent early seventeenth-century taste and practice, in order to see the degree to which such pieces were used. The volumes show a wide interest in pieces of foreign origin. Many of them bear the names *coranto* or *galliard*, types that brought the vitality of dance rhythms in triple meter to the English ear. The same is true of William Lawes's *Harp Consorts* and *Royal Consort*,[44] in which sarabands also appear. Such pieces were common in England long before the Commonwealth. Matthew Locke, on whom our interest is centered here, favored the *corant* and saraband in his consort music,[45] ample evidence that he was both aware of the Continental dances and using them in his instrumental music. His music for cornetts and sackbuts,[46] written for the King's procession the day before the Coronation, employs both of these forms. Competition for royal favor was constant; Locke did not miss the opportunity to captivate the King by including samples of his favorite musical styles. His high position with the King's Band until the year of his death indicates that he continued to please. His mastery over the instrumental idiom, his connection with the Chapel Royal, and his surviving pieces from that period make him, among all the musicians who lived in London then, the leading candidate for the adaptation of the verse anthem from organ to orchestral accompaniment. Obviously, England did not have to wait for Pelham Humfrey, who was still a treble singer at the time, to make his Continental visit in order to bring back a suitable instrumental style and skill.

In one source, Locke is credited with the composition of a large verse anthem that employs three four-part choruses, a five-part orchestra, a four-part consort of viols, oboes, flutes, and three groups of soloists, each group SATB.[47] Unfortunately, the anthem is not identified by name or location; consequently, any examination of it appears to be out of the question until it is brought forward. The arrangement of voices and instruments is extraordinary, and even improbable, in the face of what is known about that period in England. The most elaborate one of Locke's works that is available for study here—and it is one that bears a fascinating resemblance to that described in terms of multiple choirs, instrumental groups, and solo ensembles—is one that was copied by Tudway. *Sing unto the Lord, O ye saints of his*[48] is a verse anthem that may be divided into twelve sections of uneven length, as shown in Table 1.

[42] *The Fitzwilliam Virginal Book*, eds. J. A. Fuller-Maitland and W. Barclay Squire (Leipzig: Breitkopf & Härtel, 1899; various reprints).

[43] *Jacobean Consort Music*, eds. Thurston Dart and William Coates (*Musica Britannica*, IX; London: Stainer and Bell, 1955).

[44] William Lawes, *Select Consort Music*, ed. Murray Lefkowitz (*Musica Britannica*, XXI; London: Stainer and Bell, 1963), 64–68; 127–35.

[45] Matthew Locke, *Four Suites made from Consort Music*, ed. Sydney Beck (New York: The New York Public Library, 1947).

[46] Matthew Locke, *Music for His Majesty's Sackbuts and Cornetts (1661)*, transcribed by Anthony Baines (London: Oxford University Press, 1951).

[47] *MGG*, VIII, 1088.   [48] Harley 7340, 151–74.

London Printed for I. Walsh Serv.t in Ordinary to his Majesty at the Harp and Hoboy in Catherine street in the Strand. ...

FIGURE 2. *Charles II attending a religious service at the Chapel Royal. Plate from Weldon's* Divine Harmony *(ca. 1716–1717). (Photo courtesy of Baylor University Library.)*

TABLE 1

Structure of Locke's Verse Anthem, *Sing unto the Lord, O ye saints of his*

1. Symphony I, 26 measures* (violins, hautboys, 2 parts in alto clef, bass part).
2. Verse for ATBB, 34 measures, "Sing unto the Lord" (parts for four instruments).
3. Symphony I, 26 measures.
4. Verse for ATBB, 21 + 26 measures, "For his wrath endureth but the twinkling of an eye."
5. Symphony II, 18 measures (with flutes and violins in dialogue).
6. Verse for AT, 29 measures, "And in my prosperity."
    BB, 27 measures, "Thou didst turn away."
    ATBB, 14 measures, "Then I cried unto thee, O Lord."
7. Symphony I, 26 measures.
8. Verse for ATBB, 14 measures, "What profit is there in my blood."
9. Symphony III, 29 measures (flutes and strings).
10. Verse for ATBB and instrumental *tutti*, 46 measures, "Thou hast turned my heaviness into joy."
11. Symphony III, 17 measures (opening and closing sections of part 9).
12. SATB chorus, 10 measures, "Therefore shall every good man sing."
    AATB verse, 11 measures, "O my God, I will give thanks."
    Chorus, soloists, and orchestra, 9 measures, "Hallelujah."

* Where instrumental and vocal materials overlap their opening and closing material, the measures have been counted twice. The composition, therefore, is several measures shorter than the total number shown here.

It will be seen later in this chapter that the fully developed cantata-anthem differs from this piece only in the use of solo voices with the theatrical devices of recitative and aria. The text, using portions of Psalm 30, beginning with verse 4, does not lend itself to such treatment, but that does not imply Locke's willingness to use the devices in church music even though he was familiar with them outside the Chapel. Reliance on the ATBB combination for the verse sections may point to an early date for the work, for it is probable that no composer would undertake such an extensive work for soloists that were ill prepared for the task. The one certain missing item in choirs around 1660 was a supply of properly trained and experienced boy sopranos. Even when such boys were present in sufficient number in later years, however, composers were hesitant to entrust them with important solo passages. The verse anthems of later composers, notably Blow and Purcell, give some solo parts to sopranos, but not in proportion to their availability. Men, on the other hand, were not in short supply. Even if their skills were less developed than they were again in later years, they were not called upon for extravagant displays of vocal prowess. The full chorus, which includes sopranos, is called upon for a mere nineteen measures of simple music, further indicating that Locke's trust was placed on maturity and specialized solo voices.

The instrumental sections of the anthem are complete short pieces, fitting the description offered by Pepys of "instruments to play a symphony between every verse

Example 12.   Section 1 of Locke's verse anthem, *Sing unto the Lord, O ye saints of his* (Harley 7340, 151–52).

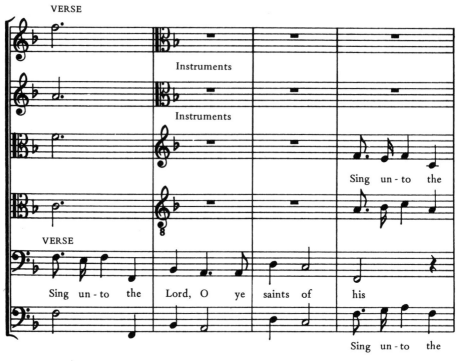

of the anthem,"[49] and having no direct connection in thematic material or mood with the material that precedes or follows as verses. Sections 1, 3, and 7 are identical in instrumentation and thematic content, calling for string orchestra and oboes (Example 12), and embodying Continental characteristics that are foreign to anthem literature in terms of length, dance rhythms, and their function as *ritornelli*. Sections 5, 9, and 11 are similar in instrumentation—flutes substitute for oboes—but the last two only are alike in musical material. Triple meter is common to the dance movements, and it is worth noting that the anthem is written in triple meter throughout except for the second half of section 4 and all of section 8, a total of only 40 measures, less than a tenth of the piece. While not all the triple-meter sections used the dotted rhythms of the courante, galliard, or saraband, the emphasis lies in that direction, even in the vocal parts.

The material of the vocal sections is not related to that of the instrumental; except for the rhythmic patterns that are common to both, the instrumental and vocal styles are different. A segment of section 4, for solo voices and instrumental bass, shows that Locke had not lost sight of the singers in his composition, even though he was forced to rely on solo voices for most of its effect (Example 13).

There are others of Locke's anthems that show less of the use of instruments to separate the verses. One of them relies on soprano voices to a greater extent, showing that the problem of finding boys' voices was not constantly a deterrent to varied composition, even in those early years after the Restoration. *When the Son of man*[50] is a verse anthem in seven sections (Table 2), simpler in style than *Sing unto the Lord, O ye saints of his.*

TABLE 2

Structure of Locke's Full Anthem with Verses, *When the Son of man*, Matt. 24: 31–40

1. Chorus, SSATB, 14 measures, "When the Son of man" (no instrumental parts).
2. Verse, bass solo and strings, 35 measures, "Come, come, ye blessed of my Father."
3. Choral recitative, SSATB, 4 measures, "Then shall the righteous answer him, saying."
4. Verse, SSAATB, 14½ measures, "Lord, who saw ye an hungry" (no instruments are specified).
5. Choral recitative, SSATB, 3½ measures, "And the King shall answer and say unto them."
6. Verse, bass solo and strings, 8 measures, "Verily I say unto you."
7. Final chorus *a 10*, SSAATBB and strings, 10 measures, "Hallelujah" (chorus in alternation with a verse section).

When the Son of man is entirely in duple meter, a fact that may be related to the slight attention devoted to the orchestra and, consequently, to dancelike sections. The two works compared here are different in a number of other ways also. The longer anthem has no two vocal sections in succession, the orchestral *ritornelli* assume a prominent position, it has no individual solo sections, and the piece is conspicuously free of

[49] See n. 28.   [50] Harley 7340, 142–50.

Example 13.   Section 4 of Locke's verse anthem, *Sing unto the Lord, O ye saints of his* (Harley 7340, 157).

demands upon sopranos. The shorter piece, on the other hand, uses string orchestra for accompaniment only, depends upon a solo bass for two arialike sections, uses the chorus in recitative fashion (Example 14), and encloses the entire piece in a choral framework. As to the musical style of each, the former work naturally has a more secular flavor, not only from the presence of the orchestra, but because of the rhythms that are used. Dotted rhythm patterns in triple meter point more strongly than any other ingredient to Continental influence. The use of a "hallelujah" chorus to close each piece, always a rousing way to bring a multisectional work to an end, provided something the English could supply in no other way. The Germans could call into use an appropriate chorale tune whenever they so desired, but the Anglican faith had no body of sturdy hymns from which to select appropriate and pithy stanzas. The use of a generally acceptable formula, while tedious when viewed from later centuries, may still have provided a fresh conclusion to musical sections at that time. Notably, Locke's "hallelujah" sections take on a character heretofore unnoticed in the anthem. A sharply dotted pattern supplants the fluid lines of the "hallelujahs" favored by Child and others of the earlier generation.

One other feature of *When the Son of man* must also be mentioned. It begins with chorus rather than a verse section, even though it contains parts designated as solo or verse. It has been common practice to distinguish between full and verse anthems, but this piece does not belong clearly to either category. The full anthem is properly a work for chorus without any sections for solo singers, either individually or in groups;

Example 14. The choral recitatives from Locke's full anthem with verses, *When the Son of man* (Harley 7340, 146; 147–48).

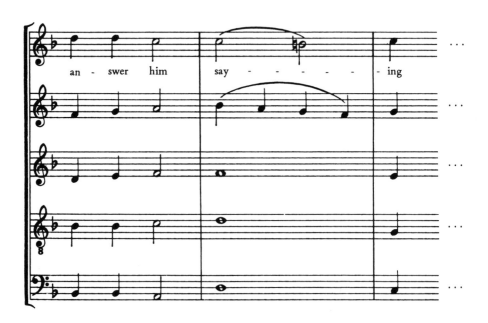

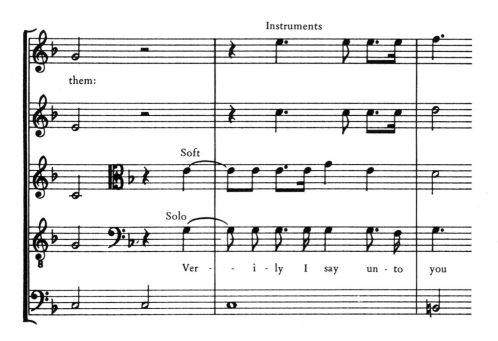

the verse anthem correctly begins with solo voice or voices, either with or without preliminary instrumental material. The other type, illustrated by this piece, is a full anthem with verses—i.e., an anthem beginning with a choral section, but containing verses at later points. Such an anthem places the chorus and soloists in a more balanced emphasis, and relies less on the accompaniment than does the verse anthem. If there is a norm for the full anthem with verses, Locke exceeded it here in his choral recitative sections.

Considerable space has been devoted to the first years after the Restoration of the Crown, partly because the period is generally avoided by writers as unfruitful and unimportant. The contributions of this first dozen years are of singular importance to the development of the anthem, leading directly into the cantata-anthem of the masters of this century, Blow and Purcell. We can see, also, through an examination of these few anthems, the musical taste of the England that Pelham Humfrey left when he made his visit to France and Italy, and we place in better perspective the contributions he made upon his return.

Between Locke and Humfrey, only Robert Creyghton (1639–1734) has retained a place in the annals of history, and even that place has become dimmed by the greater light that is cast by his fellows of the Chapel. His best known anthem, *I will arise*,[51] is a simple four-part setting that shows considerable skill in setting text on a modest scale. His *Praise the Lord, O my soul*[52] is an effective setting of the opening verses of Psalm 104, SATB, in the form of a full anthem with verses. No instrumental parts are supplied by Tudway, and, since the piece cannot be dated, it is impossible to determine

TABLE 3

Structure of Creyghton's Full Anthem with Verses, *Praise the Lord, O my soul*

1. Chorus, SATB, 10 measures, "Praise the Lord, O my soul."
2. Verse, ATB, 7 measures, "Thou deckest thyself with light."
3. Chorus, SATB, 2½ measures, "And spreadest out the heavens."
4. Verse, ATB, 7 measures, "Who layeth the beams of his chambers."
5. Chorus, SATB, 3½ measures, "He maketh his angels spirits."
6. Verse, SAB, 9 measures, "He laid the foundations of the earth."
7. Chorus, SATB, 2 measures, "The waters stand above the hills."
8. Verse, SAB, 2 measures, "At thy rebuke they flee."
9. Chorus, SATB, 2½ measures, "At the voice of thy thunder."
10. Verse, SSA, 1½ measures, "They go up as high as the hills."
11. Chorus, SATB, 1½ measures, "And down to the valleys beneath."
12. Verse, ATB, 6 measures, "O Lord, how manifold are thy works."
13. Chorus, SATB, 2 measures, "The earth is full of thy riches."
14. Verse, SSA, 12 measures, "I will sing unto the Lord."
15. Chorus, SATB, 12 measures, "Hallelujah."

[51] Boyce, *CM*, II, 145–47; Harley 7338, 299–300.   [52] Harley 7339, 114–18.

whether any existed or whether unaccompanied performance of all sections was intended. The composition alternates regularly between chorus and verse sections, some of them so short that they carry only half a hemistich of the psalm text in syllabic form (Table 3).

The opening choral statement covers the entire opening verse. Subsequent verses are sung in alternation by soloists and chorus, divided between the two groups, or, as with section 3, have the chorus repeating the second hemistich after it has been sung by the solo group. Neither the chorus nor the solo groups have a monopoly on important texts; the chorus predominates only by virtue of its position at the beginning and end of the composition. Its prominence, and the regular use of soprano voices in the verses, indicate a confidence on Creyghton's part that the boys to perform this music would be present, even though no extraordinary skill was required of either group. The piece proceeds in an unvarying duple meter until the middle of section 13, where it shifts to triple meter. This final surge of exuberance, culminating in a "hallelujah" section, contains nothing extraordinary. The result is a satisfying, but somewhat studied, alternation of forces.

Creyghton was not in the mainstream of choral activity, but it is certain that he knew the importance of developments at the sophisticated Chapel Royal. His sphere of activity was to the west of London. He was canon and precentor of Wells Cathedral, and his father had been Bishop of Bath and Wells. The elder Creyghton preached a number of times to the Royal Household, at times being openly critical of the profligate Charles' adulterous liaisons.[53] His son also preached there later,[54] and it may be assumed that his musical curiosity was not put aside on those occasions. His use of the full anthem with verses cannot be dated, but his avoidance of instrumental interludes is not necessarily related to the chronology of his pieces. The sections of *Praise the Lord, O my soul* connect in such excellent fashion that no accompaniment was needed; if any was added, it would have been of the *colla parte* variety. There is no place to insert any other type.

The use of a style characteristic, by Creyghton or any other composer, does not indicate that he was following in a stream of tradition or that other people imitated his practice. Consequently, we may not employ Creyghton's example as a yardstick for future full anthems with verses. We shall see again the alternation of tiny fragments of text and music in Humfrey's anthems, but there is no reason to say that one influenced the other, nor is there any proof of where the original idea of such alternation may have been seen.

Of the new generation of Restoration composers, there are five who may be designated as the St. James group, inasmuch as they were the first students of the new system within the Chapel and were influenced by the surviving members of the old Chapel tradition. These, the principal composers of the Restoration school appearing as Children of the Chapel under Henry Cooke as early as the middle of 1660, were

[53] *The Diary of Samuel Pepys*, I, 383, 597, 865; II, 611, 644.
[54] *The Diary of John Evelyn*, III, 623; IV, 23, 97, 181, 465.

Pelham Humfrey, Michael Wise, John Blow, Thomas Tudway, and William Turner. The first of this group to develop as a composer seems to have been Pelham Humfrey (1647–1674). Pepys mentions having heard an anthem on Sunday, November 22, 1663, "being the fifty-first psalme, made for five voices by one of Captain Cooke's boys, a pretty boy."[55] Henry B. Wheatley, editor of the Pepys diary, asserts that "the 'pretty boy' was Pelham Humfrey, and his anthem is printed in Boyce's 'Cathedral Music'."[56] One discrepancy, however, is apparent—Humfrey's setting of Psalm 51, as found in both Boyce and Tudway, is SATB with ATB solos, and not for five voices as Pepys observed. Since no other setting of this psalm appears among the extant works of those composers who make up the St. James group, it is probable that the Humfrey setting is the one performed on that date, and that Pepys may have imagined more voices than he actually heard.

A spirit of fraternal friendship is evident in the *Club Anthem* (*I will always give thanks*),[57] which was written by three of the boys of the Chapel choir—Pelham Humfrey, John Blow, and William Turner. Humfrey is said to have written the first part, Turner the section beginning with the bass solo, and Blow the closing section.[58] It would be absurd to suggest a direct link between Humfrey and Locke, existing before 1664 when Humfrey went to the Continent to learn the French taste. Still, it must be recognized that the instrumental introduction to the piece shows a familiarity with the type of writing we have observed in Locke's pieces. The opening Symphony (Example 15) obviously had an ancestor that was still active. The *Club Anthem* was a hasty job, not to be compared critically with works that were deliberately created over a period of time. Due to the short time available for its creation—certainly not much more than twelve hours—it is probably a *pasticcio* of works the young composers had completed earlier. Thomas Tudway, their contemporary in the Chapel, describes the work's genesis:

> The news of a great victory obtain'd over the Dutch at sea, by the Duke of York, coming to King Charles the 2d. on a Saturday at night, His Majesty was desirous of having an Anthem of Thanksgiving the next day at Chappell; which none of his composers being willing to undertake, 3 of the Children of the Chappell aforenam'd, undertook it & it was perform'd to the King, the next day accordingly.[59]

Here was an opportunity for three youngsters among the Chapel's Children to command the attention of the King. In view of Humfrey's later reputation as a sycophant, it is not difficult to see him as the instigator of the joint effort. There is some confusion about the date of this anthem, but it may easily be due to Tudway's faulty memory, since he was writing some years after the event.[60]

---

[55] *The Diary of Samuel Pepys*, I, 781.   [56] *Ibid.*   [57] Harley 7339, 471–76.   [58] *DNB*, X, 237.
[59] Harley 7339, 471.
[60] *Grove's*, IV, 404, points out that the Duke of York's victory over the Dutch dates from June, 1665. Humfrey was in France at that time, and could not possibly have engaged in a group project. On the other hand, evidence supplied by Rockstro, that "in 1664, there was a naval engagement in which the English captured 135 vessels," is quoted as counterevidence by Henry Bryce Jordan, "The Music of Pelham Humfrey" (unpublished Ph.D. dissertation, University of North Carolina, 1956), 18.

Example 15. Humfrey's opening Symphony to *I will always give thanks*, the *Club Anthem* by Humfrey, Blow, and Turner (Harley 7339, 471).

The *Club Anthem* contains the only surviving anthem material by Humfrey that can be positively dated before his departure for the Continent in 1664. Meager as it is, we are left with only these few measures as a basis for comparison. That it was intended for performance at the Chapel is without doubt; that it builds on a pre-existent pattern is most probable; that the pattern was laid down by Matthew Locke is a distinct possibility.

It is alleged that Charles II sent Humfrey to Paris specifically to study with Lully,[61] and that he traveled to Italy as well.[62] While still abroad, he was appointed Gentleman of the Chapel Royal in 1666, and was sworn into office October 26, 1667, upon his return to England.[63] At the death of Captain Cooke in 1672, he was appointed Master of the Children, a post he held until his death in 1674.

Arrogant and conceited by nature, Humfrey evidently was unbearable after his return from France. Pepys relates an interesting encounter between the two on November 15, 1667:

> Thence I away home, calling at my mercer's and tailor's, and there find, as I expected, Mr. Caesar and little Pelham Humphreys, lately returned from France, and is an absolute Monsieur, as full of form, and confidence, and vanity, and disparages everything, and everybody's skill but his own. The truth is, every body says he is very able, but to hear how he laughs at all the King's musick here, as Blagrave and others, that they cannot keep time nor tune, nor understand anything; and that Grebus, the Frenchman, the King's master of the musick, how he understands nothing, nor can play on any instrument, and so cannot compose: and that he will give him a lift out of his place; and that he and the King are mighty great![64]

The French style, which Charles II was intent upon fostering in his own Chapel Royal, came into full flower in the works of Humfrey, for of his fifteen extant anthems, all but three are written with string symphonies. Reference has already been made to the use of dance rhythms, especially the saraband, in the works of Matthew Locke. These same dance rhythms are also found repeatedly in the symphonies of Humfrey's anthems. One of his works in this form, *O give thanks*,[65] is a full anthem with verses, based on Psalm 118. The opening symphony consists of twelve measures in duple meter followed by twenty-four measures in triple meter, a procedure of alternation frequently followed by Humfrey. Saraband rhythms are used throughout the triple-meter section (Example 16). The main body of the anthem falls into the following major sections:

1. SATB chorus alternating with *ritornelli*.
2. TT, AT, and B alternating with *ritornelli*.
3. SATB chorus, ATTB verse, and *ritornelli* in alternation.
4. Opening chorus repeated with added cadence in duple meter.

[61] *Hullah's Lectures on the Third or Transition Period of Musical History*, 1865, p. 201, cited in *OCB*, 213.

[62] Jordan, *op cit.*, 18–19, states that there is no evidence to show that Humfrey studied with Lully, nor is there any to prove conclusively that he went to Italy.

[63] *OCB*, 14.   [64] *The Diary of Samuel Pepys*, II, 712.   [65] Harley 7338, 122.

Example 16. Saraband rhythms in *O give thanks*, Pelham Humfrey (Harley 7338, 123).

Example 17. *By the waters of Babylon*, Pelham Humfrey (Harley 7338, 113–14).

The four solo voices are again drawn from the lower ranges, indicating that only adults were entrusted with such responsibilities. The solo soprano voice is seldom used in Humfrey's anthems, probably due to the continuing dearth of boys with reliable solo voices.

A feature of special interest is found in *By the waters of Babylon*,[66] where a violin *obbligato* accompanies the bass solo (Example 17). The use of *obbligato* solo instrument with voices is unknown in England, and this may be one of the true fruits of Humfrey's Continental experience. Generally, the strings are silent in the verse sections of this anthem, and it appears that Humfrey wished to enhance the poignancy of the text with this special effect.

Hear, O heavens[67] is perhaps Humfrey's most unusual anthem. It employs Italian declamatory style extensively. It is also one of three anthems in which Humfrey does not use any accompaniment other than the *basso continuo*. The piece opens with the bass soloist declaiming, "Hear, O heavens, and give ear, O earth, for the Lord hath spoken." The text is made to stand out in bold relief by the unrelenting sustained accompaniment of the opening phrase (Example 18a).

Another Italianate feature is the use of melodic chromaticism to create a sense of tension and urgency (Example 18b). Still another expressive passage occurs on the text, "Ah! sinful nation," where the three solo voices successively introduce the phrase with sighing *appoggiature* (Example 18c). In yet another instance, the melodic and textual continuity is carried by the three voices in succession (Example 18d). It may not be beyond the scope of probability to suggest that Humfrey knew such writing from Locke's *Lord, let me know mine end*[68] or another similar earlier piece.

Much has been written concerning Humfrey's role as an innovator of French musical style at the court of Charles II. To be sure, he made extensive use of string symphonies, dotted rhythms, and frequent meter changes. But these, as we have already noted, were introduced by earlier composers. He did, however, make a unique contribution to the English anthem by his introduction of a declamatory style capable of more intense and direct expression than was known prior to his time.

It is difficult to assign Henry Aldrich (1647–1710) a place among his contemporaries because his position in the musical world is that of an interested amateur rather than a professional who needed to win acclaim in order to survive. It is generally conceded that he contributed little to the development of church music, but produced a large amount of material that found a way into standard repertories for a couple of generations. Possibly, this evaluation may be inaccurate. Music was at best a fascinating hobby for him, but hobbies often loom larger in men's lives than do their professions.

He was a canon of Christ Church, Oxford, a man well versed in logic, architecture, theology, and letters. His essays into composition, though numerous, were not of

[66] Harley 7338, 113.   [67] Boyce, *CM*, III, 186; Harley 7338, 200–204.
[68] *CMC*, 149–50, has a brief discussion and examples from Locke's anthem. The complete anthem is printed in *TECM*, III, 21–35.

Example 18.   *Hear, O heavens*, Pelham Humfrey (Boyce, *CM*, III, 186–87).

(c)

(d)

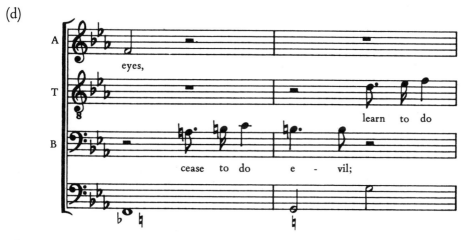

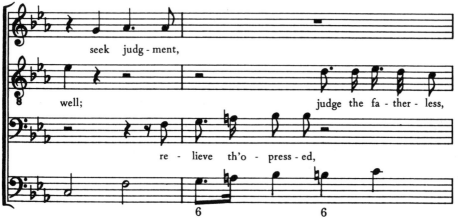

such quality that they provided him with either an enviable reputation after his death or a livelihood during his life. His greatest impact was probably through the many arrangements he made of works from the masters of the late Renaissance and early Baroque periods. He arranged fewer works from the English tradition than from the Continental, a fact that brought the style of Catholic motet composition back into the orbit of Anglican limitations; his "alterations" of polyphonic works provided a body

Example 19.   *Out of the deep have I called unto thee*, Henry Aldrich (Boyce, *CM*, II, 135).

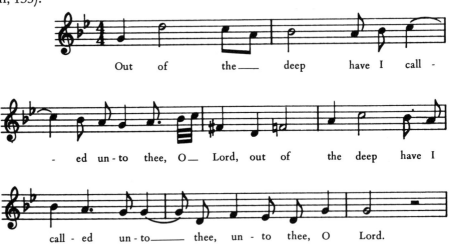

of material that had the solidity of imitative writing while it was forced into syllabic English settings. His accentuation of text often left something to be desired; he was forced into artificial divisions of words in order to produce the necessary number of syllables (Example 19), an unfortunate concomitant of his translating activities. His product was apparently held in high esteem by compilers, and his pieces were handed on to succeeding generations through the efforts of Tudway, who included twenty-seven of his works, original and arranged;[69] Boyce, who printed two;[70] Arnold three;[71] and Page, two.[72] Such a representation by his contemporaries and successors is too generous a tribute to ignore, but the quality of his work has usually been deemed such that it was thought best to stir little of its dust. His excursions into the motets of Italian masters gave him an understanding of the delights of textural alternation, and he often used high and low groups of voices in succession, as in *God is our hope and strength*,[73] SSATB, a full anthem with verses (Example 20).

[69] Harley 7338–7340, *passim.*   [70] Boyce, *CM*, II, 135–39; 104–44.
[71] Arnold, *CM*, I, 276–83; 290–93; 294–97.   [72] *HS*, I, 50–57; III, 61–64.
[73] *HS*, I, 50–57.

Example 20.   Alternation of high and low voice groups in *God is our hope and strength*, Henry Aldrich (*HS*, I, 54).

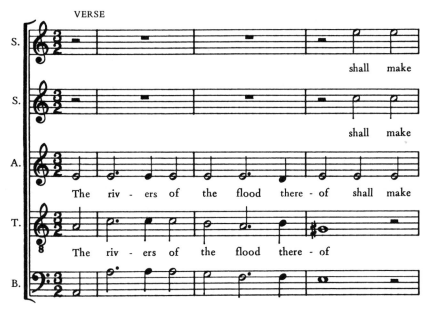

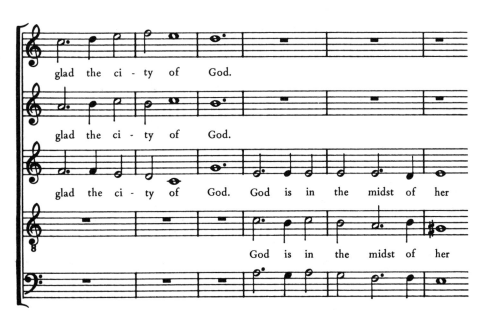

Example 21.   Opening measures of *How are the mighty fall'n*, Michael Wise (Harley 7339, 185), and Henry Aldrich's modified version, *Thy beauty, O Israel, is slain* (Boyce, *CM*, III, 208).

* Tudway has omitted a measure here.

A certain amount of editing, even to the extent of tampering, was also practiced on his own contemporaries and predecessors. He altered the works of Blow, William Lawes, Farrant, and others, sometimes providing a distorted idea of what the original material may have been, improving one feature while diminishing the finer qualities of another. He did much to give English musicians a better understanding of Continental polyphonic style, but some of the effect was lost through the necessary adjustment to English text. Unfortunately, any lessons he learned in this fashion had small results in the next generations. A half century after Aldrich's death, the inexorable decline of

English church music that was to continue for nearly a century had begun in earnest.

One of the compositions that Aldrich arranged is a verse anthem, *How are the mighty fall'n*,[74] by Michael Wise (ca. 1648–1687). In the apparently original version Tudway has left us, the text comes from II Sam. 1:19–29, using most of that text beginning with the second half of verse 19. The composition has a brief organ introduction, verse sections by solo voices and solo groups, and choruses SATB. It exhibits a fine understanding of contrapuntal writing in short points of imitation, a sensitive use of chromaticism, and the use of pathetic intervals on selected words.

The Aldrich version of the piece is quite another matter. Its title is different, since Aldrich was not satisfied to begin with the second half of the opening scriptural verse. He added the first half, thus producing a piece identified as *Thy beauty, O Israel, is slain*.[75] The style of his initial phrase is less direct and agitated than Wise's original material, and it seems incongruous with what follows. The difference in the opening sections is illustrated in Example 21. Wise had also omitted verse 21, probably to obtain better continuity of the material, but Aldrich restored it as a verse for solo bass. The student who comes unsuspecting upon Aldrich's version will believe that Wise was a leader in the development of rhapsodic expression for solo voice in Restoration anthems, but the extended passage shown in Example 22 is an Aldrich accretion, interesting but unidentified as to authorship.[76] At other places, sections of text are repeated, music is modified, and the piece becomes an entirely different one from Wise's original. The end of the foregoing example contains another feature that was to become common in English music, coming to full realization with Handel, the declamatory statement that covers a wide range within a single phrase, and which ends on a firm cadence. Such phrases occur in both the Wise and Aldrich versions of this piece.

Wise's anthems available in Tudway and Boyce total nine, all of them verse anthems with organ. Often a *ritornello* is indicated, a possible clue that an orchestra was intended or used. None of the pieces favors the alto as a solo voice, although Wise was a countertenor of considerable distinction. Solos are given to all voices without apparent favoritism. In addition to his use of imitation, chromaticism, and pathetic intervals on sensitive text fragments, Wise made good use of the delayed accent on strong opening words, an Italian characteristic. He also employed text-painting of a type that had been missing for some years, as on "trumpet" in *O praise God in his*

---

[74] Harley 7339, 185–88.

[75] Boyce, *CM*, III, 208–14. Aldrich expanded the works of other composers as well, probably with mixed success. His treatment of Blow's *And I heard a great voice* is described in *CMC*, 153–54.

[76] The authors are certain that other comparisons are possible, but the scope of this book does not permit such distant excursions, however interesting they may be. An example of what can be accomplished by thorough comparison of all existing versions of a work is seen in such publications as *TECM*. There, however, the results are hidden in arcane symbols that confuse the casual reader or moderately interested student. The proper place for further study of such features will continue to be the master's thesis and the doctoral dissertation.

Example 22. A rhapsodic solo section added to Wise's *How are the mighty fall'n,* by Henry Aldrich (Boyce, *CM,* III, 209–10).

Example 23. *O praise God in his holiness*, Michael Wise (Harley 7339, 102).

holiness[77] (Example 23), and some florid writing for chorus that anticipates the Handelian style.

Again we must reiterate that the presence of these specific ideas in Wise's music does not point to him as their originator, although we are sure of no other composer who employed them with equal facility and enthusiasm. He was one of those unfortunate composers who, were it not for their involvement in a poorly appreciated period of history, would long ago have been dignified by thorough study. The brief examination of Wise's music undertaken here does not exhaust his contributions. Some of the other developments to which he may have been a party include further development of the recitative idea, the development of florid passages that appear first for soloists and are repeated by the chorus, and the use of the echo device.

It is not possible to follow the fortunes of all the important or prolific composers of any period, and some deserving men must always be overlooked. Perhaps some lesser members of the St. James group fall into this number, and it is likely that Robert Smith[78] (ca. 1648–1675) is representative of such composers. The words to six of his anthems are listed by Clifford,[79] while only five by Humfrey are printed there, and three by Blow. Since Clifford collected his texts no later than 1664, he simply reflected the promise of these youngsters, and cannot be blamed for lack of foresight. Apparently Smith's anthems were being sung when he was still in his middle teens, but no copy seems to have been preserved. Furthermore, secular composition was more to his taste, so no church works of his maturity exist. Our search for significant composers, then, is limited not only by records of those in important positions, but further by the departure of apparently talented men to the pursuit of rewards found in composing for the theater and the drawing room.

On the other hand, the skill of William Turner (1651–1740), whose contribution to the *Club Anthem* was mentioned earlier (p. 60), is a matter of record and of considerable interest. None of the texts given by Clifford are from Turner's anthems, indicating at least that he had no anthems copied into the part-books before 1664. There is, however, a clear indication that he produced his verse anthem, *Behold now, praise the Lord*,[80] before 1685, since Tudway states that it was "compos'd in King Charles' time."[81] It is a notable work for two reasons: the presence of a part for *obbligato* violin in a verse section, and the use of a ground bass as a constant unifying device throughout the entire composition. The ground is three measures long, and it appears in three different forms in the piece (Example 24). The manner in which the text is divided and allocated to the voices is best illustrated in Table 4. The text is taken from *The Book of Common Prayer*, which continued in the use set forth by the Great

---

[77] Harley 7339, 194–98.

[78] Not Richard, as erroneously stated in Ralph T. Daniel, *The Anthem in New England before 1800* (Evanston, Ill.: Northwestern University Press, 1966), 21.

[79] James Clifford, *The Divine Services and Anthems usually Sung in His Majesties Chappell and in all Cathedrals and Collegiate Choires in England and Ireland* (2nd ed., London: W. G., 1664), 361–67; 415–16.

[80]   Harley 7341, 151–56.   [81] *Ibid.*, 151.

Bible, and Turner used the same source for the piece next mentioned. The setting of the Lesser Doxology to music at the close of this paslm is also unusual.

Turner wrote an anthem for the St. Cecilia's Day observance in 1697, *The King shall rejoice*,[82] taken from Psalm 21. He had made a setting of Nahum Tate's text for the 1685 celebration, but that was an entirely secular affair.[83] It is worth noting that for the occasion on which Turner composed his anthem, the sermon was preached by Tate's collaborator in the "New Version" of the metrical psalms, Nicholas Brady. The close relationship between the secular and religious observances is again evident in the

TABLE 4

Structure of Turner's Verse Anthem, *Behold now, praise the Lord*, Ps. 134

1. Symphony, ₵, 6 measures, 2 statements of ground.
2. Verse, AT with violin *obbligato*, "Behold now, praise the Lord," 8 statements of ground.
3. Ritornello, 6 measures, strings with new material, 2 statements of ground.
4. Verse, ATT, instrumental bass only, "Lift up your hands in the sanctuary," upper parts imitative over 9 statements of ground.
5. Ritornello, $\frac{6}{4}$, strings with new material, 5 statements of ground.
6. Chorus, SATB, ₵ with dotted figures, no instruments specified, "Glory be to the Father," 5 statements of ground.

fact that Brady had written the secular ode for the 1692 celebration, and the composer of its musical setting was Henry Purcell. Now again, in 1697, Purcell's *Te Deum and Jubilate in D*, with trumpets, was performed as part of the religious observance, along with Turner's anthem. The convenience of bringing trumpeters to St. Bride's for two pieces in a single service is of some significance—for Turner's anthem calls for *obbligato* trumpets, as we shall see—and it must not be overlooked that Brady's text for the day mentioned the instrument also: "It came to pass, as the trumpeters and singers were as one, to make one sound to be heard in praising and thanking the Lord. . . ."

Turner's piece is an extended one, as befits the occasion. The opening Symphony is a long, two-section piece for strings and trumpets that begins in duple meter and proceeds to a triple-meter section on a ground bass. It is substantial enough to stand by itself as a separate instrumental composition, although its alternating fast and slow

[82] Harley 7339, 245–72.

[83] Divine Services at St. Bride's Church in Fleet Street, with specially composed music and a sermon in praise of church music, were held beginning in 1693. These continued at least until 1714, after the secular concerts had ceased. Services were regularly held at St. Bride's in London, except for the 1699 meeting, which was held in St. Paul's Cathedral. A number of places outside London also carried on the tradition of having a special St. Cecilia sermon. The best information on this tradition is found in *Two St. Cecilia's Day Sermons (1696–1697)*, with introduction by James E. Phillips, Jr. (The Augustan Reprint Society, Publication Number 49) (Los Angeles: William Andrews Clark Memorial Library, University of California, 1955), i–vii.

Example 24.   The three forms of a ground bass in *Behold now, praise the Lord,*
William Turner (Harley 7341, 151–56).

(c)

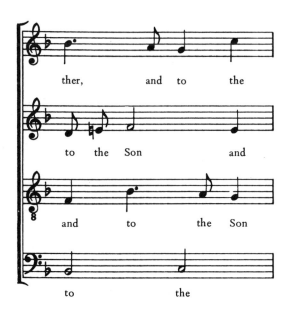

sections mark it clearly as an introductory piece to a festive work of considerable size. Except for the alternation of tempi in the opening section, the piece follows the outlines of a French Overture in matters of speed sequence, dotted rhythms, and running passages.

Example 25. *The King shall rejoice*, William Turner (Harley 7339, 259–60).

The text is assigned principally to a series of verses separated by *ritornelli*. Two solo sections for countertenor are accompanied by strings and *obbligato* trumpets and violins. The solo instruments are not confined to passages that are idiomatically their own, but derive their patterns from the vocal materials (Example 25). Two verse sections for ATB call for considerable flexibility from the soloists, and the *ritornelli* that follow both sections are again derived from the preceding vocal material. In addition, there are short recitative sections for bass, and a closing chorus that alternates the SATB choir and instruments with an SSATB verse group. The composition is remarkably unified, its sectional structure notwithstanding. Thematic ideas are transferred and developed from one section of the piece to another, so that materials sound familiar although not repetitious. Several developments from a single thematic idea are illustrated in Example 26.

The significance of Turner's use of violins and trumpets as *obbligato* instruments lies not in his calling for them generally in the score, but in his use of them to enhance the vocal solos. Such use of instruments was uncommon, although instrumental accompaniment as such was a normal feature of Lutheran and Catholic works—as well as of Anglican works for the Royal Chapel—by the third quarter of the seventeenth century. The Continental practice, being part of a longer uninterrupted tradition, developed more generally than did the English usage which stopped, except for festival works, upon the death of Charles II. Whether Purcell, Blow, Turner, or some other composer was the first to undergird solo voices with prominent instrumental passages in England is not of primary importance. We can assign the device to this period, and we know it was a feature in the works of several of them.

As various foreign and theatrical features made their way into the larger anthems for the Royal Chapel, we are able to discern a tendency among composers to produce large-scale works that we call cantata-anthems. These generally employ some—or ideally, all—of the following features: preliminary or interstitial orchestral sections, arias, recitatives, verse sections employing ensembles of soloists, and choruses with or without orchestral support. The segments of the cantata-anthem are often separated into sections that stand complete by themselves rather than simply being parts of a continuous piece that shifts density and texture. Their way is predicted in the works of Humfrey and Wise, and is brought to its culmination by Turner, Blow, and Purcell.

One of the key figures of the St. James group was John Blow (1649–1708), who, like Humfrey and Turner, was one of the boys of the Royal Chapel under Captain Cooke. His distinguished career included such appointments as organist of Westminster Abbey in 1668, Gentleman of the Royal Chapel in 1674, Master of the Children there upon the death of Pelham Humfrey in the same year, and Almoner and Master of the Children at St. Paul's Cathedral, 1687. At the death of his famous pupil and friend, Henry Purcell, in 1695, Blow returned to Westminster Abbey as organist, assuming this duty in addition to his post at St. Paul's. In 1699 he was named Composer for the Royal Chapel, a new position to which he was the first appointee.

Example 26. Related thematic fragments in *The King shall rejoice*, William Turner (Harley 7339, 252–71).

(a)

Ex - ceed - ing glad

(b)

He ask - ed life of thee

(c)

And make him glad

(d)

So will we sing

(e)

So will we sing, so will we sing

Blow's influence on cathedral music in the latter part of the seventeenth century was considerable. His reputation as a teacher was certainly enhanced by the accomplishments of Henry Purcell, and his productivity as a composer of church music is evident in the eighty-nine anthems that are extant in various manuscript sources.[84] In addition, the texts of three of his early anthems are contained in Clifford's *Divine Services and Anthems* of 1663, evidence of his early acceptance as a composer of promise in his youth (see p. 76). Most of Blow's anthems are the verse type and, of these, more than twenty employ string orchestra. Insofar as they can be dated, it appears that almost all of the anthems with symphonies were written during the reign of Charles II.

Coronation anthems were an important part of Blow's musical contribution. He wrote three such anthems for the coronation of James II in 1685, and the fact that other prominent composers—Purcell, Turner, Lawes, and Child—were represented with one or two anthems each, indicates the high esteem in which Blow was held at that time. Two of his three anthems for that occasion, *Let thy hand be strengthened*[85] and *Behold, O God our defender*,[86] are short, five-part, full settings. However, the third anthem, *God spake sometimes in visions*,[87] is a work of massive proportions. It is scored for SSAATBBB and string orchestra and is 372 measures in length. Full choir, verse sections, and instrumental *ritornelli* alternate in the usual manner. Two features, however, are noteworthy: The opening vocal section is full rather than verse, and the verse sections employ eight solo voices of the same disposition as the chorus. Here, contrary to the usual practice of limiting the verse sections to adult voices, the boys are trusted with solo soprano parts, although stability is always insured by the presence of one or more adult voices with them. At least three solo voices sing at any given time. Blow protected himself against any catastrophic lapses of quality by supporting the boys' parts with mature, experienced singers. Again, four years later, Blow provided three anthems for the coronation of William and Mary. Two of these are short, four-part, full anthems, and the third is a more extensive verse anthem with string orchestra.

The unusually large dimensions of *God spake sometimes in visions* were not entirely due to the fact that it was a coronation anthem. No doubt the grandeur of this momentous occasion prompted Blow to conceive the piece on a large scale, but this was by no means an isolated example. A number of his works fall into the cantata-anthem category. In fact, this form, already seen in the works of Turner, and forecast by Humfrey and Wise, is brought to full flower by Blow. A case in point is *And I heard a great voice*,[88] an extensive verse anthem 362 measures in length.[89] Another work by Blow, *The Lord is my shepherd*,[90] must also be considered a cantata-anthem.

---

84 *Grove's*, I, 772–74.

85 John Blow, *Coronation Anthems; Anthems with Strings*, eds. Anthony Lewis and Harold Watkins Shaw (*Musica Britannica*, VII; London: Stainer and Bell, 1953), 46–47.

86 *Ibid.*, 48–50.   87 *Ibid.*, 1–45.

88 *Ibid.*, 62–77.

89 Discussed, along with Aldrich's modification of it, in *CMC*, 153–55.

90 *Musica Britannica*, VII, 93–108.

While not quite as long as the two previously mentioned pieces, this 298-measure anthem is of major proportions. It has the features associated with a cantata-anthem: (1) an independent orchestral overture which can stand alone apart from the vocal sections, (2) well-defined solo and chorus sections, several of which are contrasting in character, interspersed with instrumental *ritornelli*. The sectional nature of the work is quite pronounced. Another remarkable feature of this anthem is the degree of thematic unity it contains. The material of Example 27 *a* is contained in the second section of the overture; Example 27 *b* shows the use of the same theme in the opening solo verse. In Example 27 *c*, the theme is again given to the violins, and the bass solo is derived from the bass line of Example 27 *b*. Again, a modification of the same theme is found in the tenor solo (Example 27 *d*). In addition, the original thematic material (Example 27 *a*) reappears twice in short instrumental *ritornelli*.

Not all of Blow's anthems, however, were large-scale works. Some of his full anthems are relatively short and tightly constructed. *My God, my God, look upon me*[91] is of this type. Written in 1697, the piece reflects the general trend away from the large verse anthem with orchestra so popular during the reign of Charles II, and was probably indicative of the more conservative tastes of William and Mary, who were known to prefer Hampton Court to the Chapel Royal.

Time has not dealt favorably with most of the anthems of John Blow; only a few of them are available in modern editions. But that he was a central figure in the development of the Restoration anthem is seen in the fact that eighteen of his works were included in the Tudway collection early in the eighteenth century. That Boyce printed ten of his anthems in his *Cathedral Music* is evidence of their continued use in that century. Four of his works, including *My God, my God, look upon me*, have remained in the repertoire at more than ten English cathedrals.[92] One can only assume that the pieces have also had some continued use in a number of parish churches.

Henry Purcell (1659–1695) wrote nearly seventy anthems, some of them in several versions, and a few of them incomplete. His interest in church choral music was greatest in the years between 1680 and 1688, and it is significant that most of the anthems come from the first five of those years. After that time his attention appears to have been increasingly turned to solo songs, odes, and theatrical music. By far the largest percentage of the anthems is of the verse type, they being more in demand at the Chapel Royal until the death of Charles II in 1685. This preference, and its effect upon the general musical style of the times, is reflected in Purcell's full anthems as well, for most of them have verses. The interspersed verses sections may be one or more, and they are usually surrounded by full chorus sections as befits the class of anthem we know as "full with verses," and they contain no instrumental parts other than the *basso continuo*. Most works of this type fall into the first two years of the anthem decade, indicating that he preferred the complexity and length of the verse anthem to the

---

[91] Boyce, *CM*, II, 130–34.

[92] *Sixty Years of Cathedral Music [1898–1958]* (Church Music Society Occasional Paper No. 24; London: Oxford University Press, [1958?]), 17, 23, 27.

Example 27.   *The Lord is my shepherd*, John Blow (*Musica Britannica*, VII, 93, 94, 96, 103).

(a) 1st Violin

(b) Tenor solo

The Lord is my shep - herd, there - fore can I,

(c) 1st Violin and bass solo

He   shall   feed   me   in   a   green

pas - ture,   shall   feed   me

(d) Tenor solo

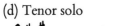

Thou shalt pre - - pare a ta - ble be - fore me,

Used with permission of The Royal Musical Association, c/o Stainer & Bell Ltd., Reigate, Surrey.

direct expression of the full or full with verses, or that verse anthems and cantata-anthems were more in demand.

Lord, how long wilt thou be angry?[93] belongs to his early, simpler type. Written sometime between 1680 and 1682, it is a setting of parts of Psalm 79 (Great Bible version) for SSATB chorus, ATB verse, and organ. The opening chorus is a restrained piece of imitative writing featuring a melodic diminished fourth in each voice along

Example 28. *Lord, how long wilt thou be angry,* Henry Purcell (Harley 7339, 455–56).

Lord,——   how   long   wilt   thou   be   an - - gry?

Shall   Thy   jeal - ous - y   burn   like   fire,   like

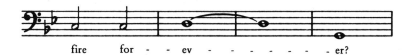

fire   for - - ev - - - - - - er?

with considerable chromatic motion (Example 28). The only verse section of the piece begins after twenty-one measures of choral writing, and the three-part verse continues to develop short chromatic fragments suited to the poignant text, "O remember not our old sins." The closing choral sections are varied in style, the final thanks-and-praise portion moving briskly into triple meter as a contrast to the otherwise quadruple material.

In the full anthem, *Remember not, Lord, our offences,*[94] with text from the Litany, a brief passage of text is expanded through repetition. A middle section of imitative counterpoint is enclosed between two chordal sections, and no single voice of the SSATB chorus is isolated for special attention.

When dealing with the solo voice, especially if the singer was to be the famous bass of the Royal Chapel, John Gostling, for whom Purcell intended many of his bass solos, the entire effort was devoted to displaying the fine vocal skills of the soloist. The stylistic restrictions that still clung to the full anthem disappeared completely from

[93] Henry Purcell, *The Works of Henry Purcell* (London: Novello and Co., 1878–), XXIX, 19–27; Harley 7339, 455–60.
[94] *Ibid.,* XXXII, 19–22.

solo anthems, and theatrical considerations were the order of the day. *Sing unto God*,[95] a portion of Psalm 68, is such a display piece, given entirely to the soloist with support of a *basso continuo*, and using the chorus only for two interjected Alleluia sections and a pair of closing Amens. Even more lavish is the treatment accorded the solo part in *My song shall be alway*,[96] a cantata-anthem for bass, strings, organ, and chorus. The opening Symphony testifies to the composer's knowledge of the French Overture in matters of length, meter change, and characteristic rhythms. Its opening section is in slow quadruple meter with some dotted rhythms in homophonic style; the second section is in imitative style and triple meter; and while no tempo change is indicated, the implication of greater motion is quite obvious from the context. A long solo passage for the bass follows, accompanied only by the *basso continuo*, a short instrumental *ritornello* gives the singer a breathing space, and he follows with a slow solo section, after which the entire Symphony is repeated. The second half of the piece follows a similar arrangement of parts, and the chorus finally enters to sing a perfunctory seven measures of Alleluia, a small contribution to an anthem of 373 measures. The veritable explosion of a solo anthem into the equivalent of the Italian solo cantata as it finally made its way into the Lutheran service truly had no need of the chorus except as a sop to convention, a gesture to insure that the dignity of worship was not completely lost. As remarked earlier, the Anglican musical practice was unable to supply the convenient vehicle available to the Lutherans, the summarizing chorale verse, and Alleluias and Amens were their only recourse.

The cantata-anthem in its normal form suffered no abuse from Purcell, for he maintained a more suitable balance among the solo, ensemble verse, chorus, and instrumental sections. *I will give thanks unto the Lord*,[97] one of several such cantata-anthems, illustrates such a balance of the parts. It consists of a large number of sections for instruments, solo voice, solo ensembles, and chorus, all of them organized with as much attention to balance and variety as to the appropriateness of text given to the performers. The attention to smaller details of balance is evident in such things as the use of modified sequence (Example 29). It is obvious that similar examples can be found in Purcell's secular works. Stylistic consistency is not necessarily a weakness; it may, in fact, be evidence of a composer's producing his very best work regardless of the medium or function of the composition.

One means of achieving variety does not appear consistently in the long cantata-anthem at this time, that of variety in key. *I will give thanks unto the Lord* remained firmly attached to the key of G minor, making excursions into closely related keys only for the duration of a single phrase or less. That the strong movement into related keys for several phrases or complete sections of an anthem was recognized as desirable by Purcell is evident in a number of cases. *Behold, I bring you glad tidings*[98] may be used as an example. Its opening Symphony is in C with brief excursions into D minor and

---

[95] *Ibid.*, XXXII, 23–29.   [96] *Ibid.*, XXIX, 51–67; Harley 7338, 459–67.
[97] Purcell, *Works*, XXVIII, 139–56.   [98] *Ibid.*, XXVIII, 1–27.

A minor. The opening verse sections move freely in keys related to C, and subsequent sections rest firmly in C minor, briefly in D minor and G, and again firmly in
G minor before returning to the closing chorus in C.

Purcell's interest in the organization of an entire piece, his control of the features
of unity and variety, is especially apparent in such a piece as *It is a good thing to give
thanks*,[99] which uses an arch form as its integrative device, and in his occasional use of

Example 29.   *I will give thanks unto the Lord*, Henry Purcell (*Works*, XXVIII,
144, 145).

Sought   out   of   all   them   that   have   plea - sure   there -

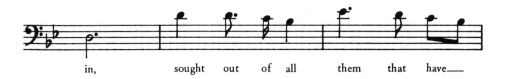

in,   sought   out   of   all   them   that   have____

plea - - - - - - - - sure   there - in.

Copyright by Novello & Co. Ltd. Used by permission.

ground basses that are found in other anthems. Generally, his solo writing for individuals and for solo ensembles is quite demanding, his choral writing relatively simple,
and his orchestral material full of vitality. Solo soprano voices are generally avoided
except in verses that call for several other parts; the adult male voices—countertenor,
tenor, and bass—are required to carry the burden of solitary singing.

The composers of the St. James group brought the anthem to a peak of complexity
and artistic expression that it would never again achieve as a large form. When the
orchestra ceased to be a desirable feature after the death of Charles II, the cantata-
anthem lost its most important element. The *ritornelli*, having to be modified, reduced
to organ, or omitted altogether, were avoided by the next generation of composers,
although they tried to continue with other features of the large anthem forms. When
James II succeeded to the throne in 1685, the Chapel must have suffered both lack of
interest and support, neither of which James, as a Roman Catholic, could offer.
Matters were no better under the next monarch, for William III and Mary were not

[99] *Ibid.*, XIV, 1–20. The anthem is discussed in detail in *CMC*, 158–61.

sympathetic to the Anglicans. "It was another of history's humors that the Anglican Church, which for a century had been persecuting Calvinists (Presbyterians, Puritans, and other Dissenters), should now accept a Dutch Calvinist as its head."[100] The court was moved to Hampton Court shortly after 1689, deserting Whitehall and London as principal areas of activity, and Mary delivered a further crushing blow when she "abolished the singing of prayers in the Chapel Royal at Whitehall and introduced Sunday afternoon sermons there."[101]

The result was almost catastrophic; a period of decline ensued which, while not completely laden with inferior compositions, produced too many pieces that owed their charm, grace, and appeal to the theater and popular taste. Composers had next to learn how to produce anthems that again depended on choral effects rather than on instrumental brilliance or interest in solo voices. It was to be nearly a century before consistent success in such efforts would become evident.

[100] Will and Ariel Durant, *The Age of Louis XIV*, Part VIII: *The Story of Civilization* (New York: Simon and Schuster, 1963), 301.
[101] *DNB*, XII, 1245.

CHAPTER THREE

A Century of Adjustment

The reasons for the great changes in English choral music during the eighteenth century are complex and numerous, and their beginnings may be seen in the late years of the seventeenth century. The great tradition of the Chapel Royal was on the wane; the paternalistic transfer of responsibility from teacher to student was to have one more spurt of life under the students of John Blow before its strength was dissipated. Tastes were becoming increasingly secular—or at least the distinction between religious and secular styles was becoming diffuse—and musicians were finding it profitable to win public favor when their skills were sufficient, or they were forced to submerge themselves in a dreary round of church-music activities when they were not. Attention was turning—but only slightly at first—to the parish churches and their musical problems, problems that were not to be solved easily, but that would supply a simpler kind of music than the cathedral choral service. The increased industrialization of England, the rising costs of maintaining musical establishments and of sustaining their personnel, and the gradual rise of a non-Anglican segment of the population to the surface of English society all had their impact upon life and upon the changing shape of church music. A survey of each of these factors would be outside the scope of our book, but some consideration of their effects is essential to an understanding of the state of English church music after the heyday of the St. James group and Henry Purcell.

Up to this point our concern has been with cathedral music and with composers who lived in the London area, principally those of the Chapel Royal. This has been true for a number of reasons. First, there was a lack of printed music books, and the few that came into existence reflected the cathedral practice, either because they were compiled from materials on hand and by people closely associated with the Chapel Royal, or because they were intended to perpetuate its traditions. Clifford's collection of texts and Barnard's anthem collection[1] served this purpose well, but they were aimed at the continuation of an esoteric practice. Second, there is little information about the practice at most of the cathedrals. We must assume that the musical practice at those places was simply a dim shadow of what happened in the services of St. Paul's, St. James's, St. George's, and Westminster Abbey. The notable composers and performers were, so far as we can determine, almost entirely confined to this small orbit, feeding upon each other's talents and nourishing no outside establishment. After the reestablishment of the Chapel Royal under Captain Cooke, when any boys in cathedral choirs who showed promise were simply appropriated for his training, the musical growth of cathedrals outside London was negligible. Third, parish churches existed, both large and small, but on a relatively primitive basis so far as music was concerned. Organs were rare in the smaller churches, for even where they had existed in the early years, they were often removed after the issuance of an Order of Council in 1664 calling for "the speedy Demolishing of all Organs, Images and all manner of Superstitious Monuments in Cathedrall, Parish Churches and Chappells."[2] Choirs were virtually nonexistent, and the only music available to the congregations (when they sang at all) was the metrical psalm. Bands of amateur gallery musicians often performed as instrumental support to the singing, attracting so much interest that it was common practice for the parishioners to turn their backs upon the altar during the music and face the gallery where the musicians were seated.[3] In some cases the only singing group was made up of the charity children of the parish.[4] The musical practices of these smaller churches and their influence in the creation of a new kind of anthem will be examined in the next chapter, along with a consideration of influence from Nonconformist groups.

Large parish churches were undoubtedly better favored in their music, but the regular use of choirs should not be taken for granted, even in the largest. Between 1749 and 1760 Charles Burney was organist at two fairly large parish churches, St. Dionis' Backchurch in London and St. Margaret's in King's Lynn. His responsibilities appear to have been quite small, and those in connection with a choir seem to have been minimal.

---

[1] John Barnard, *The First Book of Selected Church Musick, consisting of Services and Anthems, such as are now used in the Cathedrall, and Collegiat Churches of this Kingdome*, 1641.

[2] Quoted in K. H. MacDermott, *The Old Church Gallery Minstrels* (London: SPCK, 1948), 1–2.

[3] *Ibid.*, 1.

[4] Not necessarily those supported by alms. They might simply be the children of the free school for the poor or the Sunday School children. See Percy A. Scholes, *The Oxford Companion to Music* (9th ed., London: Oxford University Press, 1955), 38.

As far as one can gather he would play some composition (or extemporize) three times—firstly, as a prelude to the service, secondly, before the first lesson or the sermon, and thirdly, at the end of the service.

He would also accompany a metrical psalm (probably rarely an anthem) and that would usually be all he had to do.[5]

It should be remembered that the distinction between parish church and cathedral is not one of size, but of function and the consequent complexity of the service. Parish churches often exhibited the same degree of careful planning, architectural personality, and spacious beauty as a notable cathedral, the difference being only that the latter was more amply staffed as befits the principal church of a bishop. Parish churches varied from low, thatched-roof structures to lofty buildings with vaulted naves, towers, and many of the features commonly associated with cathedrals.[6] Much of the musical history of these churches remains undiscovered and, unfortunately, may remain so because documents appear to be scarce. For the present, then, we must continue to trace the traditional practice in Anglican cathedrals until the rise of a new practice becomes apparent.

As the fortunes of the Establishment declined during the eighteenth century, the quality of music produced for and by the choirs deteriorated to a large extent. Members of the Chapel Royal who remained active in composition for the Church were perpetuating a tradition that embraced both musical and liturgical practice. They inherited the cantata-anthem, a composition of such proportions that its performance was more a concert than an act of worship. They had available choirs that were well staffed, but that were increasingly hard to maintain because of the gulf between assigned responsibilities and financial return and because of the seductive beckonings of secular activities to both composers and singers. Of the truly successful composers, few were church musicians first and foremost. Such men as Greene, Boyce, Arnold, and Croft were esteemed for their instrumental and theatrical works as well as, or even more than, their anthems and Services. They are ranked among the leading church composers of their day because of their compositional skills generally, not because their works were uniquely suited to the Church. Many of their contemporaries were mediocre composers, known to history simply because they were there, and because so few of greater stature existed in their time.

It will be most convenient to deal with these composers in three groups, divided chronologically. The first group will comprise those men who died by the middle of the eighteenth century; the second those whose lives did not extend beyond that century; and the third those who died in the first quarter of the nineteenth century. Separation into groups by this manner is not an infallible method for assigning composers to patterns of similarity, for some have twice the life-span of others, and they

---

[5] Percy A. Scholes, *The Great Dr. Burney* (2 vols., London: Oxford University Press, 1948), I, 59.

[6] See J. C. Cox and C. B. Ford, *Parish Churches*, rev. Bryan Little (London: B. T. Batsford, 1961), for illustrations and descriptions.

overlap two groups during their productive years. On the other hand, it does, how-ever artibrarily, classify those who fall mainly under certain influences, musical or social, religious or secular.

The first group has as its most important figures Jeremiah Clarke (ca. 1670–1707)[7] and William Croft (1678–1727). Of lesser stature are John Goldwin (ca. 1670–1719), John Weldon (1676–1736), and Charles King (1678–1748). Other names can be brought to light, but they do not identify significant figures, although their bearers were some-times ambitious, as witness the prodigious efforts of the elder James Hawkins (ca. 1660–1729), who produced seventy-five anthems. The members of this group were all mature, employed, or dead before Handel became an important figure in English music. Any similarities of style will almost certainly not be traceable to Handel, through either direct contact or musical osmosis. Only two of these men, Weldon and King, would have been sufficiently exposed to Handelian ideas to transmit them in their own music.

Why do we make such a point of Handel's influence? The veneration for his music that overtook the English in the second half of the eighteenth century has so clouded the scene that contributions of native composers, and the continuing develop-ment of musical ideas from earlier decades, have often been overlooked or falsely attributed to Handel. The choral idiom for which he is best known, and through which he could have cast some influence on the anthem, stems from the Chandos Anthems (not earlier than 1718), occasional anthems for state occasions (all later than the Chandos Anthems), or the oratorios, which could have influenced only King.

Clarke and Croft were choristers under John Blow at the Chapel Royal; King was a chorister under Blow at St. Paul's, and he may have been there still when Clarke became master of the choristers. However, if King received his B.Mus. degree at Oxford in 1707,[8] and Clarke was not appointed to that post at St. Paul's until 1703—rather than 1693 as supposed by some authorities[9]—King would have known him there only in his earlier capacity as organist. The continuation of Blow's influence is a certainty; Clarke followed Blow at St. Paul's, whatever the date, and Croft succeeded him as organist at Westminster Abbey and as composer and Master of the Children at the Chapel Royal. Weldon, a pupil of Purcell's (therefore at least a musical grandchild of Blow) inherited Blow's position as organist to the Chapel Royal. Notwithstanding the fact that inherited positions sometimes come about through connections as much as through abilities, a thread of tradition is visible as far back as Pelham Humfrey, a tradition that guaranteed placement of the favored heir (and probably the best qualified most of the time) in the musical chair while its seat was still warm from the previous occupant.

Although Clarke was active as a composer of secular pieces during his entire musical maturity, his approach to the anthem was not entirely colored by what was

<hr/>

[7] See *MGG*, II, 1462, concerning the possibility of other dates for Clarke's birth.
[8] *Grove's*, IV, 754.   [9] *Ibid.*, II, 331.

the best theatrical fare. Some imitative writing may be found for solo ensembles and chorus, and he did not avoid the full anthem, although he ranged far afield from the sober pattern generally encountered in his *Praise the Lord, O Jerusalem*,[10] which shows signs of an eagerness to captivate the listener through variety in its use of six meter-signatures in the course of a seventy-eight-measure composition. Of the six sections, two are cautiously imitative and one is an uninspired Hallelujah chorus.

For the most part, Clarke favored the verse anthem. It was designed principally for displaying solo voices, and since the regular use of instruments at the Chapel Royal had ceased and it had never been a practice at St. Paul's, soloists, individually and in ensemble, were the best conveyors of excitement left to the composer. *Bow down thine ear*,[11] a cantata-anthem for alto solo, ATB ensemble, and SATB chorus with organ, is devoted mainly to the display of the solo voice. With the exception of the central solo that displays the singer in rather dramatic fashion (Example 30), the anthem is a succession of short pieces. In two sections the ATB group is given an imitative phrase to sing, each voice making one entry as in a fugal exposition, and then concluding in chordal fashion. Except for those two brief passages, the piece is solidly homophonic.

The favored place given to the solo voice is emphasized even more in *How long wilt thou forget me?*[12] where all but twenty-eight measures of the 190-measure anthem belong to the soloist. The chorus sings entirely in block-chord style, emphasizing the soloist's importance even more. Reliance on the solo voice is carried to extremes in *O be joyfull*,[13] a long solo anthem Clarke wrote for one of the annual meetings of the Sons of the Clergy,[14] and given entirely to a solo voice except for four measures of Amen for SATB chorus. The solo is in six sections of varied character and meter; one of them is on a ground, several of them are florid, and portions of two feature alternating runs between the accompaniment and the soloist. The Hallelujah section is of that type, the organ stating the material and the voice answering it. Dependence on solo performance was to become more important with other composers as well, but the chorus would retain a degree of importance, as we shall see later in this chapter.

John Goldwin, the only member of this first group not to fall directly under the influence of either Purcell or Blow (and consequently not a recipient of one of Blow's positions), was a pupil of William Child, to whose position he succeeded at St. George's Chapel, Windsor Castle. He shows less of the theatrical contamination that pervades this period than do his contemporaries, probably because neither he nor his teacher had any connection with the advanced styles of the Chapel Royal in the Restoration years.

[10] Boyce, *CM*, II, 179–82; Harley 7340, 492–95.

[11] *HS*, II, 26–34; Harley 7340, 495–502.

[12] Boyce, *CM*, II, 285–88; *TECM*, III, 114–21; R. J. S. Stevens, *Sacred Music for one, two, three & four Voices*... (3 vols., London: Charterhouse, [ca. 1796–1802]), II, 96–99, without chorus section; *Divine Harmony* (London: I. Walsh, [1716–1717]), II, 18–21.

[13] *Divine Harmony*, II, 6–10.

[14] The earliest music festival in Britain, it began as a charity sermon in 1655, and became more a musical service after the Restoration. An orchestra was added to the service in 1698. The date of Clarke's anthem is not given. See Scholes, *The Oxford Companion to Music*, 351.

Example 30. Solo section for alto (countertenor) in *Bow down thine ear*, Jeremiah Clarke (*HS*, II, 31).

While Child was an organist at the Chapel Royal, Tudway, who was a chorister there, later reported that he and the other composers of the older generation "hardly knew how, to comport themselves with those new fangl'd ways, but proceeded in their compositions, according to the old style, and therefore, there are only some Services and full Anthems of theirs to be found."[15] What must have appeared to Tudway as a stubborn inability to accept modern ideas is to us evidence of a sturdy tradition, about to expire because of secular encroachment. It is evident that Goldwin was well schooled in the old ways; an examination of some of his anthems reveals consistent use of materials and devices that his contemporaries either shunned or could no longer handle skilfully. His use of the solo voice is infrequent. There is an alto solo in *O praise God in his holiness*,[16] part of which is written over a four-measure ground-bass pattern. A solo anthem, *O Lord, how glorious*,[17] has no chorus at its close, but this may be due to the organization of the volume in which it appears. The title page advertises that the book was "very proper not only in private Devotion but also for Choir's," and the title page of the first volume states also that its anthems (all are of the solo type) may be "Sung either by a Treble or Tenor." The commercial age of anthem publication had dawned!

In full anthems with verses, a number of features may be discerned that prove Goldwin's firm grasp over his craft. He develops contrapuntal sections farther than an initial entrance for all voices in many instances, and especially so in *O Lord God of hosts*,[18] which opens with SSAATB chorus, has a verse section AATB, and returns again to the full choral group. In some anthems he alternates a bright texture against a darker, e.g., SSA and ATB. In *Thy way, O God, is holy*,[19] the verse section begins with SAB, shifts color with a section for AATB, and expands to SAATB solo group before returning to the original choral SSATB combination. His most unusual work is probably the verse anthem *Ascribe unto the Lord*,[20] which opens with a verse for three basses and organ. This is followed by a solo for bass, a duet for basses, and a closing Hallelujah section for SATB. The gravity of bass voices is suitably joined to the serious content of Psalm 29. Few of Goldwin's contemporaries approached the setting of text with as much care as he.

William Croft was a prodigious composer of anthems. It would be possible to survey the various types of his works simply by referring to his two-volume collection.[21] It contains anthems for from two to eight voices, if we are to believe the title page, but actually there are solo anthems as well. In addition, each volume contains an elaborate cantata-anthem for voices and instruments, although there is no indication of where these might have been performed at such a late date. Other anthems of his are published in the collections of Arnold, Boyce, Tudway, Page, and Stevens. It is difficult to tell, in some cases, what the original form of an anthem may have been. The

15 Dedication to Harley 7338, [ii].   16 *HS*, I, 227–33; Harley 7342, 382–90.
17 *Divine Harmony*, II, 30–32.   18 Harley 7341, 387–93.
19 *Ibid.*, 393–98.   20 Harley 7342, 272–79.
21 William Croft, *Musica Sacra: or, Select Anthems in Score*... (2 vols., London: J. Walsh, [1724]).

Stevens collection, for instance, has portions of complete pieces as well as arrangements and adaptations. Croft's setting of Psalm 118:14–29, *The Lord is my strength*,[22] appears in his collection as a cantata-anthem of six sections (see Table 5). In the Stevens collection[23] only the opening AB duet is printed, with an organ introduction not provided by Croft. Nothing there warns the reader that only a part of the entire composition is printed. Such alteration of material begins to be sufficiently common that one must be wary of accepting at face value any anthem that appears in only one source. In addition to tempo designations, Croft has supplied some dynamics. The bass part supplied for the organist is carefully figured throughout.

TABLE 5

Structure of Croft's Verse Anthem, *The Lord is my strength*, with figured bass

1. Verse, AB, 37 measures, ₵, "The Lord is my strength."

2. Verse, bass solo with *obbligato* passages in parallel thirds for organ,$\frac{3}{4}$, Brisk, "The voice of joy and health is in the dwellings of the righteous," 82 measures.

3. Verse, SA, 65 measures,$\frac{3}{2}$, Slow, "This is the day which the Lord hath made."

4. Verse, alto solo with organ interludes, ₵, Slow, 37 measures, "Help me now, O Lord."

5. Verse, ATB and SATB chorus in alternation,$\frac{3}{2}$, Brisk, 43 measures; ₵, Slow, 8 measures, "Blessed be he that cometh in the name of the Lord."

6. Verse, SATB in alternation with SATB chorus,$\frac{3}{2}$, Brisk, 76 measures, "O give thanks unto the Lord."

It is evident from Croft's corpus of anthems that the verse anthem was not relegated to a place of unimportance after the death of Charles II and the reversion to organ-accompanied pieces at the Chapel Royal. His verse anthems make considerable use of organ, often demanding an interplay of motivic material between the instrument and the solo voices, the forecasting and repetition of material in introductions and interludes, and they demand a high degree of skill from the solo voices. The two anthems that include instrumental parts are also built on a large scale. His setting of Psalm 33, *Rejoice in the Lord*,[24] bears also the designation "A Thanksgiving Anthem." It calls for an orchestra of strings and oboe, and the instruments accompany throughout the anthem, whether the passages are for solo or chorus. The instrumental parts are well written, and the introductory passages to the various sections are set with melodic interest and rhythmic vitality that is completely removed from the dance-

---

[22] Croft, *Musica Sacra*, I, 67–78.   [23] Stevens, *Sacred Music*, III, 30–32.
[24] Croft, *Musica Sacra*, I, 143–76.

related material of the two generations before him. Likewise, *O give thanks unto the Lord*,[25] a festive setting of Psalm 118:1–7, calls for an orchestra of strings throughout, except during the alto solo that occupies the central position of the work. It calls for a "Trumpet *or* Haut:" *obbligato* with organ. These instruments participate in figurations that are taken up in the vocal line later, as in the introduction where the organ states a motive that is picked up by the trumpet (or oboe) and, after nine measures, becomes the opening material for the vocal phrase. The instruments concertize, punctuate, and imitate, having the least to do during the course of a long melisma that is an obvious effort at text intensification (Example 31). Croft was aware of the need for key variety in works of this length; he was also careful to wander only into nearby areas. *Rejoice in the Lord* begins in E flat, moves to G minor for its principal solo, and returns to E flat for the final chorus. *O give thanks unto the Lord* begins in G minor, moves to D for its middle section, and concludes in G.

The two anthems with instruments are both on texts that speak of thanksgiving, but the particular occasion for which they were intended is not evident. Had they been written to commemorate some military victory or other nationally significant occasion, one would expect a reference to that fact in the published material. The custom of signalizing the Harvest Festival in musical fashion can be dated back only so far as 1843,[26] and the custom of using instruments in the course of a normal anthem performance appears to have stopped some time before these works could have been written. It appears probable, however, that the pieces were intended for some specific occasion; the time when composers wrote pieces without some immediate performance or common observance in mind was still in the future.

Full anthems with verses are not readily adaptable to the cantata-anthem pattern. The verses are usually less numerous, and the sections are not separated by full cadences, thereby lessening the effect of set pieces such as one finds in the operas and oratorios of these and the succeeding years. Croft took advantage of such anthems to employ contrapuntal choruses, commonly the opening one and sometimes another in the course of the piece. His *We will rejoice in thy salvation*[27] begins with an easily remembered theme (Example 32) that is the subject of a fifty-two-measure fugue. What distinguishes this from the usual imitative writing of the early eighteenth-century English composer is the complete statement of the subject before entry of the answer, and the use of a countersubject. A final example that displays Croft's use of imitative technique is *O Lord, rebuke me not*,[28] for SSATTB chorus, ATB verses, and organ. The imitative writing differs sharply from that of the preceding anthem in that imitation begins after two notes of the *dux* have been sung, rather than after the complete subject.

John Weldon placed more emphasis on highly ornamented solo material. *O God, thou hast cast us out*[29] has a carefully written ornamented line, so that the soloist must

25 *Ibid.*, II, 117–32.

26 Percy A. Scholes, *The Mirror of Music: 1844–1944* (2 vols., London: Novello & Co., 1947), II, 561.

27 Croft, *Musica Sacra*, I, 31–39.   28 *Ibid.*, I, 79–86; *TECM*, 124–39.   29 Arnold, *CM*, I, 266–75.

Example 31. Section of countertenor solo, "Let Israel now confess," from *O give thanks unto the Lord*, William Croft (*Musica Sacra*, II, 124–25).

ev - - - er, for ev - - - - - - - - - - -

6   5   4   3   4
                                   2

6

6
5

6   [er]
5

Example 32.   Fugue subject from *We will rejoice in thy salvation*, William Croft (*Musica Sacra*, I, 31).

Example 33.   Opening solo from *O God, thou hast cast us out*, John Weldon (Arnold, *CM*, I, 266).

demonstrate his grasp of the techniques that were equally favored in the theater (Example 33). The first two choruses are identical short sections; the closing one makes a few imitative entries before concluding in homophonic fashion. A full anthem SAATTBB with ATB verse, *Who can tell how oft he offendeth?*[30] is without any of these excrescences of the popular taste of the day. It is also undistinguished as a piece in the older style.

Charles King, the last member of this first group, is known to many for the quality of his Services, which were useful but unimaginative. His SATB anthem with ATB verse, *O pray for the peace of Jerusalem*,[31] is of the same family, for it plods dutifully through repetitions of a brief text, although King tries to mitigate its tedium by giving the repeated sections to alternate light and dark combinations of voices. The plague of repetition is also visited on an otherwise interesting verse anthem, *Wherewithall shall a young man cleanse his way?*[32] for three trebles and chorus. The use of three sopranos to represent the young man mentioned in Psalm 119:9–16 is especially appropriate, but the use of every text segment four or more times renders the piece tiresome, and the tedium is not lessened by the entry of the SSATB chorus for the last seventy-nine measures, for it is required to reiterate its material as well.

Thomas Tudway (1650–1726) wrote a number of anthems, but they do not point strongly either to the old tradition or to a new one. The fact that they did not influence later generations to any extent is evident in the absence of his pieces from collections other than that which he compiled. Of the later compilers, only Arnold saw fit to print one of Tudway's pieces.

The composers of this first group after the St. James composers showed several results of being deprived of a ready orchestra to support their anthems. They returned, as best they were equipped, to some use of contrapuntal material; they stressed the interplay of organ and solo voice; they ornamented the solo parts to a greater extent than was common with most of their predecessors, although the move in this direction is evident in Purcell's anthems; and they showed a reluctance to write full anthems unless they contained verse sections. We shall now see how the direct contemporaries of Handel approached the anthem.

The greatest importance of George Frideric Handel (1685–1759) to the course of English church music lay not in the compositions he produced in that genre, but in the impact he made upon English taste in general, and on church composers in particular. His largest body of anthems was the twelve Chandos Anthems[33] dating from before 1720, and this was supplemented by a number of occasional pieces to commemorate a coronation, two royal weddings, a royal funeral, a military victory, and a charity.[34] None of these works were intended to become a part of the cathedral practice of that time, and Handel made no attempt to accommodate the taste in church music that then

---

30 *Ibid.*, II, 207–15.
31 *Ibid.*, II, 121–27.   32 *Ibid.*, III, 156–68.
33 The first and sixth Chandos Anthems are discussed in *CMC*, 165–70.
34 See the list in *Grove's*, IV, 54.

existed. It is fortunate that he did not, for the works might have been of far less substance. All of the anthems call for an orchestra, a resource that was no longer common
for regular religious observances, even at the Chapel Royal. Such an orchestra was
available at Cannons, the country home of the first Duke of Chandos, who was then
Handel's patron. Instrumental groups could also be called into existence for the other
important occasions for which Handel wrote anthems, but none of these were normal,
everyday activities. The largest of his coronation anthems, *Zadok, the priest,* calls for a
brilliant orchestra of three trumpets and timpani, a pair each of oboes and bassoons,
violins divided into three sections, and *continuo* to support an SSAATBB chorus.[35]
The funeral music for Queen Caroline, *The ways of Zion do mourn,*[36] is more modest
and restrained, but still employs a pair of oboes with the string orchestra. The occasional pieces, of course, were generally useless for general service music because of the
topical nature of their texts.

Compilers, however, did not hesitate to snip and patch, modify and arrange, to
suit their purposes in riding the wave of Handel's veneration that swept over England
in the second half of the eighteenth century. It is not possible to single out one person
among Handel's imitators and editors as the most important of those who thrust his
music before the public. It is certain, however, that William Boyce (1710–1779) was
influential in this respect. Boyce did no composing after 1769,[37] when his deafness
forced him to retire from active musical life. In addition to his own compositions,
which will be considered later in this chapter, he edited a large number of pieces. Not
only those that appeared in his *Cathedral Music* should be considered, but certainly the
numerous Handel pieces he extracted from larger works and scaled down to be performed without instruments.

John Page's collection was not published until two decades after Boyce's death,
but it contained six Handel pieces arranged by Boyce. There is an anthem excised from
Israel in Egypt, beginning with the chorus, "Moses and the children of Israel," and continuing through duets, recitatives, and short choral sections to the chorus, "The Lord
shall reign for ever and ever."[38] There are also the "Four Occasional Anthems, the
Words selected from the Works of George Frederick Handel Esqr. By his present
Majesty, and by his Command adapted to Voices only by William Boyce Mus:Doc:
Organist and Composer to his Majesty."[39] These four are taken from *Messiah,* and are
designated for various days of religious importance. For Christmas the selection begins
with a truncated version of the "Pastoral Symphony" and continues in order through
"His yoke is easy."[40] The "Anthem for Whit-Sunday" begins with "Thou art gone
up on high" and concludes with "The mouth of the Lord hath spoken it."[41] For Good

[35] *Georg Friedrich Händels Werke,* ed. F. Chrysander (96 vols. and 6 supplements, Leipzig: Breitkopf &
Härtel, 1858–1894, 1902), XIV.

[36] *Ibid.,* XI.

[37] Not 1758, as was stated in Foster, *op. cit.,* 97.

[38] HS, III, 153–77.   [39] *Ibid.,* III, 178.   [40] *Ibid.,* III, 178–90.

[41] *Ibid.,* III, 212–25.

Friday the anthem is made up of material from "Behold the Lamb of God" to "Let all the angels of God worship him,"[42] and the Easter anthem opens with "Behold, I tell you a mystery," and concludes with "Since by man came death."[43] Each of the pieces consists of solo and choral material, the former strongly flavored with recitative because of its original connection with oratorio. The works are not anthems in any sense of traditional practice, but serve the same purpose as did some of the earlier borrowed pieces of Henry Aldrich. The reference to "his present Majesty" indicates that the monarch whose taste is reflected here would be George III. Royal approval of musical material is no guarantee of its acceptance by the general music-loving public, but in this instance it appears to have been consistent with popular taste.

Handel's music was altered to suit every convenience and occasion, and few hymn or psalm collections of those years failed to reach for the sure success guaranteed by including something by Handel and the current European masters, no matter how meager those examples might be. Fellowes states that "it was Theodore Aylward [1730–1801] who first introduced the custom of choosing excerpts from Handel's *Messiah* and other such works for performance as anthems in the choir of St. George's Chapel, Windsor."[44] However, Aylward was not appointed to his position there until 1788, nine years after Boyce's death. To Boyce must go the credit—if such it be—for cutting anthem material from the oratorios at an earlier date.

Some idea of the extent to which modifications were made in Handel's music can be seen in the various versions of the sixth Chandos Anthem that were placed before the public. Handel made four different versions of the work. The Chandos version was for STB chorus with orchestra; another, apparently for the Chapel Royal, begins with an SAATBB chorus, and continues *a 4*. It also uses orchestra. Another version keeps the same voice arrangement, but calls for organ. The fourth version is based upon the third. There was already considerable variety in these versions. The compilers, however, were not content; they changed the material further, often selecting only a portion of the original composition. In 1791, Samuel Arnold and John Wall Callcott published a volume intended for use in parish churches. They included a truncated version of the opening chorus from that anthem,[45] compressing the original fifty-three measures of material to forty, and setting the text (Psalm 42) as a strophic piece of five stanzas. For those who did not care for Handel's material, or who could not master it, they offered an option, stating that "this may be sung to any Tune of Common Measure." The SATB version matches none of Handel's exactly, but is pointed directly at the highest level that could be expected of parish churches. The anthem was also published in its entirety, but again without instruments, about the

---

[42] *Ibid.*, III, 191–99.

[43] *Ibid.*, III, 200–211.

[44] Edmund H. Fellowes, *English Cathedral Music: From Edward VI to Edward VII* (4th ed.; London: Methuen & Co., Ltd., 1948), 200.

[45] [Samuel] Arnold and J. W. Callcott, *The Psalms of David for the Use of Parish Churches* (London: Printed for John Stockdale and G. Goulding, 1791), 50–51. See pp. 164–65 for further discussion of this volume.

year 1800,[46] in a form that appears to stem from the Chapel Royal version for the most part, but modifying the arrangement of voices. The soprano solo, "Tears are my daily food," was printed separately about the same time, but using the version as written for Cannons.[47] The same source provides five other solos and a duet from the Chandos Anthems, all of them scaled down to organ accompaniment, but in most other respects still as Handel wrote them.

This distribution of material was multiplied in other collections. The English ear was saturated with music from Handel's oratorios and anthems, and it is understandable that the high esteem in which it was held did not wane in the face of its weaker competition. Handel's style, after all, was not that of the cathedral. He combined the characteristics of the German church cantata and the Italian secular cantata, mixed them with dramatic devices that were common to church and theater, and created a small corpus of religious music unlike anything the English themselves had written, and that was beyond their capacities to imitate. Even had imitation been possible, the loss of the orchestra from the normal practice of the Chapel Royal prohibited any continuation of such elaborate pieces except for events of national significance. Furthermore, at this period the parish churches were beginning to engage in musical activity on a scale that was to change the nature of English church music to a great extent.

One admirer and sometime associate of Handel's was Maurice Greene (1695–1755). His skill in music is evident from the variety and importance of his positions. In 1718 he became organist at St. Paul's, in 1727 he was appointed second organist and composer to the Chapel Royal, and in 1730 he succeeded Tudway as Professor of Music at the University of Cambridge. "He thus held, before he was forty years of age, all the chief musical appointments in the country."[48] His strong interest in the development of cathedral music caused him to undertake the collection of numerous anthems and Services, which he edited with a view of publishing as the best music of its type. He did not live to complete the project, but had the foresight to bequeath the materials to his friend, Boyce. He, in turn, finished the work and, in publishing the material as his monumental *Cathedral Music*, gave credit to Greene for his part in the undertaking.[49] The collection has long stood as the storehouse of the cathedral tradition, and the absence of Greene's own works in it is due to a limitation he himself placed upon it. Boyce wrote: "Had I not been under a restriction by the last Will and Testament of the late Dr. MAURICE GREENE, I should have inserted some valuable pieces of his."[50]

Many of Greene's anthems are of the verse variety or are full anthems with verse, but he wrote some full anthems as well that look to the past for their structural features. They are based on the "points of imitation" principle, each phrase of text having

[46] *HS*, II, 198–218.   [47] Stevens, *Sacred Music*, I, 58–61.   [48] *DNB*, VIII, 507.

[49] John Alcock (see p. 109) had also begun to collect works for such a publishing project. He had handed his material to Greene at an earlier date.

[50] Boyce, *CM*, III, vi.

Example 34. Section of *Bow down thine ear, O Lord*, Maurice Greene (*HS*, III, 18).

a characteristic musical figure that clings to its every statement. Each text-phrase is presented one or more times by each voice, the parts reach a cadence together, and the next text and music section is introduced, this procedure continuing to the end of the piece. This technique of composition was new and exciting in the sixteenth century, when it was a common feature of Continental music, and was incorporated into English music as well. By the eighteenth century, however, the treatment was anti-quarian, probably stemming from Greene's interest in and familiarity with earlier cathedral works. One such full anthem, *Bow down thine ear, O Lord*,[51] SSATBB, employs only four note-values in unimaginative fashion (Example 34), and the set of six SSATB anthems[52] published more than half a century after his death by Richard Clark (1786–1856) show the same studied care and lack of vitality. Most of Greene's anthems take their texts from the psalms. This is evident in his published collection of forty anthems which appeared first in 1743. One notable exception is a verse anthem for Christmas Day, *Behold, I bring you good tidings*.[53]

Greene appears to have been sensitive to choral textures in his verse anthems, even though textural variety was severely lacking in the full anthems. In this case, the voice selection is strongly toward the treble side. The piece opens with a verse for soprano solo, the following SSSATB chorus alternates with a duet for sopranos, and this emphasis on light voices continues through the closing Hallelujah chorus, which jubilates unrelentingly for sixty-eight measures. His solo anthem, *Praise the Lord, O my soul*,[54] in which the solo alternates with SATB chorus after the opening solo section, calls for a "Tenor Bass" (baritone?) soloist. His *Hear my crying*[55] is for two basses and chorus, closing with a fugal chorus that is still far short of the Handelian ideal he must have held, although it is more skillful and imaginative than the imitative full anthems. His approach to the Handelian style may be seen in the contrapuntal final chorus of *The Lord is my strength and my song*,[56] a verse anthem for ATB and SATB chorus. The melodic figure has some of the vitality of Handel's fugal subjects (Example 35), but Greene carries it through only a single exposition.

Among Greene's many anthems are some excellent passages, but the writing is not consistently strong. His successors apparently held him in high esteem, for Greene's works were printed, complete and altered, by Arnold, Page, and Stevens, and fragments found their way into hymnals as well. The full anthem with verses, *Arise, shine, O Zion*,[57] and the full anthem, *O clap your hands*,[58] are available in a modern edition, and some works are also printed in octavo copies for practical performance.

The number of composers who wrote for the cathedral tradition in the eighteenth century seems immense when one reflects on the limited market. Certainly not all

[51] *HS*, III, 17–24; Harley 7342, 453–59.

[52] Maurice Greene, *Six Full Anthems, for Five Voices* (Westminster: Richard Clark, 1812).

[53] Maurice Greene, *A New and correct Edition of Forty Select Anthems in Score, Composed for One, Two, Three, Four, Five, Six, Seven and Eight Voices* (2 vols.; London: R. Birchall, 1795), II, 39–49.

[54] Arnold, *CM*, II, 51–58.   [55] *HS*, II, 42–50.   [56] *Ibid.*, II, 122–30.

[57] *TECM*, III, 152–70.   [58] *Ibid.*, III, 171–83.

cathedrals were in a position to undertake daily choral service. The choirs were of various sizes and qualities; conflicts between clergy and organists, and between organists and choirs, existed. Many of the men who rose to eminence as organists tried their hands at composition, either hoping to improve their own choral situations or providing something uniquely suited to their forces. The case of John Alcock (1715–1806), organist at Lichfield Cathedral, is extreme, for few choral situations could have been worse than his—or worse than he thought it to be. He apparently expected the best and experienced the worst. Whether the fault was partly his or not, the quality of choral music at Lichfield must have been as distant from the Chapel Royal ideal as one can imagine.

Example 35. Fugue subject from *The Lord is my strength and my song*, Maurice Greene (*HS*, II, 128).

The   Lord   shall   reign   for   ev - er   and__   ev - er

I may venture to affirm, no *Choir* in the Kingdom is so much neglected by the Members thereof as this; one of them attending no more than five Weeks in a Year, another five Months, some seven, and few of them so often as they might do; sometimes only one Priest-Vicar at *Church*, and at other Times, but one Lay-Vicar, both on *Sundays* as well as the Week-Days, tho' there are Eleven of them, which has occasion'd some People of the Town to write upon the *Church* Doors, *My House shall be called the House of Prayer, but ye have made it a Den of Thieves.*

> . . . .

If the Singers are not skill'd in the Musical Part of their Duty, Disputes must unavoidably arise betwixt them and the Organist; for the natural Consequence is, that when they sing wrong, the Fault is laid on him, no Matter how great his Merit is; and he having no one to appeal to that understands Music, the former of course get the better of the latter, as it generally happens in these Cases, that those People who make the greatest Noise, and talk most fluently, are thought to have the true Side of the Argument, especially if they are perfectly acquainted with the Nack of Lying *judiciously*: . . . I can't forbear relating one very extraordinary Thing I have heard a certain Pretender to Music advance, tho' rather too ridiculous to trouble you with, which is, that the Organist, in the *Services* and *Anthems*, shou'd always keep with the Singers, so that if one sings extremely slow, another extremely fast, and others moderately, all at one Time (which is what I have frequently heard,) he must nevertheless play with each of them.[59]

Alcock's complaint, addressed to the Dean of the cathedral in the Introduction to his volume, was not an isolated one, although it may have been exaggerated, stem-

[59] John Alcock, *A Morning and Evening Service,* . . . (London: Printed for the Author and Jno. Johnson, 1752), [iii–iv].

ming from his frustrations at having to attempt the cathedral tradition with an inadequate group of singers. A few years later William Hayes (1741–1790) published a set of suggestions for singers and organists. He had been appointed minor canon to Worcester Cathedral in 1765. It may signify something about the state of music there that his brief paper was written in that same year. The samples quoted here indicate that the Chapel Royal traditions were not a matter of common concern at Worcester:

> With regard to a long grace at the end of any part of an anthem, I think it should be very cautiously avoided, because it breaks in too much upon the seriousness and dignity of church musick. But if a singer should be determined to favour the congregation with a *gratioso*, I would advise the organist to play a little short voluntary as soon as the grace is quite finished, in order to qualify the singer to go on with a *quantum sufficit* of breath for the remaining part of the anthem.
>
> · · ·
>
> The practice of singing the octave above instead of the octave below, (and so *vice versa*) has a very unnatural effect. Singers often take too much liberty in this respect, little considering that although it may be the same with regard to the laws of composition, yet there seems to be an obvious difference in nature.
>
> · · ·
>
> In the winter season the organist should never presume to play upon the organ in gloves, unless there is a great necessity for it.
>
> · · ·
>
> If the chantor desires a rehearsal of any musick, all the members must comply, and more particularly so if the chantor should desire it in a polite, genteel, and friendly manner.[60]

Not all the composers of this period were faced with situations of this kind. Still, there were not as many excellent cathedral positions as there were men to fill them; some remained farther down the ladder of prestige, at least until the top rungs were vacated. James Kent (1700–1776), although trained in the Chapel Royal practice under Croft, found himself for some fourteen years of his early life as organist of the parish church in Finedon, Northamptonshire. Since he received the appointment at age seventeen, the stay may have been less than onerous. His later appointments were to churches that followed the cathedral tradition. John Travers (ca. 1703–1758), a pupil of Greene's, likewise held positions in his early years as organist of St. Paul's, Covent Garden, and later of Fulham Church. Significantly, both of these men composed for the limited market they served in their mature years, that of the cathedral tradition; however, Travers saw the need for music in the growing market of the parish church, and he produced a book of psalms that was aimed at the larger group of singers.[61] His compositions for the cathedral tradition are obviously examples of his best work. The

---

[60] William Hayes, "Rules necessary to be observed by all Cathedral-Singers in this Kingdom," *The Gentleman's Magazine, and Historical Chronicle*, XXXV (May, 1765), 213–14.

[61] John Travers, *Whole Book of psalms, for one, two, three, four and five voices with a thorough bass for the harpsichord*. . . (2 vols.; London: Printed for J. Johnson, [ca. 1750]). The reference to harpsichord probably means the work was intended for use in the home rather than the church.

solo anthem *Ponder my words*[62] employs the affective, stylized patterns of theatrical melody seen in Example 33, but its SSATB Hallelujah shows familiarity with the older traditions in its nonvertical structure. A verse anthem, *Ascribe unto the Lord*,[63] has a florid tenor solo (Example 36 *a*), employs changing meters and a change of key for variety during the various solo passages, while the SATB chorus is given little to do. The solo for bass has a variety of melismatic sections that stem from an earlier period, but it is difficult to say whether the composer was more influenced by Purcell or Handel (Example 36 *b*). Pieces of this kind required excellent solo voices more than an outstanding chorus, although the choral writing is better than perfunctory.

William Boyce, with whose efforts as arranger and editor of Handel's works we have already dealt, and whose *Cathedral Music* has been a source of much music from earlier periods, is recognized as one of the best composers of this second half of the century. He composed for the stage and for instrumental groups; he wrote a considerable amount of secular choral music, and a large number of anthems make up his contribution to church music, along with several Services. Fellowes suggests that some of the church works found in manuscript after his death were simply copies of other composers' works, and not his own,[64] but allowing for this possibility, the total would still be large. In any case, his name would survive in the history of the anthem had he not written a single note, for the importance of his *Cathedral Music* as the only significant collection of cathedral pieces until the last decade of the century is firmly established. The music published under his name is of the same wide variety as that of his active contemporaries. There are a large number of verse anthems and a lesser number listed, according to the practice of the time, as full anthems. These latter pieces are actually full anthems with verses. The full anthem for choir alone rarely appears and, as was seen in the case of Greene's pieces, comes off badly in comparison. Solo anthems are quite common, usually with one or more chorus sections. All the foregoing were written to be accompanied by organ. On the other hand, there are festival or commemorative anthems similar to the cantata-anthems of the Restoration, spiced with Continental touches that may derive from Handel. While they are not numerous and do not represent the usual repertory of the cathedral composer, some notice of their style must be taken, since they are the highest level of church music to which the English composer of that century could aspire.

A study of four Boyce cantata-anthems with orchestra forms part of a survey of his large choral works with orchestra.[65] The funeral anthem for George II (*Souls of the righteous*) and three anthems bearing the common title *The King shall rejoice* have been transcribed from their manuscript sources and considered in some detail. The occasions for which the three were intended—one was for St. Paul's Cathedral, the others

[62] Arnold, *CM*, III, 59–63.
[63] *Ibid.*, III, 257–69; *TECM*, III, 184–99.
[64] Fellowes, *English Cathedral Music*, 184–85.
[65] John Robert Van Nice, "The Larger Sacred Choral Works of William Boyce (1710–1779)" (3 vols., unpublished Ph.D. dissertation, State University of Iowa, 1956).

for the coronation and wedding of George III—caused Boyce to adapt and re-use
material from one to the other. This was common practice among composers who
wrote copiously in those days, and instances of borrowing among other composers of
the eighteenth century are well known. The similarities displayed in the three versions of *The King shall rejoice* are large-scale borrowings and are quite obvious to eye

Example 36a.   Beginning of tenor solo from *Ascribe unto the Lord*, John Travers
(Arnold, *CM*, III, 257).

Example 36b. Melisma from bass solo, *ibid.*(Arnold, *CM*, III, 262–63).

Example 37.   Parallel settings of the text, *Blessed is he*, by William Boyce.

and ear. For example, the wedding anthem and the one for St. Paul's are almost identical for the first eighty-four measures, and the coronation anthem differs from the others mostly in instrumentation for that section of the work.[66] Other less obvious differences exist as well. There are probably numerous other instances that may be found where Boyce has re-used his own material. One such is seen in his anthem for tenor and bass, *Blessed is he that considereth the poor*,[67] which parallels the music of his cantata-anthem with orchestra that is also based on part of Psalm 41.[68] The larger work was dedicated to the Stewards of the Sons of the Clergy, and the text is altered from that shown in the title, possibly as a gesture toward the charitable nature of the organization, to "Blessed is he that considereth the sick." The opening musical material, while not being bodily lifted from one to the other, shows an unmistakably common parentage (Example 37). While it is not profitable to pursue thematic parallels further here, it may be that later studies will produce other related pieces.[69]

The cantata-anthem calls for an orchestra of flutes, trumpets and timpani, oboes, bassoons, and strings; the chorus sections are SATB, and verses for solos and ensembles appear also. The orchestral writing is of high quality, both in the vocal sections and in the instrumental introductions and interludes. Another equally lavish work is *Lord, thou hast been our refuge*,[70] also composed for the Sons of the Clergy and apparently performed at the annual festival at St. Paul's in 1755. The text of this work is a conflation of several psalm verses and another scriptural passage. Boyce set the text, "Remember, O Lord, what is come upon us: Consider and behold our reproach. We are orphans and fatherless, our mothers are as widows,"[71] for an SSS choir, bolstering the unstable boys' voices by doubling their parts with three oboes. The verse sections generally have independent accompaniments, but doubling of the choir was common. In doubling full choir, however, Boyce vitalized the rhythm by sometimes letting the winds play at unison with the voices while the strings played repeated notes of half the value (Example 38).

Solo vocal style in the anthems is quite florid, especially for the adult voices, and the recitative passages smack strongly of the dramatic. Boyce was not above using the obvious in his text-painting; long passages on "generations," bouncing triplets on "pleasure," and predictably diatonic runs on "praise," "thanksgiving," and the like are found in abundance. He understood the need for alternating between polyphonic fluidity and forceful vertical sonorities, and he took full advantage of the variety to be

[66] *Ibid.*, I, 72.

[67] William Boyce, *A Collection of Anthems,...For 1, 2, 3, 4, 5, and 8 Voices* (London: Printed for the Author's Widow, 1790), 94–98.

[68] William Boyce, *Blessed is he that considereth the Poor* (London: For Mr. Ashley by Bland & Wellers, 1802), 73 pp.

[69] Another dissertation on Boyce's anthems is in progress by Phillip W. Sims at Southwestern Baptist Theological Seminary.

[70] William Boyce, *Lord, thou hast been our refuge* (London: For Mr. Ashley by Bland & Wellers, 1802), 87 pp.

[71] Lamentations 4:1, 3.

achieved by changing key, meter, and tempo within a multisectional piece. Whether or not he was influenced by the simpler music that was being heard in parish churches, he was not above using a direct style of expression, as can be found in the Easter anthem, *If we believe that Jesus died*[72] (Example 39).

Directness is an obvious feature of the anthems of James Nares (1715–1783). His best work was apparently done in other areas of composition, for his church music is generally correct but uninteresting. His *Blessed be the Lord God*[73] consists of three short sections: a chordal SATB section; a verse for two sopranos singing, for the most part, in parallel thirds; and another short choral section that, after a single imitative entry,

Example 38. Rhythmic doubling of voice parts in *Lord, Thou hast been our refuge*, Boyce, 83.

continues in block chords. Three anthems in Arnold's *Cathedral Music* are equally brief. The choral parts are not difficult, and the verse sections are given to two sopranos, their parts moving in comfortably safe parallel motion. *O Lord, grant the king a long life*[74] is typical. The sections alternate regularly between choir and soprano duet, no section except the final chorus extending more than ten measures. The choir is given a more active role than it was in many of the solo and duet anthems of the day, but its responsibility here is usually that of completing the sentences begun by the soloists. Nares expressed a concern over the proper distinction between church music and secular music. He stated that proper tempo was one mark of propriety, and he wrote further: "In my Compositions for the Church, it has been my Endeavour to preserve the true Character of Church Music, without Regard to these Diversities of Fancy. I have been very sparing of Divisions, thinking them too airy for the Church, though proper enough in Oratorios."[75] Sparing he may have been, but the graces,

[72] William Boyce, *Fifteen Anthems, together with a Te Deum and Jubilate, in score for 1, 2, 3, 4, & 5 Voices, Composed for the Royal Chapels* (London: Printed for the Author's Widow and Family, 1780), 52–60.

[73] *HS*, II, 195–97.   [74] Arnold, *CM*, III, 96–99.

[75] James Nares, *Twenty Anthems in Score for 1, 2, 3, 4, and 5 Voices* (London: Printed for the Author, 1778), quoted in *TECM*, III, 260.

trills, and runs he wrote in *The souls of the righteous*,[76] printed in the same book for which he had written those remarks, are more abundant than in the music of most of his contemporaries. The text for that anthem is taken from the apocryphal Wisdom of Solomon, an unusual selection. Even though the apocryphal books were not com-

Example 39.   *If we believe that Jesus died*, William Boyce (*Fifteen Anthems*, 52).

pletely rejected by the liturgical faiths, they rarely became the source of musical texts.

It has not always been the high quality of a composer's work that causes him to deserve attention. Some men mirror their times more accurately than do their musical betters. Joseph Key (fl. 1790–1795), whose music is published in a set of four books

[76] *TECM*, III, 225–35.

dating from after 1792,[77] clearly followed a new direction that music was taking: the movement of parish church musicians to the west gallery,[78] where they held forth with their instruments and voices. Key's books are definitely intended for Anglican churches, and not for the Nonconformist market; the contents are occasional anthems, settings of Propers for the Communion Service, Collects, carols, and so on. Many of them call specifically for instruments—viz., violin, hautboy, and bass, or two hautboys and a bassoon. The second volume of the set is further identified as "being particularly design'd for the Use of Parochial Choirs."[79]

The exactly specified instrumentation places these books apart from the kind usually found in the country parishes; there the performers used whatever instruments were conveniently at hand, and their books did not designate instrumentation. Key's volumes call for a certain instrumental skill, but not high professional mastery. Apparently the instruments were intended to double the voice parts except in introductions and interludes. Instrumental and vocal parts share the same staves, and it is impossible to know for certain whether the instruments rested during the singing, or whether they continued to play. The rural practice, as we know,[80] was to play with the singers, but the practice may have differed in this more sophisticated material. Only two clues are found in the four volumes. In one anthem an optional version of the music is provided for "whenever the above Anthem is performed with Voices alone."[81] At another place, following a section of thin texture, the voices enter together and the word "Repiano" (ripieno) appears at the same time, indicating that possibly some instruments had been playing and the rest should now join in. The term could have been familiar to Key through Handel's use of it—among other places, in Messiah. Key's knowledge of that work, and possibly his admiration of it, can be seen in his Easter anthem, Now is Christ risen,[82] from which he borrowed in spirit, if not in fact. Some passages sound as if Messiah is being performed from memory—with errors (Example 40).

[77] The first volume was sold by Messrs. Thompson, No. 75, St. Paul's Church Yard, and by several other music sellers. The Thompson imprint in this form is not found before 1792 (see Grove's, VIII, 429). The second book included the name of a Mr. Bland, No. 45 Holborn, as one of its sellers. John Bland, of that address, died or retired in 1795 (Grove's, I, 752), so that volume was printed prior to that date. Key was dead before the third and fourth volumes appeared. The third book was printed for, "and sold by Mrs. Eliz. Key," and the fourth bears the inscription, "composed by the Late Mr. Joseph Key."

[78] The "west gallery" was across the back of the church. Since the altar was traditionally placed at the east end, the gallery position placed the music at the rear of the congregation. The divided chancel, employing decani and cantoris division of a choir, was generally restricted to the cathedral practice. Few parish churches aspired to such elaborate ritual. The gallery placement of singers made it possible to employ women in the singing, since they were not usurping a priestly function.

[79] Joseph Key, Eleven Anthems on General and Particular Occasions, Interspersed with Symphonies and Thorough Basses, For Two Hautboys and a Bassoon; Being particularly design'd for the Use of Parochial Choirs (Nuneaton, Warwickshire: Printed for & Sold by the Author. [ca. 1794]).

[80] See Chapter 4.

[81] Joseph Key, Eight Anthems on Various Occasions (2nd ed.; Nuneaton, Warwickshire: Printed for, & Sold by the Author, [ca. 1792]), 7.

[82] Ibid., 1–7.

Example 40. *Now is Christ risen*, Joseph Key (*Eight Anthems*, 3–4).

We can only speculate on how these books were used. They apparently sold well. At least some of the surviving copies appear to have been used often. Full anthems of the polyphonic type are completely absent from their pages; organ parts, in the form of figured bass lines, are likewise not found there. Although completely removed from the cathedral tradition, the pieces are written with skill, if not imagination. Many other books for use in the parish church were on the scene by the century's end, but few of them expected so much of the singers and players.

The first quarter of the nineteenth century saw little new church music of high quality in England. The composers whose lives extended into that period showed little interest in producing for the Church, and those few who did write anthems produced most of them before the end of the previous century. The creation of anthems and Services was no longer their first interest. It was more important to a man's prestige and self-esteem to be known as a successful composer for the theater, to attain membership and recognition in The Glee Club or The Noblemen and Gentlemen's Catch Club, among whose members were numbered most of the London residents who wrote for the Church as well. Coupled with lack of interest and support from within the Church, these secular attractions added to the deterioration of choral composition.

The interests of William Jackson (1730–1803), known as "Jackson of Exeter" to differentiate him from William Jackson of Masham (1815–1866), were divided between his position at Exeter Cathedral and the London scene. His duties kept him at the former, but he managed to achieve some successes in the theaters of the latter. While his secular music attained popular acceptance, his anthems and Services were quite ordinary, and they are now generally held in low esteem. One feature of his religious pieces, published after his death by James Paddon, does warrant consideration. The accompaniments to all his published pieces are written out in full.[83] It is most improbable that Jackson wrote out the full accompaniment in his manuscripts, and it is certain that Paddon did not institute the practice of writing them out when he undertook the publication of Jackson's works, for it is known that Vincent Novello (1781–1861) aroused the disapproval of the entire body of English organists in 1811 by providing full accompaniments to his first publication rather than supplying the usual figured bass.[84]

Jackson's anthems demand no attention in our time, but they show a change in expression to direct, forceful statement of text, and it may be that their present low regard stems not entirely from their own weaknesses, but from the fact that composers who followed him dealt with such direct expression less obviously. The melodic lines are strong, taking every advantage of leaps that have strong chordal implications, and using scales not as melismatic expansions of a single syllable, but as thrusting passages to emphasize positive text segments (Example 41). Earlier music had often suffered

[83] Three volumes appeared under Paddon's editorship. *Anthems and Church Services* (Exeter: Printed for the Author [Paddon], [ca. 1820]); *Two Anthems and a Complete Church Service* (Exeter: Printed for the Author, [ca. 1820]); and *Sacred Music* (London: Goulding and D'Almaine, [ca. 1825]).

[84] *Grove's*, VI, 137.

Example 41. Typical scale passage from *Praise the Lord, O my soul,* William Jackson (*Anthems and Church Services,* 97–98).

from poor accentuation of text; Jackson joined text and music accents with a lack of subtlety that does not encourage modern performance.

The six readily available anthems of Jonathan Battishill (1738–1801) show a wide range of styles. *O Lord, look down from heaven*,[85] a restrained full anthem of varying textures, employs a modified "points of imitation" technique with characteristic melodic material for each text segment. The anthem opens with SATB choir, broadens to SSATB, expands again to SSATBB, then SSAATB, and finally SSAATTB. At its climax, the fragments of text are sung in block chords, repetitions of two words being emphasized by full or half measures of rest, an effective contrast to the preceding imitative material. *Call to remembrance, O Lord*,[86] a full anthem with verses, employs a similarly varied selection of voices for the chorus sections, first SATB, then SATBB, SSAATBB, and SSATBB. In one instance, a solo group SSA alternates with another ATB, and there is a "pathetic" verse for SAB (Example 42). Fellowes calls these "the only two pieces of his Church music that have any value at all."[87] While the other anthems show some variety of approach, the result is indeed without distinction. *Behold, how good and joyful*[88] is a full anthem with verses; the full sections are prosaic, and the verses are, by contrast, overly theatrical. The closing Hallelujah is an exercise in endurance for both singer and listener. *How long wilt thou forget me*,[89] a solo anthem for treble with a closing chorus, explores the varied skills of a soloist with more regard to gymnastics than to propriety. *Deliver us, O Lord*,[90] a full anthem SATB, suffers from unfortunate attempts at text-painting; and *I will magnify thee, O God*[91] has a fine opening chorus, but its verses and lengthy Hallelujah chorus detract from its general effect.

The tendency in Battishill's time was toward simplicity in anthems, especially as the number and quality of singers failed to remain at the high level of earlier years. Battishill wrote as if the solo voices he knew in the theater were available in the choir, which, unfortunately, they usually were not.

There were other composers for the Church during this time, but they are of little importance to our understanding the trend of the period. Their names have been recorded in a number of sources, where they may be sought by those making a detailed study of the literature.[92] It remained for a Roman Catholic, Samuel Webbe (1740–1816), to produce further pieces that were intended for Anglicans in their churches, and for them and the general public to use at home. Since Webbe had no church positions outside the Catholic embassy chapels of Sardinia and Portugal, any anthems he wrote were frankly commercial ventures. That he had a sharply critical eye is evident in the changes he made in his pieces. His first collection contained eight anthems, and its title clearly indicated that he hoped to find a market wider than that which composers

---

[85] *TECM*, IV, 9–17.   [86] *HS*, I, 92–103.
[87] Fellowes, *English Cathedral Music*, 192.   [88] *HS*, III, 1–16.
[89] *HS*, II, 187–94.   [90] *HS*, III, 75–78.   [91] *HS*, III, 137–52.
[92] Among others, John S. Bumpus, *A History of English Cathedral Music* (2 vols.; London: T. Werner Laurie, 1908); M. B. Foster, *op. cit.*; and Fellowes, *op. cit.*

Example 42. "Pathetic" trio from *Call to remembrance, O Lord*, Jonathan Battishill (*HS*, I, 96).

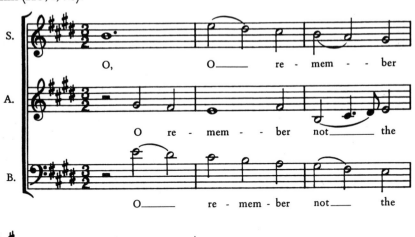

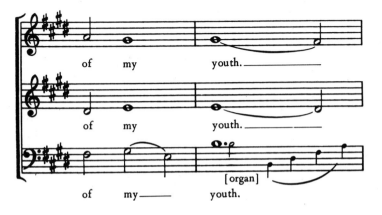

writing for the cathedral practice envisioned for their publications.[93] The chorus parts do not call for any group more complex than SATB, and the solo parts make no great demands upon the singers. Furthermore, Webbe indicated that the treble and tenor parts were interchangeable, further guarding against loss of sales through small choral groups fearing to undertake them. Webbe also placed a descriptive title at the head of each anthem, indicating the affection it was the intention of "the Author to excite in the Minds of those who either perform them or hear them performed."[94] The anthems also have their

> texts taken from various portions of the Bible and chosen in such a manner as to amplify the heading. Thus, the first anthem, entitled *Public Worship*, begins with Psalm 121:1, "Unto Thee, O Lord do I lift up mine eyes, from whence cometh my help." The next section is taken from Psalm 43:3 and begins "O send out Thy light." The third anthem contains texts from Luke, Philippians, and Acts, as well as the Psalms.[95]

Webbe must have learned something about the public demand and taste from his first publication, for the pieces of his second collection[96] are simpler and more directly pointed to the home market while being useful to the small choir at the same time. Most of the choir sections are scaled down to SAB, the rhythmic patterns are simple, and block chords are the rule rather than the exception. Webbe explained his intentions in the foreword to the volume:

> The following little Pieces are humbly submitted to the Perusal of those who on Days set apart for Devotions, might wish to take the Aid of Music, in raising the Mind to a Contemplation of the DIVINE GOODNESS to Man. The Subjects are General and (as in the Eight Anthems for Cathedrals) the Words are Selected from different parts of the HOLY WRITINGS, so as to accord with the Title prefaced to each Anthem.
>
> In Order to render them the more useful for Families, or private musical Parties, they seldom require more than Three Voices; but the Effect may be considerably improved by more Voices joining in those Places marked TUTTI.
>
> The Solos and Duets are in the Treble Cliff, yet they may be sung by Tenor Voices; for the Tenor Cliff is only introduced in Chorus where it could not be avoided. Repeats may be made where it seems necessary, very few being marked: and Figures are purposely omitted except where the Harmony might appear to be doubtful.[97]

That Webbe, a Catholic, saw promise of financial gain from a kind of music that was of no use to him in his chapel positions is evidence of a growing market. He was highly respected, his excellence as a composer of catches and glees was widely known,

---

[93] Samuel Webbe, *Eight Anthems in score, for the use of Cathedrals and Country Choirs* (London: Printed for the Author, [1788]).

[94] *Ibid.*, [i].

[95] James H. Richards, "Samuel Webbe as a Church Composer" (unpublished Master's thesis, Baylor University, 1965), 121.

[96] Samuel Webbe, *Twelve Anthems Particularly Calculated for Families or Small Choral Societies* (London: R. Birchall, [1798]).

[97] *Ibid.*, 1.

and his good judgment in meeting a marketable level of taste insured the success of his publications.

Publishers also saw that anthems in inexpensive collections could find a ready public. The collection published by John Johnson (d. ca. 1762), nearly three decades before Webbe's first volume appeared, recognized the purchasing power that was developing outside the limits of the cathedral choirs and the London churches.[98] Since the composers of his pieces were long dead, any sale of the anthems meant a clear profit to the publisher. Johnson did not identify his "Eminent Composers," and not all the works can be traced through earlier sources. Four have been found, however, in the collections of Arnold, Boyce, and Tudway. Two of them, *We have heard with our ears* and *Out of the deep*, are by Henry Aldrich. *Behold now, praise the Lord*, by Benjamin Rogers, and *O Lord God of my salvation*, by Vaughan Richardson (?–1729), are also included.

The collections of Johnson and Webbe, and others like them, were for the smaller Anglican churches. They made no attempt to meet the needs of Nonconformist groups, nor did they serve the instrumental practices in country churches that Joseph Key sought to interest in his publications. Those churches found an entirely new kind of printed music developing for their use. It is to that important, but little known, line of composition that we turn next.

[98] *Ten Full Anthems Collected from the works of several Eminent Composers, Published principally for the Use of Country Churches* (London: J. Johnson, [ca. 1760]).

CHAPTER FOUR

The Anthem in Nonconformist Chapels and Parish Churches, 1700–1825

The seventeenth century was a time of religious and political turbulence in England. The unrest that brought about the Commonwealth, and in turn effected the Restoration, gave evidence of a nation seeking religious and political stability. The root of the trouble could be traced to the Marian exiles who, following the death of Queen Mary in 1558, returned to England bent on recasting the Anglican Church in the mold of Calvinism. To those Puritans, much in the Anglican Church was corrupt and unscriptural.

> They demanded express Scriptural warrant for all the details of public worship, believing that all other forms were popish, superstitious, idolatrous, and anti-Christian. They attacked church ornaments, vestments, surplices, rochets, organs, the sign of the cross,...and put corresponding emphasis on preaching, Sunday observance, Church government by presbyters, and the 'tablewise' position of the altar.[1]

Puritanism flourished in the time of Elizabeth and James I, and the more extreme elements of the movement withdrew from the Established Church, creating fellowships such as Congregationalists, Presbyterians, Baptists, and Quakers—groups subsequently known under the collective titles of Dissenters or Nonconformists.[2]

---

[1] *The Oxford Dictionary of the Christian Religion*, ed. F. L. Cross (London: Oxford University Press, 1966), 1127.

[2] Dissenters were those who disagreed with the doctrines of the Established Church, while Nonconformists were those who refused to conform to the ritual and discipline of the Church, especially the various

Restrictions placed on the Nonconformists after the Restoration were so severe that organized church life was all but impossible for them. The Conventicle Act of 1664 imposed imprisonment on anyone found attending a Nonconformist religious meeting, and the Five Mile Act of 1665 prohibited a dissenting minister from coming within five miles of any city or town unless he took a nonresistance oath, agreeing not to attempt any alteration of Church or State government.

Nonconformists labored under these severe limitations until the passage of the Toleration Act of 1689, a reflection of the more liberal policies of William and Mary. Although Roman Catholics did not benefit from the Act, Nonconformists were now free to carry on their activities and turn their attention to internal matters.

The general musical picture in Nonconformist churches at the turn of the century was simply this: They sang versified psalms, unaccompanied, and nothing more. No doubt the Sternhold and Hopkins "Old Version" was widely used, but it tended to be regarded with some disfavor because of its association with the Established Church. More to Nonconformist liking was the Ainsworth Psalter of 1612, which not only lacked this association with the Establishment, but had the added advantage of a Separatist authorship.

In all of this the Nonconformist churches lagged behind the Anglican Church. A significant innovation was in the making, however; it was the introduction of hymns of "human composure" into worship services—that is, hymns based on scriptural ideas, but not confined to the psalms or other specific Scriptures. To be sure, these hymns were not new to England—they had been in existence since the early seventeenth century—nor was their use in worship services entirely new, for Benjamin Keach (1640–1704), pastor of a London Baptist church, had introduced such hymns into his services as early as the 1670s.[3] Widespread acceptance of the hymnic writing of Isaac Watts (1674–1748) followed the publication of his *Hymns and Spiritual Songs* in 1707, which firmly established hymns of human composure in Nonconformist churches, and would have done so in the Anglican Church had not her commitment to the versified psalms been so great. All of this has a bearing on the anthem, as we shall see, for, in the latter half of the eighteenth century, the hymn tune underwent such stylistic change as to make it a quasi-anthem. This is clearly seen in tune-books of the period designed for parish churches as well as Nonconformist chapels, where the differences between hymns and anthems, in some cases, was simply a matter of stanzaic versus prose texts.

Musical conditions in parish churches at the beginning of the eighteenth century were more or less the same as those of the Nonconformist chapels, but for different reasons; Nonconformists restricted their musical activity to the unaccompanied singing of psalms and hymns because they believed organs were "popish" and not ordained

Acts of Uniformity. In general use, however, the terms are synonymous. See Albert Edward Bailey, *The Gospel in Hymns* (New York: Charles Scribner's Sons, 1950), 20.

[3] Robert H. Young, "The History of Baptist Hymnody in England from 1612 to 1800" (unpublished D.M.A. dissertation, University of Southern California, 1959), 39.

for New Testament worship; on the other hand, many parish churches were obliged to sing the psalms unaccompanied, due to the widespread destruction of organs in parish churches as well as cathedrals during the Commonwealth. Furthermore, the dearth of organ builders at the time of the Restoration made replacement of the instruments exceedingly difficult. Hawkins' commentary on the problem is interesting:

> Organs being thus destroyed, and the use of them forbidden in England, the makers of those instruments were necessitated to seek elsewhere than in the church for employment; many went abroad, and others betook themselves to such other occupations for a livelihood, as were nearest related to their own; they became joiners and carpenters, and mixed un-noticed with such as had been bred up to those trades; so that, excepting Dallans, Loose-more of Exeter, Thamar of Peterborough, and Preston of York, there was at the time of the restoration scarce an organ-maker that could be called a workman in the kingdom. Some organs had been taken down, and sold to private persons, and others had been but partially destroyed; these, upon the emergency that called for them, were produced, and the artificers above named were set to work to fit them up for use; Dallans indeed was employ-ed to build a new organ for the chapel of St. George at Windsor, but, whether it was through haste to get it finished, or some other cause, it turned out, though a beautiful structure, but an indifferent instrument.[4]

Parish churches found an answer to the problem in what came to be known as the West Gallery tradition. Bands of amateur instrumentalists and singers were formed in churches to provide music after the Third Collect at Morning Prayer or Evensong. The tradition appears to have originated in the seventeenth century, continuing to the middle of the nineteenth century.[5] The musicians carried on their activities in the west gallery of the church (or a special singing pew if the church lacked a gallery), and when it came time for them to perform, members of the congregation simply turned around to listen and observe. Membership in such groups was a matter of considerable pride, and a lively spirit of competition prevailed in many areas. MacDermott states that the musicians were proud

> of themselves and their performances, and it was quite a common boast either that the choir or band was the best in the neighbourhood, or that at least it had one of the finest voices in the country.
>
> Wadhurst was stated to have two of the best and most powerful voices in England, a tenor and a bass. Donnington, a tiny village near Chichester, claimed that its singing was the best of any village church in the country; but that claim was ignored by Hallingly (also in Sussex), who had the best choir in the neighbourhood!
>
> ·　　·　　·
>
> At Courteenhall, Northants, early in the nineteenth century, the minister remonstrated with a member of the choir for using trombones, bugles, etc., for the church band, and asked them to make less noise. The offended singer replied, "Well, sir, I've heard many quires, and I've heard quires and organs in cathedrals, but I think they are no-ways to be compared to *our* band and quire!"[6]

---

[4] Hawkins, *op. cit.*, II, 689.　　　[5] MacDermott, *op. cit.*, 1.　　　[6] *Ibid.*, 7–8.

Unlike the more sophisticated works of Joseph Key, where particular instruments are specified (see p. 118), West Gallery players formed their bands of any instrumentalists available. Among the instruments most frequently employed were violins, flutes, clarinets, violoncellos, bassoons, trombones, oboes, and cornets.[7]

There is some indication that West Gallery musicians could, and frequently did, bring considerable pressure to bear on a vicar who dared to cross them in some way. MacDermott tells of a John Pennicott, the bandmaster of the church at Amberley for many years, who evidently viewed the church solely as a convenience for the musicians:

> On one occasion, through some misunderstanding with the vicar, the bandsmen, although present in church, refused to play, and the vicar, who was between eighty and ninety years of age, asked from the pulpit, "Are you going to play or not?" To which Pennicott answered for himself and the bandsmen, "No!" The parson rejoined, "Well, then, I'm not going to preach," and forthwith came down out of the pulpit in a rage. Later, after the service was over and the parson walked down the village street, the band came out with their instruments and gave him "horn-fair" or "rough music" to the vicarage. On another occasion, the same band went out on strike. As they would not play at the service of the church, the vicar called upon all the inns in the village, and was successful in "freezing the taps"—that is, the landlords agreed not to serve any of the band with liquor. The bandsmen retorted by whitewashing the vicar's windows from top to bottom of the house during the night.[8]

The West Gallery tradition also affected the churches of Nonconformity. Although documentation concerning musical activity in Nonconformist chapels is scarce, the limited evidence at hand indicates that, at least in some areas, groups of the West Gallery type did exist. For example, the "Deighn Layrocks," or the "Larks of Dean" as they were also called, carried on a musical tradition, both vocal and instrumental, in the Baptist Chapel at Lumb, a few miles north of Manchester. Evidently, the group originally had met for rehearsal in homes about the community. However, following the religious conversion of their leader, John Nuttall, in the 1740s, the Larks centered their activity in the church, establishing a tradition that continued for a century.[9] Annie Buckley quotes Thomas Newbigging's vivid description of a Sunday School Charity at Lumb Chapel in 1841, for which the Larks had made diligent preparation.

> The impression produced upon my mind by a visit paid some years ago in the month of June, to Lumb Chapel, on the occasion of the anniversary services there, will not be easily effaced from my memory. It was quite a field day among the 'Deighn Layrocks,' and they mustered in strength as though bent on maintaining the reputation they had acquired for their musical display. The singers' gallery was thronged to excess. In the forefront was a dazzling row of buxom girls with ruddy faces and sparkling eyes. . . . Behind the girls were the males of every age—from the youthful tyro to the hoary and spectacled patriarchs of the Valley; in the rear with scarcely room to exert their powers were the instrumentalists, amongst whom the fiddlers, large and small, predominated. The mellow flute and the

[7] *Ibid.*, 20.   [8] *Ibid.*, 23–24.   [9] Young, *op. cit.*, Chapter VII.

clarionet had their representatives, and dotted here and there might be seen a brass instrument, reflecting the bright sunshine that gleamed through the windows of the humble edifice. It may indicate a want of taste on my part, but I confess to having experienced a pang of regret that the old-fashioned instruments at Lumb Chapel have been supplanted by the more fashionable, but also more formal organ.[10]

Percy Scholes indicates that the Lumb Chapel was not unique among Baptists:

> There were other places in the north of England and in the midlands where Baptist church services were enlivened with instrumental and choral music. Indeed, the Baptist musicians in general came at last to play their full part in that eighteenth- and early nineteenth-century activity amongst simple-minded musical people which made the choir pew, both in the Establishment and in Nonconformity, a centre of orchestral and choral culture.[11]

There is some indication of a similar practice among Methodists, although ministers may not always have regarded their musicians with favor. Scholes tells of a Methodist minister who, on a particular Sunday in 1803, "stopped a performance of 'The horse and his rider',[12] which was being performed with 'trumpets, horns, violins, hautboys, bassoons, bass viols, and double bass', with the cry, 'Put that horse into his stable; we've had enough of him for today'."[13] Instruments were in wide use in Methodist chapels at the turn of the nineteenth century, although they were not officially sanctioned, for a Conference in 1805 declared that no instruments should be allowed in the singers' seats except a bass viol if needed by the principal singer.[14]

Two major influences in the religious and musical life of eighteenth-century England had a profound effect on music in parish churches and Nonconformist chapels. These influences were (1) the religious awakening under John and Charles Wesley, and (2) the dominant role of Handel in English music. The two are not unrelated; the positive, aggressive preaching of the Wesleys demanded a musical expression of the same quality, and the bold Handelian style was infinitely more suited to the new evangelism than were the old stately, but sometimes dull, psalm tunes. In fact, Handel wrote three hymn tunes for the Wesleys.[15]

While the influence of Handel may clearly be seen in the various hymn-tune and anthem collections of the period, the Wesleyan influence is not as readily apparent. Rather, it was felt in a general quickening of religious interest throughout England, even among the churches that were not in total sympathy with Wesleyan doctrine.

There were numerous collections, published in the eighteenth century for both church and chapel, that contain both hymns and anthems. Such collections create a peculiar problem in that the pieces are not always clearly identified; the anthem fre-

[10] Annie Buckley, *History of the Providence Baptist Chapel, Lumb* (Rawtenstall: A. Riley, "Free Press" Office, 1928), 49–50.

[11] Scholes, *The Oxford Companion*, 83.

[12] Undoubtedly this refers to the chorus from Handel's *Israel in Egypt*.

[13] Scholes, *The Oxford Companion*, 638.   [14] *Ibid.*, 639.

[15] James T. Lightwood, *Hymn-Tunes and Their Story* (rev. ed., London: The Epworth Press, 1923), 174–75.

quently was scaled down and simplified to the extent that it became hymn-like in character, and the hymn, in many instances, was so embellished and extended that performance of it by a congregation would appear to be all but impossible. Hence, in dealing with the collections, we shall attempt to trace the evolution of the simple psalm-tune book into a more involved and specialized source of material which, though still designed for country and village choirs, approaches to some extent the cathedral tradition.

One of the earliest collections designed for parish churches was Henry Playford's *Divine Companion*, first published in 1701. The subtitle declares it to be

> A Choice Collection of New and Easy Psalms, Hymns, and Anthems. The Words of the Psalms being Collected from the Newest Versions. Compos'd by the best Masters, and fitted for the Use of those, who already understand Mr. *John Playford's* Psalms in Three Parts. To be used in Churches or Private Families, for the greater Advancement of *Divine Music*.[16]

That Playford intended the work to fill a specific need in parish churches is evident from his preface:

> We have, 'tis true, had Anthems long since sung, and continued in our Cathedrals and Chappels, which have rendered our Divine Music not Inferiour to that of Italy. . . . But our Parochial Churches, which are equally dedicated to God's Glory, and innumerable, in res[p]ect to those mention'd, have been altogether destitute of such necessary Assistances to praise their Maker by. . . . This has made me be importunate with my Friends to compile such a set of short and easy Anthems as may be proper for the Places they are design'd for.[17]

The friends whom Playford importuned to contribute musical settings for the collection are interesting. William Turner, John Church, William Croft, Jeremiah Clarke, and John Weldon—all Gentlemen of the Chapel Royal, and prominent composers in the cathedral tradition—are represented. Two contributors, however, are not associated with church music; they are Robert King and Samuel Akeroyde (dates of both unknown), court musicians and songwriters who contributed to the Restoration stage. One might expect that the anthems written by these secular musicians would differ stylistically from the others. Such is not the case. These, and the other anthems contained in the collection, are short, simple pieces that are similar in musical style to the psalms and hymns, and, judging from the uniformity of the compositions, it appears likely that Playford may have prescribed their general format. Example 43 reveals the simplicity and tunefulness of pieces in the collection, and further indicates that the styles used here by Jeremiah Clarke and Robert King are similar.

---

[16] Henry Playford, *The Divine Companion; or, David's Harp New Tun'd* (4th ed.; London: Printed by W. Pearson, 1722), title page. The first edition, 1701, consisted of 96 pp.; a second edition with large additions, 1707, contained 180 pp.; the third edition, 1709, was reprinted in 1715.

[17] *Ibid.*, [ii–iii].

Example 43. *My song shall be of mercy and judgment,* Jeremiah Clarke (Playford, *The Divine Companion,* 103).

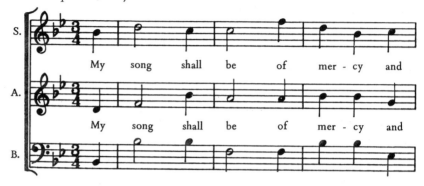

I will always give thanks, Robert King (*ibid.,* 105).

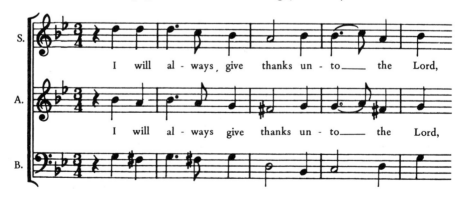

Two anthems of quite different style are found near the end of the collection. The first is a four-part verse setting of *O pray for the peace of Jerusalem* by John Blow, and the second is a two-part verse setting of *I charge you, O daughters of Jerusalem* by Michael Wise. These appear to be truncated versions of larger anthems, representing an effort to adapt the cathedral anthem to less sophisticated use.

It is not possible here to deal with all of the numerous collections that appeared during the eighteenth century in the wake of Playford's *Divine Companion*. Several collections, however, gained wide popularity, and they will be examined as representative of the anthem material that was sung (or, at least, attempted) in parish churches and chapels. For the most part, the collections follow the Playford pattern; they contain psalms, hymns, and anthems; and frequently chanting tunes for the various parts of Morning and Evening Prayer are included. Another feature common to many of the collections is a theoretical introduction dealing with the gamut, or scale, clefs, signatures, note values, and other musical signs.

The first important collection after Playford's was James Green's *Book of Psalmody*, the third edition of which is dated 1715. The eleventh and final edition appeared in 1751, indicating a wide acceptance. Not much is known about Green except that he was organist at Hull and a noted campanologist.[18] The collection contains chanting tunes, psalm tunes, and eighteen anthems which the title page of the third edition indicates are composed by the "best masters." It has not as yet been possible to identify these composers; however, the fact that four of the anthems are also found in John Chetham's *Book of Psalmody* (1718) suggests a common and well-known source. There is, of course, the possibility that Chetham pirated these pieces from Green's collection, although this is not likely, since Chetham's version of *O clap your hands* has an entire section not found in the Green version.[19]

The general style of the anthems in Green's collection is that of the Restoration composers. Closing Hallelujahs are used in seven of the anthems, and passages of parallel thirds with dotted rhythms, like those found in Purcell and Croft, are frequently employed. A syncopated cadence, characteristic of Michael Wise, is found in the setting from Isaiah 12:2,6, *Behold, the Lord is my salvation*, suggesting the possibility of his authorship (Example 44). The eighteen anthems are uncomplicated in that the settings are limited to SATB, but there is a surprising degree of complexity in the numerous melismatic passages which are almost always involved in descriptive word-painting. There are no independent instrumental accompaniments or organ reductions, and it may be assumed that any instrumental participation would have been *colla parte*. The three familiar anthem types are present: full, full with verse, and verse. *Thou, O God, art praised in Sion*, taken from Psalm 65, is a rather curious verse setting. Four solo voices are heard in a succession of two-measure phrases, almost as though the com-

---

[18] The third edition of his *Campanalogia Improved* (London: Printed for A. Bettesworth and C. Hitch, 1733) is advertised in this collection.

[19] Cf. James Green, *A Book of Psalmody* (8th ed., corrected and enlarged; London: W. Pearson, 1734), 100–104, and John Chetham, *A Book of Psalmody* (6th ed., corrected; Wakefield: Joseph Lord, 1741), 130–38.

Example 44. *Behold, the Lord is my salvation* (Green, *A Book of Psalmody*, 21).

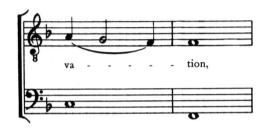

The ways of Zion, Michael Wise (Boyce, *CM*, III, 205).

Example 45.   *Thou, O God, art praised in Sion* (Green, *A Book of Psalmody*, 62).

Tenor alone

Thou,   O   God,   art   prais - ed   in   Si - - on,

Bassus alone

Thou,—   O——   God,   art   prais - ed   in   Si - - - on,

Contra alone

Thou,   O   God,———   art   prais - ed   in   Si - - - on,

Treble alone

Thou,   O   God,———   art   prais - ed   in   Si - - - on,

poser intended for the parish choir to make a display of the best local talent (Example 45).

Reference was made to the appearance of a theoretical introduction in eighteenth-century collections of this type, and while no claim can be made that Green was the innovator of this feature, his inclusion of an instructor in this collection appears to be one of the first. It is quite simple. In six pages Green deals with scales, clefs, the greater and lesser third, the use of the sharp and flat, note values, and time signatures. He frequently sets rules in rhyme, which he evidently considers an effective means of memorization. A rule concerning flats and sharps is thus stated:

> The Effects of *Flats* and *Sharps*, as to the Sound, may be remembered by these two Lines.
>
> > *Under each* Flat *a* Half-Note *lies,*
> > *And o'er the* Sharp *the* Half *doth rise.*[20]

Green also supplies interesting information concerning the relationship of triple and common time, and the use of the hand in marking these times, intended, no doubt, primarily as an aid to the director:

[20] Green, *op. cit.*, [v].

If this $\frac{3}{2}$ Mark be set before a Tune, it denotes *Triple-Time*, which is one third swifter than *Common-Time*; and you must sound three *Minims* in this *Time*, as you do a *Semibreve* in *Common-Time*; and three *Crotchets* in the same *Time*, as you do a *Minim* (or two *Crotchets*) in *Common-Time*, &c. And here the way of Keeping of *Time*, is to Sing two *Minims* with the Hand down, and but one with it up (or as many lesser Notes as come to the length of *Sound*) so that the Hand is as long again down as up. The Hand should fall at the beginning of every *Bar*, both in *Common* and *Triple-Time*.[21]

The obvious purpose of the introduction was to acquaint unlearned parish musicians with the rudiments of music so that their rendition of the psalms and anthems might be more effective. That Green's effort was successful is evident in the large number of such instructors, ever more complex, that followed in the wake of his early effort.

A second important collection appearing in the first quarter of the eighteenth century was the previously mentioned *Book of Psalmody* by John Chetham. The collection, first published in 1718, ran through eleven editions by 1787, and was revised and enlarged several times in the nineteenth century, indicating that its popularity exceeded that of Green's book. On the title page, Chetham stated that the fourteen anthems contained in the collection are "all set in *Four Parts*, Within such a Compass as will most naturally suit the Voices in *Country Churches*, yet may be Sung in *Three* or *Two*, without any Disallowances,"[22] obviously providing a method of performance for those choirs unable to muster four parts. In his preface, the author expounds on the nature and present state of psalm singing, stating that

> it has that Force upon the Passions, as to compose our Thoughts, to dissipate our Sorrows, and to enliven our Devotion. It suits the Spirits when heavy with Grief, or exalted with Joy, and brings them into a Temper of grateful Seriousness. How ravishing and delightful is this Exercise when perform'd with Skill in a becoming Manner? And how much unlike itself when made up of harsh and disagreeable Sounds? They must have very inharmonious Souls, who can hear the one without Pleasure, or the other without Pain: I may appeal to a great many of our Country Congregations for the Truth of this; and yet with how much difficulty are they persuaded to Sing in Tune, or to forsake that they have been accustomed to? What terrible Outcries do they make (such Force has Prejudice) against any Alterations? and if their Understanding does not help 'em to any Arguments against the thing itself, they immediately cry out *Popery*! A frightful Word, often made use of by such as have neither Knowledge enough to judge a thing nor Prudence to let it alone.
>
> The Design of this Undertaking is to better and improve this excellent and useful Part of our Service, to keep up an Uniformity in our *Parish Churches*, and bring them as much as may be, to imitate their Mother Churches the *Cathedrals*.[23]

Chetham's desire to imitate cathedral practice is reflected in the anthems, which are, on the whole, like those contained in Green's volume. Again, the degree of melodic complexity is surprising. *Sing we merrily*, one of the four settings common to both collections, is a case in point (Example 46). A passage such as this would not be sung without

---

[21] *Ibid.*, [vii].   [22] From the title page.   [23] Chetham, *op. cit.*, [iii–iv].

Example 46. *Sing we merrily* (John Chetham, *A Book of Psalmody*, 160).

difficulty by present-day volunteer choirs. How could these anthems be sung by rough, untrained parish and country church choirs? The answer to this question may at least partially be found in the rise of the West Gallery tradition. These village musicians took great pride in their groups (see p. 128), and spent a considerable amount of time in rehearsal. Evidence of this is seen in the activities of the previously mentioned Deighn Layrocks:

> Limitations of time and space were no obstacles to them. Alderman Compston tells a typical "Layrock" story of a youth who tramped over the hills from Dean to Haslingdon to attend a rehearsal. When the practice had gone on until after midnight, he said he ought to be going because he had "to be up middlin' soon on 'i th' morning," whereupon an old enthusiast exclaimed, "Dost yer what awm sayin' to thi? Tha'll ne'er mek a musicianer as long as tha lives; tha'rt i' too big a hurry."[24]

Such investment of time and enthusiasm was bound to result in accomplishment; the mastering of a difficult anthem would have been a matter of pride. Another aid in the performance of these pieces was the *colla parte* accompaniment of instruments characteristic of the West Gallery tradition. The distinctive timbres of the various instruments would have been a great help in clarifying parts for the singers.

An entirely different approach was taken by Nathaniel Gawthorn in his *Harmonia Perfecta*.[25] The collection is chiefly devoted to psalm tunes, many of which were drawn from the Ravenscroft Psalter. In connection with this study, the importance of Gawthorn's book is limited, since it contains only four anthems; however, of particular interest is his use of the treble clef for all voices except the bass. The influence of the collection was limited, it having only three printings, all of them dated 1730.

Yet another type of collection, *A Compleat Melody*, was published by William Tans'ur (1706–1783) in 1734.[26] It reached a fifth edition by 1743, and thereafter appears to have been supplanted by a similar work, *Royal Melody Compleat*, a sixth edition of which was printed in America in 1771.

The work is divided into three books: the first is an extensive theoretical introduction of seventy-two pages, the second consists of settings of the versified psalms, and the third is made up of hymns and anthems composed by the author. Apparently an eccentric, Tans'ur's strange turn of mind is seen in the prefatory pages where, after rapturous praise of church music, he launches into a tirade against unseen enemies of this art, finally consigning them to the judgment of God:

> Oh! How do the Blessed Spirits Rejoyce! to behold Man prostrating his Soul in this pathetical Method; pouring out his Soul in such a Warmth of Piety! How can the most hardened Sinner but have Veneration and be softened, when he hears the Praises of our

---

[24] Buckley, *op. cit.*, 16.

[25] Nathaniel Gawthorn, *Harmonia Perfecta: A Compleat Collection of Psalm Tunes, in Four Parts* (London: William Pearson, 1730).

[26] William Tans'ur, *A Compleat Melody; or The Harmony of Sion* (4th ed.; London: Printed by Alice Pearson, 1738).

CREATOR described in the most expressive Harmony? When it was his Great and infinite Goodness to bestow, and frame to us the Nature of Harmony, only for the very same Divine and Holy Use: And we are in Duty and Gratitude bound to Praise him with it, both in our publick, and private Devotions.

But alas! in this our Age, the right Use of Musick is not only prophan'd, but also condemn'd by many ignorant and blind Zealots; who do not, nor will not endeavour to know the Excellency thereof: The Reason of which is (as I conceive,) they have no Taste or Relish of true Godliness; they are Enemies to all Piety and Learning, and their Lives are Inharmonical: They envy all that are not worse than themselves, and hate to see others perform what they cannot attain to. But though they cast so much Contempt and Scorn on such as perform this Part of Divine Worship in this World, I doubt not but they would gladly be Partakers of that sweet Concert, and Harmony which is incessantly performed in that which is to come; Bearing their Parts with the Angels in Heaven. But alas! Unwise Men do not consider this: Neither do Fools understand it.—Destruction and Unhappiness are in their Ways; the Way of Peace they have not known: Neither is the Fear of God before their Eyes.—He that dwelleth in the Heavens shall laugh them to scorn; and shall bruise them in pieces like a Potter's Vessel.[27]

The massive ego of Tans'ur is further seen in the printing of a verse just before Book I, reading as follows:

A Poetical ENCOMIUM, written on the Author Mr. Tans'ur.
By a Lover of Divine-Musick.

Ingenious Tans'ur! Skilled in Musick's Art,
Which please the Ear, likewise affect the Heart;
Thy Works Melodious, and sweet inflame
Each pious Breast to imitate the same.
This Noble Art thou fully hast survey'd,
Where all its curious Rules are open laid:
May all the World receive thy good Intents.
And Tune to them both Voice and Instruments.
Some God-like Angel did thy Soul inspire
On Heav'nly Mirth, to raise a Heav'nly Quire
On Earth; to praise our GOD with Sacred Love,
To do that Work as Angels do above.

.   .   .

Rewarded may'st thou be as thou dost merit,
And after death a Golden Crown inherit:
In heav'n be plac'd, amidst the Heav'nly Throng,
And Hallelujahs thy perpetual Song.
Whose Tuneful Notes a Monument will raise,
Like Marble Lasting, to declare his Praise.[28]

The foregoing extensive quotations are given in order that the reader might better understand the eccentricities of Tans'ur's anthem composition. For example, his

[27] *Ibid.*, [vi].   [28] *Ibid.*, [xiv].

Example 47a. *Sing unto the Lord*, William Tans'ur (*Compleat Melody*, 101).

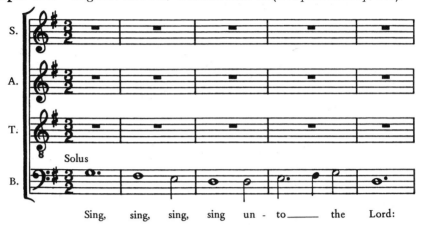

Example 47b. *Ibid.*, 102, 103.

setting of Psalm 33 opens in a conventional manner (Example 47 a), but in measure 16, he surprises the singers with an intricate rhythmic passage that virtually defies performance (Example 47 b), and, to compound the problem, a solo voice is specified for the easy line, and *tutti* for the difficult! Nor is this an isolated case; faulty textual accentuation and uncommonly difficult rhythmic figurations mark almost all of his anthems. Nowhere is this more clearly seen than in the setting of Psalm 47, *O clap your hands* (Example 48).

Example 48. *O clap your hands*, William Tans'ur (*Compleat Melody*, 112).

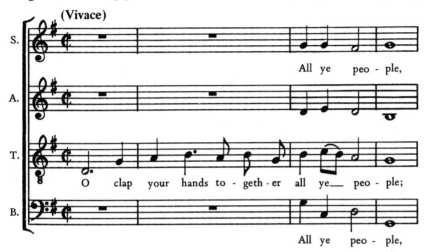

Every anthem in this volume ends with either a short Hallelujah section or the Lesser Doxology. Tans'ur writes fewer of these closing formulas than he does anthems, directing the singers at the end of an anthem to proceed to the "Hallelujah as Page 105" or to the "Glory be, &c. Page 119." Unfortunately, since the closing formulas are too few for the number of anthems, there are cases where an anthem with one sharp in its signature is linked to a coda in three sharps (Example 49).

Yet, in spite of these faults, the work of Tans'ur was popular, at least for a time, in both England and America.[29] No doubt the rustic simplicity of the harmonic structure, which consists mostly of primary chords in root position, held a certain appeal for the singers in country choirs.

The work of Tans'ur, however, was soon overshadowed by that of William Knapp (1698–1768), who was parish clerk at St. James's Church, Poole, for a number of years.[30] His most popular collection, *A Sett of New Psalms and Anthems*, was published in 1738, and ran through an eighth edition by 1770.

---

[29] For an account of Tans'ur's influence on the anthem in America, see Daniel, *op. cit.*, 52–57.
[30] *Ibid.*, 57.

Both Knapp and Tans'ur used dialogue between an imaginary master and scholar to achieve interest in their theoretical introductions, but Knapp's dialogue is the more colorful.[31] Theophilus is the teacher (here Knapp may have had in mind the second-century Christian teacher and writer who was Bishop of Antioch), and Philemon is the student. The reader will appreciate the way in which Knapp tried to overcome the inherent dullness of a theory manual.

> *Theophilus.* Good Morrow, Philemon.
>
> *Philemon.* Good Morrow, good Theophilus, pray what makes you so early Abroad this morning?
>
> *Theo.* I suppose the same Reason that gives you the Opportunity of asking the Question, *viz.* the lovely Season and Weather which seem united to invite us hither.
>
> *Phil.* You are entirely right; Who can forbear frequenting these pleasant Fields, both Morning and Evening, which are now so sweetly adorned with all blooming Beauties of the youthful Spring?

---

[31] Such dialogues appear, among other places, in Sebastian Virdung, *Musica getutscht* (Basel, 1511), and Thomas Morley, *A Plaine and Easie Introduction to Practicall Musicke* (London: Peter Short, 1597).

Example 49.   Anthem excerpt and closing formula from Tans'ur's *Compleat Melody*, 126, 119.

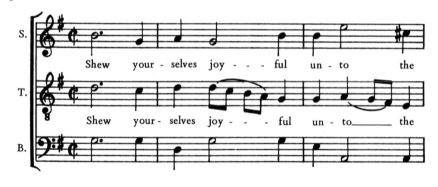

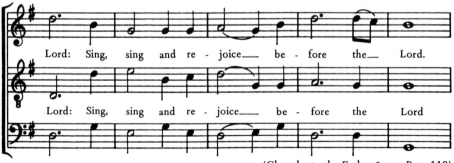

(Glory be to the Father &c. as Page 119)

Theo. It is true; besides the Morning is the fittest Time for Study, which is another Reason of my being here so early; hoping to have some Moments to myself; for to tell you the Truth, I have had a new Lesson in Psalmody lately given me, which I had a Mind to peruse this Morning.

Example 50. *Bless God, my soul,* William Knapp (*A Set of New Psalms and Anthems,* 41–42).

Example 51. *Unto us a Child is born*, William Knapp (*A Set of New Psalms and Anthems*, 53–54).

Example 52.   *I heard a great Voice*, William Knapp (*A New Set of Psalms and Anthems*, 71).

Phil. Since you have named Psalmody, methinks I am sorry that my early Appearance has disappointed you of your desired Solitude, because it gives me the wished-for Occasion of my acquainting you with the Knowledge of that delightful Art; and wish you could recommend me to some Person for my Instruction therein.

Theo. Your Desire is very commendable, since the Knowledge of Music enables us to sing our Maker's Praises with Understanding; and if you will accept so small a Proficient as myself for your Instructor, I shall be ready to serve you.

Phil. I thank you for your kind Offer, and will begin when you please, Sir.[32]

In this instructional preface, Knapp gives us an interesting insight concerning the actual duration of the semibreve. After an explanation of time values, Philemon asks how one can know the length of each note, to which Theophilus replies: "A Semibreve is as long in singing as while you can tell four Strokes of a large Pendulum Clock."[33] This offhand answer conflicts with his later statement that, "Of *Common-Time*, there are three Kinds. . . .The First denotes a very slow Movement, the second a middling Movement, and the two last a quick Movement."[34] Obviously, a flexible duration for the semibreve existed, even in Knapp's own use.

The collection contains nine hymns—or actually psalms—and twelve anthems; and, except for the last two anthems, all of the compositions appear to be Knapp's own. The well-known tune, "Wareham," is here set to Psalm 36 from the Tate and Brady Psalter, and, although the melody is in the tenor, slightly more embellished, its form is quite similar to that found in present-day hymnals. Several psalms in the collection, however, are not conventional. In "Litchet" tune, a setting of Psalm 104, Knapp uses a continuous melody, but assigns successive phrases to different voices in solo fashion, similar to the style of a verse anthem. Only in the last eight measures do all the voices sing together (Example 50). Knapp also used this same device frequently in his anthems (Example 51).

Imitation, however, was his favorite compositional device, and he employed it frequently. The points of imitation are generally brief, and after the entry of the fourth voice, the parts are quickly united in a homophonic texture (Example 52). Another feature relating Knapp's anthems to the hymn tune is his frequent placement of the melodic line in the tenor, especially when the texture is homophonic.

Unlike that of Tans'ur, Knapp's rhythmic vocabulary was simple and straightforward. Nevertheless, his frequent use of dotted rhythms gives his compositions a vital, impelling drive, similar to that found in the music of Handel. Knapp's harmonic material is also simple, consisting mostly of primary chords in root position, thus producing a bold and predictable bass line.

Certainly Knapp's formula was made to order for the country choir, and it is not surprising that this collection retained its popularity for nearly forty years.

---

[32] William Knapp, *A Set of New Psalms and Anthems in Four Parts: On Various Occasions* (5th ed.; London: Printed by Robert Brown, 1752), 9–10.

[33] *Ibid.,* 13.

[34] *Ibid.,* 20.

A third important collection, continuing in the Tans'ur and Knapp tradition, was John Arnold's *Compleat Psalmodist*, published in 1741. An enlarged second edition was published in 1750, and a seventh edition was reached by 1779.

Arnold was born in Essex in 1720 and died in 1792, but details of his life and activities are not known. However, the extent of his publication, which, besides *The Compleat Psalmodist*, includes *The Psalmist's Recreation*, *The Leicestershire Harmony*, *Church Music Reformed*, and *The Essex Harmony*, indicates that music was more than an avocation with him.

The Compleat Psalmodist is divided into four books: an introduction to the grounds of music, a set of Services, together with anthems, psalm tunes, and a set of divine hymns. Arnold indicates in the title page that the collection is intended for the use of country choirs, and that the anthems have been composed after the cathedral manner. In the preface to the second edition—which Arnold wrote in 1749, the year before publication—he stated that he had "very much enlarged the whole Work, by an additional Number of choice Anthems, Psalm-Tunes, &c. a great many of which are properly my own Compositions."[35] It has not yet been possible to determine which of the twenty-four anthems contained in this enlarged edition are by other composers, but it appears likely that most of the pieces are Arnold's.

The anthems in *The Compleat Psalmodist* reveal more structural organization and refinement than do those found in earlier collections of the same type. The setting of Psalm 111, *I will give thanks unto the Lord*, opens with a canon for tenor and bass. The imitation is strict for the first eight measures, after which the voices come together for the cadence (Example 53). The remainder of the anthem employs frequent imitative sections of the same type in an otherwise chordal setting. Another unusual feature of this piece is the SSATB setting of the closing part of the *Gloria Patri*. Since anthems in these collections seldom exceed four parts, this five-part close may indicate that it is the work of a composer other than Arnold, perhaps drawn from the cathedral repertoire. Another feature of interest is a key change from C major to C minor in the middle section. To be sure, this compositional device is to be found in the cathedral repertoire at least as far back as the works of Henry Purcell, but while meter changes were frequent, key changes had not been a regular feature of anthems designed for parish and country choirs.

A simple, but compelling, melodic line is characteristic of Arnold's work. His setting of Psalm 66 illustrates this (Example 54). Note here the bass line, which outlines the tonic chord in fifth and octave leaps, and invests the piece with a straightforward, rugged quality. Word-painting is also frequently used. In the setting of Psalm 47, *O clap your hands together*, the trumpet is vividly portrayed in a bass solo line (Example 55). Considered as a whole, *The Compleat Psalmodist* appears to represent an advancement in the type of material created for country churches.

In the first half of the eighteenth century, materials for country choirs had been composed and published by Anglicans. Nonconformists no doubt drew on these

[35] John Arnold, *The Compleat Psalmodist* (3rd ed.; London: Robert Brown, 1753), [iii].

Example 53. *I will give thanks unto the Lord* (John Arnold, *The Compleat Psalmodist*, 77).

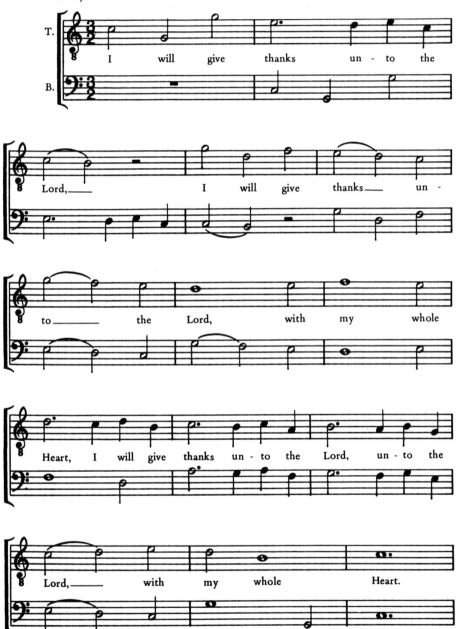

Example 54. *O be joyful* (John Arnold, *The Compleat Psalmodist*, 143).

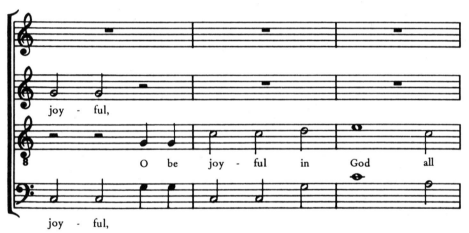

Example 55. *O clap your hands together* (John Arnold, *The Compleat Psalmodist*, 183).

Example 56. *By the rivers of Babylon*, Caleb Ashworth (Hubbard, *A Volume of Sacred Music*, 17).

Example 57. *By the rivers of Babylon*, Caleb Ashworth (Hubbard, *A Volume of Sacred Music*, 18, 19).

sources and, occasionally, as in the case of the Deighn Layrocks, composed their own hymns and anthems. This condition changed to some extent, however, in the latter part of the century. In 1760 Caleb Ashworth (1722–1775) published *A Collection of Tunes*, and in 1762 added a second part which contained anthems. The Ashworths were Baptists, and a prominent part of the Deighn Layrocks in Rossendale, Lancashire; but Caleb, evidently not in sympathy with the Baptist movement, studied for the Independent (Congregationalist) ministry under Philip Doddridge and became headmaster of an academy at Daventry.

Ashworth's setting of Psalm 137, *By the rivers of Babylon*, although somewhat less involved than the anthems of Knapp and Arnold, effectively conveys the meaning of the text. The E-minor tonality, the frequent meter changes, and the pairing of voices, usually running in thirds, all combine to enhance the plaintiveness of the psalm (Example 56). Text-painting is also seen in the treatment of the word *song*, where a quasi-imitative melisma is employed (Example 57).

In the last quarter of the eighteenth century, collections of the type published by Tans'ur, Knapp, and Arnold began to wane in popularity; they were gradually supplanted by a new type quite different in character and purpose. Several distinguishing features of the new collections may be enumerated:

1. The compositions were not chiefly the work of the compiler, as in the case of Tans'ur, Knapp, and others. Instead, they were drawn from a number of composers. In this respect they were similar to those of Playford, Chetham, and Green.

2. The music of European composers was drawn upon. Most of these composers were living in London, at least temporarily.

3. Classical, rather than Baroque, stylistic features predominate.

4. The hymn-type anthem and the anthem-type hymn are virtually one and the same.

5. Several collections were designed for the use of "charity children," whose singing was in vogue during this period.

The first of these charity-children volumes, a collection for use at the chapel of Lock Hospital, was compiled and published in 1769 by Martin Madan (1726–1790). Madan, an Oxford graduate preparing for a career in law, became a Wesleyan convert and entered the Anglican ministry. After taking Holy Orders he founded and became chaplain of the Lock Hospital, Hyde Park Corner, where he acquired a reputation as both preacher and composer.

Of immense popularity, Madan's collection reached a thirteenth edition by 1794, and it was also published in America. The influence of the work was further felt in other collections, both in England and America, where many of Madan's pieces were reprinted. Although the volume could have netted Madan a considerable profit, it is interesting to note that he assigned the proceeds to the hospital. He dedicated the collection to the administrative officers and

Example 58a. *Not all the blood of beasts,* Samuel Arnold (Lock Hospital Collection, 117).

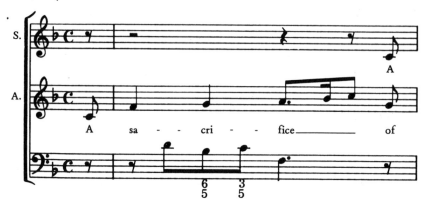

Example 58b.   *Ibid.*, 118.

to the rest of the Governors of the Lock Hospital, near Hyde-Park Corner, to whom the
entire copy of this Collection of Hymn and Psalm Tunes is presented as a benefaction to the
hospital, that the profits arising from the sale of it may be applied for the benefit of the
Charity.[36]

The texts in the collection are exclusively hymns, and would ordinarily be outside
the scope of this study. It is here, nevertheless, that the aforementioned fusion of hymn
and anthem is first seen on an extensive scale. The length and nature of many of the
pieces give evidence that they were intended for use as anthems. Characteristic of this
hymn-anthem type is Samuel Arnold's setting of Isaac Watts's hymn, *Not all the blood*

[36] Martin Madan, *The Collection of Psalm and Hymn Tunes sung at the Chapel of the Lock Hospital* (from
the last London edition; Boston, Mass.: West & Blake, and Manning & Loring, 1809), [iii].

of beasts.[37] It is a two-part setting with figured bass, through-composed, and seventy-two measures in length. Although the vocal texture has no imitation, it is, to a degree, contrapuntal (Example 58 a). The middle section of the anthem, in triple meter, is for solo voice and is framed with organ interludes. The melodic line flows with a light grace typical of composition in the Classical Period, a style no doubt well suited to the singing of the charity children (Example 58 b).

In addition to Samuel Arnold, several other English composers are represented in the collection. John Worgan (1724–1790), Musgrave Heighington (1679–1774), and the famed music historian Charles Burney (1726–1814) were musical contributors, and several pieces are Madan's own work. Three Italian composers are also represented: Felice Alessandri (1742–1798), Felice Giardini (1716–1796), and Mattia Vento (1735–1776), all of whom were involved in opera and the theater in London during this period. No doubt Madan's influence and wide circle of acquaintance is responsible for the introduction of these Continental composers into the stream of English church music. It is in this collection that Giardini's well-known hymn tune, since named "Italian Hymn," first appeared. That Madan was closely associated with the composer is indicated by the fact that Giardini's oratorio, *Ruth*, was performed at the Lock Hospital Chapel in 1765.[38]

Although most of the compositions by the three Italians are short stanzaic pieces, Giardini's setting of *Father, how wide thy glory shines!* is of a more extended nature. Here the form is:

A (19 measures in $\frac{4}{4}$ time)

B (27 measures in $\frac{3}{4}$ time)

C (16 measures in $\frac{6}{8}$ time, marked "Siciliana").[39]

Although the piece has no hint of polyphony, a considerable degree of variety is produced by the through-composed treatment and the changes of meter.

Madan's collection, then, was not rooted in either the cathedral tradition or in the country church music that had arisen in the early part of the century; rather, it was a new type of church music—one that draws stylistically from the stage and, in spite of its manifest superficiality—a style that became immensely popular in English and American churches.

Another collection of much the same type appeared in 1774. It was *Psalms, Hymns, and Anthems Used in the Chapel of the Hospital for the Maintenance and Education of Exposed and Deserted Young Children.*[40] The music is set for one and two treble parts.

---

[37] *Ibid.*, 117.   [38] *Grove's*, III, 628.   [39] Madan, *op. cit.*, 128–30.

[40] Although the compiler of this collection remains anonymous, William Russell (1777–1813), organist of the hospital chapel, published a revised edition of the work in 1809 under the title *Psalms, Hymns, and Anthems for the Foundling Hospital.*

An instrumental bass, mostly figured, underlays the voice parts, and instrumental introductions and interludes are numerous. Most of the psalms are three-part settings in the old style, although a few are somewhat elaborate. The hymns are musically similar to the anthems, the distinguishing feature being the nature of the texts.

More than half of the pieces are anonymous, and the remaining ones are designated only by last names, most of whom can be identified. John Worgan and Musgrave Heighington, both contributors to Madan's collection, are represented here. Two pieces are by the German-born John Christopher Smith (1712–1795), an organist and composer who was closely associated with Handel in England. Smith was the first person to be appointed organist at the Foundling Hospital Chapel (1754),[41] and it is possible that he may have been instrumental in the compilation of the collection. His close association with the hospital is seen in that the first piece in the collection, entitled *The Foundling's Hymn*, bears his name and appears to be something of a theme song. Benjamin Cooke (1734–1793) and John Stanley (1713–1786), both fairly prominent as composers and organists, are also represented.

An unusual feature of the book is the inclusion of some anthem texts (without music) at the end of the volume. One of these, entitled *Anthem Taken From the Late Mr. Handel's Works*,[42] is actually a cantata drawn from his *Messiah*. Except for the opening recitative, the selections are entirely from the joyous sections of the oratorio (Table 6).

TABLE 6

Anthem Excised from Handel's *Messiah*

Recitative, "Comfort ye."
Aria, "Every valley shall be exalted."
Chorus, "And the glory of the Lord."
Aria, "O thou that tellest good tidings to Zion."
Chorus, "For unto us a Child is born."
Chorus, "Hallelujah."

This lifting of the Hallelujah section out of context, still very much a custom in our time, may have originated here, or this may be merely an indication of an already established practice. The other anthem texts are to be sung to the music intended for them by either John Stanley or Maurice Greene, as the case may be. The Greene anthems are *Acquaint thyself with God* (alto solo and SATB chorus), *O God, thou art my God* (ATB soli and SATB chorus), *O God of my righteousness* (ST soli and SATB chorus), *The Lord is my shepherd* (AA soli and SATB chorus), *My God, my God, look upon me* (tenor solo and SSATB chorus), and *Behold I bring you glad tidings* (SS soli and SSATTB chorus).[43] The music for all the foregoing anthems appears in Greene's *Forty*

---

[41] *Grove's*, VII, 854.   [42] *Psalms, Hymns, and Anthems*, 126.   [43] *Ibid.*, 130, 131, 134–37.

Example 59. *Hymn for Easter (Psalms, Hymns, and Anthems used in the Chapel of the Hospital, 77–79).*

(a) Duet

(b) Solo, slow

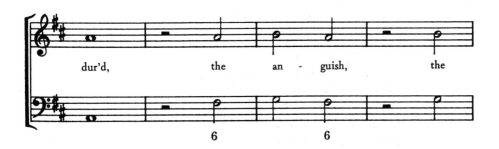

Select Anthems. The fact that no music was provided in the Foundling Hospital collection indicates that copies of Greene's two-volume work were widely distributed. The Greene anthems are in every case longer than the pieces published with music in the collection, and are more difficult as well. While the solo parts are mostly within the range of children, it is questionable whether such casually trained youngsters could have sung them well.

The main item of interest in the collection is a piece entitled *Hymn for Easter*.[44] It is essentially both the text and tune of the well-known hymn from the *Lyra Davidica* of

44 *Ibid.*, 77–79.

1708 (and now known by that name) arranged in anthem form. Anthem-type settings of hymn texts have been previously encountered, but none was based on a preexistent hymn tune, and this example may well mark the beginning of the hymn-anthem, a type that has become increasingly popular to the present time. The original hymn tune and several sections of the anthem are here quoted to facilitate comparison. In the opening section, only two measures of the hymn tune are stated, after which there is a rhapsodic development on the first line of the text (Example 59a). The entire tune and first stanza of the text are then stated by a solo, duet, and chorus in alternation. The second stanza is sung by a solo voice, the melodic material being related only in general

TABLE 7

Form of *Hymn for Easter*

Introduction (15 measures).
 Interlude a (2 measures).

Section A, basic hymn tune (15 measures).
 Interlude b (2 measures).

Section B, new material (12 measures).
 Interlude a (2 measures).

Section C, new material plus part of B (20 measures).
 Interlude a (2 measures).

Section A repeated plus Interlude b serving as a final cadence.

mood and style to the hymn tune. The mood changes sharply in the opening of stanza three, but in the last half of the stanza the music is almost identical with that in the corresponding section of stanza two (Example 59b). The anthem is then brought to a close with the repetition of the entire first stanza. Instrumental interludes are employed frequently throughout. Table 7 shows the form of the entire piece.

The formal organization of the piece is quite similar to that found in many present-day hymn-anthems.

Yet another innovation may be observed in this volume; that is the placement of the melody in the first treble rather than the tenor, as had been the case almost invariably in earlier collections. This, no doubt, was the result of necessity. The music being intended for the use of children, there was no tenor part. The melody, being displaced from its accustomed position, had to be assigned to one of the two surviving higher parts. This new sound may well have helped to pave the way for the eventual change to this style with the melody clearly audible above the other voices. In fact, further evidence of this trend was seen just one year after the publication of the Foundling Hospital collection. In *Psalmody Improved*, a book of psalm tunes and anthems intended for country choirs, James Williams Newton, curate of Wrentham, explained why the principal melody was placed in the tenor in the early development of psalm singing.[45] He roundly condemned the practice, and attacked the prejudice that sustained it:

> Performers of the tenor part have been so long accustomed to the principal melody, that they cannot readily conform to another part, which may be less pleasing to *themselves*: therefore they are disposed, from prejudice, not to approve a contrary method, though it be far more consistent with propriety.

. . .

> It is a lamented truth, that very few Psalms, performed in full chorus, are grateful to an audience; because, either composers have erred in the arrangement of the parts; or compilers have *carefully transposed* the treble of those Psalms, whose parts have been properly arranged into the tenor cliff; for one or more of the purposes already assigned. Several Anthems have been subject to the same fate; and are equally disagreeable to an audience, for the same reason. . . . With all deference due to the opinion of others, he [the author] thinks it may safely be affirmed, that *That property* [leading part] *invariably belongs to the first treble voice.*
>
> This fundamental rule has been too generally disregarded; and, either from perverseness, or want of taste, composers and compilers of psalmody have substituted another rule, very insufficient to produce the effect, universally intended to be produced, by good vocal harmony. To restore this rule to its proper authority, is an improvement greatly to be desired. An attempt toward such an improvement is offered to the public, in this little Preface, and in the annexed specimen of psalmody.[46]

It is evident from the foregoing quotation that the transfer of the melody from tenor to first treble was not easily accomplished, and that it would be some time before the new method would be universally adopted in England.

Further evidence of a growing interest in church music among Nonconformists is seen in the publication of *A Selection of Psalm and Hymn Tunes*, ca. 1791, by John Rippon (1751–1836), a prominent Baptist minister in London. Thomas Walker (fl. late 18th c.), of whom nothing else is known, served as Rippon's musical editor. The tune-book was intended as a companion to Rippon's *Selection of Hymns from the Best Authors* (1787), which became enormously popular in England and America. In his Preface, Rippon makes reference to this popularity, and explains the circumstances that prompted the compilation of the tune-book:

> Having had the honour of publishing a Selection of Hymns...which has met a favourable reception among good men of *different denominations*, at home and abroad, and obtained a circulation of near *Twenty Thousand copies* in a few years; repeated enquiries have been made for Tunes suited to many of the Hymns, especially such as are in peculiar metres. These enquiries have been partly answered, sometimes by mentioning one Author, and then another; but the purchase and use of *several* Tune Books being found inconvenient, it was thought that *One* Volume might be published, which should remedy this evil, contain a

---

[45] James Williams Newton, *Psalmody Improved: In a Collection of Psalm Tunes and Anthems* (Ipswich: Printed for the Author, and sold by John Shave, 1775), [i]–iii.

[46] *Ibid.,* vi–viii.

greater variety than any other book extant—and be calculated to unite London and the Country in singing.

With this in view it appeared advisable, not only to adopt those which are allowedly the best Tunes sung in the Dissenting Meetinghouses, and other societies in the Metropolis, but also to obtain lists of such as are used in the principal congregations throughout England; paying, at the same time, a due regard to others which are highly esteemed in some of the foreign churches.[47]

This was, of course, a tune-book primarily intended for congregational use, but there can be no doubt that some of the more extended and complex pieces were intended as anthems, even though they were not so named. Evidence of this intention is seen in Rippon's discussion of some of the four-part pieces, where he makes reference to their beauty when sung by a choir.[48]

Martin Madan, Musgrave Heighington, Samuel Arnold, and others are represented by extended anthem-type compositions. The editor, Thomas Walker, included a number of his own works, one of them 247 measures in length, enough to try the patience of any congregation![49] The popularity of Handel's works is evident in a lengthy, anonymous anthem entitled *Easter Ode*.[50] Based on a hymn by Walter Shirley, "From heaven the loud angelic song began," the piece extends to 122 measures, and concludes with a truncated version of the "Hallelujah, Amen" from Handel's *Judas Maccabaeus*, in which the text has also been altered.

It is doubtful that Rippon's tune-book attained a popularity anything like that of his *Selection of Hymns*, for much of the music is too complex for congregational use, but the selection no doubt found its way into many choir lofts, especially in country churches.

In the last decade of the eighteenth century, two anthem composers of the cathedral tradition turned their attention to the problem of parish and country churches. Brief reference was made in Chapter 3 to *The Psalms of David for the Use of Parish Churches*, compiled by Samuel Arnold and John Wall Callcott in 1791. The purpose of the collection is made evident in the opening part of the Preface:

> The country parochial Choirs make psalmody their principal study; which, consisting generally of simple counterpoint, is in every respect the easiest for them. The various collections of anthems which have done so much honour to the learning and genius of this nation, are too difficult for those places where generally no other bass than a violoncello, or bassoon, is used; especially as in their intermediate symphonies the accompaniment of an organ is almost absolutely necessary. At present, the gradual improvement of the singers has advanced them beyond simple counterpoint; and several productions, published for their use, of psalms and anthems composed in the choral style, with imitations and fugues, have been so incorrect and deficient, both in melody and harmony, that some among them scarce deserve the name of music.

---

[47] John Rippon, *A Selection of Psalm and Hymn Tunes* (5th ed., enlarged; London: Sold by Mr. Rippon, [n.d.]), iii.

[48] *Ibid.*, ii.   [49] *Ibid.*, No. 268.   [50] *Ibid.*, No. 253.

To remedy this defect, and to assist the country Choirs in their cultivation of this species of music, the following collection of music has been made.[51]

The texts for the collection were compiled by Adam Gordon. The entire psalter is represented in versified form, and, for the most part, the psalms are drawn from the Tate and Brady New Version. However, Gordon restricted each setting to a maximum of five stanzas. In addition, twelve hymns are included.

While the musical settings are chiefly the work of Arnold and Callcott, there are numerous adaptations from the works of prominent English and Continental composers such as Handel, Arne, Pergolesi, Jomelli, and Graun. Many of the compositions are short and simple, but at the same time musically interesting. For example, Callcott's strophic setting of Psalm 81 consists of only seventeen measures, yet interest is achieved through melodic movement in the voices and short points of imitation (Example 60). In this instance the tenor appears to have the primary melody in the opening measures, while it is given to the treble at the close. Not only are the majority of the pieces short, strophic settings, many of them are also designed for choirs with limited forces, for there are numerous two- and three-part settings. On the other hand, some of the compositions are considerably more ambitious. Arnold's setting of Psalm 147, *To God the Lord a hymn of praise*, is a full anthem with verses extending through ninety-four measures. The chorus is SATB, and the verse sections employ TB, SAT, and SA solo voices in succession, after which the anthem concludes with a lively, extended Hallelujah.

The work of Arnold and Callcott was more or less imitated by John Whitaker (1776–1847) early in the nineteenth century with his two-volume collection, *The Seraph*, which contained traditional psalm and hymn tunes as well as selections from Handel, Haydn, Mozart, Pleyel, and numerous English composers.[52] In addition to being a composer, Whitaker was organist at the Church of St. Clement, Eastcheap, London, and a partner in Button and Whitaker, a music publishing firm.[53]

An unusually clear picture of contemporary English church music, at least as Whitaker saw it, is found in the prefatory material. The author contended that psalmody, as it had traditionally been practiced in the Church of England, was not suited to the expression of contemporary religious poetry:

> In the Church of England it appears that the model for composing a Psalm Tune, was formed about the time of the Reformation, and is still adhered to, with very few exceptions. But its style is so antiquated and monotonous, that cultivated genius and refined taste (produced by progressive improvement in the Science of Music) have become satiated with its dulness and insipidity. The model itself, however pleasing it might have been in those days (when the knowledge of the theory of music was so confined) will be found to be little else

---

[51] Arnold and Callcott, *op. cit.*, iii.

[52] John Whitaker, *The Seraph, A Collection of Sacred Music, Suitable to Public or Private Devotion* (2 vols.; London: Whitaker and Company, 1818).

[53] *Grove's*, IX, 274.

Example 60.   *Psalm 81*, John Wall Callcott (*The Psalms of David . . .* , 91).

than a succession of chords without any reference either to melody, or pathos; and any musical composition...without these great requisites, will never win the uncultivated ear. In this system the Composers of our Church Psalmody have so constantly persevered, even up to the present day, that I presume they have either conceived it impossible to improve this model, or, that they have never given the subject one moment's reflection: it is, however, certain, that such a mere dry combination of sounds can never embrace the imagery of poetry.[54]

Whitaker then commented on the manner in which psalmody was being performed in parish churches:

The consequence then is, that a congregation so situated is compelled to hear compositions which are sameness personified, applied indiscriminately to the language of the Psalmist, whether *joyful* or *melancholy*. Thus I have frequently heard in parish churches some scores of charity children, who, in singing a *penitential psalm*, or *invoking the mercy of the Deity*, have been so vehement, that their *vocal efforts* have rather resembled *a shout* or *a scream*, than the impressive tones of *repentance* or *humility*; and to heighten the effect, they have been accompanied on a fine and powerful organ by a miserable performer, who has been selected more as an object of charity than as a person of talent: the congregation being thus nearly deafened by such a sacrifice of sense to sound, becomes as indifferent to this essential and delightful part of divine worship, as they would be to the noise of passing carriages in the streets.[55]

The author was somewhat more charitable in his evaluation of music in Nonconformist congregations. Here he found much to commend, even though theoretical aspects of the music were found wanting:

In Dissenting Congregations, I have heard with wondering pleasure their efforts to laud the Deity; I have also heard with astonishment such bold and impressive flights of fancy in their melodies, that would have done honour to first-rate musical talent; but I have at the same time found most of them so encumbered with *false harmony*, *forbidden progressions*, and *injudicious and fruitless attempts at counter-point*, that my pleasure and astonishment have given place to regret. In some of these compositions I have even found endeavours to produce *harmony* so completely abortive, that a combination of sounds has been substituted *which could not be found in any theoretical scale of music whatever*. Still the effort is laudable, although it does more honour to the *heart* than to the *head*.[56]

Naturally, the purpose of Whitaker's collection was to correct the musical defects of both Anglicans and Nonconformists. His texts were drawn from England's famous hymnists: Watts, the Wesleys, William Cowper, Anne Steele, Joseph Addison, and others. Perhaps the most significant feature of the collection is the number of instances where works of the famous composers previously mentioned were adapted to hymn texts. For example, Handel's "Dead March" from the oratorio *Saul* is set to Isaac Watts's hymn of similar sentiment, *Hark from the tombs a doleful sound*.[57] The entire march is employed with only such rhythmic alterations as are necessary to accommodate the text. A shortened version of "The heavens are telling," from Haydn's

[54] Whitaker, *op. cit.*, I, 1–2.   [55] *Ibid.*, I, 2.   [56] *Ibid.*, I, 3.   [57] *Ibid.*, I, 8–11.

oratorio *The Creation* is set to Charles Wesley's hymn *Come away to the skies*.[58] Again the original and substitute texts bear a similarity. The main point of interest, however, lies in Whitaker's adaptations from secular sources. The hymn *O praise ye the Lord! prepare a new song* is set to the music of the closing chorus, "Amanti, costanti seguaci d'onor," Act III, of Mozart's *Don Giovanni*.[59] Even farther removed from tradition are the adaptations from symphonic literature. Here the theme from the second movement of Haydn's Symphony No. 53 (L'Impériale) provides the melodic material for Watts's hymn *I love my Shepherd's voice*.[60] And again, the theme from the second movement of the same composer's Symphony No. 73 (La Chasse) becomes the melody of Wesley's hymn *Happy soul, that free from harms*.[61] For the most part, the borrowed material remains unchanged, although occasional minor alterations result from textual requirements.

Whitaker's borrowing from identifiable secular sources appears to be far more extensive than had been the case with any previous compilers—many more instances occur than have been mentioned here—and it would probably be equaled or surpassed only by Lowell Mason some years later in America.

From the foregoing study it is evident that the eighteenth century gave rise to a tradition of choirs and religious choral music in parish churches and Nonconformist chapels. In short, the anthem had ceased to be the sole property of royal court and cathedral; it had caught the popular fancy, and now belonged to the common people. Stylistic changes, no doubt reflecting popular taste, are evident; from the comparatively simple adaptations of cathedral style found in Playford, Green, and Chetham, to the roughhewn, folksy collections of Tans'ur, Knapp, and Arnold, the more refined charity children collections, and those works designed to "correct" alleged abuses—all of these suggest that the anthem would henceforth more quickly and accurately reflect the changing tastes of the people.

---

[58] *Ibid.*, II, 173–78.   [59] *Ibid.*, II, 186.   [60] *Ibid.*, I, 6.   [61] *Ibid.*, II, 6.

CHAPTER FIVE

The Beginnings of the American Anthem

Despite several excellent studies of the early American anthem, any examination of its introduction to America—specifically to New England, since our first evidence of imported examples appears there—invites a number of questions, not all of which can be answered successfully. Our task in assigning importance to English models or native ingenuity would be immeasurably simpler if we knew exactly which books were introduced from England, how early they were first known here, how widely they were distributed, and whether their appearance in American collections reflected a growing taste in this country or simply the hopes of compilers and publishers. Our understanding of the anthem in America will benefit from knowledge of whether the transplanted product in any way reflected the cathedral practice, that of the parish church, or that of the Nonconformist chapel. Some answers will be quite clear, others will leave some doubts, and, worst of all, certain vague references, hints, and incomplete records will prove to be tantalizing in their promise, but will remain ever out of our grasp.

It is essential that we review the situation in this country at the middle of the eighteenth century, when the first evidence of religious choral pieces more elaborate than a hymn is seen. That there is a relationship between the religious bent of certain colonies and the popularity of tune-books may be worth pursuing first.

The settlers of Virginia were, for the most part, not fleeing from the authority of the Established Church. As Anglicans they were content with the old ways for a longer time than their neighbors to the north. Still, they were not able to continue the cathedral practice in their new home, and they could not adopt modified practices without disturbing their traditions. It is not to these settlers that we may look for the first American anthems.

The other colonies of the South—the Carolinas and Georgia—were dominated by Anglicans, but populated by a larger labor force that failed to make itself felt in religious and musical matters. Social conditions generally separated the classes in the South. They failed to encounter each other as equals in or out of church, and the tightening of religious bonds continued among members of the dominant group, while the emergence of a folk practice is found in the subordinate one. New York and New Jersey, largely settled by Anglicans, and Pennsylvania, nominally Quaker, burst the confinement of limited religious practice because they were quickly settled by people from many backgrounds and callings. As centers of commerce, learning, and population they took on the cosmopolitan qualities that no region under a single theocratic control could have done. These northern centers appear as publishers' locations, distribution centers for ideas, and desirable locations for music teachers and businessmen.

The New England Colonies, on the other hand, were essentially Puritan in their outlook. This included the Separatists, who had broken completely with the Church of England, and those who, bearing the title of Puritan, were still in the Church. Disapproving much of the Church of England's dogma and practice, the settlers of the New England Colonies held in common an unbending Calvinistic theology. The major point of difference, however, was in polity rather than theology. The Puritans believed in an established church; the Separatists did not. But the tide was running in favor of the Puritans, and the principle of establishment was dominant in New England.

In a discussion of Puritan religious thought and life, Clifton T. Olmstead observes that

> at the center of Puritan theology stood a God who controlled all events according to His eternal arbitrary purpose. Every circumstance of life, however nonsensical from man's purview, was decreed by God. It was for man to accept and not to fathom the divine logic. All that man needed to know about the divine will was revealed by God in the Scriptures, the final rule in all matters of faith and life. For the Puritan, the Bible was a book of law, an infallible text which was authoritative not only for the religious life but for the social and political order. His duty, as a follower of the law, was to promote its observance in society through exhortation and, if necessary, by force.[1]

The theocratic order in the Colonies extended its rule over all citizens, whether they were members of the church or not.

---

[1] Clifton E. Olmstead, *History of Religion in the United States* (Englewood Cliffs, N.J.: Prentice-Hall, Inc., 1960), 77.

Outside the church membership were the unregenerate inhabitants of the community. They could not participate in either church or civil affairs but were expected to attend services of worship, conduct themselves in an approved manner, and contribute to the support of the church. Thus was preserved the rulership of the redeemed—a prerequisite to the establishment of the Kingdom.[2]

The Puritan intolerance of dissent is evident in the case of Roger Williams, who had the audacity to oppose the concept of an established church in Massachusetts, and was subsequently banished from the colony there.

Austerity also characterized Puritan religious musical expression. While it is true that Puritans have been unjustly accused of a general negative attitude toward the arts, it nevertheless remains that their practice of church music was limited by the traditional Calvinistic concept—the versified psalms could be sung in unison without accompaniment, and nothing more. Thus the first implements of church music brought to this country were the Sternhold and Hopkins psalter and Henry Ainsworth's *Booke of Psalms*, both direct products of Calvinistic biblicism. It is not surprising then that a psalter, the Bay Psalm Book of 1640, has the distinction of being the first printed book in the Colonies.

Even these limited resources were gradually laid aside in favor of the "lining-out" practice in which the deacon or leader, reading or intoning a single line of the psalm, would pause while the congregation rendered it musically, a deadly custom to be sure, and one no doubt offensive to persons of musical sensibility. Whether the practice grew out of a shortage of psalters or an increasing illiteracy, the certain result was a musical illiteracy and a shrinking psalm-tune repertory. Moreover, a certain amount of improvisation resulted from the oral tradition, and the handful of tunes in common use was sung according to the whim of local custom.

Such was the scene of musical disrepair in New England's churches at the turn of the eighteenth century, and it was to it that the Reverend Thomas Symmes addressed his treatise *The Reasonableness of Regular Singing*, in 1720. His brief but lucid essay was only the first thrust against what he called the "Anti-Regular-Singers," a group he slyly referred to by an abbreviated form of that term.[3] The burden of his essay is apparent from quotations in several volumes.[4] A few of his points follow:

1. Singing by note is the true old way; lining-out is a new, wrong way.
2. Singing by note is supported by Scripture.
3. The usual way of singing is enough to make one join the Papists, they sing so much better than one finds now.
4. Music study with notes was undertaken at Harvard from its founding.

[2] *Ibid.*, 78.

[3] Irving Lowens, *Music and Musicians in Early America* (New York: W. W. Norton & Co., 1964), 19.

[4] See Daniel, *op. cit.*, 13–14; Gilbert Chase, *America's Music: From the Pilgrims to the Present* (2nd rev. ed., New York: McGraw-Hill Book Company, 1966), 27; Leonard Ellinwood, *The History of American Church Music* (New York: Morehouse-Gorham Company, 1953), 19–20; and Lowens, *op. cit.*, 19–20.

Symmes turned the criticisms of the "A. R.S.es" upon themselves by supporting his argument with scriptural references, and he put the old practice in what seemed to him a proper light by bringing an established center of literacy and culture into the picture. Urbanization and a higher level of literacy were to be strong forces in bringing Symmes's hopes to reality. Lining-out was destined to become the last resort of the unlearned and rural folk.

Symmes's viewpoint was shared by other enlightened ministers, many of whom stood to gain from the growth of singing by note, since they were able to write, compile, and publish books that could be used in the singing-school movement. In addition to Symmes, John Tufts (1689–1750), Nathaniel Chauncey (dates unknown), and Thomas Walter (1696–1725), all ministers, wrote in support of regular singing. The remarks of Walter are particularly interesting. In *The Grounds and Rules of Musick Explained*, 1721, he compared the need of singing by note to that of general literacy:

> We don't call him a *Reader*, who can recite *Memoriter* a few Pieces of the Bible, and other Authors, but put him to read in those Places where he is a Stranger, cannot tell *ten Words in a Page*. So is he not worthy of the Name of a *Singer*, who has gotten eight or ten Tunes in his Head, and can sing them like a *Parrot of Rote*, and knows nothing more about them, than he has heard from the voices of others; and shew him a Tune that is new and unknown to him, can't strike two notes of it.[5]

Continuing his argument in support of rules for singing, Walter commented on contemporary practice in psalmody:

> They [the rules] will instruct us in the right and true singing of the Tunes that are already in Use in our Churches; which when they first came out of the Hands of the Composers of them, were sung according to the Rules of the *Scale of Musick*, but are now miserably tortured and twisted, and quavered, in some Churches, into an horrid Medley of confused and disorderly Noises. . . . Our Tunes are, for Want of a Standard to appeal to in all our Singing, left to the Mercy of every unskilful Throat to chop and alter, twist and change, according to their infinitely divers and no less odd Humours and Fancies.[6]

Walter further attested to the small repertory found in use, stating that "at present we are confined to *eight or ten Tunes*, and in some Congregations to little more than half that number."[7]

A number of well-known psalm tunes in three-part settings are found in the closing section of the book, a matter of considerable significance, since the traditional Puritan practice had been unison singing.[8] Such a departure from established custom

---

[5] Thomas Walter, *The Grounds and Rules of Musick Explained: Or an Introduction to the Art of Singing by Note. Fitted to the meanest Capacities* (Boston: printed by J. Franklin for S. Gerrish, 1721), 2.

[6] *Ibid.*, 2, 3.   [7] *Ibid.*, 4.

[8] It should be noted that the ninth edition of the Bay Psalm Book, 1698, contained thirteen psalm tunes in two-part arrangements (see Lowens, *op. cit.*, 33). It is doubtful, however, that any part other than melody was sung. Lowens points out that these tunes were drawn from John Playford's *Brief Introduction to the Skill of Musick*, which probably accounts for the two-part arrangement.

required a biblical explanation, and it was forthcoming the following year when Walter was called upon to preach in Boston before the Society for Promoting Regular and Good Singing. The *New England Courant*, March 5, 1722, carried an account of the meeting, and reported that, in addition to Walter's sermon, "the Singing was perform'd in Three Parts (according to Rule) by about Ninety Persons skill'd in that Science, to the great Satisfaction of a Numerous Assembly there Present."[9]

Walter appears to be the first to publish the psalm tunes in three-part settings, for although John Tufts' *Introduction to the Singing of Psalm-Tunes* probably antedates Walter's, it was not until the fifth edition of Tufts' work in 1726 that the tunes were set in three parts.[10] It is obvious that except for three tunes Walter drew his settings from John Playford's *Whole Book of Psalms*, 1677, since the former agrees with the latter in all but the smallest details.

A curious aspect of Walter's format is the way in which he set up tunes of double length—i.e., tunes of sixteen measures rather than the traditional eight measures. Instead of running the three parts together in a continuous score, he put the second eight measures of the *cantus* directly under the first eight, and dealt in like manner with the *medius* and *bassus*. The following diagram will clarify Walter's design:[11]

$$
\begin{array}{ll}
\text{Cantus} & \text{———————————} \\
\text{continued} & \text{———————————} \\
\text{Altus} & \text{———————————} \\
\text{continued} & \text{———————————} \\
\text{Bassus} & \text{———————————} \\
\text{continued} & \text{———————————}
\end{array}
$$

Even though Walter's intentions are quite clear, the resultant score has led at least one unwary observer to call it a six-part setting.[12]

In his lengthy sermon, entitled *The Sweet Psalmist of Israel*, Walter set about to prove the validity of singing from Old Testament practice. Among other points, he dealt with the matter of part-singing, claiming it had been established by David:

> The *Music* of the Temple, as it was under the Management and Direction of our *Sweet Psalmist* of Israel, was a *Chorus of Parts*. The Singers and the Players upon Instruments, were divided into *Three* Sets of Quires. One for the *Bass*, another for the *Medius* or inner parts; the third for the *Trebles* or *Altus's*.[13]

The sermon was sufficiently popular to pass through a number of editions in the following decades, suggesting that it was widely used by those who carried on the

---

[9] As quoted in Chase, *op. cit.*, 27.   [10] Lowens, *op. cit.*, 51, n. 18.   [11] *Ibid.*

[12] See Marvin Charles Genuchi, "The Life and Music of Jacob French (1754–1817), Colonial American Composer" (unpublished Ph.D. dissertation, University of Iowa, 1964), I, 3–5, where the writer mistakenly reads six-part settings in the tune collections of both Walter and Tufts.

[13] Thomas Walter, *The Sweet Psalmodist of Israel: A Sermon Preach'd at the Lecture held in Boston, by the Society for promoting Regular and Good Singing, and for reforming the Depravations and Debasements our Psalmody labours under, In Order to introduce the proper and true Old Way of Singing* (Boston: printed by J. Franklin for S. Gerrish, 1722), 8.

battle for regular singing. In the dedicatory material, Walter indicated that other singing lectures were being held in the surrounding territory, and he expressed the hope
that those opposed to regular singing would soon be won over:

> The *Society for promoting [Reg]ular Singing* are to be Applauded for their good and generous
> Design:. . .I am glad to hear of the Attempts made in another County in prosecution of the
> same noble Design, and that the Rever[e]nd Mr. *Brown* of *Reading* has justified and put
> Respect upon their Undertaking, by preaching a Sermon at a *Singing Lecture* there. I would
> feign hope it will not be long e'er the Ignorant will be convinced that they have mistaken
> *Novelty* for *Antiquity*, and will be brought to own, that the *present Depravations of our Tunes*,
> which they now so pertinaciously adhere to, and unreasonably insist upon, can lay no
> manner of Claim to their beloved Title and Denomination of, THE GOOD OLD WAY.[14]

While Walter labored under a misconception concerning ancient Hebrew psal-
modic practice, his eloquent argument no doubt influenced many of his contemporaries
to accept part-singing, and in turn paved the way for the introduction of anthems later
in the century.

Among the reactionaries of that time was one John Hammett (d. 1773), who, rather
than concern himself with the debate that was just then finally dying down, stood
against the generally accepted practice of using metrical psalms in any form. In defense
of his position, he wrote in his *Promiscuous Singing* ([Boston], 1739), "'Tis evident to
me, that David's Psalms were not in Poetical Rhyme, as our Singing Psalms are, but in
Prose, and were sung by some agreeable Tone."

Into this field of continual and often vituperative dissension about the singing of
congregational music came the anthem, an imported product from the country the
New Englanders and their ancestors had left. The collections that arrived in New
England containing such pieces were not used by choirs, for choirs as performing
groups in churches simply did not exist except in a few of the principal cities, and even
there they were probably simply the best singers who gathered together for organized
psalmody.[15] The presence of anthems in collections of psalm tunes and hymns may be
viewed as the carrot before the donkey, an inducement to master the rudiments and
exercises at the front of the book, to sing the psalm tunes well, and to move on to the
ultimate in group singing, choral hymns and anthems. The last were done more as a
recreational exercise than a religious one. Anthems at first were the end result of
singing schools; only later did they become regular ornaments to worship.

The use of the term *anthem* in New England is found as early as 1752 in a collection of tunes by James A. Turner in Boston. Daniel observes that the piece to which
the name is attached is no different from any other in the volume, it being worthy of
attention only because it is entitled "Anthem to 100."[16] The word apparently was
used in random fashion in other instances. Without the music at hand, one is intrigued
by the references, but titles and advertisements are small help in establishing musical

---

[14] *Ibid.*, [iv].   [15] See Daniel, *op. cit.*, 16–17, for quotations from pertinent documents.
[16] *Ibid.*, 39.

practice. In 1755, for example, there was advertised "The Anthem That is to be Sung at St. George's Chappel,"[17] but we lack the essential details about who was to sing, what kind of piece it was, and what the occasion may have been.

The year 1760 is important, for it marks the beginning of the first fruitful decade in American anthem publication, and it is in those years that the first two American-born composers of any music make their first appearance. Francis Hopkinson (1737–1791) and James Lyon (1735–1794) are the first to qualify for consideration as American composers. Their initial efforts in church music date from the beginning of the 1760s, and as has been known for some time, they were aware of each other's work. Hopkinson's compositions are found in a manuscript book in the Library of Congress,[18] in which is copied "An Anthem from the 114th Psalm," dated 1760. The piece is for two sopranos and bass, and carries evidence that keyboard accompaniment is intended, for the bass part is figured.[19] His setting of *The 23rd Psalm*, using the text from the Tate and Brady New Version, also appears in that manuscript. It is for two trebles and unfigured bass. Words appear below both the treble parts, their convenience to the bass part making it apparent that it is to be sung as well as played. Several features remove the piece from the category of psalm tune or unison hymn. The melody is in the top part, the second section has a florid passage leading to its cadence, and a wordless section apparently for keyboard instrument closes the piece (Example 61).

Hopkinson's setting of *The 23rd Psalm* was quite popular. James Lyon included it, as a four-part piece without instrument, in his *Urania*, which was published in 1761. Hopkinson used it again in *A Collection of Psalm Tunes with a few Anthems and Hymns*[,] *Some of Them Entirely New for the Use of the United Churches of Christ Church and St. Peter's Church in Philadelphia*, 1763, this time adding figures to the bass part because he foresaw the need of such music for the time when organs would be installed in both those churches. His prefatory remarks in the volume are in the form of a letter to the Reverend Mr. Richard Peters:

Reverend Sir,

Among your many Designs for the Promotion of Religion in general, and the Good of the Churches more immediately under your Care, permit me to hope this Attempt to the Improvement of our *Psalmody*, or *Church Music*, will meet with your favourable Acceptance and Encouragement. Something of this Kind was thought the more necessary, as it is highly probable there will be Organs erected in both our Churches, before it be long; which would be but a needless Expence, if the Congregations could not join their Voices with

[17] Charles Evans, *American Bibliography, 1639–1820 A.D.* (14 vols., New York: Peter Smith, 1941–1959), item 7350, attributes the anthem to William Tuckey (1708–1781), who emigrated from England in 1753. He is discussed in some detail by Daniel, *op. cit.*, 71–75, and mentioned by Ellinwood, *op. cit.*, 87–88, and Chase, *op. cit.*, 118–19.

[18] ML 96.H83.

[19] Robert Stevenson, *Protestant Church Music in America* (New York: W. W. Norton & Company, Inc., 1966), 47. It is printed in O. G. Sonneck, *Francis Hopkinson, the First American Poet-Composer (1737–1791), and James Lyon, Patriot, Preacher, Psalmodist (1735–1794): Two Studies in Early American Music* (Washington, D.C.: H. L. McQueen, 1905; reprint, New York: Da Capo Press, 1967), 200–201.

Example 61.   Opening and closing sections of Francis Hopkinson's *The 23rd Psalm.*

them in the singing of Psalms. For this Purpose I have made this Collection of Psalms, Hymns and Anthems, and prefixed a few Rules for Singing, in as clear and easy a Manner as possible; so that Children, with very little Attention, may understand them. . . .

Hopkinson's work appeared none too soon, for an organ was built at St. Peter's the same year his book was published.[20]

Hopkinson wrote about congregational psalm-singing in his preface, and he avoided entirely mentioning the several anthems in his collection. The term *psalmody* appeared there as a general equivalent for *church music*. We must assume that the anthems were printed for eventual use when the congregation would be able to join in their singing, or when a regular, trained choir should be available. In the same volume he was supplying the teaching materials to bring the singers to a level where anthems could be undertaken.

All but ten of the volume's thirty-six pieces are psalm settings. The remainder differ from them quite markedly. The texts for those ten are from Tate and Brady's New Version, from Isaac Watts, or from Joseph Addison. The musical settings are, at their simplest, single stanzas or strophic pieces, and one closes with an eight-measure Hallelujah chorus. Hopkinson's setting of *The 4th Psalm* is made up of seven musical phrases. The first two are *a 3* (two trebles and bass); the third is for two trebles; the fourth, for bass; and the last three are again *a 3*. Surely this, and *The 23rd Psalm*, which follows it in the volume, are not for congregational use, and it is doubtful that any of the last ten pieces in the book were intended for people who were accustomed to unison singing only. The pieces are similar to, if somewhat simpler than, the short ones found in English Nonconformist tune-books of about the same decade.

It was observed in Chapter 4 that the English anthem was becoming hymnlike and the hymn anthemlike. The state of affairs that made it increasingly difficult to distinguish between one type of piece and another requires that pieces be examined whether they bore the specific title *anthem* in earlier publications or not. We cannot permit ourselves the luxury of considering only pieces so named in the early American period, especially since the early books appear to be pointed at two levels of skill—that of the beginning singer and that of the experienced one, the latter probably the product of the singing-school or the itinerant private instructor. Hopkinson's title referred to anthems, but the word was not applied specifically to any single piece in the volume. All pieces that appear to call for skill in group singing will have to be considered, at least for the duration of this chapter.

In the case of *Urania*,[21] the distinction between anthems and non-anthems is fairly clear, although, as we shall see, there are included a few anthemlike pieces that are not designated as anthems. Identification of the *Urania* pieces has not been attempted recently, and most current opinion is based on work done early in this century by O. G. Sonneck, who approached the problem more from the bibliographical side than

---

[20] Stevenson, *op. cit.*, 47.

[21] James Lyon, *Urania or a choice Collection of Psalm-Tunes, Anthems and Hymns From the most approv'd Authors, with some Entirely New* . . . ([Philadelphia: 1761]).

the musical. As a result, most later discussions include one false attribution to Lyon, traceable to Sonneck, and, in addition, fail to pursue the contents farther than Sonneck did, a gross oversight, since some of the remaining pieces might possibly be identified if they were sufficiently publicized. Sonneck's study was printed in a limited edition of 200 copies. Its limited availability provides some excuse for the lacunae in studies involving *Urania*, but its issue in reprint and the availability of *Urania* on microforms opens the way for a revaluation of the entire problem of America's first printed collection of anthems. While the use of *Urania* as a tool for the identification of the first printed American anthem is important, the examination of its contents as a showcase of anthem repertory is even more so. Unaccountably, no such examination has been made. The table of titles and incipits given in Table 8 may serve to encourage further study. The listing and identification of psalms and hymns must be left to those whose interests lie specifically in that area; only mention of them will be made here.

Sonneck identified about forty pieces by tracing them to earlier sources or by recognizing them as Lyon's own compositions. Left unidentified are fourteen tunes that have names, twenty-four numbered psalm tunes, seven of the twelve anthems, and eleven hymns, these last being either *a 2* or *a 3*. The first two groups and the last one concern us little here, but since Hopkinson's *23rd Psalm* appears in the numbered set it must be mentioned again shortly. The anthems are of enough significance that they will be discussed individually, including those that have been identified earlier. They appear as a group, between pages 90 and 169, all of them specifically called anthems except a two-section setting of two verses by Sternhold and Hopkins. The latter piece is sufficiently different from the volume's hymn settings to be considered among the anthems, and its presence in the midst of them seems to indicate that Lyon recognized it in that light. Added to this dozen pieces must be Hopkinson's psalm setting. Let us examine each piece in the group, beginning with a few more words about *The 23rd Psalm*.[22]

Sonneck correctly identified Hopkinson's setting when it appeared in *A Collection of Psalm Tunes*, and he printed a facsimile of it to support his discussion.[23] In his essay on Lyon, however, Sonneck attributed the piece to that composer as an original one,[24] at the same time providing a fragment of it as an example. His failure to collate the examples and other information must be mentioned, especially since no writer since Sonneck's day has clarified the situation; most of them, in fact, help to perpetuate the misattribution through direct title reference, page-number reference, or blanket acceptance of Sonneck's material. The problem arose initially through Sonneck's interpretation of a marginal note in the *Urania* index, stating that "All Tunes marked with an Asterism are new." Unfortunately, some copies lack asterisks on certain pages, others lack the index, and other differences between examples may be found. Sonneck felt, concerning the absence of asterisks on two pages, that "after the book had been delivered to subscribers either Dawkins the engraver, or the author or others noticed the

---

[22] Printed in *Urania*, 50–51.
[23] Sonneck, *op. cit.*, 80, 91–92.   [24] *Ibid.*, 180, 185.

omissions and Dawkins corrected either one or both."[25] Assuming this to be the case, the presence or absence of asterisks does not influence any evidence pointing to Lyon as a composer. That the tunes were new is perfectly possible, but "new" does not mean "by Lyon." Sonneck was convinced in his early pages that Hopkinson had written *The 23rd Psalm*, and his conclusions were based on unshakable evidence. His attribution of the same piece to Lyon in an essay apparently written at another time, and without reference to his other evidence, has erected a bibliographical hurdle that has been unsuccessfully negotiated ever since. Let it now stand that Lyon wrote no setting of the Twenty-third Psalm, but printed Hopkinson's in expanded texture, as we saw earlier in this chapter. Lyon's original contributions must, then, number five at the most, and not six.

The other anthems in *Urania* are listed by Lyon without titles, but bear the heading, "An Anthem taken out of the . . . Psalm." Titles given in Table 8 are derived from text incipits, as is usually the case with material from this period and earlier.

It will be observed from Table 8 that the selection of clefs, the positioning of sharps and flats high or low on the staff in key signatures, and the octave in which the alto part was written vary from piece to piece. Since Lyon must have taken the convenient way of compilers in copying things as he saw them, rather than revising them all into a single system of his own, another road is open to the identification of anthems through these features. For example, the two pieces attributed to Lyon, the

TABLE 8

The Anthems in Lyon's *Urania*

Derived title	Source	Location in Urania
Preserve me, O God	16th Psalm	90–96

Unidentified

25 *Ibid.*, 144.

I will bless the Lord   34th Psalm   97–102

Unidentified

O be joyful   100th Psalm   103–110

Unidentified

O sing unto'the Lord   96th Psalm   111–117

The bass imitates the tenor in the second phrase; soprano has a nonimitative melisma on "sing"; then three parts (B, T, A) make fuging entries on the following pattern, after which the piece proceeds *a 4.*

Unidentified

O clap your hands together   47th Psalm   118–124

O   clap_____ your   hands_____   to-

geth - - - - - - - - - er,   all   ye   peo - - ple

The piece continues *a 4.*

Unidentified

Two Celebrated Verses by   125–132
Sternhold & Hopkins set to music

The   Lord _____ de - - scend - ed   from a - bove

After 12 measures this is followed by an SATB setting of the same material; then, on p. 127 follows the second verse of material to new music. SATB sections are notated in three treble clefs and a bass clef. The alto is notated an octave higher than it sounds.

The complete text reads:

> *The Lord descended and*
> *bow'd the heavens most high*
> *and underneath his feet*
> *he cast the darkness of the sky.*
>
> *On cherubs and on cherubim*
> *full royally he rode*
> *and on the wings of mighty winds*
> *came flying all abroad.*

Sternhold and Hopkins Psalter (1588), 8. Psalm XVIII, verses 9–10

Generally accepted as a Lyon original; Sonneck, *op. cit.*, 207–8, prints it complete.

Jehovah reigns   97th Psalm   133–141

Composed by William Tuckey (1708–1781). The anthem is identified as his by Sonneck, *op. cit.*, 174, and Stevenson, *op. cit.*, 49–50. Daniel, *op. cit.*, 72, devotes a full page to Tuckey and this anthem, but does not know of its existence in *Urania*, attributing its first appearance to Stickney's *Gentleman and Lady's Musical Companion* of 1774, from which he takes the example he prints.

I will magnify thee, O God   145th Psalm   142–150

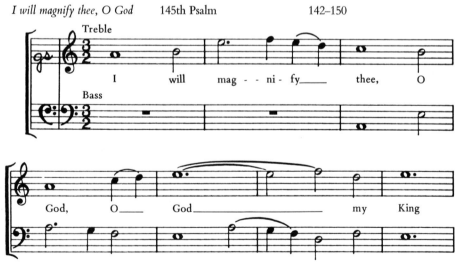

Sonneck identifies this as a slightly altered version of Anthem XIII in Arnold's *Compleat Psalmodist*. Sonneck, *op. cit.*, 175.

O give thanks unto ye Lord   105th Psalm   151–153

The first two pages are for soprano and bass; page 153 is SATB, with "Hallelujah" as the only text. "Ye" is used consistently for "the."

Unidentified

O praise ye Lord of heaven   148th Psalm   154–155

The piece is for soprano and bass throughout. The use of "ye" for "the" is consistently found, possibly pointing to an English source.

Unidentified

Is there not an appointed time   Job 7:[1–?]   156–164

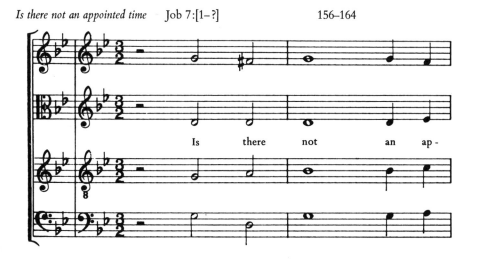

point - ed   time   to   man   up - on   earth

Sonneck, *op. cit.*, 174, traces this to Knapp's *New Set of Psalms*.

Let the shrill trumpets warlike   150th Psalm   165–169
voice

Let   the   shrill   trum - - - - -

Let ___   the   shrill   trum - - pets

Let ___   the   shrill   trum - - pets

Generally accepted as Lyon's own work.

FIGURE 3. *A page showing James Lyon's anthem,* Let the shrill trumpets warlike voice, *from* Urania, 1761. (*Photo courtesy of Baylor University Library.*)

Two Celebrated Verses and *Let the shrill trumpets,* share common clef arrangements and positioning of the sharps in their signatures; moreover, no other pieces in the set have those characteristics. They are thereby removed from such relationship with any of the other identified or unidentified pieces in the volume. A number of other anthems in the table share common features in clef arrangement and sharp placement. What can this mean to the student? Near the middle of the eighteenth century, English psalm books that contained anthems were fairly consistent in the use of certain patterns in regard to these features. A careful study of such books, their printers, and their compilers may bring to light further evidence of possible composers for the unidentified *Urania* tunes. A representative set is provided in Table 9.

TABLE 9

Clef and Signature Patterns in Pre-*Urania* Volumes

By itself, Table 9 proves nothing. As an example of how a complete tabulation of clef and signature patterns for English publications of the period before 1760 could be compiled, it illustrates how a picture of volumes that could have provided Lyon with his anthems might emerge.

After the appearance of *Urania* and Hopkinson's published collection, a rapid increase in publication of hymns and anthems is evident. The anthem material is derived to a large extent from imported volumes, and some American anthems take on English characteristics so far as their composers can imitate them successfully. The name of William Tans'ur is prominent among contributors to the early volumes; his pieces make up in quantity what they lack in quality, and for a time they serve to fill both his own volumes and those of native compilers. His most popular book, *The Royal Melody Complete*, was known to be in this country before Hopkinson's collection came into print. Evans[26] lists an advertisement for that volume under the 1761 imprint of McAlpine and Bayley of Boston. However, the *Boston News-Letter* of June 11, 1761, referred to the work as "lately imported." Whatever the facts of publication or shipment, it is certain that Tans'ur's music was in this country, and possibly widely distributed, since it proved so popular with compilers who were too wise to overlook a successful item.

In 1764 Josiah Flagg (1737–1794) published his first volume.[27] It contained two pieces specifically called anthems, and several others that are anthemlike. One of the former is an anonymous *O praise the Lord*; the other is a setting of *O give ye thanks unto the Lord* by Tans'ur.[28] The latter is printed here in part (Example 62). The piece is significant for two reasons: it is one of the first three imported anthems to be published in New England, and it is not a typical Tans'ur product in its structure. Psalm 136 is excellently suited to responsorial litany treatment, such as Tans'ur undertakes in this setting which was taken by Flagg from *The Royal Melody Complete*. Employing eight of the first nine verses of the psalm, Tans'ur assigned the first hemistich of each verse to solo or solo ensemble; the second, with its constant text, to the chorus. Flagg made an excellent choice of pieces for singing-schools, for the chorus part is easy to learn, appears frequently, and can be sung with completely untrained voices while the varied melodies may be assigned to singers only slightly more skilled. Flagg included the work in his second collection (to be discussed), and it appeared in all later editions of Tans'ur's *Royal Melody Complete* as well as in Stickney's *Gentleman and Lady's Musical Companion*.[29] To return to Flagg's 1764 volume, it contained also hymn tunes by Battishill and Blow, some fuging tunes, and Tans'ur's "St. Luke's" tune, an anthemlike piece with the text, "O come, loud anthems let us sing." Another extended piece

[26] Evans, *op. cit.*, item 9021.

[27] Josiah Flagg, *A Collection of the best Psalm Tunes, in two, three, and four Parts. . .to which are added some Hymns and Anthems the Greater part of them never before Printed in America* (Boston: Paul Revere and Josiah Flagg, 1764).

[28] Daniel, *op. cit.*, 40, indicates that the Tans'ur piece was unidentified. However, in Flagg's volume, above the first line of music on p. 46, there is printed "An Anthem Ps. 136 Set by W. Tans'ur."

[29] Published by Daniel Bayley, Newburyport, 1774.

Example 62. Two verses of Tans'ur's litany-anthem, *O give ye thanks unto the Lord* (Flagg, *The Royal Melody Complete*, 46).

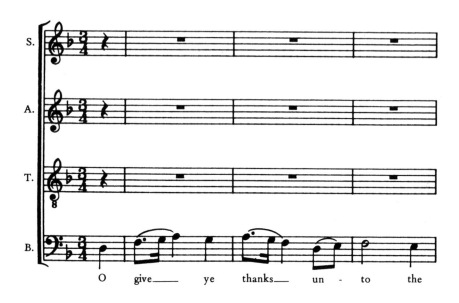

with a closing Hallelujah sets the text, "Hail, hail, all glorious Lamb of God" (Example 63).

Flagg's idea of borrowing liberally from all available sources was the pattern that was to be followed by compilers for the rest of the century. He wrote, in his Preface,

Example 63.   Opening measures of *Hail, hail, all glorious Lamb of God* (Flagg, *A Collection . . . ,* 50).

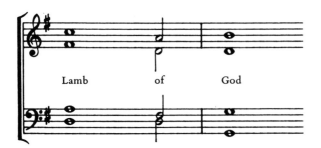

"The Editor. . .has taken from every Author he has seen, a few Tunes, which he judges to be the best." From this, and from the often-quoted apology "for offering to the Publick, a *new* Collection of Psalm Tunes," printed in the same Preface, we may safely theorize that many imported volumes were in the hands of American singing-school teachers and their pupils by this time. What was needed was a home-grown product, and this the compilers could not produce until composers appeared who would be regularly published.

Flagg's other collection dug even more deeply into imported materials. Its title clearly shows it to be an eclectic volume,[30] and its contents prove it to be taken

[30] Josiah Flagg, *A Collection of All Tans'ur's and a Number of Other Anthems from Williams, Knapp, Ashworth, and Stephenson* (Boston: J. Flagg, [1766]).

entirely from English sources. Predominating over all others are the anthems of Tans'ur, numbering ten. There are also four by Knapp, two by Stephenson, and one each by Ashworth, Williams, and Handel.[31] That the compositions of Hopkinson and Lyon did not find a welcome here may be because Flagg hesitated to print what was obviously another person's unique contribution. American compilers showed no such reserve in appropriating the works of English composers.

Other than our previous references to Tans'ur publications that were imported some years earlier, and speculation about what other books may have been imported, little can be said as to the sources of the American repertory. Irving Lowens gives titles of several volumes by Aaron Williams, John Arnold, Abraham Adams, and William Knapp that were in circulation here before the date of Flagg's second book.[32] His views can be supported by an advertisement that lists the following imported titles for sale as early as July, 1766, at the bookstore of John Mein in Boston:[33]

> Williams's Universal Psalmodist
> Knapp's new Set of Psalms and Anthems
> Arnold's Complete Psalmodist
> ————Church Music reformed
> ————Leicestershire Harmony
> Green's Body of Psalmody
>
> [Spelling and capitalization as in the advertisement]

The following year (1767) saw the first American edition of Tans'ur's *Royal Melody Complete*. The immense popularity of this work must date from earlier, for we have seen the notices of publication or importation of his book as early as 1761, and this may not have been the first time it circulated here. Until he was superseded by composers of greater skill and sophistication, his anthems, clumsy at times, forced at others, served the appetites of American singers just as they had those of the English singers in country churches and chapels. Daniel Bayley (ca. 1725–1799), one of the enterprising publishers who moved into this new field of opportunity, combined Tans'ur's volume with Williams' *Universal Psalmodist*, the two appearing under the new title, *The American Harmony*. Thus a basic repertory of English material was placed upon the American market, to serve singing-schools and, later, their products in moments of religious musical utterance, and possibly still more often in the home than the church.

At this point it is well to pause for a comparison of the situation in England and New England, for there is, as we have already seen, more than a simple transfer of a full-grown art of composition and performance involved. The functions, distribution, performance practice, and sophistication of the anthems differ greatly between the two places in which they were to continue as flourishing expressions of religious song.

---

[31] Daniel, *op. cit.*, 163–64.   [32] Lowens, *op. cit.*, 246–47.

[33] William Arms Fisher, *One Hundred and Fifty Years of Music Publishing in the United States* (Boston: Oliver Ditson Company, Inc., 1933), 33.

English anthems were tied firmly to religious observances; their types became simpler as the eighteenth century passed, but their functions were not removed from church and chapel. They had, at most, sifted down to a lower, less musically trained, stratum of society. In New England, the practice of singing anthems as part of regular church services was not firmly established. So far as can be determined now, anthems represented the achievement of the singing-school group, a kind of music that continued in the community after the teacher had moved to another place. The movement toward organized church choirs—or even of separating the skilled singers from the unskilled—took place in the last four decades of the century. Daniel prints three parish actions that set the trained singers above the congregation,[34] and a few other references help to show that the interest in regular singing was high, even in small towns. In a sermon delivered at a singing-lecture, March 18, 1773, the Reverend Joseph Strong sharply criticized the nonsingers in the church. The title page of the sermon[35] states that it was delivered in Simsbury "On Occasion of introducing regular Singing into public Use in the Worship of God there."

A few years later we find printed criticism of mannerisms among singers, a sure indication that the practice of singing is in such common use that it will not be driven out by comparative judgments. Chauncey Langdon, after speaking of the need for proper accent in the music, goes on to say:

> It ought likewise to be the Care of every Performer to behave with Decency and Solemnity, especially when singing sacred Words, and to avoid as much as possible all aukward [sic] Gestures, such as looking about, whispering, standing or sitting not erect, having their Faces distorted with Wrinkles, their Eyes strained, and their Mouths open too wide: all which frequently disgust Spectators. The best Rule that can be given is to aim entirely at Ease; to let the Voice flow freely, but not harshly. In singing a Solo the Voice ought to be a little more soft and shrill, but with a little more Spirit than when the Parts move together.[36]

Such instructions and complaints are markedly different from any that might have been given in England, for the training of cathedral and parish church singers usually prevented the need for such advice. What we know of the West Gallery tradition there indicates that such problems were common, but apparently not of great concern to those taking part.

The American anthem singer was likely to be an entirely different type of person from his English counterpart. Self-taught or the product of a singing-school, he sang where no tradition of choral music had been developed. The best pieces he sang were rarely above the lowest level of English parish anthems, and when American composers appeared on the scene, their anthems were generally unskilled imitations of the

---

[34] Daniel, op. cit., 16–17.

[35] Joseph Strong, The Duty of Singing (New Haven: Thomas and Samuel Green, 1773).

[36] Chauncey Langdon, Beauties of Psalmody (New Haven: D. Bowen, 1786), [2].

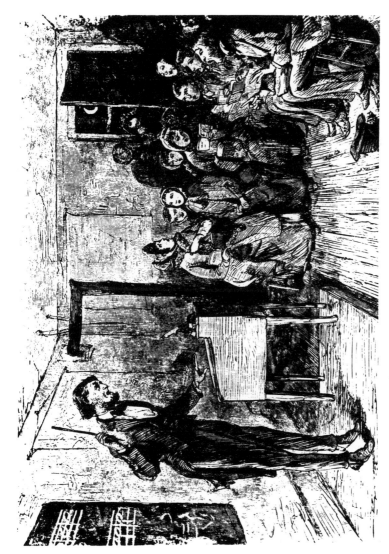

FIGURE 4. *Old time singing school.* (*Photo courtesy of the Bettmann Archive.*)

English model, despite the composer's disclaimer of European influence. Emerging nationalism is evident in the title of the early books, but the music breaks away more slowly from the English prototype unless some of its features are wrenched free by an individualist like Billings. As was the case in rural England, women sang in the choirs, having been trained in the singing-schools along with the men and older boys. There is no evidence of the unchanged boy's voice having any significant part of the American musical interest. No tradition of choral Services existed here until a later time.

We have one excellent document that describes the final concert given by members of several neighboring singing-schools who gathered at the Presbyterian Church at Neshaminy to demonstrate their newly acquired prowess. The discourse on that occasion—a sermon or lecture was customary at all such events—was delivered by Samuel Blair (1741–1818), who had his remarks printed the same year. The singing-school had been conducted by a Mr. Spicer, described as a Master in Sacred Music. His success may be judged from a letter printed in the Preface to Mr. Blair's sermon, written by a "lady of judgment and taste in music":

> I find by your last, that you have not seen the account, which I have given our friend, of the concert in Neshaminy. Had you been of our party, as proposed, I am persuaded, that, independently of the facility you would have enjoyed on the road, and in "the feast of reason, and the flow of soul" at ——— the evening before, you would have been highly gratified, both with the Discourse, and the musical entertainment, which followed. For the latter, we had about two hundred and fifty singers; who were arranged in the order of the art, on the front floor of the gallery. They were all, I may say, well dressed; that is, in rurul [*sic*] simplicity and elegance. Many of the girls were, really, very handsome. This circumstance, added to the sweetness and harmony of their voices, and the sweeter harmony and innocence of, what may be called, the *toute ensemble* of their appearance, must have inspired you with a very charming sentiment. They all, indeed, seemed to be well taught and practiced in the tunes, and different forms of music, which they sang; and many of their voices were remarkably fine. The several parts of counter, treble, tenor, and bass were so judiciously adjusted and proportioned, and the time was so accurately observed, that not a jar, or any kind of insipidity, or dissonance, offended the ear. A very pleasing order, decency, and, indeed, solemnity, was maintained throughout the performance. One blunder, however, I know not from what cause, was committed. But they recovered it, at the instance of their monitor, with so much address, that, in the event, it did them not a little honour. I was not sensible of its having produced the least confusion. The auditors, as I was informed, consisted of between eleven and twelve hundred persons. They were apparently attentive to the preacher, and delighted with the music.[37]

This condescending account appears to come from an urban female who received better entertainment than she anticipated. The speaker that evening remarked that "public worship hath assumed, comparatively, a celestial grace; and the temples of religion, instead of drolling out tones of ill-measured dullness, or jarring with harsh

---

[37] Samuel Blair, *A Discourse on Psalmody* (Philadelphia: John M'Culloch, 1789), 4–5.

discord, as before, now resound with vibrations of well-ordered, and commanding melody."[38] In a lengthy, but illuminating, footnote, he continues:

> I cannot omit mentioning, in this place, the obligations of society to Mr. *Adgate*, for his assiduity and amiable conduct in promoting these improvements, particularly in the city of Philadelphia. The man, who has signalized himself by such successful exertions; and who, from the benevolence of his heart, hath made so many sacrifices, in a design of so much utility to the morals of the people, ought, doubtless, to be held in great estimation, both as a citizen and as a Christian. It is much to be desired, that his important services may continue to be encouraged by the wise and the good of all denominations.
>
> I will only add what has been suggested by others, that it would contribute not a little to the benefit of religion, as well as to the satisfaction of many Christian worshippers, if proper choruses were instituted in the several churches; consisting of a competent number of the best performers in each; and stationed, either, in the front of the galleries, or in pews, appropriated to that use. In this case, the whole congregation, may unite, and follow with ease, in the best execution. At the same time, the predominant melody and address of the chorus will cover, or rectify, any mistakes, or other defects, which may occur in the general performance.[39]

The movement toward grouping of the best voices, formation of actual choirs, and preparation of music other than the regular psalm-tunes and hymns for performance during church services were part of the American scene when American composers first began working. We shall see that, whether the men who tried to supply this market deliberately imitated English models, or claimed to provide a uniquely American product, they were strongly influenced by the works that had appeared in the first American collections, works that had probably had a wide circulation in imported copies as well.

It is William Billings (1746–1800) who is the first native-born composer of anthems after Hopkinson and Lyon. He dominated the scene for the first decade after 1770, giving way gradually to men who provided a more varied, but not necessarily more interesting, diet of anthems.

Between 1770 and 1794, Billings published six books containing anthems, the total number of anthems reaching forty-seven. While this is merely a part of his total compositions, it is only this class of pieces that concerns us here. An analytical study of his church music generally discusses the anthems;[40] other volumes to which reference has been made in this chapter isolate such details as fuging tunes, anthems, psalm tunes, and the like for special consideration. Examination of a few anthems here will serve to place him in relation to other composers of his time.

Most readily accessible of his volumes is *The Continental Harmony*, which appears

---

[38] *Ibid.*, 25.
[39] *Ibid.*
[40] J. Murray Barbour, *The Church Music of William Billings* (East Lansing: Michigan State University Press, 1960).

Example 64. *The dying Christian's last farewell,* William Billings (*The Continental Harmony,* 164, 168).

(a)

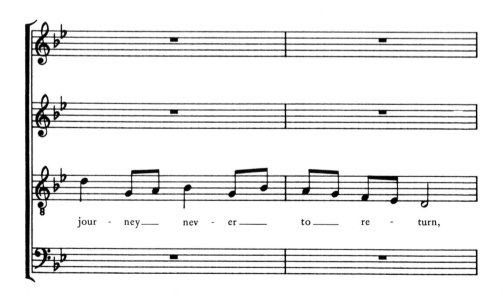

(b)

in a facsimile reprint with a critical introduction by Hans Nathan.[41] All the anthems in the volume are Billings' own, as is the case in all his books, and a good assortment of pieces can be examined conveniently. The texts come mainly from the psalms, but the Old and New Testaments furnish most of the remaining words. Tate and Brady provide part of the text for a single anthem, *O thou to whom all creatures bow*,[42] but even there the major part of the text is scriptural. One other anthem, *The dying Christian's last farewell*,[43] a lugubrious piece that has the principal character's part "spoken in the tenor," has an unidentifiable text, though the idea underlying it may be derived from Pope's "Vital spark." The opening dialogue is repeated (Example 64 *a*), then followed by a long section *a 4* extolling the joys of the hereafter, and the piece closes with a modified version of the opening section, the closing measures symbolically omitting the tenor (Example 64 *b*). This piece, as also a number of others by Billings, has certain crudities, apparently resulting from Billings' inability to notate exactly what he had in mind. The modern user of Billings' music is faced with a decision whether to retain these flavorful passages, or to correct or even recast entire sections in other metrical arrangements.[44] The former renders some few passages unpalatable; the latter places upon the music a veneer of sophistication that Billings obviously lacked.

Two pieces in *The Continental Harmony* take their text from The Song of Solomon. They and their companion from the same biblical source, *I am the Rose of Sharon*,[45] are odd companions for the other anthems. Unabashed love songs, the anthems cannot be assigned to any religious occasion as most others of his can. The solo melodies of *I am come into my garden*[46] are lyrical, among the most subtle that are found in this ordinarily straightforward composer's work. The opening phrase (Example 65 *a*) contains the seed of the first two basic motives in the anthem, the rising fifth. It is seen again in the first phrase *a 4*, soprano; it is the interval most frequently outlined or emphasized by leap; and the melody is strongly recalled in the last solo entry (Example 65 *b*). The other part of the anthem emphasizes the upward leap of a fourth, to a lesser degree, and as the basis of a shorter section. The other anthem with text from the same source is *I charge you, O ye daughters of Jerusalem*.[47]

It should no longer surprise anyone that Billings displayed a variety of musical ideas. Two decades ago it was customary to cast Billings as a rough, uncouth buffoon, making music vigorously but clumsily. Barbour rose sharply to his defense,[48] and both Daniel and Chase had earlier dealt more fairly with the composer than any

---

[41] William Billings, *The Continental Harmony, containing, A Number of Anthems, Fuges, and Chorusses, in several Parts* (Boston: Isaiah Thomas and Ebenezer T. Andrews, 1794), reprint, ed. by Hans Nathan (Cambridge: The Belknap Press of Harvard University Press, 1961).

[42] *Ibid.*, 105–16.   [43] *Ibid.*, 164–68.

[44] Barbour, *op. cit.*, 14–42, discusses the problem of meter in Billings' music. A number of rebarred samples may be examined there.

[45] Published in a number of Billings' books, but first in *The Singing-Master's Assistant* (Boston: Draper & Folsom, 1778).

[46] Billings, *The Continental Harmony*, 76–81.

[47] *Ibid.*, 155–59.   [48] Barbour, *op. cit.*, xi–xii.

writers who preceded them.[49] Billings was capable of the tender sentiment, and crudity was not his constant product. He apparently read widely about music and examined much that had been written; he was aware of what went on outside his own country, and he accepted what he pleased, perhaps being influenced by more than he recognized.

Example 65a.   First phrase of *I am come into my garden*, William Billings (*The Continental Harmony*, 76).

Example 65b.   Final solo entry, *ibid.*, Billings (*ibid.*, 80).

The Continental Harmony contains the usual tutor of music, explaining the notes, clefs, tempo, and so on. It is followed by a Master-Scholar dialogue which reveals Billings as more knowledgeable than some of his contemporaries. When the Scholar asks who invented the gamut, the Master replies:

> The first invention is attributed to several Grecians; but the form in which the scale now stands, is said to have been projected between 7 and 800 years ago, by *Guido Aretinus*, a Monk; whose name deserves to be recorded in the annals of fame, in capitals of gold.[50]

[49] Chase, *op. cit.*, 128–33, and Daniel, *op. cit.*, 102–3. It must be remembered that Daniel's dissertation, though unpublished, was available in 1955. It was quite widely read, and probably deserves credit for a large amount of the enlightened evaluation of Billings.

[50] Billings, *The Continental Harmony*, xii.

Example 66. *Universal Praise*, William Billings (*The Continental Harmony*, 97).

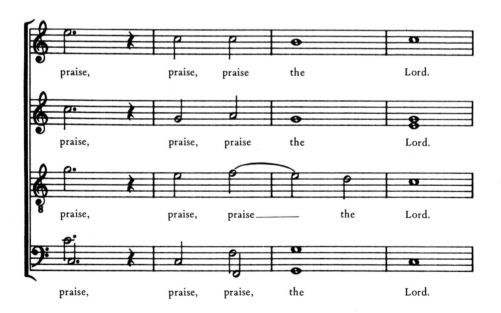

Billings makes known his acquaintance with such later important figures, important to the American scene, as Williams, Stephenson, Arnold, and Tans'ur. His avoidance of certain features in English and European common practice was probably deliberate and rational rather than resulting from his isolation and unfamiliarity with established procedures. He knew the music that had come from the country-church composers. Too often those who have criticized his nonconformity have expected him to emulate the composers of the cathedral tradition. Similarities need not be sought here, but they can be found in the works of those men who were known in New England during Billings' lifetime.

Three Billings anthems are printed complete by Daniel,[51] and other publications make possible the study of his style through still other pieces.[52] It will suffice, then, to point out that Billings succeeded in forging a uniquely American group of pieces at a time when the American taste and repertory were largely dependent upon English importations. His knowledge of those pieces did not hinder his own mode of expression, but he drew on such features as he cared to use, even to borrowing the already popular fuging tune as the basis for single compositions and as a stylistic feature for parts of his longer anthems. He sought variety through normal means, changing textures in his always unaccompanied pieces by adding or dropping voices within the SATB framework, changing meter to achieve variety and to emphasize certain passages, and retaining those features of his English printed teachers that he chose to use, the success depending upon his mastery of them. Generally he clung to the tenor as the conveyor of his principal melodic material, but broke free from that restriction in passages of imitative entry, where the voices took on fleeting equality. Not all his imitative sections are plagued with the simplicity of fuging entries; some of them approach the dignity of true points of imitation, a European term Billings probably would have scorned.

There remains the matter of form. Billings exhibited considerable variety in this feature, using everything from simple repetitions to closed forms and rondolike arrangements. The variety of these forms may be examined easily in *The Continental Harmony*, where Billings appears as a man of imagination and variety, but not without discipline. Whether close examination of all Billings anthems would show a preference for the simpler forms or the complex is beyond our study, but it may be noted that generally the Billings anthems are no shorter than English pieces that appeared here, and they fall into as many sections as do the imported pieces, at times exceeding them in both features. One direct parallel may be cited—whether it was an imitation of the English model cannot be determined—in the litanylike anthem, *Universal Praise*,[53] on

[51] Daniel, *op. cit.*, contains a setting of *As the hart panteth after the water brooks*, 229–38; *I love the Lord because He hath heard the voice of my pray'r*, 239–43; and *I will love Thee, O Lord*, 244–51.

[52] W. Thomas Marrocco and Harold Gleason, *Music in America: An Anthology from the Landing of the Pilgrims to the Close of the Civil War, 1620–1865* (New York: W. W. Norton & Company, Inc., 1964), 111–19. Barbour, *op. cit.*, gives many examples of style features.

[53] Billings, *The Continental Harmony*, 97–104.

Example 67. *Lift up your eyes,* William Billings (*The Suffolk Harmony,* 30).

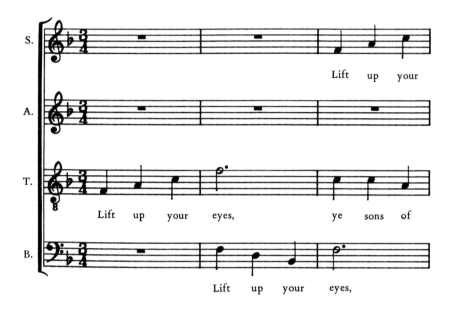

the text "O praise God," from Psalm 149 and others. The piece employs a short choral refrain in *falsobordone* style (Example 66). The similarity of treatment to that of Tans'ur's *O give ye thanks unto the Lord*, the fact that Billings had every opportunity to know the Tans'ur model, and the rarity of pieces with litany characteristics would seem to indicate a direct imitation of Tans'ur by Billings.

The future of the American anthem lay beyond Billings' generation, full of promise and hope. He was perhaps prophetic when, in his vigorous setting of *Lift up your eyes*[54] (Example 67), he displayed a fine grasp of choral style in an anthem featuring changing meters and textures. His instructions for the closing six measures are "shout and swell," which the composers and singers of American anthems have done ever since, through trash and treasure, producing a deluge of anthems that has no seeming end.

[54] William Billings, *The Suffolk Harmony* (Boston: The Author, 1786), 30–33.

CHAPTER SIX

American Compilers and Borrowers

We have seen how the pioneering efforts of James Lyon and Josiah Flagg established the anthem firmly on the American scene, where it was vigorously cultivated by William Billings. In the wake of their efforts followed numerous collections of psalms, hymns, and anthems compiled by men active in the singing-school movement, men who were anxious to supply the growing demand for such publications. Most prominent among the compilers were Daniel Bayley and Andrew Law (1748–1821).

Bayley has been mentioned before as one who helped disseminate English anthems as early as 1769. Of his several publications, *The New Universal Harmony* was the most important as far as anthems are concerned.[1] It contained twenty anthems and six hymns, all by English composers, save one piece by Lyon, entitled *A Marriage Hymn*.[2] This piece does not appear in *Urania*, and Sonneck speculated that it may have been part of another collection of Lyon's compositions which was not published.[3]

Of equal importance as a compiler was Andrew Law. Born in Connecticut, he graduated from Rhode Island College in 1775, and was later ordained to the ministry. Much of the time he seems to have been engaged in disputes over what he claimed was

---

[1] Daniel Bayley, *The New Universal Harmony or, A compendium of Church-Music containing, A Variety of Favorite Anthems, Hymn-Tunes, and Carols, Composed by the greatest Masters* (Newbury-Port: Printed and Sold by the Author, 1773).

[2] *Ibid.*, 24.   [3] Sonneck, *op. cit.*, 187.

piracy of his works, and went so far as to petition the Connecticut Legislature, and later the United States Congress, for copyright protection. Whether he was pirate or pirated makes an interesting study.[4] Law's *Select Harmony* was his most important anthem collection. In the preface, he indicated that "it was the Design of the Editor in this Publication, to furnish Schools with a Set of Psalm-Tunes, Hymns and Anthems, most approved, and best adapted to the Worship of God; that thereby his Glory might

TABLE 10

Anthems by English Composers in Several Important American Collections Before and After the Revolution*

	(1766) Flagg	(1773) Bayley	(1774) Stickney	(1778) Law	(1786) Anon.
	A Collection	*New Univ. Harmony*	*Gentleman and Lady's*	*Select Harmony*	*Worcester Collection*
Adams	0	0	1	0	0
Arnold	0	2	0	2	1
Ashworth	1	1	1	1	0
Brown	0	1	0	0	0
Clark and Green	0	0	1	0	1
Handel	1	0	0	0	2
Knapp	4	10	3	2	0
Selby	0	0	0	0	1
Stephenson	2	1	4	3	2
Tans'ur	10	0	11	0	0
Wanless	0	1	0	0	0
West	0	0	0	3	2
Williams	1	4	5	2	3

* Titles of the anthems may be found in Daniel, *op. cit.*, 158–71, where the contents of each volume are listed in his Bibliography.

be promoted, and his Name exalted."[5] The fact that the volume passed through several editions indicates that it was well accepted. Like the earlier collection of Josiah Flagg, those of Bayley and Law drew exclusively from English composers for their anthems. The comparison in Table 10, which includes the anonymous but popular *Worcester Collection*,[6] will identify, to some extent, those English anthem composers most highly regarded in America both before and after the Revolution.

[4] For a full discussion of this development, see Lowens, *op. cit.*, Chapter IV, "Andrew Law and the Pirates," 58–88.

[5] Andrew Law, *Select Harmony, Containing in a plain and concise manner, the Rules of Singing: Together with a Collection of Psalm-Tunes, Hymns and Anth[ems]* (New Haven: T. and S. Green, 1778), 1.

[6] *The Worcester Collection of Sacred Harmony* (Worcester: I. Thomas, 1786).

While a survey of only five compilations cannot provide conclusive evidence about the whole period, it appears that the anthems of Arnold, Ashworth, Knapp, Stephenson, and Williams were widely accepted. Tans'ur's rather crude and eccentric writing had an early vogue, only to fall by the way after the Revolution. From the evidence at hand, it is apparent that the prototype for the anthem in America was provided by English composers closely associated with the parish church and the Nonconformist chapel.

The accomplishments of most other American anthem composers in the late decades of the eighteenth century appear dwarfed when compared with the sizeable output of William Billings. Some of the lesser figures, however, contributed significantly to the growing repertory. One such person was Jacob French (1754–1817), born at Stoughton, Massachusetts. Although little is known of his life and activities, he is remembered as the compiler of three collections: *The Psalmodist's Companion* (Worcester, 1793), *The New American Melody* (Boston, 1789), and *The Harmony of Harmony* (Northampton, 1802), each of which contained some of his own anthems. Daniel lists ten anthems by French,[7] while Genuchi attributes twelve to him.[8] His *O sing unto the Lord*, printed in its entirety by Daniel,[9] goes through several keys in search of variety, but its constant dependence on block chords robs it of rhythmic vitality. His "Harmony,"[10] an anthemlike setting of Watts's versified text to Psalm 148, has a fuging entry that shows some variety from the common type in its melodically modified entries.

Although less productive as a composer, with only six anthems to his credit, Daniel Read (1757–1836) was, nevertheless, very active in the cause of religious music during his life. Also a native of Massachusetts, he served in the Revolutionary War, and spent the balance of his life as a merchant, composer, compiler, and publisher. His first volume, *The American Singing Book* (New Haven, 1785), passed through several editions. One of its two anthems was *Down steers the bass*,[11] a piece whose text has no religious significance whatever, and whose interest lies largely in its attempts at text-painting. Read may have been influenced by the earlier setting of Billings,[12] which also followed closely the descriptive possibilities of the text. Three issues of *The Columbian Harmonist* were published in New Haven. The third (1795) contained two Billings anthems, two *Messiah* fragments—Read was a great admirer of Handel—and four anthems of his own composition. One of these may be conveniently examined. *O be joyful in the Lord*[13] follows the form of a full anthem with verses. There are indications that instruments were intended to be used in its performance, both in an interlude and as accompaniment to a bass solo. If the term *full anthem with verses* falls strangely on our ears at this point, it is because composers had been tied so firmly to the chapel and

[7] Daniel, *op. cit.*, 122.   [8] Genuchi, *op. cit.*, 51.

[9] Daniel, *op. cit.*, 252–56.   [10] Marrocco and Gleason, *op. cit.*, 148–50.

[11] *Ibid.*, 127–37.

[12] First printed in *The Psalm-Singer's Amusement* (Boston: Billings, 1781).

[13] Daniel, *op. cit.*, 257–62.

parish church prototypes that they had not encountered it. Read's appreciation of the more formal tradition from England is apparent in the instrumentally supported solo section, greater skill in contrapuntal writing than shown by his fellows, and the approximation of a formal scheme that is traceable to the cathedral tradition. By the beginning of the nineteenth century, composers were ready to look with interest at fresh European models, finding need for improvement in their homespun works.

A word must be inserted here about the attention given to performance of pieces in the proper tempo. Tans'ur's instructions were widely known, and they probably had a great influence on early composers and performers in New England. Instructions were given for common time, triple time, and compound time, all of which are easily translated into metronome equivalents for our use.[14] The resulting metronomic instructions would call for one, one-and-one-half, two, or two-and-one-half beats per second. Billings attempted to improve on this system, translating his method into elapsed time for the measure, and giving specifications for a pendulum that would provide the exact duration of a beat.

> The first, or slowest mood of time, is called Adagio, each bar containing to the amount of one semibreve: four seconds of time are required to perform each bar; I recommend crotchet beating in this mood, performed in the following manner, viz. first strike the ends of the fingers, secondly, the heel of the hand, then thirdly, raise your hand a little and shut it up, and fourthly, raise your hand still higher and throw it open at the same time. These motions are called two down and two up, or crotchet beating. A pendulum to beat crotchets in this mood should be thirty-nine inches and two tenths.[15]

He takes his reader through duple, triple, and compound meters, and the results have been tabulated into modern equivalents for convenience of comparison and performance.[16] The instructions of both Tans'ur and Billings cover details of tempo and meter.

Another approach to the problem was made by Andrew Law.[17] His tempo instructions are explicit as to the frequency of beats, but make no reference to meter. The method for determining how to differentiate between the various fractions of seconds in elapsed time is left entirely to the performer, as well, resulting in a number of differences when the system was put into practice, we may be sure.

The need for such more or less elaborate systems finds its explanation in the general lack of understanding or common use of the standard tempo and mood terms that were current in European art music. Rather than adopt the rather forbidding

---

[14] Daniel, *op. cit.*, 48–49, prints Tans'ur's explanation from *The American Harmony*, and gives a table with modern metronomic equivalents.

[15] Billings, *The Continental Harmony*, vii. Billings' instructions for constructing pendulums provide an interesting insight into his concern for proper performance.

[16] Nathan provides such a table in the Introduction to the reprint of *The Continental Harmony*; Marrocco and Gleason, *op. cit.*, 99, provide a similar table.

[17] Andrew Law, *The Musical Magazine Containing a Variety of Favorite Pieces, Number Second* (Cheshire, Connecticut: William Law, 1793).

terminology that would explain these matters, American singers were probably quite willing to follow Billings' instructions to "make a pendulum of common thread well waxed, and instead of a bullet take a piece of heavy wood turned perfectly round, about the bigness of a pullet's egg, and rub them over, either with chalk, paint or white-wash, so that they may be seen plainly by candle-light."[18] The American singing public need not be criticized for requiring simple means for solving problems of performance practice; neither need their composers be downgraded for filling the need. While some of the public were ready for a higher level of material, and showed it by absorbing European imports of a higher quality, the bulk of the public had been trained to an easy, pleasant, and somewhat stereotyped kind of anthem. The market

TABLE 11

Billings' Tempo Instructions Translated into Metronomic Equivalents

Very slow	A second and a quarter	M.M. 48
Slow	A second and an eighth	53.3
Moderate	A second	60
Cheerful	Seven eighths	68.5
Lively	Two thirds	90
Quick	Five eighths	96
Very quick	Half second	120

for such pieces continued to be filled, and the need for new composers was apparent to many, if we may judge by the preface to one work, which invited composers to submit material, stating that "original Pieces, accompanied with the Authors' names, . . . will be gratefully received by the Public's obliged Servants, THE PUBLISHERS."[19]

The word *anthem* made its way into places where one ordinarily would not expect to find it, even though the meaning of the word was not synonymous with that of general use. In a volume that printed the words of music sung at a Catholic church, the word was used generally throughout the collection as a substitute for *antiphon*, a curious parallel to the manner in which the term originally evolved. Each so-called anthem in the collection is really the antiphon text for one of the principal church festivals rendered into English.[20]

Many composers inhabited this scene, some of them extremely successful and competent, others exhibiting greater success than competence, and still others having neither. Only a few names emerge as leading figures, and they follow quite divergent paths. One might settle on William Billings and Oliver Holden (1765–1844) as the two most important and influential American composers of the late eighteenth

---

[18] Billings, *The Continental Harmony*, vii.

[19] *The Modern Collection of Sacred Music* (Boston: Isaiah Thomas and Ebenezer T. Andrews, 1800). The volume is sometimes attributed to Holden. It is almost identical with his *Union Harmony*.

[20] *Anthems, Hymns, &c. usually sung at the Catholick Church in Boston* (Boston: Manning & Loring, 1800).

century. Billings' importance has already been stressed. As a rustic, self-taught composer following an equally rustic English tradition conveyed by William Tans'ur, he infused this style with his own particular genius, and imparted to it a quality as uniquely American as New England itself. Holden, on the other hand, set a new trend. Although there is much about his compositions that suggests a distinctly American style, he adopted, in due course, the more sophisticated European Classical style of the late eighteenth century. This basically secular style was adopted in England as early as Madan's Lock Hospital Collection of 1769 (see Chapter 4), and used extensively among Nonconformists and Anglicans at the parish level. In America, the adoption of this style appears to have begun with Holden.

He spent his entire life in Massachusetts, living in Charlestown from his twenty-first year. There he prospered in real estate, built and pastored a Puritan church, and for a number of years represented Charlestown in the Massachusetts House of Representatives.[21] He operated a music store, conducted singing-schools, directed choirs, and worked extensively as a composer and compiler.

Holden's first music book was *The American Harmony*.[22] It contained psalm tunes and four of his anthems, revealing the continuation of a style already firmly established in America. But his work began to take new directions the following year with the publication of his two-volume *Union Harmony*.[23] There he expressed his reservations concerning the fuging tune which had been so prominent a feature with Billings, Read, and Lewis Edson (1748–1820), whose tunes remained in the repertory longer than most others:

> Fuging music in general is badly calculated for divine worship; for it often happens that music of this description will not admit of a change of words without injuring the subject. In such cases it would be better to reject the tune, than to obscure, or injure the words; but, when a tune is so contrived as to admit of changing the words with propriety, the parts falling in by turn serve to convey the meaning and impress the importance of the words more forcibly than otherwise they would, especially if the subject be praise.[24]

This is only a qualified reservation, however, for a number of fuging tunes are included in the first volume of *Union Harmony*, tunes that evidently met his requirements for text meaning. One would be at a loss to know whose compositions would be rejected, since the most prominent exponents of the fuging tune—Tans'ur, Billings, and Edson, among others—are represented here. That he was attempting to supply a need regardless of personal preferences is suggested in the Preface, where he stated that

> in a work intended for general use, it is probable that some tunes which are in high estimation with some performers, will be less approved of by others; this is utterly unavoidable,

[21] See Frank J. Metcalf, *American Writers and Compilers of Sacred Music* (New York: The Abingdon Press, 1925), 125.

[22] Oliver Holden, *The American Harmony* (Boston: Isaiah Thomas and Ebenezer T. Andrews, 1792).

[23] Oliver Holden, *The Union Harmony, or Universal Collection of Sacred Music* (2 vols.; Boston: Isaiah Thomas and Ebenezer T. Andrews, 1793).

[24] *Ibid.*, I, iii–iv.

considering the high variety of airs which are produced by the different composers in ancient and modern times, and the diversity of taste which will always exist among numerous practitioners of music. These circumstances have claimed and received particular attention. . . . It is therefore presumed that in so large a work as this, every school or singing society into whose hands it may fall, will find a sufficient number of tunes adapted to their purpose and adequate to their wishes.[25]

Holden's personal tastes, however, are probably better reflected in the contents of the second volume of *Union Harmony*, which came off the press within a very short time after the first. Here only three pieces—"Omega" and "Rapture" by Holden, and

[25] *Ibid.*, I, iii.

Example 68. "Epsom," Martin Madan (*Union Harmony*, II, 126).

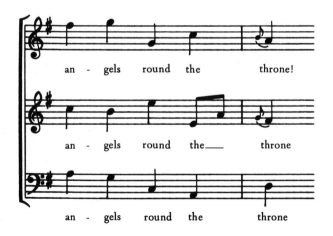

"Cambridge," Felice Giardini (*Union Harmony*, II, 155, 159).

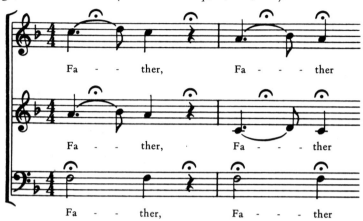

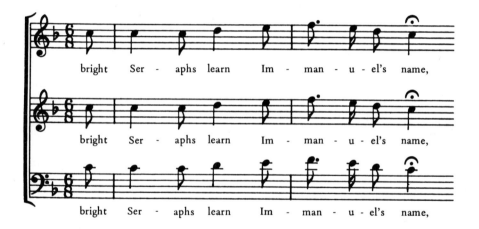

"Dismission" by Stephenson—could be considered genuine fuging tunes. To be sure, points of imitation occur in the anthems; these, the bulk of which were drawn from the English composers Selby, Stephenson, and Williams, represent a style already quite familiar.

Of the three anthems by native American composers, one is by Billings, a second is by Jacob Kimball (1761–1826), and the other is Holden's own *Hear my cry, O God*.[26] It is a sectional piece, in no way unusual except for the *a 3* setting, a texture that was to become a favorite of Holden's.

[26] *Ibid.*, II, 3–7.

The real interest in the second volume is found in the extended pieces that are anthemlike, but are not so named. Again, the distinction has to do with texts—those pieces are invariably based on hymns or other versified material rather than on Scripture in prose form. Evidently Martin Madan and the Lock Hospital Collection greatly influenced Holden's choice of materials and general style. Five pieces in the second volume are drawn from Madan, although there are slight alterations in some instances. Three of the pieces were composed by Madan, one is by Giardini, and the other is anonymous.

Daniel points to Hans Gram (1754–1804), a Danish organist-composer who settled in Boston, as the foremost influence on Holden's style.[27] It is true that Holden studied with Gram and was undoubtedly influenced by him; however, the three features that Daniel specifically mentions—frequent use of the *fermata*, "sighing" figures in repeated suspensions, and sudden unison passages—are all to be found in both Madan and Giardini where Holden also gained familiarity with them. In fact, these features are seen repeatedly in the works of both composers as they appear in Holden's second volume (Example 68). Here Madan used both the *fermata* and the suspension in the opening measures of "Epsom," and symbolically employed unison writing for the words, "the whole creation join in one." Giardini made lavish use of the *fermata* in "Cambridge," and dramatically joined the voices in unison on the text, "bright Seraphs learn Immanuel's name."

The stylistic features just mentioned are seen in the compositions of Holden, though not to the extent that they occur with Madan and Giardini. Actually, Holden's work is a mixture of the rugged, angular American style and the suave grace that characterizes European style in the late eighteenth century. In the opening measures of "Messiah," an extended piece that Holden listed as an ode, the melodic line, replete with the "sighing" suspension, is typical of Classical style (Example 69). In "Apollo," another ode, Holden makes sudden use of unison in an otherwise harmonic texture (Example 70).

Further evidence of Holden's high regard for Martin Madan and the Lock Hospital Collection is seen where Holden is listed among the subscribers for the first American edition of that work. That edition, published in 1809, followed *Union Harmony* by a number of years, but there can be no doubt that the English editions were widely circulated in America during the last decades of the eighteenth century, and Holden's liberal borrowing of those materials attest to his having had access to an earlier edition.

Finally, we may examine an American volume to which Holden had regular access, and of which he edited the sixth and later editions.[28] *Laus Deo!* was the product of Isaiah Thomas, and its profitable existence began in 1786. The contents changed from edition to edition, and we may be sure that when Holden was given charge of the sixth

[27] Daniel, *op. cit.*, 132.
[28] *Laus Deo! The Worcester Collection of Sacred Harmony...The Sixth Edition, Altered, Corrected and Revised with Additions*, by Oliver Holden (Boston: Isaiah Thomas and Ebenezer T. Andrews, 1797).

Example 69. "Messiah," Oliver Holden (*Union Harmony*, II, 90).

Example 70. "Apollo," Oliver Holden (*Union Harmony*, II, 33).

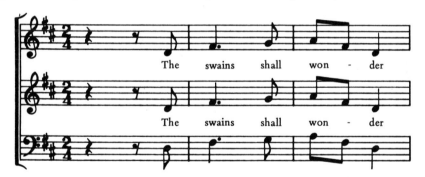

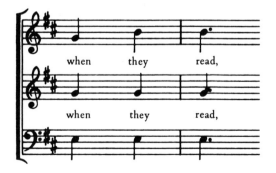

edition, it underwent another shift that represented his own preferences. It contained psalm tunes, fuging pieces, anthemlike pieces, and a few anthems. Rather than concern ourselves with the anthems, inasmuch as they form such a small part of the whole, let us consider briefly the composers known through the collection, for they are probably a true index to the leading popular figures of the period. The most prominent is Daniel Read, of whose work sixteen examples appear. Second in importance is Billings with twelve pieces, one of which is an anthem. Other men with three or more pieces are [Abraham] Wood (1752–1804), Stephenson, Williams, Supply Belcher (1751–1836), Timothy Swan (1758–1842), Madan, Kimball, and Holden. Handel is given credit for three pieces, but one is Croft's "Hanover," misattributed to Handel. After the same fashion, "Old Hundred" is attributed to Martin Luther, a common error in American books of the period. Among other sources, we find seventeen borrowings from *Union Harmony*, and the presence of the names of Arne and Sacchini shows an increasing awareness of the secular European musical scene.

It is interesting to compare the foregoing with the next edition of the same work,[29] for *Laus Deo!* continued to be modified through the remaining editions. The seventh was again under Holden's editorship. It differed in two respects: The introductory material was cut to a minimum, an indication that tutorial material for singing-schools was needed to a lesser degree than formerly, and the identification of composers was no longer continued in the body of the work, their names appearing only in the index. The seventh edition contains five anthems. Only two are identified in the index: a funeral anthem, *I heard a great voice*, by Kimball,[30] and the Easter anthem, *The Lord is risen indeed*, by Billings.[31] Unidentified is Holden's *Man that is born of a woman*,[32] but it can be traced back to the sixth edition and to its earlier printing in *Union Harmony*. Holden may have felt that the prior appearances made it unnecessary for him to identify himself with it again, but that would not account for the two other unidentified pieces listed with the anthems.

One of those is a three-voice setting of Pope's popular text, *Vital spark of heavenly flame*,[33] widely known on both sides of the Atlantic under its other designation, "The Dying Christian." Billings had earlier made a setting that found its way into a number of collections, but this is not the Billings piece.[34] Holden apparently took this one directly from an English source. It may be found in Rippon's *Selection of Psalm and Hymn Tunes*[35] in the same form as it appears in *Laus Deo!* and is attributed to Edward Harwood (1707–1787), who is supposed to have composed the piece prior to 1786.[36]

The remaining piece bears the heading "Dedicatory Poem," but is listed among the anthems in the index. *With joyful hearts and tuneful song*[37] is a long piece on a metrical text. It achieves variety through changes of meter, shifting textures, use of

29 *Ibid.* (7th ed., 1800).   30 *Ibid.*, 20–21.   31 *Ibid.*, 130–34.   32 *Ibid.*, 137–39.
33 *Ibid.*, 116–20.
34 The Billings version is printed in *The Psalm-Singer's Amusement* (Boston: [Billings], 1781), 99–102.
35 Rippon, *op. cit.*, No. 182. The 5th edition dates from around 1791.
36 *Grove's*, IV, 127–28.   37 *Laus Deo!*, 98–104.

solo and duet sections, and some differences in tempo. The probability that it is Holden's is considerable, even though it is not listed among his anthems by Daniel. It opens with a bold unison phrase and proceeds into a variety of voice pairings (Example 71). The closing Doxology likewise begins with a unison section, one of Holden's hallmarks.

In 1801 a "Dedicatory Poem," most probably this same one, was sung as part of the dedication program for a Baptist meetinghouse in Charlestown, Holden's place of residence. The music is not printed with the document that contains the dedicatory prayers and sermon,[38] but the prominent mention of the musical piece, coupled with Metcalf's statement that, during Holden's Charlestown years, "when a new Baptist church was organized he gave the land on which to erect the building,"[39] provides more than a coincidental chain of events.

There is a danger of assigning too much importance to Holden, significant though he may be. There are other composers of the period who, while relatively obscure, were aware of the attraction of English and European models which, while they had certain features that associated them with the stage, had an engaging impact that made them excellent material for the promotion of their collections. In addition, the works of Englishmen who had adopted those models, but had not written for the stage themselves, were brought back into the picture. Prior to the publication of Holden's first book, Andrew Adgate (?–1793), mentioned earlier in connection with Samuel Blair's *Discourse*, published a volume[40] that borrowed from the Lock Hospital Collection, and which included, in addition to anthems, Madan's anthemlike setting of the portion of Watts's poem, *Sing to the Lord with joyful voice*, beginning with the text, "Before Jehovah's awful throne," *a 3*, and identified as "Denmark."[41]

This composition, SSB in four varied sections, continued to appear in various books for well over half a century after its first appearance. (See Figure 5 for two others in which it was printed later.) Its popularity is evident not only from its longevity, but from the arrangements in which the voice parts were printed, from its appearance in shaped notes, and from the editorial emendations it suffered. As early as 1802, Elias Mann (1750–1825) had made an arrangement of the piece, inserting a new seventeen-measure section into its middle, and identifying the composition as one by "Madan and Mann"[42] (Example 72). The arrangement of the two upper voices changed as the

[38] *Sacred Performances at the Dedication of the Baptist Meeting-House in Charlestown, May 12, 1801* (Boston: Manning & Loring, [1801]).

[39] Metcalf, *op. cit.*, 125.

[40] Andrew Adgate, *Philadelphia Harmony* (Philadelphia: John M'Culloch, 1789), 54–56. Adgate published a secular collection the same year, in which glees, catches, and *God save America* (to the tune of *God save the King*) were printed, the volume depending entirely upon English sources. He used a pseudonym, publishing it under the name Absalom Aimwell, *The Philadelphia Songster* (Philadelphia: John M'Culloch, 1789).

[41] See John Julian, *A Dictionary of Hymnology* (2 vols. 2nd rev. ed.; London: John Murray, 1907. Dover reprint, 1957), II, 1059.

[42] Elias Mann, *The Northampton Collection of Sacred Harmony* (Northampton: Daniel Wright, 1802), 107–110. The piece had also appeared in A[ndrew]. Adgate, *Philadelphia Harmony, or A Collection of Psalm Tunes, Hymns, and Anthems* (Philadelphia: Mathew Cared, [1801]), 74–76.

Example 71. *With joyful hearts and tuneful song* [Oliver Holden] (*Laus Deo!*, 98).

FIGURE 5. Before Jehovah's awful throne ("*Denmark*"), *as it appeared in Little and Smith*, The E Instructor, 1798 (*above*), *and in Lowell Mason's* Carmina Sacra, 1842 (*below*). (*Photos courtesy Baylor University Library.*)

when like wand'ring sheep we stray'd, He brought us to his fold again, He brought us to his fold again. We are his

people, we his care, Our souls and all our mortal frame; What lasting honors shall we rear, Almighty maker, to thy name.

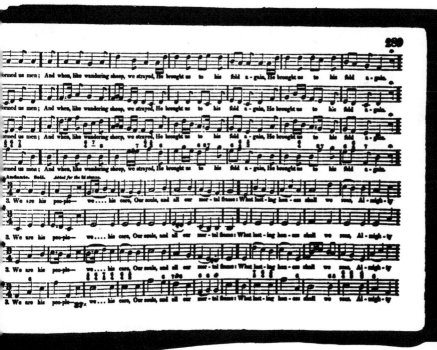

formed us men; And when, like wandering sheep, we strayed, He brought us to his fold a-gain, He brought us to his fold a-gain.

3. We are his peo-ple— we .... his care, Our souls, and all our mor-tal frame: What last-ing hon-ors shall we rear, Al-migh-ty

piece went from publisher to publisher. Originally the melody lay in the middle voice.[43] but early American printers put it in the upper.[44] It was restored to its original position in *The Essex Harmony*,[45] where it appeared with pieces by Arne, Burney, Chetham, Arnold, Handel, Wanly (Wanless), and Claude le Jeune, to name only a few, even though the title of the volume stressed its continuation of the practice of reprinting American composers. It is possible that American purchasers of tune-books were habituated to the American product, that the increasing number of English pieces were forced upon compilers by the absence of a fresh indigenous expression. It would be fruitless to compare the contents of the various volumes, for some lean toward imported anthems, whereas others continue in the proven tradition of reprinting American works by Billings, Kimball, and others. The increasing flow of English pieces, and the apparent rediscovery of the cathedral composers and the better ones of the parish-church practice, is significant in the light of general opinions that place this renascence as late as the heyday of Lowell Mason and Thomas Hastings.

Another imported work that appeared to catch the fancy of compilers was Harwood's *Vital spark* ("The Dying Christian"). Its appearance in *Laus Deo!* was noted earlier. It appeared again in Atwill's collection;[46] along with "Denmark" restored to its original American voice arrangement—i.e., with the voices reversed from their original English position. Also present are two enduring Billings anthems—the funeral anthem, *I heard a great voice*, and the Easter anthem, *The Lord is risen*. Tracing the courses of these two kinds of music in the nineteenth century would be an interesting pursuit, but it must be left to more specialized studies than this. We may note, however, that by the last quarter of the century, a volume apparently intended to reflect the quaint past surviving in the repertory contained eight anthems and choruses.[47] They included Billings' Easter anthem, his *I am the rose of Sharon*, "Denmark," and two choruses from *The Creation*. The Billings materials obviously did not disappear early in the nineteenth century, to await their restoration by twentieth-century editors.

The interest in European materials and their wide dissemination to the American public continued to be reflected in the 1804 volume Samuel Holyoke (1762–1820) compiled for the Baptists.[48] He drew heavily upon Rippon, Watts, and Joshua Smith, and he included two anthems that are unidentified. They are a *Hear our prayer*[49] and an *O be*

---

[43] Rippon, *op. cit.*, No. 87; *The Collection of Psalm and Hymn Tunes sung at the Chapel of the Lock Hospital*, 106–7.

[44] Holden, *The Union Harmony*, 77–81, as well as in Mann, *op. cit.*, and Adgate, *opp. cit.*

[45] *The Essex Harmony, Part II, Consisting of Original Pieces by Kimball, Holyoke, and others . . .* (Salem: Cushing & Appleton, 1802), 60–64.

[46] Thomas H. Atwill, *The New York Collection of Sacred Harmony* (Lansingburgh: Abner Reed, 1802), 73–77.

[47] *Ye Centennial. A Quire Booke for Folke Old and Younge. Made by ye Compiler* (Boston: Oliver Ditson & Co., 1875).

[48] Samuel Holyoke, *The Christian Harmonist . . . designed for the Use of the Baptist Churches in the United States* (Salem: Joshua Cushing, 1804).

[49] *Ibid.*, 181–83.

Example 72. Elias Mann's addition to Madan's "Denmark" (Mann, *The Northampton Collection of Sacred Harmony*, 108).

joyful.[50] Their three-voice texture (SSB) points to England either directly or through Holden. The following year Benjamin Carr (1768–1831), a London-born composer who moved to Philadelphia and turned to publishing, compiled a volume for Catholic churches. It contained a number of pieces called anthems. One is an anthem for Easter, *Our Lord is risen from the dead*,[51] by Samuel Arnold. It opens with a chorus section for SAB with organ, the instrument performing from the unfigured bass vocal part. A duet for sopranos follows, and the opening chorus is apparently repeated to conclude the piece. Among the other anthems in the volume is *My song shall be of mercy and judgment*,[52] by James Kent. It follows Kent's English edition exactly until the closing section. Where Kent has the Lesser Doxology introduced by two sopranos and continued by SATB chorus in alternation with the soloists, Carr substituted a chorus *a 3* by Raynor Taylor (ca. 1747–1825) to the text, "Praise ye the Lord, Amen." A number of other interesting pieces may be found in the volume, but the most curious is a *quodlibet* of music by Handel, Corelli, and Haydn, employing sections of familiar and lesser known music in fragments as small as two measures from each composer. The whole is entitled *Anthem for Christmas*.[53] The use of the word *anthem* in a volume designed for Catholic use is worth mentioning. When such anthems are lifted from Anglican sources with only a few modifications to suit local performance practice or available singers, they point to a universality of practice and to a search for wider commercial outlets by publishers. The material in this volume was drawn from music selected for the choir of St. Augustine,[54] and was published because

> there being no books of sacred music for this purpose published in this country, arranged for different voices, it was suggested, that a work of the present kind might be of essential service to the different choirs in the United States, by being conducive to their singing in parts; and the clergy, and some leading members of the congregation, having kindly offered to promote, all in their power, such an undertaking, the following sheets are with defference [*sic*] presented to the public. Should they be the humble means of improving the choirs in general, by adding *harmony* to their *melody*, the author will not think his labour ill bestowed.[55]

Carr went on to mention Samuel Webbe's collection of Masses, published in London,[56] and then went on to say

[50] *Ibid.*, 193–95.

[51] Benjamin Carr, *Masses, Vespers, Litanies, Hymns & Psalms, Anthems & Motets Composed, Selected and Arranged for the Use of the Catholic Churches in the United States of America* (Baltimore: J. Carr, [1805], 100–105.

[52] *Ibid.*, 85–90. See James Kent, *Twelve Anthems* (London: Printed for the Author by William Randall, 1773), 45–51, for the original.

[53] *Ibid.*, 96–99.

[54] *Ibid.*, [iii]. Whether in New York, Philadelphia, or Baltimore is uncertain; Carr had business interests in all three places.

[55] *Ibid.*

[56] In view of the modifications that were made to choral pieces in this volume, Carr probably was referring to Webbe's *A Collection of Masses, With an Accompaniment for the Organ* (London: T. Jones, 1792). Most of its material was simple, being limited to three-voice texture.

if they wish hymns or anthems, with English words, this continent supplies many collections of sacred music; particularly one published in New-York, by Mr. W. Pirson, under the auspices of Dr. Jackson, and one Mr. John Cole of Baltimore, both highly deserving of public patronage: Further augmentations of English anthems Great Britain can supply in abundance, in publications of the works of Handel, Purcell, Blow, Boyce, Greene, Stanley, Arnold, and a long list of names of high repute that it is needless to enumerate; but no choir, who are able to accomplish the performance of it, should be without Handel's *Messiah*—it is a library in itself, that would furnish appropriate pieces for almost any day throughout the year, for any Christian church of whatever denomination.[57]

In the early years of the nineteenth century, terminology was becoming less specific in reference to choral pieces. It has been observed repeatedly that anthemlike pieces deserved consideration alongside the compositions specifically labeled anthems, and our examination of such pieces has been conducted in the light of that conviction. We may see again, in a volume apparently intended for use in Episcopal churches, but offered on the open market[58]—a number of single and double chants are included along with the usual psalm tunes and a larger than usual number of anthems and extended anthemlike compositions—that the anthems and set pieces are set apart in the Index in a category called "Pieces." "Denmark" is the first of these, and it is followed by Harwood's "Dying Christian," although without the composer's name to identify him. Among the other pieces, we also find *Now is Christ risen*,[59] unidentified by composer. It is a virtually unaltered reprint of Joseph Key's anthem of the same name.[60] The rest of the volume also leans on the English chapel tradition, borrowing liberally from Madan, Aaron Williams, and Stephenson.

The direction for the first quarter of the nineteenth century was thus established. Two lines of activity were to be present: the continuation of the native American tradition in the reprinting of pieces by Billings and a few others, and the renewed flow of materials from distinguished names of the parish church and cathedral practice of England, along with a sampling of materials from the European continent. In both cases the materials came from the previous generation of composers. No new Americans of significance were on the scene from whom the compilers could draw their material. They were content to reprint from the works of men already recognized when they themselves were in their youth.

The trend toward the adoption of European composers, already apparent in the works of Oliver Holden and Benjamin Carr, continued through much of the nineteenth century. In the first decade, numerous compilers brought out collections that contained the most popular works of both American and European composers, a process that continued into the second half of the century. However, an incipient trend,

---

[57] Carr, *op. cit.*, [iii–iv].
[58] G. E. Blake, *Vocal Harmony, Being a Collection of Psalms, Hymns, Anthems & Chants, Compiled from the Compositions of the most Approved Authors* (Philadelphia: G. E. Blake, 1805).
[59] *Ibid.*, 88–93.
[60] Key, *Eight Anthems, on Various Occasions*, 1–7.

perhaps confined to more sophisticated circles, favored European composers to the virtual exclusion of Americans. A case in point was the posthumous publication in 1814 of a collection of thirty anthems compiled by John Hubbard (1759–1810).[61]

Hubbard chose only English composers. The list represents cathedral practice as well as that of the parish church and Nonconformist chapel. Only one anthem, *O praise the Lord, all ye nations*, by William Selby (1739?–1798), could be considered American in any sense. Selby was an established musician in London when he immigrated to Boston in 1771 or 1772, where he became organist at King's Chapel. Evidently this anthem was written in America, since its publication was announced in the *Boston Gazette*, August 26, 1782.[62]

Representative of the English parish church and Nonconformist chapel are such familiar names as Aaron Williams, Caleb Ashworth, William Knapp, and Joseph Stephenson, all of whom had long been favorites in America. On the other hand, the selections from cathedral composers were no doubt much less familiar to Americans, some of them probably being introduced to this country for the first time.

Hubbard not only brought in the cathedral tradition, but he reached back to the Tudor period with the inclusion of a piece by William Byrd entitled *Bow thine ear, O Lord*.[63] The work is especially interesting here since it was not drawn from the composer's anthem repertory, but was taken from the *secunda pars* of the motet *Ne irascaris, Domine*.[64] How this fell into Hubbard's hands, or who provided the English translation, is not known.

Other cathedral composers represented here are John Weldon, Jeremiah Clarke, and Henry Purcell. Clarke's *The Lord is full of compassion*[65] is one of three pieces printed here by that composer. Certain alterations are apparent when the anthem is compared with the original; ritornellos are omitted since the Hubbard collection contains no accompaniments, the original ATB verse setting becomes SAB, with the upper parts an octave higher, and twenty-three measures of the original verse section are deleted.[66]

Purcell is represented here by three pieces, one of which is the well-known anthem *O give thanks*.[67] The original employs ATB verse in alternation with an SATB chorus; in Hubbard, these parts are run together in a continuous SATB setting (Example 73). Again, ritornellos are removed, and an extensive bass solo is omitted.

The works of Handel contained in the volume reveal an even greater degree of alteration. In *We praise thee, O God*, an anthem bearing the heading "Taken from the 'Grand Dittengen [*sic*] Te Deum'," everything in the original version that might create a performance problem is removed. The anthem is pieced together from the first four movements of Handel's work; solos, involved choral passages, and, of

[61] John Hubbard, *A Volume of Sacred Music, containing Thirty Anthems, selected from the works of Handel, Purcel, Croft, and other eminent European authors* (Newburyport: E. Little & Co., 1814).

[62] Daniel, *op. cit.*, 86.

[63] Hubbard, *op. cit.*, 28–33.

[64] *The Collected Vocal Works of William Byrd*, II, 158–65.

[65] Hubbard, *op. cit.*, 83–87.   [66] *Ibid.* Cf. *Divine Harmony*, II, 11–17.

[67] *Ibid.*, 64–72.

Example 73. *O give thanks,* Henry Purcell (*A Volume of Sacred M*

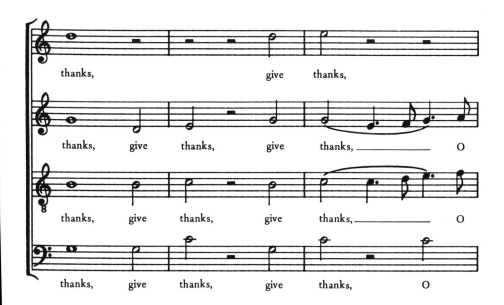

course, the accompaniment are omitted so that a continuous block-chord structure results.[68] A seven-part setting of "Glory be to the Father," not related to the *Te Deum*, closes out the piece.

Another of Handel's works underwent a similar type of editing; *Hail Judea, happy land*,[69] drawn from *Judas Maccabaeus*, is a much-cut version of the famous "Hallelujah! Amen" from the same work.

Whether Hubbard or another hand is responsible for the extensive alterations found throughout the volume is not certain. It does appear, however, that Hubbard's purpose was to introduce to the American scene works from England more sophisticated and extensive than had previously been known, yet to simplify them and to tailor them to the capabilities of American singing societies.

Another volume influential in the first quarter of the nineteenth century was *Templi Carmina*, otherwise known as the *Bridgewater Collection*.[70] Originally compiled in 1802 by Bartholomew Brown (1772–1854) and Nahum Mitchell (1769–1853) under a slightly different title, the collection reached a twenty-seventh edition in 1839.[71]

In addition to a large number of the usual hymn tunes, the volume contains thirty compositions that are classified in the index as anthems or set pieces. Several English composers—Kent, Callcott, Clarke, and Madan—already familiar on the American scene are here represented, as well as the works of several lesser-known contemporary Englishmen. This latter group consists of Capel Bond (1730–1790), suborganist at St. Michael's and Holy Trinity churches in Coventry; James Peck (n.d.), an engraver-publisher and composer who resided in London; Samuel Chapple (1775–1833), composer and organist at Ashburton; and William Mason (1724–1797), composer, author, and clergyman. The work of these composers represents the tedious mediocrity that characterizes the bulk of English composition during this period; nevertheless, many of the pieces have a quality of easy tunefulness that undoubtedly made them attractive to American choirs and singing societies.

Two other features of the collection must be mentioned. One is the inclusion of pieces edited from the larger works of Haydn and Mozart; the other is the appearance of an anthem by a Moravian composer.

In Chapter 4, reference was made to John Whitaker's *Seraph*, in which adaptations from the larger instrumental and vocal works of Haydn and Mozart appear (see pp. 167–168). Evidently the compilers of *Templi Carmina* drew from Whitaker to a considerable extent, for several of the same adaptations are found here. In addition, six of Whitaker's own compositions, some of an extended nature, were included.

The borrowing of materials from Germanic sources marks what may be the earliest instance of such use in America, foreshadowing the practice that was to be so

---

[68] *Ibid.*, 106–17. Cf. Handel, *Dettingen Te Deum* (London: Novello & Co., 1951), 1–26.

[69] *Ibid.*, 99–102.

[70] *Templi Carmina. Songs of the Temple, or Bridgewater Collection of Sacred Music* (10th ed., Boston: Richardson & Lord, 1822).

[71] For further details concerning editions, see Metcalf, *op. cit.*, 151, 168–69.

prominent in the work of Lowell Mason and his contemporaries. It has been established that the edition cited here is the earliest one to contain the adaptations and compositions of Whitaker. The ninth edition is without them, although the Moravian piece, to be discussed, appeared there.[72]

The printing of an anthem from a Moravian source in an early nineteenth-century American collection is something of a curiosity. Although Moravians had been in America since the middle of the eighteenth century, they had not become involved in the mainstream of American life; rather, they had preferred to maintain an insular colonial society. The anthem in question here, *Hosanna, blessed is he that comes*,[73] is the work of Christian Friedrich Gregor (1723–1801), a prominent Moravian bishop who traveled extensively in Europe and spent some time in Pennsylvania where, among other things, he instructed Johann Peter in composition. The anthem is different from the others in *Templi Carmina* in its use of an opening dialogue, melodic sequence, and, later, the opening melodic material returning in a five-part texture (Example 74). Whether the composition originally used instruments, as did so many Moravian anthems, cannot be discovered from the version printed here. It has been previously assumed that this piece first appeared in the *Stoughton Collection of Church Music* (Boston, 1831).[74] It is to be found, however, as early as the ninth edition of *Templi Carmina*, and it may have appeared in an even earlier source. It is interesting to note that of the extended compositions in the collection, only Gregor's survives in present-day repertory, an indication of its high quality in comparison with the other pieces in the volume, and of Moravian music in general.

Indeed, Gregor was the senior member of a substantial group of Moravians in America who, in the later part of the eighteenth century and the first of the nineteenth, produced anthems of astonishingly high quality. He wrote a number of texts for other composers, among which *Go, congregation, go!* by John Antes (1740–1813) is an anthem of rare beauty. Antes shares with Johann Friedrich Peter (1746–1813) and Johannes Herbst (1735–1812) a position of leadership in the composition of Moravian church music. To Jeremiah Dencke (1725–1795) goes the honor of being the first composer in America to write anthems with orchestral accompaniment, and it is this characteristic feature that makes Moravian religious music unique. It is no less than amazing that these unassuming disciples of Pietism, many of them ministers and missionaries as well as musicians, could and did produce vocal and instrumental music of a quality comparable to that of the Classical European professional musicians.

Unfortunately, the Moravian influence did not work into the mainstream of American music, and only in recent years have a few of these fine anthems become widely known through octavo editions and recorded performances.

---

[72] *Templi Carmina* (9th ed., Boston: Richardson & Lord, October, 1821).

[73] *Ibid.*, 10th ed., 303–6.

[74] Donald M. McCorkle, "The Moravian Contribution to American Music," *Music Library Association NOTES*, XIII (September, 1956), 605.

Example 74.   Dialogue, sequence, and return of melodic material (in brackets) in *Hosanna, blessed is he that comes*, C. F. Gregor (*Templi Carmina*, 303, 304).

It has been seen that nineteenth-century compilers began to import a greater amount of European material and place it before choirs, congregations, and singing societies. It has generally been thought that Lowell Mason (1792–1872) was the first American to bring about this wholesale shift in taste, from the homespun American product to the translated extracts from the European masters. This, we now know, was far from fact, although Mason's place in the development of American religious song is not less firm because he followed in a path already clearly marked.

His first significant publication dates from 1822, and it is often confused with another of similar name. Since the two volumes concerned differ greatly in every respect, it is important that they be compared at this point. Both were produced under the sponsorship of the Boston Handel and Haydn Society, an organization founded in 1815 for the purpose of improving the style of church music and promoting the works of the established Classical composers. The earlier of the two works had no connection with Lowell Mason, although its title superficially resembles that of his own publication of a year later.[75] It consists principally of pieces taken from oratorios, along with a few anthems. It was not intended for the use of either church choirs or congregations; at least, the contents seem completely out of line with the accomplishments of such groups as we know them in that year. The oratorio cuttings are principally from works by Handel, in the form of recitative and air, air and chorus, or chorus alone. There is printed as the central point of interest what appears to be a complete oratorio, *The Intercession*, by Matthew P. King (1733–1823). The work had been well received at Covent Garden Theatre in 1816, one of its airs achieving great popularity; and now, only a few years later, the Society was presenting it to the American public as the featured item of its collection along with anthems from the cathedral practice by Kent,[76] borrowed material from Mozart and Beethoven, and a piece of chant ascribed to Thomas Tallis.[77] This last, a fragment of eleven measures of music, is supplied with parts for *clarini*, horns, timpani, and strings. It is without parallel in American publications of that period as a pompous display of poor taste, and it is quite out of character with the rest of the volume. The collection contains not a single psalm tune or hymn melody. Its contents are aimed at the skilled performer who has been through the training of at least the singing school, and who has been accepted into regular singing groups. The accompanying reproduction of the Index pages shows the emphasis placed on works from the stage, and generally not adaptable to American church services (Figure 6).

---

[75] *The Boston Handel and Haydn Society Collection of Sacred Music, Consisting of Songs, Duetts, Trios, Chorusses, Anthems, &c. Selected from the Works of the Most Celebrated Authors. Arranged for the Organ or Piano Forte. By the Handel and Haydn Society.* Vol. I. (Boston: The Handel and Haydn Society, Thomas Badger, Jr., Printer, 1821).

[76] *Give the Lord the honor*, 41–52, is from James Kent, *A Morning & Evening Service with Eight Anthems*, rev. and arr. by Joseph Corfe ([London]: Printed for the Editor, [ca. 1780]), 52–63; *The Lord is my shepherd*, 165–75, printed in Kent, *op. cit.*, 74–82.

[77] *The Boston Handel and Haydn Society Collection*, 144–45.

INDEX.

TO VOL. I.

A.

AIR,	Arm, arm, ye brave,	*From the Oratorio of Judas Maccabeus.*	Handel.	90
CHORUS,	We come in bright array,			95

B.

AIR,	Begin my soul rejoicing,		*Purcell.*	143
CHORUS,	Behold the morning sun,		*Mornington.*	166
AIR,	Blessed be the power,	*From the Oratorio of Theodora.*	Handel.	76
CHORUS,	Blessing, honor, adoration,			

C.

CHORUS,	Come sweet spring,	*From the Oratorio of the Seasons.*	Haydn.	57

F.

AIR,	Fallen is thy throne,		Martini.	8
TRIO,	Fallen is thy throne,		Martini.	10

G.

ANTHEM,	Give the Lord the honor,		Kent.	44

H.

CHORUS,	Hallelujah, Amen,	*From the Oratorio of Judas Maccabeus.*	Handel.	163
CHORUS,	He sees, and he believes.		Bishop,	68
ANTHEM,	Holy, Lord God of hosts,		Mozart.	175
AIR,	How green our fertile pastures look,	*From the Oratorio of Solomon.*	Handel.	53
AIR,	How willing my paternal love,	*From the Oratorio of Samson.*	Handel.	70

INTERCESSION.

AN ORATORIO.

M. P. King.

RECITATIVE,	Father, thy word is past,		101
AIR,	I for his sake,		102
RECITATIVE,	But he shall rise victorious,		103
CHORUS,	The multitude of Angels,		104
RECITATIVE,	Thus they in heaven,		113
AIR,	Why comes not death,		115
RECITATIVE,	The great Archangel,		118
AIR,	Must I leave thee, Paradise?		119
SEMI-CHORUS,	Lament not Eve,		121
DUETTO,	With sighs the air frequenting,		125
SEMI-CHORUS,	Thus they in lowliest plight,		126
AIR,	See, Father, what first fruits on earth are sprung,		131
SEMI-CHORUS,	The heavenly choir,		134
CHORUS,	Hallelujah, Amen,		131

I.

CHORUS,	Is there a man?		Handel.	38

L.

QUARTETTO*,	Lovely is the face of nature,		Haydn.	29

M.

ANTHEM,	My God look upon me,		Reynolds.	184

N.

RECITATIVE,	Next the tortured soul release,			188
AIR,	Thus rolling surges,	*From the Oratorio of Solomon.*	Handel.	188
CHORUS,	Thus rolling surges,			189

O.

CHANT,	O all ye nations praise the Lord,		Tallis.	144
CHORUS,	O first created beam,	*From the Oratorio of Samson.*	Handel.	24
ANTHEM,	O Lord who hast taught us,		Marsh.	83
AIR,	O Lord whose mercies,	*From the Oratorio of Saul.*	Handel.	66
DUETT,	O lovely peace,	*From the Oratorio of Judas Maccabeus.*	Handel.	32
ANTHEM,	Our Father who art in heaven,		Denman.	5

R.

AIR,	Rejoice O Judah,	*From the Oratorio of Judas Maccabeus.*	Handel.	160
CHORUS,	Hallelujah Amen,			163
DUETTO,	Sion now her head shall raise,	*From the Oratorio of Judas Maccabeus.*	Handel.	149
CHORUS,	Tune your harps,			151
AIR,	Sound an alarm,			16
AIR,	Sound an alarm,	do. do.	Handel.	140
CHORUS,	We hear the pleasing dreadful call,			18

T.

TRIO,	The bird let loose,		Beethoven.	73
AIR,	The holy one of Israel,	*From the Oratorio of Samson.*	Handel.	78
ANTHEM,	The Lord is my Shepherd,		Kent.	167
QUARTETTO*,	The saffron tints of morn appear,		Mozart.	11
ANTHEM,	They play'd, in air the trembling music floats,		Stevenson.	93
AIR,	Thou who lov'st the desert wild,		Mozart.	52
AIR,	Thus rolling surges,	*From the Oratorio of Solomon.*	Handel.	188
CHORUS,	Thus rolling surges,			189
CHORUS,	To fame immortal go,	*From the Oratorio of Samson.*	Handel.	81
AIR,	Total Eclipse,	do. do.	Handel.	22
CHORUS,	Tune your harps,	*From the Oratorio of Judas Maccabeus.*	Handel.	151

W.

CHORUS,	We come in bright array,	*From the Oratorio of Judas Maccabeus.*	Handel.	95
CHORUS,	We hear the pleasing dreadful call,	do. do.	Handel.	18
ANTHEM,	While with ceaseless course the sun,		Webbe.	116
RECITATIVE,	With might endued,			77
AIR,	The holy one of Israel,	*From the Oratorio of Samson.*	Handel.	78
CHORUS,	To fame immortal go,			81
QUARTETTO*,	Winter has a joy for me,		Attorbury.	68

*These may be sung as Choruses.

FIGURE 6. *Index pages from* The Boston Handel and Haydn Society Collection of Sacred Music, 1821. *This is the volume often confused with Lowell Mason's publication of a similar title. (Photo courtesy of Baylor University Library.)*

The presence of the King oratorio, as well as the uncut verse anthems of Kent, makes it virtually inconceivable that the volume was intended for church use. Its importance here is still considerable, however, since the collection is sometimes unwittingly identified with the Mason volume of similar title.

Lowell Mason edited, but did not have his name on the title page of, a volume of greatly different content in the following year.[78] His aim was to supply an improved version of the kind of tune-book that was already in existence, with psalm tunes, hymns, anthems, and the anthemlike compositions that had now become commonly known as set pieces. The fifth edition, and probably the earlier ones as well, outshone such impressive earlier volumes as *Templi Carmina* in sheer size, number of set pieces, number of psalm tunes, and variety of composers, especially with the new emphasis on European masters, small though their individual contributions in excised sections of larger works set to religious text may have been. The Preface makes clear the aims of the Society and, of course, of Mason, who was still lurking behind the scenes, thinly garbed in decreasing anonymity as editor.

> The Handel and Haydn Society, having been instituted for the purpose of improving the style of Church Music, have felt it their duty to keep two objects continually in view; the first to acquire and diffuse that style and taste in performance, without which even the most exquisite compositions lose their effect; the second, what was indeed a necessary prerequisite, to furnish the public with a selection of the most approved and useful compositions, from both ancient and modern authors.[79]

The Society was content to follow the dictates of taste as Mason saw them, rather than carry on in the oratorio-borrowing path they had begun to follow the year before. His collection was directed to the attention of unschooled singers—a fortunate circumstance, since that large market was responsible for the phenomenal sale the work achieved—its slant being evident in the presence of a tutorial section and the large number of tunes that were set syllabically. The anthems and set pieces included a number of the tried-and-true group, among them "Denmark" and "The Dying Christian," but also showed an increasing number of pieces from the Germanic tradition, although the German emphasis is less than one would expect from general statements that circulate about the volume's contents. There are only three pieces among the longer ones of the fifth edition that are incontestably Germanic in origin. A set piece, *Sons of Zion, come before him,* by Naumann,[80] *Hallelujah to the God of Israel,*[81] and *Lo! my shepherd is divine,*[82] both by Haydn, are included with several Handel pieces. But Handel was generally viewed as English in all but name. There is an anonymous piece that seems Germanic. Its title is given as *That I may dwell in the house of the Lord,* but it is

---

[78] [Lowell Mason], *The Boston Handel and Haydn Society Collection of Church Music; being a Selection of the Most Approved Psalm and Hymn Tunes; together with many Beautiful Extracts from the Works of Haydn, Mozart, Beethoven, and other Eminent Modern Composers* (5th ed., [Boston]: Richardson and Lord, 1827).

[79] *Ibid.,* [iii].

[80] *Ibid.,* 308–10.   [81] *Ibid.,* 312–15.   [82] *Ibid.,* 318–22.

preceded by a recitative on the text, "One thing have I desired of the Lord, which I will require."[83] The two parts are separated by a twelve-measure section of minuet-like character. A piece attributed to the Bohemian Brethren, and probably acquired through a German source, completes the list. The set of anthems itself is, naturally, English and American in its makeup. The use of the term *anthem* in the general sense of meaning any part-song of religious nature did not yet exist here. Mason was not behind his fellows in appropriating materials from the cathedral tradition. Three of his pieces are by Kent. *Blessed be thou, Lord God of Israel* is printed complete,[84] in the same form as it appears in *Templi Carmina*—i.e., with the long verse *a 4* set for chorus, although Mason's figured bass is more carefully thought out, and is closer to the original. *Sing, O heavens*[85] is an abridged version of Kent's anthem,[86] continuing only through the first chorus. *Salvation belongeth to the Lord*[87] is the closing chorus of Kent's full anthem, *Lord, how are they increased that trouble us.*[88] Callcott, Madan, Harwood, Clarke-Whitfeld, Jackson, and Bishop complete the English group, far outweighing any Germanic intrusion in the anthems and set pieces. Among the hymn tunes there is a stronger feeling of Continental imports, German and Italian. The names of Viotti, Wranitzky, Pleyel, Giardini, Pergolesi, Mozart, Corelli, and Koželuch are among those that indicate contact with the polite and social tastes of the period, and a number of chorales make their appearance here as well. From the English front there is an expansion on the horizon; names that were little known are now to be found—Busby, Purcell, John Milton, Heighington, and numerous others. The Moravians are represented, there being pieces without composer identification, and others by Christian Ignatius Latrobe (1757–1836). It seems probable that these tunes arrived through England. Latrobe, at least, was well established and widely known there.

One may ask, what does the character of the hymn tunes have to do with anthems now when it had so little to do with them earlier? Two answers, at least, may be provided. One, that taste had become static, the same materials were being fed into the presses for book after book, and the substitutions that were made provided no great difference in style. Second, that with the avowed purpose of the Boston Handel and Haydn Society to improve the style of church music, and "to diffuse that style and taste in performance, without which even the most exquisite compositions lose their effect," they brought onto the scene a new body of music that actually did improve the level of taste. The congregational music that was sung and heard when Mason's volume was put into use had a stronger melodic thrust, a more vigorous relationship of chords, better accentuation, and the reflected glories of great names which, when compared to the shabby anthem material that was common to some collections, created a taste for better quality choral music. It is not to be expected that choral societies and church choirs rushed immediately to publishers demanding translations of works by the European masters, but the satisfaction they received from performing

---

[83] *Ibid.*, 323–25.   [84] *Ibid.*, 287–96.   [85] *Ibid.*, 297–301.
[86] Kent, *Twelve Anthems*, 1–7.   [87] [Mason], *op. cit.*, 302–303.   [88] Kent, *op. cit.*, 96–100.

skillfully written fragments certainly influenced their selection of materials during the next decades. That the tunes were not originally written for the church is unimportant. They seemed better in many respects than what had been in tune-books, and they were eagerly received. As a result, *contrafacta* from other traditions and denominations, from the stage and concert hall, were now a part of the American singing tradition. Some of them, divested of any former associations, remain in current hymnals and octavo anthem files.

Mason's introduction of Beethoven's music to the American church repertory has been overemphasized, for his music had been known slightly before this volume. Still, six of his tunes appeared in the first edition of the collection. They are identified and discussed by Otto Kinkeldey,[89] who traces them back to the *Sacred Melodies* of William Gardiner (1770–1853), a group of volumes published in 1812 and later years. Gardiner, an English amateur, aimed at "the regeneration of English psalm- and hymn-singing by the improvement of the poetic quality of the words and by a strong injection of Haydn, Mozart and Beethoven melody and harmony into the music."[90] From those volumes Mason chose six Beethoven tunes—originally found in longer instrumental pieces—and, by the fifth edition, still retained five of them.[91] Of great importance to the study of anthems and set pieces is *Lo! my shepherd is divine*,[92] a piece Mason lists as an extract "from the Oratorio of Judah" by Haydn. The material does come from a Haydn Mass, but concerning the oratorio connection, Kinkeldey writes, "In 1821 Gardiner manufactured a pasticcio of Haydn, Mozart and Beethoven music to which he adapted English words in a more or less connected story. This he entitled *Judah*."[93] The piece, printed by Mason, has continued in the repertory in one arrangement or another to the present time.

In summary we may observe that Mason's first collection did the following: (1) It brought in a large amount of hymnic material of a new type, much of it Germanic; (2) it dispensed with the anthems of the Billings and Holden type; (3) it introduced materials from the parish and cathedral tradition, drawing upon the same sources as other volumes of its time in the works of Kent, among others; and (4) it raised the general level of craftsmanship higher than that of earlier volumes, even in the short pieces, thereby providing singers with music likely to elevate their taste, whether they recognized those qualities or not.

The veneration of European masters that is apparent in the foregoing collection was evident in most of the volumes Mason produced later, either independently or in conjunction with some other figure prominent in church music. Titles either gave a

---

[89] Otto Kinkeldey, "Beginnings of Beethoven in America," *The Musical Quarterly*, XIII/2 (April, 1927), 217–48.

[90] *Ibid.*, 218.

[91] "Vienna," "Weston," "Waltham," "Ganges," and "Germany" still appear in the fifth edition. "Havre" is listed in the index, but is not printed.

[92] [Mason], *op. cit.*, 318–22.

[93] Kinkeldey, *loc. cit.*

list of specific composers, most of them associated with the highest level of concert stage and opera, or referred in general terms to "distinguished European composers," "the most classic authors, ancient and modern," or "eminent German, Swiss, Italian, French, English, and other European musicians." No longer were pieces to be taken from the existing corpus of material in this country, but they were to be borrowed, introduced, modified, translated, and improved for the next edition of a work. Only those men who supplied most of the pieces for their own volumes themselves ignored the great reservoir of materials that could be drained from Europe simply by extracting sections of pieces and supplying them with suitable text for the American market.

Mason's publications of religious music over the next half century are representative of the best that America could offer. A number of other people who appeared on the scene either differed sharply with him or followed the same path as he. A few of those names may be considered as typical of the principal approaches to anthem writing.

Nathaniel D. Gould (1781–1864) is best remembered as the author of an anecdotal volume on church music dealing with the period about 1770 to 1850.[94] He produced several volumes of music as well, the earliest of which is contemporaneous with Mason's first collection. *Social Harmony*[95] was a multipurpose volume intended for the home, the singing society, and, only as another possible source of revenue, the church. While the title implies that it is a volume of religious music, only a portion of its contents can be considered in that light. Keyboard accompaniments are printed with some pieces, figured basses for others, but some have only an unfigured bass line, while the choruses are printed with only vocal parts. Gould evidently attempted a collection different from most of those then in existence. This he accomplished by avoiding any psalm and hymn tunes, and by selecting pieces that were not in common use by other compilers. In this second matter, however, he showed poor judgment, or it may be that there were no suitable pieces other than those already in print. His collection is generally a shabby set of inferior pieces in the then popular taste, unable to endure beyond their brief moment of fame. His choice of composers was severely limited, for he seems to have avoided any duplication of items already in print. His list includes such generally unknown names as J. G. May, John Hall, G. Bellas, Pring, Widdub, and a host of other forgotten figures. The extracts from Mozart, Haydn, and Handel are without distinction, and the one example taken from Kent, *When the Son of man shall come*,[96] is a severely truncated and arranged version of the original.[97] Gould chose also the popular air "Must I leave thee, Paradise?" from *The Intercession*, by King. Since the entire work had been in the 1821 Handel and Haydn Society volume,

[94] Nathaniel D. Gould, *Church Music in America* (Boston: A. N. Johnson, 1853).

[95] N. D. Gould, *Social Harmony, or A Compilation of Airs, Duetts and Trios. Calculated for Private Devotion: Most of which are Fitted for the Organ, or Piano Forte; Also, A number of Anthems and Chorusses, Suitable for Churches and Singing Societies. The Whole Selected from the Most Approved Authors* (Boston: Printed by Thomas Badger, Jr., 1823).

[96] *Ibid.*, 80–84.   [97] Kent, *op. cit.*, 52–61.

and both collections were prepared by the same printer, Gould's source for this piece is evident. The most enduring piece in the entire collection is the Russian *Vesper Hymn*, printed here and in *Templi Carmina* simply as a Russian air, but later attributed to Bortniansky. It has come down into modern octavo editions without revision in a number of instances.

As early as 1816 the combining of two previously existent collections into *Musica Sacra*,[98] by Thomas Hastings (1784–1872) and Solomon Warriner (1778–1860), provided the public with yet another set of pieces, some familiar and some new. The third edition contains some of the time-tried anthems of the dying generation, but adds a set of chants especially for use in the Episcopal churches. At this point no wholesale importation of European materials can be noticed in the collection. Of the two compilers Hastings was to become the more significant.

Hastings' *Dissertation on Musical Taste*, first printed in 1822, apparently was widely read, for it dealt with many matters of musical interest and importance on a higher plane than had been found in the introductory sections of psalm-tune books up to that time. The sermons preached at the singing-society performances were usually vague and windy. Hastings got to the heart of the matter in discussing style and technique, and he considered anew the problems of congregational participation and the use of choirs. As he wrote in the preface to the edition of 1853, "the most important criticism offered respecting it was, that the work appeared one generation too soon."[99]

Improvement in musical practice between the two editions was sufficient that Hastings could say it had "advanced, to say the least, quite to the level of the *Dissertation*. Meanwhile, the work had been so often referred to, and quoted, and made to furnish the basis of pamphlets and speeches, and newspaper articles, that some of its contents may strike the reader as familiar acquaintances."[100] One of those who made use of Hastings' ideas was Lowell Mason, in an address he delivered twice publicly in 1826, and in the printed version of which he referred directly to the Hastings volume.[101] Hastings' place is firmly established through the *Dissertation*,[102] but some of his reputation in his own time came from his association with other music collections. He joined forces with William B. Bradbury (1816–1868) in *The Mendelssohn Collection*,[103] a volume that appears to have taken full advantage of Bradbury's presence in Leipzig at the time of Mendelssohn's death. The biographical sketch of Mendelssohn printed in the volume does nothing beyond supplying information to a culturally curious public; the number of pieces by Mendelssohn is extremely small; the increased number of

---

[98] Thomas Hastings and Solomon Warriner, *Musica Sacra; or Springfield and Utica Collections United* (3rd rev. ed., Utica: William Williams, 1822).

[99] Thomas Hastings, *Dissertation on Musical Taste* (New York: Mason Brothers, 1853), [v].

[100] *Ibid.*

[101] Lowell Mason, *Address on Church Music* (Boston: Hilliard, Gray, Little, and Wilkins, 1827).

[102] The volume is discussed in considerable detail by James Edward Dooley, "Thomas Hastings: American Church Musician" (unpublished Ph.D. dissertation, The Florida State University, 1963), 118–30.

[103] Thomas Hastings and William B. Bradbury, *The Mendelssohn Collection, or Hastings and Bradbury's Third Book of Psalmody* (New York: Mark H. Newman & Co., [1849]).

Example 75. *O magnify the Lord*, William B. Bradbury (*The Psalmodist*, 306).

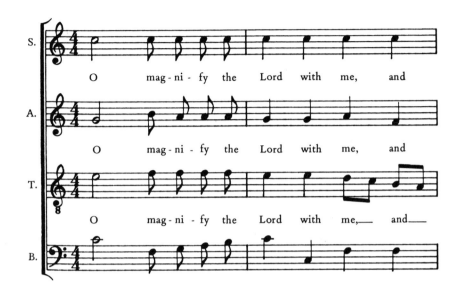

tunes by Germans reflects Bradbury's two years of study in Germany; and the presence of new pieces by Bradbury, Hastings, Isaac Woodbury (1819–1858), and George F. Root (1820–1895) is more truly indicative of the volume's direction than any other feature.

Examples of composition by the foregoing, or any of a number of others among their contemporaries, would prove that anthem composition of early nineteenth-century Americans fell far short of the imported patterns that were attracting compilers. Interest was largely achieved by alternating full chorus with semichorus, and duet or quartet with the choruses. The whole of American anthem composition, being generally homophonic, direct, and simple, lacked the variety that may be found in many English anthems of the period. Bradbury's O magnify the Lord[104] (Example 75) may be considered typical of these American works.

Compilers and composers (if the latter term may be used to dignify the efforts of some of these men) found the business of compiling tune and anthem books so profitable that they were able to amass small fortunes by the sale of their products. While some exaggeration may be involved, it is reported that sales on some of these books ran over a hundred thousand copies; in fact, Bradbury's works are estimated to have sold over two million copies in all.[105] Since fifty-nine books bore his name,[106] either as principal editor and composer or as co-compiler, the figure is entirely within the realm of possibility. Lowell Mason was even more prolific, for his collections of religious music, excluding all single pieces, congregational collections, and any books intended especially for children, in or out of church, number forty-six.[107] A number of single items were published as well, their exact place in society being difficult to determine because they could be sung by any kind of group from the parlor gathering to the church choir (see Figure 7). Watchman, tell us of the night[108] was sung at the "Monthly Concert" of a church, and certainly not at a regular morning service. In volumes that he prepared by himself, and in those compiled with the assistance of others, Mason added pieces to the repertory of American singing groups, or popularized by repetition anthems and set pieces that had appeared in lesser-known volumes.

Whether Mason made any consistent attempt to put himself forward as a composer is difficult to ascertain. If he did so, it was without fanfare, but not all unidentified works in his collections should be attributed to him, if indeed any can be with certainty. At one point he and George J. Webb (1803–1887), his associate in the Boston Academy of Music, indicated that "for those tunes which appear without the author's name, or without any designation of the source from whence they are derived, the

---

[104] Thomas Hastings and Wm. B. Bradbury, The Psalmodist (20th ed., New York: Mark H. Newman & Co., [1844]), 306–7.

[105] Metcalf, op. cit., 277.   [106] Ibid.

[107] Arthur Lowndes Rich, Lowell Mason: The Father of Singing Among the Children (Chapel Hill: The University of North Carolina Press, 1946), has a bibliography of all Mason's works. It is difficult to determine the specific function of a few of the works by title alone, and the number may be larger than indicated here. See pp. 138–72 of Rich.

[108] Lowell Mason, Watchman, tell us of the Night (Boston: C. Bradlee, 1830).

editors must, in general, be held accountable; though, in some instances, well-known old tunes will be found without any notice of their origin, and, in other cases, tunes by living composers, other than the editors, are inserted anonymously."[109] There is, obviously, no easy way to recognize which of the pieces might have been composed by Mason.

The publication of new pieces continued unabated, and if some tunes were not entirely new, their printing in Mason volumes was more complete or different from other volumes. Samuel Chapple's verse anthem, *I'll wash my hands in innocency*,[110] is printed by Mason and Webb with some interesting modifications. The contraction that opens Chapple's version is restored to a "correct" and less vital form, and the American version skips entirely the opening verse section, although the term *verse* was unwittingly retained by Mason and Webb to describe the piece.[111] They may have had no concept of the verse anthem as the English used it. It is certain that they could not, at any rate, have used such a piece without making drastic alterations in it. The keyboard part that appears as introduction and interludes is omitted, but the vocal parts contain instrumental cues that are designated "Sym." The second solo in Chapple's piece is not repeated as a chorus in the original version, but Mason and Webb alter it in that fashion rather than omit it. The piece introduces the chapel and country-church music of England again to a new kind of audience, indicating that Mason and his fellows ranged far in search of materials. The same volume contains the short anthem usually attributed to Farrant, *Lord, for thy tender mercies' sake*,[112] previously unnoticed in American collections, and gives in complete form the motet of Nicola Zingarelli (1752–1837), *Go not far from me, O God*,[113] the opening adagio of which had appeared a year earlier from different arrangers as a funeral motet entitled *Blessed are the dead*.[114] It must remain clear that there was no firm line between anthem and set piece, whether the latter was originally a motet, a Mass section, or an oratorio chorus, when the adaptation to publication was at stake. Any piece could function as an anthem outside the Episcopal churches (and sometimes in them), and this freedom has continued to mark the American practice. As a result, the Americans were able to incorporate set pieces more easily than the English, and the term *anthem* becomes applied more loosely to various types of pieces in America.

The terms *anthem*, *motet*, and sometimes *hymn* continue to be used in almost indiscriminate fashion in later books.[115] What was being done in original American com-

---

[109] Lowell Mason and George James Webb, *The Psaltery* (Boston: Wilkins, Carter, & Co., 1845), [3].

[110] Samuel Chapple, *A Second Sett of Six Anthems, In Score, Figured for the Organ & Piano Forte* (London: Goulding, D'Almaine, Potter & Co., [ca. 1820]), 8–12.

[111] Mason and Webb, *op. cit.*, 310–13.

[112] *Ibid.*, 280–81. The anthem is probably by John Hilton (1599–1657).

[113] *Ibid.*, 282–85.

[114] Hastings and Bradbury, *op. cit.*, 304.

[115] Lowell Mason and William Mason, *Asaph, or The Choir Book* (New York: Mason Brothers, 1861), shows these terms used with little distinction, but with *hymn* being the simplest of the three, filling the gap that had existed between psalm tune and set piece.

position was, fortunately, little. Only the large-scale importation of musical material from England and the Continent made it possible for American publishers and compilers to survive. The American examples of this period are shabby at best. It is small wonder, then, that when an American who was trained in the European tradition appeared on the scene as a composer of religious music, he was received with enthusiasm. Although Dudley Buck (1839–1909) was not a threat to the superiority of European composition, he was the best that America could then bring to the field of church music. When we next return to our study of American materials, we shall see how his influence served to advance taste and practice still another step.

CHAPTER SEVEN

The English Anthem to About 1920

The parallel developments of cathedral and Nonconformist practices we have seen in England would have been destined to an ineffective decline had it not been for one significant development, the printing of cheap music.[1] Credit for this important contribution goes entirely to the firm established by Vincent Novello, and especially to his son, J. Alfred Novello (1810–1896), who first set out to provide inexpensive editions of choral works for the growing number of English singing societies. The importance of this firm cannot be exaggerated, and its fortuitous appearance on the scene at a time when choral music captured the English fancy was of utmost significance.

Two areas of choral literature were important to the young publishing house. Alfred Novello began serious publication of choral works in 1829, continuing his father's set of *Purcell's Sacred Music*, the first complete collection to be added to Anglican materials since Page's *Harmonia Sacra*, three decades earlier. The demand for large works of cathedral style was limited, however, and the greater market was to be found in the singing societies and country choirs. The efforts and direction of this young business were strongly influenced by the work of two men whose interests lay in music teaching rather than in composing or publishing.

---

[1] The term *cheap* was used by Novello in advertising its editions. It does not imply inferiority in quality but a comparison with prevailing prices.

Joseph Mainzer (1801–1851) and John Pyke Hullah (1812–1884), although they worked independently of each other, each created a skill and taste in choral singing through their methods of teaching sightsinging to large groups. Hullah became interested in a system devised by Guillaume-Louis Wilhem (*recte* Bocquillon) (1781–1842), during his visits to Paris. He adapted the system to English, established a Singing School of Schoolmasters in 1841, and thousands of people came under the influence of his system which, although it had a considerable popularity, created great controversy. It and that of Mainzer had in common the promotion of the "fixed Do" solmization common on the Continent. As one writer put it, in referring to Mainzer's loss of acceptance, "his classes fell off, the pupils experiencing greater difficulties in modulation than his system had prepared them to cope with."[2] Regardless of his limited success in pedagogical matters, Mainzer influenced English choral practice in another manner. On his arrival in England in 1841, after sojourns in Brussels and Paris, he began publishing a periodical, first called *The National Singing Circular*, and later *Mainzer's Musical Times and Singing Class Circular*.[3] The periodical carried a musical supplement each month, and this practice was continued after its purchase and subsequent continuation in 1844 by J. Alfred Novello. The journal was of octavo size. The popularity of that size for single copies of choral music since then is the direct result of Mainzer's initial effort. *The Musical Times and Singing Class Circular*, continuing to the present day under the title *The Musical Times*, has carried on the practice of printing a choral work in each issue. As we shall see, these pieces both influenced and reflected the tastes of English choral groups, and they provide a catalogue of the leading composers in that genre.

The practice of publishing works in large format with hard covers continued, confined mostly to the cathedral tradition, and usually on subscription, since a large sale could not have been expected in view of the limited market such works served. The set of anthems published by John Stafford Smith (ca. 1750–1836) at the beginning of the nineteenth century,[4] for example, had a subscription list of less than 150 copies, of which several were multiple-copy orders to larger church establishments or to members of the Smith family, and a dozen were ordered, apparently for sale at their music shop, by the firm of Longman and Broderip. The sale of such volumes was always on a limited scale, and their presence in private collections and libraries now is not an accurate reflection of their impact on society in their day. The flimsy, unbound octavo copies were sold in far greater quantity, but time and use have removed many of them from this world; whereas the durable bindings and limited use of the large

---

[2] David Baptie, *A Handbook of Musical Biography* (London: W. Morley & Co., [1883]), 139.

[3] *A Century and a Half in Soho: A Short History of the Firm of Novello* (London: Novello and Company Limited, 1961), 19. The influence of Mainzer, Hullah, and the more lasting efforts of John Curwen (1816–1880) are detailed in Scholes, *The Mirror of Music: 1844–1944*, I, 3–19. *A Short History of Cheap Music* (London: Novello, Ewer and Co., 1887) is informative on this, as well as the entire history of English choral publishing.

[4] John Stafford Smith, *Anthems, Composed for The Choir-Service of the Church of England* (London: Printed for the Author, [ca. 1800]).

Example 76. *The Beatitudes*, John Stafford Smith (*Anthems*, 9).

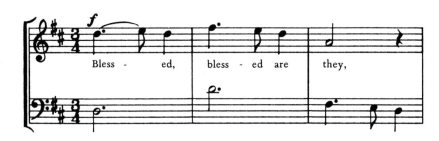

volumes have preserved them in numbers out of proportion to their importance then and now.

Still, since the Smith volume antedates the practice of single-copy publication, a brief examination of two of its pieces will remind us of what the cultivated taste in anthems was at the time of its publication. Smith's Dedication stated that the anthems were "Intended to exhibit a closer Analogy than usual between the Accent of Speech, and the Melody of Song." Although he has become better known as a writer of glees and an early arranger of the tune that has become the American national anthem, Smith was a typical product of the Chapel Royal, and his collection of twenty anthems reflects cathedral practice entirely. It is made up mainly of verse anthems and full anthems with verses. Any of the set could be used to illustrate his effectiveness in carrying out the proposal of improving accentuation, but the second one, *The Beatitudes*,[5] illustrates his methods most clearly because of the subtle modifications of text, and by his use of repeated "Hallelujah" choral sections. The piece falls into eighteen short, but unequal, sections, most of them solo statements of the nine Beatitudes, preceded by a short recitative, and except for one instance of an organ interlude, followed by choral "hallelujah" segments, no two of which are alike. The analogy between speech and song was not accomplished by any unusual melodic or rhythmic means, but appears to have been sought almost entirely in the variety of tempo, mood, and dynamics instructions that occur throughout the anthem. No short section can be considered typical of the profusion of effects Smith sought to create, but one of the shorter solo-chorus combinations (Example 76) will provide some idea of his method. All the solo material appears to be intended for tenor, and the choruses are all SATB. There is no variety of key, but there are several changes of meter from section to section. By way of contrast, his full anthem, *Come unto me*,[6] sustains a single mood throughout, but is laden with instructions for varied dynamics, including the specific demand "softening" on a sustained cadential pattern. Surely the cathedral had been invaded by theatrical effects to its greatest extent when such works as these were performed.

One of the prominent cathedral composers, who stands with one foot in the late eighteenth century, and the other in the early nineteenth, was Thomas Attwood (1765–1838). From the age of nine, he served as a chorister in the Chapel Royal. In 1783 he was sent to Italy for musical study by the Prince of Wales (later George IV), and thence on to Vienna, where he studied with Mozart. In the years following his return to England, he held a variety of important musical posts, and was highly regarded in influential circles. A favorite pupil of Mozart's, Attwood in turn recognized the potential of young Mendelssohn, and a close friendship existed between them.

Some fifteen years after his death, much of Attwood's church music was edited by

---

[5] *Ibid.*, 8–17.
[6] *Ibid.*, 78–81.

his godson, Thomas Attwood Walmisley (1814–1856), and published in London.[7] In the prefatory material of the volume, an interesting reference is made to Attwood's relationship with Mozart.

> If Attwood's veneration for his master was ardent and unchanging, the attachment of Mozart to his pupil was no less warm and sincere. Mozart loved him as a friend and brother. Kelly[8] was at Vienna during the period of Attwood's residence there, and he thus records Mozart's estimate of his talents: "I have," said Mozart, "the sincerest affection for Attwood, and I feel much pleasure in telling you that he has imbibed more of my style than any other scholar I ever had."[9]

The eight anthems in the Walmisley edition were composed in the forty-year span from 1797 to 1837. Three of them, dated 1814, are Collects proper to Epiphany, the First Sunday after Epiphany, and the Twenty-first Sunday after Trinity. They are all full anthem settings. The remaining five are based on various psalms, three of which are extended verse anthems; the last two, dated 1835 and 1837, are designated as full anthems, although they contain either solo or verse sections.

The first anthem in the collection, *Teach me, O Lord*,[10] is dated 1797, and does indeed bear a strong imprint of Mozart's style. The opening measures suggest the influence of the Viennese master from both a melodic and harmonic standpoint (Example 77). The texture has an unusual clarity, and the piece is adorned with an easy melodic grace.

Attwood's style underwent considerable change, however, in the ensuing years. His setting of *O God, who by the leading of a star*,[11] a Collect for Epiphany composed in 1814, reveals an increased complexity not found in his work seventeen years earlier. Here the independence of voices is manifest, and the musical texture, especially in the elaborate "Amen," is characterized by a fluidity not seen in his earlier work. One has the feeling that Attwood was in transition at this point to an essentially Romantic style. This is further seen in *Grant, we beseech thee*,[12] another setting of a Collect composed the same year, where the remarkable similarity of Attwood's opening theme with one found in Schubert's *C major symphony* has already been pointed out.[13] The fact that Schubert's work was composed fourteen years after that of Attwood not only rules out any indebtedness on Attwood's part, but also reveals him, in the entire work, as an early exponent of Romantic style.

In the years immediately preceding his death, Attwood's style appears to have undergone still another change, and the major influence seems to have been that of

---

[7] Thomas Attwood, *Attwood's Cathedral Music*,... *Edited, and the Organ Accompaniment, arranged, by Thomas Attwood Walmisley* (London: Ewer and Co., [ca. 1853]).

[8] Reference is made here to Michael Kelly (1762–1826), Irish tenor and actor, who was a close friend of Mozart. In 1787 he left Vienna for England in company with Attwood and others.

[9] Attwood, *op. cit.*, [v].

[10] *Ibid.*, 156–69.

[11] *Ibid.*, 170–74.

[12] *Ibid.*, 175–85.   [13] *CMC*, 346.

Example 77. *Teach me, O Lord,* Thomas Attwood (*Attwood's Cathedral Music,* 156). Note values halved.

Mendelssohn. This is easily accountable, for the two were close friends. In 1829, on his first trip to London, Mendelssohn suffered a knee injury ̇͘ latter part of his convalescence in A̶t̶t̶w̶o̶o̶d̶'s̶ ̶h̶o̶m̶e̶ ̶̶ piece for unaccompanied choru̶ wood. Thus it is not surprising tha̶ dated 1835 and 1837, bear a general sty̶

The first of these, *Let the words of my mo̶u̶t̶h̶*, pedal tones. The influence seems even stronger in the second a̶n̶t̶h̶e̶m̶ *down to the sea.*[16] Here one is reminded in a general way of *St. Paul*, which is not at all

Example 78.   *Thou, O God, art praised in Sion*, Samuel Wesley (*Original Sacred Music*, 140). Note values halved.

surprising, since the oratorio had first been performed in Liverpool one year earlier. Specific thematic similarities are not evident, but the general harmonic and melodic style of the anthem is much like that of Mendelssohn.

The degree of stylistic evolution observed in the works of Attwood has been unique in anthem composers to this point; he appears to have been progressive and open to change throughout his life, yet his earliest works are the most convincing, and one is forced to conclude that, however impressed he may have been with the Romanticism of Mendelssohn, he was still the musical descendant of Mozart.

One of the outstanding English musicians of the period under discussion was Samuel Wesley (1766–1837), son of the famous hymn writer Charles Wesley (1707–1788). A prolific composer of secular music, his church works, while of considerable quality, must be viewed as the lesser part of his total output. Obviously departing from the religious precepts of his father, he became a Roman Catholic in 1784, and the great majority of his religious music is for that church. He wrote nine anthems, of which only three have been published.

Even these, however, have been largely overlooked. The one example of his work contained in *TECM* is a motet with English translation, rather than an anthem, and he is not represented at all in *The Church Anthem Book*.[17] References to his church music

---

[14] *Grove's*, V, 680.   [15] Attwood, *op. cit.*, 220–28.   [16] *Ibid.*, 229–38.

[17] Walford Davies and Henry G. Ley, *The Church Anthem Book* (London: Oxford University Press, 1933).

are most frequently restricted to a passing comment regarding his most famous motet, *In exitu Israel*. One of the three published anthems is a full setting of Psalm 65:1,2, *Thou, O God, art praised in Sion*.[18] It is a fairly simple and straightforward setting, em-

Example 79.   *The heavens declare the glory of God*, John Clarke-Whitfeld (*The Services and Anthems*, 239).

ploying a short but strong theme first stated in the bass (Example 78). The theme is developed in an unusual way: After the opening statement, it is repeated in the tenor, and again in the bass, inverted. The next statement is in D minor—the original key is C —immediately followed by an inversion in the new key. The theme makes a final appearance near the end of the piece, first in inversion and then in its original form, having returned by this time to the original key as well.

18 Alfred Pettet, *Original Sacred Music, consisting of Psalms, Hymns, and Anthems* ([London]: Chappell & Co. and others, n.d.), 140–45.

Cla...   ...wing
achieveme.. .....s career came in 1821 when he was appointed Professor of Music at
Cambridge, a position he held until his death.

His Service and anthems were published in four volumes by Novello in 1805,[19]
with a separate accompaniment realized by Vincent Novello. The twenty-three
anthems are, for the most part, lengthy verse settings; there are, however, several four-
or five-voice full anthems.

In a verse-anthem setting of Psalm 19, *The heavens declare the glory of God*,[20]
Clarke-Whitfeld reveals a stylistic indebtedness to the Viennese Classicists in various
melodic and accompaniment figures. Moreover, he appears to have paid purposeful
tribute to Haydn in directly quoting two measures from the famous chorus from *The
Creation*, which employs the same text (Example 79).

In contrast to his lengthy verse anthems, Clarke-Whitfeld was able to write relatively short full settings. For example, his setting of the Prodigal's words (Luke 15:18–
19), *I will arise and go to my father*,[21] is confined to fifty-one measures. Here, word-
painting is used in two ways: first in a pyramid of vocal entries beginning with the
bass and culminating with the soprano on the text, "I will arise," and again in a rising
melodic sequence on the same text. Scholes notes Clarke-Whitfeld's predilection for
word-painting, observing that

> in one of his most popular anthems ('Behold how good and joyful') he graphically repre-
> sents, by a long descending solo bass passage, 'the precious ointment upon the head, that ran
> down upon the beard, even Aaron's beard: that went down to the skirts of his garments'.
> Such happy entertainment is all too rare in the sober repertory of the English Church.[22]

Another musician who flourished in the first half of the nineteenth century was
William Crotch (1775–1847). Something of a boy prodigy, Crotch toured the British
Isles at an early age. In his thirteenth year he began organ study at Oxford, and the
next year he composed his first oratorio, *The Captivity of Judah*.

Crotch's anthem output was not large; aside from a few for special occasions, his
contribution is contained in a volume of ten anthems.[23] While they are not numerous,

---

[19] John Clarke-Whitfeld, *The Services and Anthems, in vocal score* (London: J. Alfred Novello, [1805]).
Since the four volumes are bound in two with continuous pagination, only page numbers will be given in
future references.

[20] *Ibid.*, 238–52.   [21] *Ibid.*, 307–9.   [22] Scholes, *The Oxford Companion to Music*, 192.

[23] William Crotch, *Ten Anthems* (Cambridge: W. Dixon, 1798).

several of them are extremely long. A verse anthem, *The Lord, even the most mighty God, hath spoken,*[24] extends to 216 measures and, with its clear sectional structure, takes on the character of a short cantata after the fashion of the Restoration verse anthem. Another piece, *Blessed is he,*[25] is given the unusual designation, solo anthem. Here the text, drawn from the opening and closing verses of Psalm 32, is sung by a solo treble voice, with the chorus entering on the last line of text, "Be glad, O ye righteous, and rejoice in the Lord." The chorus then continues with a fifty-five-measure "Hallelujah,

Example 80.   *Blessed is he*, William Crotch (*Ten Anthems*, 92, 93).

(a)

(b)

Amen," strikingly similar to Handel's treatment of the "Amen" in *Messiah*. Crotch opens this section with a fuguelike exposition of a driving theme (Example 80*a*). The following instrumental interlude employs the thematic material imitatively in the upper register of the treble range (Example 80*b*). The subsequent full-chorus entry and the complex episodic treatment of the initial theme are so reminiscent of Handel as to suggest deliberate imitation on Crotch's part.

Not all of his anthems are lengthy, however; a setting of Psalm 84, verse 13, *O Lord God of hosts,*[26] extends for only fifty-one measures. Although it is designated as a full anthem, solo voices are called for in a six-measure passage. Quite unlike the full anthem with verses, where the sections were clearly delineated, the solo parts are introduced in the midst of a continuous musical and textual passage, an unusual if not unique procedure.

During the first half of the nineteenth century the work of Vincent Novello was often before the public, for his work as an editor and arranger did not stop when he turned the fledgling publishing house over to his son. Nor did his efforts at composition fail to find a market, for with a son in the trade, and a ready market in the form of

[24] *Ibid.*, 68–69.   [25] *Ibid.*, 90–98.   [26] *Ibid.*, 18–21.

·onthly magazine, the elder Novello produced small works in considerable number. ..ioles has listed some of the larger publications, all of which bore the Novello hall-mark of full accompaniment instead of simply a figured bass, as "thirty-four Masses by Haydn and Mozart in vocal score with orchestral parts; five volumes of Italian selec-tions from the manuscript music in the Fitzwilliam Collection...; five volumes of Purcell's Sacred Music (1832); eight of the anthems of Croft, Greene, and Boyce; fourteen of Handel's oratorios; six of organ music and so on."[27] Entirely lost from the survey of these large and important collections is any mention of the anthem and hymn material Novello provided for the market that would not or could not purchase the huge volumes that were probably too difficult to use in smaller choirs of undistinguish-ed singers. We can see something of this material in the various issues of *The Musical Times*. In No. 39, *The Easter Hymn*, on the text, "Jesus Christ is ris'n today," is pre-sented in varied stanzas for treble solo, SAT trio, and SATB quartet, with choral Hallelujahs. Novello may have known the earlier version from the Foundling Hospital Collection (see pp. 160–162). The level of his composition was not out-standing, but his taste was catholic, his knowledge of Continental works considerable, and his impact on English choral music, secular and religious alike, must have been tremendous. He favored the short anthem for the *Musical Times* supplements, a group of three appearing in No. 46, of which *There is a river* is notable for its excursion from the original key of A into a contrasting section in F. His Christmas anthem, *Sing unto the Lord*, in No. 54, and his Easter anthem, *The Lord is my strength*, in No. 58, not only pro-vided suitable pieces for the principal liturgical festivals, but were so written that un-accompanied performance would be feasible. A footnote on the first page of the Easter anthem reads: "With a view to the convenience and accommodation of those Choirs where there is no Organ, the vocal Counterpoint of this Anthem is so constructed to be susceptible of performance independently of any Accompaniment whatever." Novello certainly deserves credit for having written out the organ parts of anthems for the convenience of performers; he probably was the first to move English practice back toward the *a cappella* performance of new music as well.

It is not only because of the easy accessibility of this music that Vincent Novello was important to the English choral tradition, nor can the credit be placed on the economies of the publishing practices of the firm he founded. His compositions were firmly grounded in skillful craftsmanship, showing an accomplished understanding of the Classical harmonic idiom, slightly flavored with Romantic chromaticism, and producing an easily singable piece with immediate lyric appeal.

The Musical Times must be mentioned again as the force that spread not only Novello's compositions, but his taste in music as well as that of his heirs in the publish-ing house. They imported European works, modified and edited them, provided English translations of a number that have become standard items of church-choir performance, including what seems to be the first appearance of Friedrich Himmel's

---

[27] Scholes, *The Mirror of Music*, II, 751.

(1765–1814) solo piece, adapted to English as *Incline thine ear* by W. Patten, and arranged with a quartet version by Novello (*The Musical Times*, No. 116), and Mozart's *Ave verum corpus* (K. 618) with the English text beginning, *Saviour, source of every blessing* (No. 190). The piece is almost identical, except for its now familiar text, *Jesu, Word of God incarnate*, with a widely used American edition. The introduction of such pieces, the printing of choruses from popular Continental oratorios, the offering of short works by Farrant, Tallis, Kent, Nares, and others for the first time in octavo form, all had a direct bearing on the future of choral music in English churches—and much of this influence rubbed off on an American parallel practice later in the century, when periodicals first began to print anthems regularly, although the latter were almost entirely filled with homegrown products of inferior quality. *The Musical Times* was still, in spite of the importance of the musical supplements, a magazine of news, instruction, and advertising about choral music. It reported on the current state of musical performance throughout the area of the English reader's interest, its information usually coming from a member of the local choral society; it gave notice of the formation of new societies; it carried advertising that ranged from requests for singers and organists to the availability of new music; and certainly not the least important and entertaining feature was the letters addressed to the editor.

The Oxford Movement was the most violent internal disturbance suffered by the Anglican Church since the Puritan dissension. Beginning in 1833 with a sermon on national apostasy delivered at Oxford by John Keble (1792–1866), the Movement sought to defend the privileged position of the Anglican Church in affairs of state. Such a stance could only be made credible with proof that God favored the Church of England above others in the nation; thus the Oxford reformers attempted to prove the doctrine of Apostolic Succession applicable to their church. The resulting investigation of early church history produced an unexpected bonus; a vast store of Greek and Latin hymns, unknown to the English-speaking world, was uncovered, and scholars such as Edward Caswall (1814–1878) and John Mason Neale (1818–1866) produced translations of rare beauty. A hymnic revolution was in the making, culminating in the publication of *Hymns Ancient and Modern* (1861), which, in its many subsequent editions, had an unprecedented effect on the hymnody of English-speaking churches.

It is to be expected that such an important upheaval would leave its mark on the anthem, but the effects are less to be found on the musical idiom itself than one would suppose. We shall see that text was affected more than music, and that the adoption of texts traceable to the Movement occurred some decades after the beginnings of the reform. More significant at the time were the effects that could be seen in the surroundings and trappings in which the anthems were performed. The principal effects were (1) the removal of parish-church choirs from their traditional places in the West Gallery or the "singing pews" to the chancel; (2) the slower but eventual removal of organs from gallery to chancel or to an artificially contrived area adjacent to the chancel; (3) the establishment of male choirs when the singers were brought to the front of the church, this resulting in the need to train boys to sing soprano; (4) since countertenors were lacking, subterfuges were employed in order to incorporate women into the chancel choirs to sing alto; and (5) attempts to recreate, visually at first, the cathedral tradition by employing divided choir stalls, processions, and surpliced choirs.[28]

While the Low Church tradition must have continued without much change, the new High Church upsurge found a place for the aforementioned hymnic translations from Greek and Latin (and later from German as well). Eventually these became texts that were used in anthems as well as hymns. A few Gregorian tunes were retrieved in the course of this change, and we shall identify some of the poems and tunes as we encounter them in the composers to be discussed in the remaining pages of our book.

We have been dealing in this chapter with composers who, while they have an important position in the development of the anthem's history, have had little regular performance in American churches during the present century, and who have probably been somewhat neglected in England as well. The ones who are discussed in the remaining pages comprise, with few exceptions, those who have endured as favorites, even when they are represented by only a few published anthems. It is not their popularity that makes them the subject of our consideration here, however, but their place in the continuing growth of the anthem as a musical ornament to worship.

John Goss (1800–1880) was one of the successful nineteenth-century anthem composers—successful, that is, when measured by the number of anthems found in present-day collections and in octavo editions. Beginning as a choir boy in the Chapel Royal, Goss later studied with Attwood, and succeeded him as organist at St. Paul's in 1838, having held several posts prior to that last appointment.

No doubt the most popular of his anthems is *O Saviour of the world*.[29] Here an unpretentious romanticism quite appropriate to the text has kept the piece alive in the repertories of countless church choirs to the present time. One of the features that gives the work cohesion is the repetition of short motives, either on the same pitch or in sequence. Another anthem still available is *O taste, and see, how gracious the Lord is*.[30] Again, warm romanticism is the watchword, and a rich sonority is created in such passages as "But they who seek the Lord shall want no manner of thing that is good."

Fellowes has discussed several of the larger anthems, and refers briefly to a number of the shorter works.[31] A brief comparison of three among the latter will show that Goss had a greater variety of styles than we often assume, especially if our knowledge of his works has been limited to *O Saviour of the world*. The three anthems are conveniently printed in a single source.[32] The simplest is *God so loved the world*,[33] a setting that requires only twenty-six measures for its entirely syllabic text, and repeating only two words of that text. The anthem is reflective, almost severely reserved, but it radiates a controlled warmth. Slightly more elaborate is the treatment accorded the

[28] Scholes, *The Oxford Companion*, 38, discusses some features of the choir problem in greater detail.
[29] Davies and Ley, *op. cit.*, 352–54; B. F. Wood 411.
[30] G. Schirmer 3864.   [31] Fellowes, *English Cathedral Music*, 204.
[32] Davies and Ley, *op. cit.*   [33] *Ibid.*, 118–19.

brief text of *I heard a voice from heaven*,[34] an anthem of thirty-five measures with most text phrases repeated. The melodic outlines are typical of Goss, basically diatonic material with occasional leaps for emphasis, their interest lying primarily in the uppermost voice. The lower voices, while sharing the same qualities of diatonic emphasis, are lacking in melodic interest in such block-chord pieces. The text repetitions provide Goss with the opportunity to employ the wide range of dynamics demanded by the declamatory character of the text. Another facet of Goss's style is seen in the anthem *If we believe that Jesus died*,[35] one of the two pieces he composed for the funeral of the

Example 81.   *If we believe that Jesus died*, John Goss (*The Whole of the Music*, 2).

Duke of Wellington in 1852. The piece opens with a fugal exposition on a strong subject (Example 81), and is followed by a contrasting chordal section, after which the fugal exposition is repeated in stretto, and the chordal section reappears in major mode. A short coda on new text closes the piece. This is the most vital of the short anthems mentioned here, and the suitability of its text to the Easter season makes it worthy of reconsideration for a place in the repertory.

Goss was highly thought of in his own time; he contributed more anthems to *The Musical Times* in its second decade than any other living English composer,[36] and his works continued in favor throughout his life. Since we know little of his music in our services, we perhaps judge him by the least of his efforts. Examination of his longer works may well be rewarding, but modern religious observances are not suited to their size. Any thorough study of his anthems must probably be left to the graduate thesis or dissertation.

We have seen how the rise of Nonconformist choirs changed the face of religious choral song in England, and how the publication of good, singable, and inexpensive music came fortunately on the heels of a massive movement in sightsinging that provided England with a singing tradition. We have seen also that the publications of large

[34] *Ibid.*, 163–65.

[35] *Ibid.*, 171–78; *The Whole of the Music As performed at the Public Funeral of Field Marshal The Duke of Wellington in St. Paul's Cathedral. Edited, and in part Composed, by John Goss* (London: Addison & Hollier, n.d.), 6–11. If Goss knew Boyce's version (cf. Example 39), that knowledge is not reflected here.

[36] Scholes, *The Mirror of Music*, II, 556.

volumes perpetuating the cathedral practice underwent no corresponding growth. There was, rather, a depressing lack of interest in the continuation of such music. The effects were obvious early in the period of change; the causes were not yet clearly visible.

Samuel Sebastian Wesley (1810–1876) thought he could restore cathedral practice to a place of dignity by presenting a plan of education and financial support to the withering tradition, and this he did in a pamphlet that was published about mid-century.[37] His father had embraced Catholicism in his late teens; his music for religious groups was largely in Latin. Samuel Sebastian, on the other hand, had been a chorister in the Chapel Royal, had held responsible positions at Leeds Parish Church and Winchester Cathedral, and has lately been recognized as the most important Anglican musician since Purcell.[38] While this last may be a chauvinistic appraisal, one is hard put to find another candidate for that honor. Whatever his musical qualities were, his hopes and critical evaluations of the contemporary problem were as hopelessly out-dated as had been those of Thomas Mace (1613–1709), who, nearly two centuries earlier, had approached the same problem with a solution no more successful.[39] Both men were concerned with the quality of church music and with the availability of qualified people to perform it. Wesley placed the blame on a number of things and, most pointedly, on the use of funds that he thought were sufficient to maintain a Choral Service "but, unfortunately, the authorities at Cathedrals, to whose care the musical funds were entrusted, have, in various instances, taken them away from the musical department, and applied them to their own uses."[40] Funds were lacking indeed, for whatever reason, but the solution would not have been simple with them. People were not so involved in the life of religious establishments as they had been; society was changing while the traditionalists in church music were static; secularism was rampant; and the intrusion of a simpler style, easily found in Nonconformist circles, was more attractive to singers and listeners alike unless they had been reared in the same dignified circles as Wesley himself. His failure to see the problem clearly is evident when he says that in "viewing the Choral Service generally, and in comparison with any of the endless varieties of the Parochial, how superior is the former; . . .[and how obvious] the withering familiarity in this respect of the latter!"[41] This familiarity was, at the same time, the bane and the appeal of music outside the cathedrals.

Sebastian Wesley's works reveal a variety of stylistic features. The direct approach of chordal choruses uncomplicated by any hint of contrapuntal involvement, the use of arialike solo sections for individual soloists or entire sections, and the dramatic use of choral recitative are all seen in Blessed be the God and Father,[42] a work composed before

---

[37] Samuel Sebastian Wesley, A Few Words on Cathedral Music and the Musical System of the Church, with a Plan of Reform (London: F. & J. Rivington, et al., 1849; reprinted, Hinrichsen Edition, 1961).

[38] Fellowes, English Cathedral Music, 205.

[39] Thomas Mace, Musick's Monument (London: For the Author, 1676; reprint, Paris: Éditions du centre national de la recherche scientifique, 1958).

[40] Wesley, op. cit., 26.   [41] Ibid., 33.

[42] TECM, IV, 73–80; Davies and Ley, op. cit., 34–45.

1835 while he was at Hereford Cathedral.[43] It was not published until 1853, giving rise in some quarters to a supposition that it was a work of his later years. That he had mastery over contrapuntal techniques, and the good judgment to use them sparingly in an age that was uncongenial to them, is seen in *Cast me not away from Thy presence*[44] and *Thou Judge of quick and dead*.[45] It is unfortunate that he is known to this generation principally through shorter and simpler works than those named here, although the lesser pieces are direct and appealing, thus being within the grasp of a wide range of choral organizations, especially among volunteer choirs.

The range of styles explored by Goss and S. S. Wesley was typical of composers born in the first quarter of the century. Others of that period rarely exceeded the better qualities those two displayed, and few of them devoted themselves principally to anthems. Representative of that group are Henry Smart (1813–1879), George A. Macfarren (1813–1887), William Sterndale Bennett (1816–1875), George J. Elvey (1816–1893), and John B. Dykes (1823–1876).

When the author of a pamphlet has an obvious axe to grind and a flag to wave, there must always be the suspicion that he exaggerates, without malice but with the hope of strengthening his argument. Whether this was the case with Wesley's pamphlet cannot be proved. We have available, however, the documents of a musically alert and interested traveler, Lowell Mason. He visited England and the Continent three years after Wesley's argument was published, and attended cathedral and parish churches, although not to the extent that we might wish for a thorough report. Lowell Mason's letters,[46] intended to inform his American audience of his progress through the foreign musical scene, give us both supporting and conflicting evidence. He attended a Saturday Service at Worcester Cathedral in January, 1853, reporting that "the psalms for the day were chanted by the choir, consisting of sixteen or eighteen boys and men, who also sung the canticles set in the service or anthem form, by Dr. Nares."[47] The following day he attended the parish church of St. Nicholas, and he mentions no choir at all, although he was favorably impressed with the congregational singing. He was unimpressed with the daily Service at St. Paul's when he visited London, commenting that the choir was a little larger, but that their chanting was "confused, inarticulate, and unsatisfactory. . . . A company of hungry ones in a second or third-rate American hotel do not eat their dinner in greater speed than these humble confessions and prayers are recited."[48]

Mason's picture of English church music is equally as depressing as Wesley's, but for other reasons. Mason, while accustomed to viewing the problem as a producer at home, is in the role of observer abroad. His reaction is not that of one who is victim to the system, of one who faces it daily with no hope for change.

---

[43] *Grove's*, IX, 266.

[44] *TECM*, IV, 81–88.   [45] Davies and Ley, *op. cit.*, 439–47.

[46] Lowell Mason, *Musical Letters from Abroad* (New York: Mason Brothers, 1854; reprinted, New York: Da Capo Press, 1967).

[47] *Ibid.*, 12.   [48] *Ibid.*, 15.

On his return to London in August of 1852, after having had opportunities to observe Continental practices again, Mason was somewhat less critical in his appraisal. He reported on the singing of a Purcell anthem, with J. A. Novello as principal bass in the choir, at Lincoln's Inn Fields, but deplored the practice of "lining-out" the congregational hymns at a Baptist church and at the Scotch (Presbyterian?) Church. In addition, he wrote, "*the tunes were too difficult*, and the effect of the singing was wretched."[49]

No consistent practice was apparent in England at the places Mason visited, and one of the most unusual reports was that of his visit to the Weigh House Chapel, the church of a Reverend Mr. Binney. The Order of Service included chanting and the singing of an anthem in place of the closing hymn on some occasions. Mason wrote:

> There is no choir; the singing is congregational, and led by a precentor. It was quite good; one does not often hear a better performance of this part of the public worship, but yet it would be much improved if simple tunes, appropriate to Congregational singing, were substituted for the too difficult one attempted on the Sabbath we were present. A peculiarity of the singing here, is, that the whole congregation engage in the chanting. . . . Another peculiarity of the singing here, is, that the congregation sing anthems. They have a little book containing a collection of *three anthems for congregational use*. Smile not at the number; it is sufficient for their purpose; and, when more are required, they can easily be obtained. Anthems, however, for Congregational use, must have a simplicity such as can hardly be imagined by one accustomed to the chants that commonly prevail in choirs. We are fully satisfied that not only Congregational hymn-tune singing, but Congregational anthem singing, and chanting, may be successfully introduced where there is a desire for it, and where there is a necessary knowledge to guide in the selection of appropriate pieces; and we should not be afraid to undertake to insure success to a congregation who would give us one or two hours preparatory practice. . . . The standing posture was observed in singing, and the sitting posture in prayer and other exercises.[50]

The situation does not seem so dreary as that mentioned by Wesley, but there appears to be a wide variance in the level, size, and use of choirs. Mason's surprise at congregational anthem singing should put to rest any misapprehensions about what the American practice was earlier in that respect. The presence of anthems in psalm tune-books has sometimes caused speculation about where such pieces were used, and, it will be remembered, our contention has been that such anthems were reserved for the singing-school and its alumni.

As we have already seen, the availability of inexpensive octavo anthem editions by mid-nineteenth century wrought considerable change in the marketing of choir music. The specialized collections of anthems and Services that had been sold by subscription in the eighteenth and early nineteenth centuries all but faded from the scene in the latter half of the nineteenth.

---

49 *Ibid.*, 163.
50 *Ibid.*, 166–67.

Among the last of these is a collection of the anthems of John Larkin Hopkins (1820–1873), which was published about 1850.[51] It contains a lengthy cantata anthem and several shorter pieces that reflect the past glories of the cathedral tradition. The only signal of Hopkins' awareness of changing practices lies in his use of some New Testament texts in addition to the usual psalms and Collects. Another collection, by William R. Bexfield (1824–1853), contains anthems of five and eight parts in which the old cathedral practice of *decani* and *cantoris* division is observed.[52] A third such volume is a selection of the church music of Frederick Arthur Gore Ouseley (1825–1889).[53] Eighteen anthems are included here, most of which are short four-part pieces which lack the essential vitality that appears in the works of his contemporaries. One of the more effective pieces is *How goodly are thy tents*,[54] the brevity of which is admitted in the volume by the instruction that "it may be performed first as a Quartett, and then repeated in Chorus."[55] This is, at the same time, an admission of changing practices. For a man so steeped in cathedral traditions to recognize the existence and desirability of quartets, even though he must have envisioned them only in the parish practice, marks the deep inroads such modified choirs had made into the full choral service.

Ouseley's eight-part anthems are not noticeably better, even though he displays a technical proficiency in the handling of such devices as double fugue and changing texture. The melodic warmth and the use of Romantic harmonies found in the anthems of Attwood, Goss, and S. S. Wesley are almost totally lacking in the works of Ouseley, and one is left with the impression that his efforts represent the last gasp of the dying cathedral tradition. New forces were already at work, and had been for several decades; the old tradition, now devoid of creative spark, was moribund.

The name of Joseph Barnby (1838–1896) is chiefly associated with hymn-tune composition. Well it might be, for he wrote 246 of them, among which are such continuing favorites as "Laudes Domini," "O perfect Love," and "Merrial." He did, however, write a number of anthems, several of which are still to be found in various publishers' catalogues. Representative of these is *O Lord; how manifold are thy works*.[56] A straightforward piece, essentially chordal in character, the melodic material strikes the ear as a hymn tune. The form, AA′BAA′C, capitalizes on repetition of the principal melody much as Stainer's pieces do.

The anthems of Barnby and Arthur Sullivan (1824–1900) found early favor in America, not only in octavo form but also in the enormously popular hymn and anthem collections of the late nineteenth century. A volume published by John Sweney and William Kirkpatrick in 1881 (see p. 310) contained two of Barnby's anthems, *Sweet is thy mercy* and the previously mentioned *O Lord, how manifold are thy*

[51] John Larkin Hopkins, *A Collection of Anthems, Composed, and dedicated to...the Dean & Chapter of Rochester* (London: Surman, [ca. 1850]).

[52] W. R. Bexfield, *Church Anthems* (London: J. Alfred Novello, 1848).

[53] Frederick A. G. Ouseley, *Cathedral Music, Services & Anthems* (London: J. Alfred Novello, [ca. 1862]). A description of the contents is given in *CMC*, 347–48.

[54] *Ibid.*, 200–202.   [55] *Ibid.*, 200.

[56] G. Schirmer 5996.

works. Two of Sullivan's anthems, *Say, watchman, what of the night?* and *There is joy in the presence of the angels of God,* were included in the Palmer and Wright collection, also of 1881 (see p. 309).

It is not surprising that these two English composers would find ready acceptance, even in the least sophisticated circles of American anthem practice, for their style is altogether familiar, making few demands on the performer, and rewarding the listener with comfortable, easily remembered melodies.

There have been earlier instances where men not born to the Anglican faith have exerted considerable influence over its music, notably William Byrd, Samuel Webbe, and Vincent Novello. Another such is Berthold Tours (1837–1897), who, born in Belgium and trained there and in Germany, arrived in England in 1861, where he spent the remainder of his life. He composed pieces in quantity for the cultivated popular taste and service music for Anglican choirs. Even though Fellowes called his most widely used Service "a wretchedly poor work"[57] under the influence of Gounod, Tours had considerable popularity that demands an examination of his work now. That he admired Gounod (who was immensely popular in England and admired by other composers as well), or at least found his works worth arranging for piano solo and duet, is known.[58] That he was highly regarded in the music trade is evident from the facts that he edited and revised the piano accompaniments to Crotch's *Palestine* for Novello,[59] wrote at least ten anthems that appeared in *The Musical Times,*[60] became a musical advisor and editor to the Novello firm,[61] and moved Sir George Grove to write that "his best work is to be found in his hymn-tunes, anthems and services for the Anglican church."[62] Several of these marks of success relate to his association with Novello, but that relationship can be presumed to have been entered into with fore-thought and continued with mutual satisfaction. It is significant that his only up-to-date biographical notice, complete with a list of works, is in a German source[63] while the original comments in *Grove's* have not been revised in any way.

It is not that Tours's qualities in music have improved since his death. His position in relation to the world he knew and influenced should, however, be kept in focus as our perspective changes. It is possible that he has always been a difficult oyster to swallow, inasmuch as his success was greater than that of his contemporaries who were born into the Establishment.

The analysis of a quantity of Tours's anthems should not be necessary, for many of his techniques are used by his contemporary, John Stainer, to whom we shall devote more space. Several features to which his popularity may be attributed are found in the two works we shall examine here. His Christmas anthem, *Sing, O heavens,*[64] has an opening theme-fragment, soon and often repeated, that has a joyous swing scorned in

[57] Fellowes, *English Cathedral Music,* 232.
[58] Scholes, *The Mirror of Music,* II, 868.
[59] *Ibid.,* I, 84.   [60] *Ibid.,* II, 556–57.
[61] *Grove's,* VIII, 522.   [62] *Ibid.*
[63] *MGG,* XIII, 595.   [64] Presser (Octavo Church Music, Series I, No. 6).

these days except in Fundamentalist circles (Example 82*a*). The general level of the first section is forte, and the contrasting section, to the same text but with the interest transferred to the keyboard, surges along at a happy fortissimo. Tours was alert to the exciting possibilities of sharp contrast, for he followed this with an unaccompanied solo quartet, softly punctuated by organ chords at the ends of phrases. The following soprano solo is softly accompanied by a choir that alternates with the soloist (Example 82*b*) somewhat in the manner of American gospel-song choruses, but with the added variety of changing textures. A device to which Tours resorted in moments of climax is the division of parts, suddenly expanding three voices to six, for instance. This practice, confined to a single chord or a measure, has not been observed in earlier composers.

Tours saved his most impressive ammunition for the end of the piece. An intimation of what is to come can be found in the organ part (Example 82*c*), but the following unison choral passage immediately belies that promise. Finally, the great moment is prepared through a theatrical approach to what has been expected by the listener, the choir sounding forth "O come, all ye faithful" in unison *molto maestoso* (Example 82*d*). The appeal to singers and to congregations is not identical, but both must have derived a tremendous visceral satisfaction from such a piece after having endured the more appropriate, polite, but decidedly second-rate polyphony that came from the struggling quasi-cathedral composers. The easily singable thematic ideas, the prominence of the organ as a full, vital partner in performance, and the introduction of new ideas in unison passages before their continuation in harmonized form brought this music easily into the area where it could be enjoyed by any but the musicians who saw their standards tumbling before its onslaught. Some years earlier Vincent Novello had produced *O come, all ye faithful* as an anthem (No. 166 in *The Musical Times*), and Tours must have been aware of it, although his use of the tune as a rousing climax differs from the varied stanzaic arrangement of Novello.

His Easter anthem, *God hath appointed a day*,[65] has likewise a variety of exciting devices; trumpetlike fanfares from the organ, declamatory recitative, a crescendo passage that gains intensity from the use of insistent pedal point (Example 83), passages for solo quartet repeated by chorus, division of parts at moments of emotional intensity, repetition of short music-text segments at new pitch levels or in rhythmic modification, and finally an ever increasing pace leading to a rousing finale. We may look down our noses at the obvious appeal these pieces made, but the excitement they brought in the wake of the correct, tiresome imitations of earlier cathedral practice must have been tremendous for the thousands of singers whose experience had never included that traditional fare so lauded by the descendants of the Chapel Royal who simultaneously complained about the deterioration of the full choral Service.

The major figure in nineteenth-century English church music was John Stainer (1840–1901). By almost any reckoning he stands above his contemporaries; oddly

---

[65] G. Schirmer 3124.

Example 82. *Sing, O heavens*, Berthold Tours (G. Schirmer 4336, mm. 9–13, 76–84, 102–05, 127–35).

(a)

(b)

(c)

enough, his best accomplishments were those for which he was least known. In addition to important posts he held at Oxford, Cambridge, the University of London, and St. Paul's Cathedral, Stainer was chief inspector in music to the national Board of Education, and was active as an author, producing a treatise on harmony, another on the organ, was co-author with W. A. Barrett of a *Dictionary of Musical Terms* (1876), and edited, with his daughter, *Dufay and His Contemporaries* (1898), an important contribution to the field of musicology.

In our time, mere mention of John Stainer in connection with church music will inevitably draw derogatory comment. Much of this criticism is, of course, well deserved; his writing can be cloyingly saccharine, cliché-ridden, and embarrassingly trite. Yet, his works establish an immediate, familiar identity with the average church-goer. The reasons are not difficult to discover; Stainer provided the type of material that was wanted in his day, and he had a special flair for producing it. Fellowes relates a conversation he had with Stainer shortly before his death, in which he regretted the publication of many of his earlier anthems, but added that "they had been written in response to pressure put upon him in early days by clergy and others, who assured him that they were 'just the thing they wanted'."[66]

There is a dramatic element in Stainer's anthems not often seen in the works of his predecessors. This is the result not only of his musical vocabulary, but also of his choice of texts, many of which were taken from the New Testament. The descriptive quality of these passages provided Stainer with the opportunity to exercise his dramatic compositional talents. A case in point is the anthem for Easter, *They have taken away my Lord*.[67] Here Mary's memorable encounter with the risen Christ, as recorded in John 20, is skillfully blended with Paul's triumphant words in I Corinthians 15:55, "O death, where is thy sting? O grave, where is thy victory?" It is no wonder that such a text, given a sympathetic musical setting, provided a welcome alternative to the essentially passive nature of the psalm settings.

Indeed, Stainer capitalized on the dramatic possibilities of the texts. The opening soprano line could scarcely be more effective in conveying the plaintive voice of Mary as she discovers the empty tomb (Example 84a). One of Stainer's favorite devices is seen in the fourth measure with the melodic leap of a fifth and the resultant appoggiatura on the next accented beat. Another high point occurs when Mary suddenly realizes that she has been conversing with Jesus. Here Stainer moves harmonically from the G minor tonality to the dominant-seventh chord of D major, thus brightly framing Mary's joyful surprise, and, at the same time, preparing for the entrance of the chorus on the victorious theme, "O death, where is thy sting?" (Example 84b).

Stainer is especially skillful in the matter of accompaniments. In his more bombastic anthems, much of the effect is produced at the keyboard and in a variety of ways. He frequently uses the organ to build toward the return of the original choral material. This technique is evident in *I am Alpha and Omega*[68] (Example 85a). Another effect is created by the use of parallel inverted chords accompanying a unison choral line (Example 85b). In *Awake, awake; put on thy strength, O Zion*,[69] Stainer supports the relatively slow-moving choral parts with massive chords in the upper register that create a rhythmic drive and endow the work with heroic splendor (Example 85c).

The harmonic vocabulary found in Stainer's anthems is rich and varied. Secondary dominants, diminished seventh chords, and various augmented sixth chords are numerous. The resultant chromaticism is, however, primarily harmonic rather than melodic. In *Grieve not the Holy Spirit*,[70] chromaticism is used effectively to heighten tension and give added meaning to the text (Example 86).

In formal design, Stainer relied heavily on repetition as a binding force. For example, in *Awake, awake* the initial thematic material (Example 87) occurs, with

[66] Fellowes, *op. cit.*, 224.   [67] Presser 10826.
[68] G. Schirmer 3897.   [69] Novello Anth. 56.   [70] G. Schirmer 4383.

slight variations, no less than five times in the first forty-three measures. Such thematic saturation, when involved with the easily remembered melodies characteristic of Stainer, provides a degree of unity that cannot be achieved in any other way, and is, no doubt, a major factor in the immense popularity of his works.

Example 83. *God hath appointed a day*, Berthold Tours (G. Schirmer 3124, mm. 23–28).

By any calculation, Stainer's most widely used piece is *God so loved the world*.[71] Few church-choir libraries are without it; yet, it was not conceived as an anthem. Designed as a quartet in his famous cantata, *The Crucifixion*, the piece has been available in octavo editions for many years, and is for all intents and purposes an anthem. A basically simple, yet sympathetic setting of one of the best-loved passages in the Bible accounts for its enduring popularity, and it can be extremely effective if it is not subjected to overinterpretation.

[71] Among the numerous editions available may be mentioned Ditson 332-08621 and G. Schirmer 3798. The piece has been arranged for other voice combinations in some instances.

The stylistic traits evident in Stainer's anthems are not unique with him; virtually all of them can be found in the works of his contemporaries. Rather, his genius was the skill with which he combined these features into a total effect.

In every period there have been men able to continue in traditional ways while the world changed about them. English composers whose images were dimmed by the long shadows of Mendelssohn, Schneider, Spohr, and Gounod found it difficult to provide anything more vital than those commonly accepted idols of religious music provided the choral market. Only a few adventurous men broke away from their comfortable, patterned utterances in their own church compositions. Stanford and Parry,

Example 84.   *They have taken away my Lord*, John Stainer (Presser 10826, mm. 1–6, 23–32).

(a)

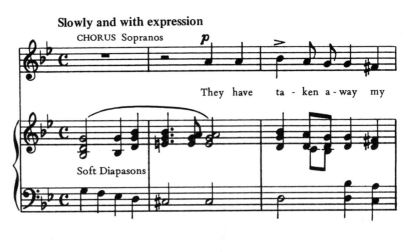

among a few others, expanded the harmonic and melodic idiom to some extent, but there was still a practice of writing in the older style of verse anthems and full anthems with verses. More interesting than the pieces of Bexfield or Ouseley, yet showing traditional practices, are the works of George C. Martin (1844–1916) and John Varley Roberts (1841–1920). The former is little known now, although his works had some vogue during his lifetime.

Employing the Easter story from the St. Matthew Gospel, Martin was one of a number of men to write an anthem entitled *As it began to dawn*.[72] An eighteen-measure organ introduction sets the mood with six statements of a three-measure

[72] H. W. Gray, **C.M.R. 130.**

phrase (Example 88) at various pitch levels, building from *piano* to *fortissimo*. The scriptural text is distributed between men's voices and chorus, and a solo voice (either soprano or tenor) takes up the piece at the segment "Fear not ye." At that point the full chorus enters with a stanza of the Easter hymn, "Jesus Christ is risen today," but using, oddly enough, two lines of text from stanza one and two lines from stanza three.

Example 85. *I am Alpha and Omega*, John Stainer (G. Schirmer 3897, mm. 27–31, mm. 55–59).

(a)

(b)

(c) *Awake, awake; put on thy strength, O Zion*, John Stainer (Novello Anth. 56, mm. 30–33).

Example 86. *Grieve not the Holy Spirit,* John Stainer (G. Schirmer 4383, mm. 42–50).

put   a - way   from   you_____   with   all   mal - ice.

put   a - way   from   you_____   with   all   mal - ice.

put   a - way   from   you_____   with   all   mal - ice.

put   a - way   from   you_____   with   all   mal - ice.

There follows a jubilant ending employing the text fragments, "Alleluia" and "He is risen from the dead." The piece is bound together by a somewhat obvious, yet effective recall of thematic materials; melodic sections that appear first with one portion of text return later with another, the accompaniment making whatever difference in mood is desired (Example 89).

Hail, gladdening light,[73] a festive full anthem with verse accompanied by organ and optional brass choir, shows the influence of the Oxford Movement. Its text is a translation from the Greek by John Keble,[74] and the general spirit of the piece recalls the impressive days of the Chapel Royal in a romantic fashion. There are melodies of noble breadth, and the closing section is a fugue, the subject of which is finally stated as a unison phrase at the opening of a pompous coda. The piece is still effective. It gives a

great deal of satisfaction to singers, and a congregation exposed to its successful production feels great things have been accomplished by the musical forces. Its size and
relative complexity, together with a taste for more direct communication, have all
conspired to minimize its appeal in this generation.

J. V. Roberts has fared badly in our time, for he is remembered mainly for his
short anthem, *Seek ye the Lord,*[75] a piece that illustrates both the appeal and the lack of
variety that infused the works of lesser composers of his day. Opening with a tenor
solo in two contrasting sections, the piece progresses to a considerably modified

Example 87.   *Awake, awake; put on thy strength, O Zion,* John Stainer (Novello
Anth. 56, mm. 1–3).

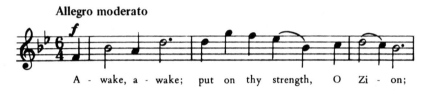

version of the melodies for soloist with choral accompaniment, broken by brief choral
interludes. What rhythmic vitality the anthem has is supplied by the constant figura-
tion in the inner lines of the accompaniment (Example 90). The solo line is constantly
supported by a prominent doubling in the keyboard part. This feature, no doubt, has
helped the piece to survive, for even the feeblest of soloists can gain confidence from
the instrumental support. *Behold, I send the promise of my Father*[76] is a full anthem with
an opening recitative for tenor. Essentially a note-against-note piece with organ support and interludes, it expands rarely into treble-dominated style and employs a few
brief imitations. The final section is made up of four statements, somewhat modified
upon repetition, of a two-phrase period that does not bear up under such extensive
treatment. What might have been made bearable by effective linking passages in the
organ becomes mundane through a lack of inventiveness and the trivial accompaniment passages that fill spaces between *colla parte* sections.

Only two anthems by C. Hubert H. Parry (1848–1918) are given extended discussion by Fellowes,[77] and both are festival works not typical of anthem literature in this
period. Neither are they examples of practical church choir material for today's
services. For example, *Hear my words, ye people,*[78] one of the two he mentions, is a
cantata-anthem reminiscent of the large-scale works of Purcell, Blow, and Boyce. An
elaborate organ part substitutes for the orchestra of earlier years, there are soprano and
bass solos, and a quartet (or semichorus) alternates with the full choir. There is variety

---

[75] Among the editions still available are G. Schirmer 3731 and Lorenz 466. The piece has been arranged
for various combinations other than SATB.

[76] Novello 554.

[77] Fellowes, *op. cit.,* 246–47.   [78] *TECM,* IV, 158–80; Novello 442.

Example 88. *As it began to dawn*, George C. Martin (H. W. Gray, C.M.R. 130, mm. 1–18).

Example 89. *As it began to dawn*, George C. Martin (H. W. Gray, C.M.R. 130, mm. 19–20, 36–38, 57–59, 61–63).

Theme a

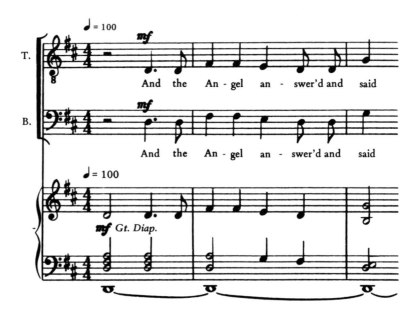

Theme b

in key and meter, the effect of the composition is grandiose, and the burden of performance is sensibly placed on the organist and solo voices. That is not to say that the
choral parts are unworthy of consideration, for they are given a varied group of
settings; unison declamation, *alternatim* passages with the quartet, and chordal sections
with a busy accompaniment. Nevertheless, the burden of part-singing lies with the
quartet, which has more complex rhythmic materials than the full chorus, has several
opportunities to sing unaccompanied sections, and generally is entrusted with the more
expressive passages that are not given to the soloists. Recognition of Parry's skill in a
large work of this nature is academic and of small help to those who hope to find
performance materials for Sunday services among his works, but it demonstrates
undeniably that his was a superior talent.

Several of his works that have had performance in English cathedrals can serve
practical needs, even though they go beyond the generally accepted limits of text
common to anthem literature. Five are listed in a recent paper,[79] one of which may
serve as typical of his shorter pieces. *My soul, there is a country*[80] is one of a set of six
motets published near the end of Parry's life. The poem is by Henry Vaughan (1621–
1695); its flights of fancy range farther into introspective realms more commonly
associated with secular pieces having religious overtones than do those texts usually
used for anthems. It is not difficult to find the musical appeal this piece had, and still
has, for choristers. The harmonies are enriched beyond those of the preceding generation; internal notes repeated as pedal tones give momentary shades of added sixth

[79] *Sixty Years of Cathedral Music,* 20.
[80] Davies and Ley, *op. cit.,* 300–308; *TECM,* V, 1–8.

Example 90.   Extract from J. V. Roberts' *Seek ye the Lord*, measures 45–49.

chords and varied types of seventh chords, and dominant seventh and diminished seventh chords resolve in irregular fashion. These, along with other post-Mendelssohn harmonic devices render the pieces satisfying to singers as did much secular music of the first third of the century. The secular world had grown accustomed to the relatively intense sound of successive seventh chords and of enriched triads, but the use of such harmonic density was still daringly experimental in church music. The piece mentioned here is broken into short sections of varied meter, tempo, and key, all of which create an emotional aura in which singers may easily enjoy themselves. Counterpoint is not employed as a major feature, but brief imitative passages occur. The most effective imitation is achieved through interlocking sequential patterns that permeate all voice parts.

At this point also should be mentioned Parry's setting of a fifteenth-century carol, *Welcome, Yule!*[81] (Example 91) that illustrates, along with other such pieces we shall encounter, the interest in recapturing traditional songs and dealing with them in dignified fashion. The use of carols was not reserved to the twentieth century, but efforts in the nineteenth had generally been poorly done, and the door-to-door singing by children had come to be regarded as a nuisance on a par with petty beggary.[82] The appearance of these pieces, set with a skill that appears ingenuous but is actually much to be admired, supplied a new kind of choral piece to groups in and out of church. This setting of Parry's deals with five stanzas of text, the fifth being a slightly expanded modification of material that appears as rapidly moving stanzas earlier. The harmonic variety of Parry's other works is not so apparent, partly because of the simplicity of the material, partly because of the constantly rapid harmonic changes.

The first English musician of our modern era who could be considered a peer of Continental composers was Charles Villiers Stanford (1852–1924). England had long been without a man who ranked with the best in all areas of composition, although she had constantly found a flow of those who were capable in writing for the stage, in setting light music, or in devoting their attentions to religious music. For the first time since Henry Purcell, there came a man, Irish-born to be sure, who was trained to the highest level of the art, who produced symphonies, concertos, chamber works, operas, oratorios, and other smaller works in addition to the usual complement of Services and anthems. For such a man to achieve eminence outside his native islands, however, was another matter. He was born into a decade over which towered Romanticism's giants: Schumann, Liszt, Wagner, Verdi, and Gounod were in their forties; the memory of Spohr, Mendelssohn, and Chopin was still fresh; Tchaikovsky, Dvořák, Brahms, and Saint-Saëns were to become widely known before Stanford emerged from his student years. It will be interesting to see whether the finest training of England and Germany could produce a man better fitted to cope with the problems posed by the English anthem than had the haphazard tuition of private instruction or the formalized apprenticeship of the Chapel Royal absorbed by others who composed in that genre.

[81] Novello (Novello's Part-Song Book, Second Series, No. 1324).
[82] Scholes, *The Oxford Companion to Music*, 155.

Among the anthems Stanford composed in the nineteenth century,[83] one of the most interesting is the one he wrote for the funeral of Henry Bradshaw in 1886. *Blessed are the dead which die in the Lord* appeared first as No. 522 in *The Musical Times* as an unaccompanied setting SATB of part of Revelation 14:13. Beginning with measure five, the soprano quotes a short section of the medieval melody *Angelus ad*

[83] *MGG*, XII, 1175–76, gives a list of anthems with dates of composition and publication in some cases. The list lacks some titles. The list in *Grove's*, VIII, 49–50, is also incomplete.

Example 91. *Welcome, Yule!*, C. Hubert H. Parry (Novello 1324, mm. 1–5).

Reproduced by permission of Novello & Co., Ltd.

Virginem[84] (Example 92), the tune of which had been brought to Stanford's attention by Bradshaw. Stanford revised the piece by the addition of about ten measures of material, mainly for solo soprano and choir sopranos *a 3* and *a 4*, taking previously unused text segments from the same source as the original version. This new anthem, given the title *I heard a voice from heaven*,[85] and appearing in 1910, has had some continuing popularity.

84 Gustave Reese, *Music in the Middle Ages* (New York: W. W. Norton and Co., 1940), 244, 390, and 404–5, discusses sources and treatments of this tune. It is printed in Harold Gleason (ed.), *Examples of Music before 1400* (New York: Appleton-Century-Crofts, Inc., 1942), 51–54, and *The New Oxford History of Music*, III, 116.

85 Novello's Short Anthems, No. 157.

Composers prior to Stanford generally sought a smoothly flowing melodic outline in setting texts, reserving large leaps for moments of excitement and emphasis. Some movement away from this diatonic emphasis may be noted in Stainer's compositions, but he achieved his effect in a number of cases through sequential reiteration of a short passage that contained a leap. By the time the passage had been repeated at different pitch levels, the impression of a large compass within a single melody was left with the listener. Stanford used large leaps more consistently, making them the means of covering a large area without motivic repetition. This is true of early anthems

Example 92.   The *Angelus ad virginem* melody as used in Stanford's *Blessed are the dead* and in its original form (transposed).

such as *Blessed are the dead* (Example 93*a*) and *The Lord is my shepherd* (1886) (Example 93*b*), and later pieces such as the motet *O living will* (1908) (Example 93*c*), and the anthem *While shepherds watched* (1923) (Example 93*d*). The instances of such breadth of phrase can be repeated from portions of other works as well, but it is evident from these few passages that these soaring examples are the immediate ancestors of the noble melodies that finally emerge in the music of Ralph Vaughan Williams, notably in such tunes as "Sine nomine" and some others to be mentioned in Chapter 9.

The organ accompaniments of Stanford's anthems are varied, rarely being limited to simple *colla parte* duplication. Pedal points, expansions of the vocal texture by duplicating the alto part in the top of the organ line, *alternatim* sections against unaccompanied choral segments, and simple sustained chords against active choral material all play a part in these pieces. While Stanford was not experimental in matters of form, harmony, or text selection, he did explore numerous possibilities in the setting of his texts, and his excursions were to become the basis for later stylistic changes.

Stanford's high position in English musical life placed him prominently before the public, and a number of young musicians were under his influence, at the Royal College of Music and elsewhere. Among his pupils were Charles Wood, Ralph Vaughan Williams, Herbert Howells, T. Tertius Noble, and still others whose place in church music will be the subject of discussion in later pages.

Apart from Stainer, John Henry Maunder (1858–1920) is probably better known among church-choir singers than any other nineteenth-century English composer. His cantatas, especially *From Olivet to Calvary*, rivaled Stainer's *Crucifixion* in popularity, and even today one can scarcely find an older church choral library where his works are not represented, even though they may no longer be performed. In the face of this, it is curious that his name does not appear in either Baker's or Grove's dictionaries. This apparent oversight was probably due to the fact that Maunder was not a product of the cathedral tradition. Scholes states that Maunder's "musical career was chiefly that of organist and choirmaster of various churches in the outskirts of London."[86] In any event, it is probably safe to assert that his works were esteemed more by volunteer choir singers than by his peers, for he had that capacity for easy and obvious melodic invention that establishes immediate rapport with the common man.

Of his several well-known anthems, *Praise the Lord, O Jerusalem*[87] is the most notable. It is a large, sectional anthem extending through 150 measures, and it carries a high degree of formal organization. Perhaps the most interesting aspect of the anthem is the combined effect of Maunder's melodic and harmonic skill. Who could ever forget the grandiose melodic sweep or the strong harmonic structure of the opening measures (Example 94), where the Psalmist's spirit of unbounded joy is so completely captured?

Nevertheless, Maunder's style was not destined to endure for long. Indications of a significant change could already be seen in the works of Parry, and they would be solidly confirmed by both Wood and Noble. The old era of obvious, comfortable, and often trite musical expression so characteristic of Victorian romanticism was giving place to a trend that would ultimately make the anthem a prominent feature of England's rising musical eminence.

With Basil Harwood (1859–1949) we again find a strong inclination to capture the past. His carol *All my heart this night rejoices* (No. 1196 in *The Musical Times*) employs a translation of the German text "Fröhlich soll mein Herze springen," made by Catherine Winkworth (1829–1878), who contributed a number of excellent German poems to the Oxford Movement. Harwood's setting is in the form of a full anthem with verse, calling for *decani* and *cantoris* division of the choir. The indications appear to be used for the sake of achieving antiphonal effects rather than as a sterile gesture toward reviving cathedral practice. Harwood drew on a John Mason Neale translation of a Latin poem for his *Draw nigh, and take the Body of the Lord* (*The Musical Times*, No. 1080), a strophic setting in the form of a full anthem with verses, the last of which is a unison statement with a sturdy accompaniment. The bold final statement of a hymn-anthem tune has become common since that time, the accompaniment furnishing a strong support for a unison melody, but the practice does not find its beginnings in the works of Harwood and his contemporaries. It is evident, however, that this is the period where it becomes a common means of closing a piece, the chorus breaking into harmony for the closing "Amen."

---

[86] Scholes, *The Oxford Companion to Music*, 614.
[87] Ditson 332-14421.

Charles Wood (1866–1926), a student of Stanford's, and his successor in a Cambridge professorship, showed the effects of that relationship. His taste for the enriched harmonies that his teacher had introduced—for the poetry of the Oxford Movement as seen in *Jesu! the very thought is sweet*,[88] and poetry of a mystical nature in *Expectans expectavi*[89] (in English, despite its title)—places him clearly in the path that led from the exploratory early decades of the twentieth century to the vital works of Vaughan Williams and his generation. While the former piece is a simple motet setting, the melodic interest is considerable, and the text is never reduced to note-against-note syllabic level. The latter piece displays to a better degree the skills and imagination of Wood. He had the advantage of good training at the Royal College of Music, and his choral settings display a skill that is not limited to the favorite devices of church composers. Harmonic enrichment may be attributed to a liberal use of nondominant seventh chords that are not restricted by regular resolutions. His choral style is as easily adaptable to the part-song as it is to the anthem, and the freedom with which texts

[88] Davies and Ley, *op. cit.*, 220–22.   [89] Summy-Birchard B-1147.

Example 93. Typical melodic contours in Stanford's compositions.
(a) *Blessed are the dead*, measures 21–28, soprano part

(b) *The Lord is my shepherd*, measures 103–12, voices in unison

(c) *O living will*, measures 12–23, soprano part

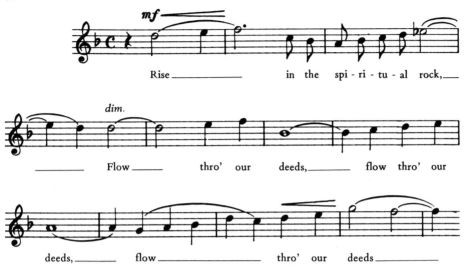

Used with permission of Stainer & Bell, Ltd., Reigate, Surrey.

(d) *While shepherds watched*, measures 28–38

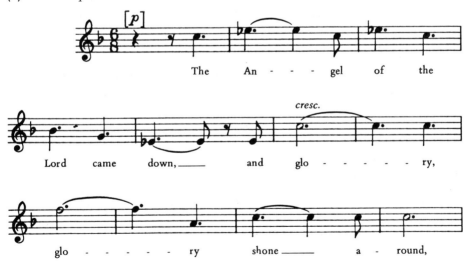

Copyright by Novello & Co., Ltd. Used by permission.

such as the one used here deal with theology makes a thin line of demarcation between one type of piece and another.

To judge a composer by what he produces as occasional music is often unfair to him if he has, in the course of such work, to write for lesser forces than is his custom. In *Summer ended*,[90] a piece Wood composed for the Harvest Festival at a preparatory school where the choir consisted of a tenor, a bass, and six each of first and second trebles, he again demonstrated his skill in producing a piece within the demands of the situation, but not beneath his dignity as a composer. There is a stanza for men's voices, another to the same tune but different accompaniment for high voices, a third of entirely different character for all voices in parts with some unison passages, and a closing setting unison and *a 4* of the opening melody. The accompaniment patterns have sufficient variety to minimize the repetition of a relatively simple melody; except for a few spots in the full sections, the harmonic interest is assigned to the organ.

Wood's contemporary, Thomas Tertius Noble (1867–1953), was a student at the Royal College of Music at the same time as Wood, and the marks of harmonic richness, wide-ranging melody, and sophisticated control of medium are to be found in his music as well, a fact that may possibly be attributed to their joint association with Stanford and their mutual exposure to other musical influences of the time. Wood's reputation was made entirely in England, with some of his publications appearing in the United States; Noble, on the other hand, moved to New York City in 1912 as organist of the newly rebuilt St. Thomas' Church, where he introduced and developed the cathedral tradition. His boys' choir attracted both students and attention, and his influence has been considerable in America. However, most of his pieces that have frequent hearings were written in England. One short, simple composition, its poem linking it with the antiquarian interest stirred by the Oxford Movement, is *Come, O Creator Spirit, come*.[91] Its modality, variety of texture, and general simplicity are appealing qualities that are fortified by a wide range of dynamic changes reflecting the text peaks of all its phrases.

Two of his anthems that have achieved great popularity in this country, although they date from before his arrival, show Noble's love of sharp dynamic contrasts. Both *Fierce was the wild billow*[92] and *Souls of the righteous*[93] use these sharply differentiated levels of volume, and both depend entirely upon the vocal forces to achieve their effects. Even though Noble was fully capable—indeed, renowned for his ability—of writing excellent accompaniments, he wrote both anthems as unaccompanied works, bringing to them the tradition of the cathedral full anthem with a new vigorous approach. His careful selection of texts accounts for much of his success as a writer of dramatic anthems. *Fierce was the wild billow* is Neale's translation of a text by St. Anatolius. It consists of a series of short phrases that invite varied expression, and it is capable of treatment that could not successfully be given to many other poems

[90] G. Schirmer 11479.   [91] Davies and Ley, *op. cit.*, 70–72.
[92] G. Schirmer 5283.   [93] Presser 20277.

Example 94. *Praise the Lord, O Jerusalem*, J. H. Maunder (Ditson 332–14421, mm. 9–13).

(Example 95). In *Souls of the righteous* Noble exposed the opposite side of his nature. Dealing with a poetic setting in long flowing phrases, the basic quality is one of quietness with a few sharply contrasted exuberant shouts. The contrast is not limited to full chorus alone, but is employed in the section for solo quartet as well. His treatment of material in *Go to dark Gethsemane*[94] (Example 96), the one work at hand that was completed after Noble's arrival in NewYork, gains in dramatic strength what it has given up in the way of sharp contrasts. The peaks of excitement are few and widely spaced, and the pictorial possibilities of the text are squeezed dry. As in his other pieces, thematic organization, sectional repetition, and harmonic modification of repeated melodies play a large part in unifying the composition.

This chapter has covered a period of approximately a century, and we have examined a product that was essentially Victorian in style. Changes that took place near the end of that period were, because of their number, more clearly apparent than those of earlier centuries. The appearance of these elements of change in simple procession does not seem of great importance, but an appraisal of them as a group indicates that they heralded the beginning of the modern period in anthem composition. It is proper that we review them briefly here before we move on to other matters, inasmuch as their various features will again be of importance in the material that follows World War I.

While the effects of the Oxford Movement were felt most directly on the cathedral ideal of the Anglican Church, certain changes were also apparent in the parish churches and the various free churches that developed from the Nonconformist chapel practices. We have already considered the musical changes that stemmed from the movement of organs and choirs from the West Gallery. We should consider the possibility that the return of women to the choirs, after they had moved to the front of the church, laid open the way for music of wider dynamic range than when only boys sang treble. Fortunately, poetry of greater emotional variety was introduced at the same time. Translations of texts from other times and traditions, newly conceived poetry by English writers of the nineteenth century, and some poetry from English writers of an earlier time made their way into choral settings. An indefinable, but positive feeling of mysticism pervaded some of the texts, and their emotional appeal, different from that of scriptural passages, was strong indeed.

Musically there was a freedom in melodic outlines, their quickly recognizable features being longer spans of melody, wider ranges in the single voice parts, enriched harmonies that moved freely out of the confined patterns that reflected Mendelssohn, Gounod, and Spohr, and into the wider range of ideas that can be traced, at least in part, to Wagnerian musical liberties. While anthems had been made up of short sections prior to this time, the sections became less clearly defined and the necessity for each to be a complete unit grew less. As the sections flowed into each other, they were often linked by imaginative organ parts. If the anthems were unaccompanied, vocal

---

[94] H. W. Gray, C.M.R. 501.

Example 95. *Fierce was the wild billow*, T. Tertius Noble (G. Schirmer 5283, mm. 10–18).

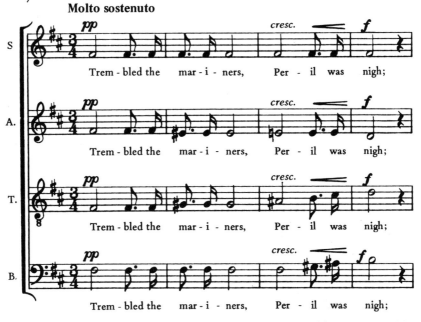

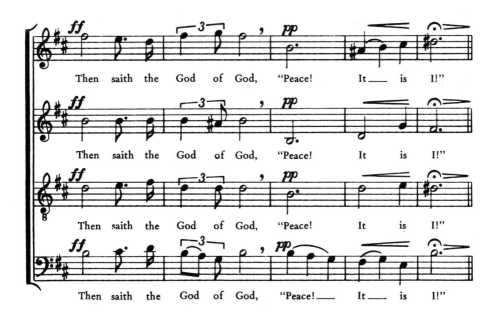

Example 96. *Go to dark Gethsemane*, T. Tertius Noble (H. W. Gray, C.M.R. 501, mm. 47–53).

Copyright, 1918, by The H. W. Gray Co., Inc. Renewed 1946. Used by permission.

links gave thrilling possibilities to singers who had earlier been dependent upon choral platitudes or formal organ bridges for modulations or the introduction of new sectional themes. Accompanied anthems were supported by organ parts that were elaborations of the vocal lines or that served as substitutes for orchestra. The unaccompanied anthems, while printed with *colla parte* keyboard scores, were intended to be sung *a cappella*, returning the choral sound to the ideal of the Renaissance full anthem.

Emerging with a new vigor was the hymn anthem. As simple material that could be sung in unison, with simple harmony, or as an elaborate set of variations, it had the possibilities that the chorale had once given Lutheran Germany, even though it could not fashionably be adapted to multimovement pieces as had the chorale to the cantata. The hymn anthem was destined to continue in favor, not only in churches where choral forces were meager, but in those richly endowed with singers.

After the Oxford Movement it became increasingly difficult to know whether a published piece of music was intended specifically for the resurgent cathedral practice or for the country church—the two practices tended to merge as the latter imitated the former. As commercial publishers began to print anthems as single octavo copies or as parts for periodical publications, the earlier identification tags, "for Cathedral Choirs" and "for use in Parish Churches," slipped away, for no publisher wished to limit his market when a piece could be sold to several kinds of purchasers. For this reason it has been necessary to make fewer references to exact use, and we shall continue to use general terms of reference in the future unless a piece is marked specifically for one practice or the other.

The development of commercial publication also gave opportunities to composers who were outside the cathedral tradition. Their publications reached the same wide market as those of men who were trained in the Establishment. The distinguishing marks between High Church and Low, cathedral and parish church, Anglican and Nonconformist, were less visible. The quality of the musical setting was finally becoming more important than the composer's birthright.

CHAPTER EIGHT

The Rise of an American Market for Choral Music

Until the middle of the nineteenth century, the American publisher and performer depended upon the imported materials from English publishers, either in their original books or as part of American collections, for most of their music. Native composers had been few, their following had either been localized or short-lived, and the glories of European masterpieces had always been lauded as superior. With the second half of the century, there began the regular traffic of promising young Americans to the musical centers of Europe—especially to the German conservatories—for training in performance and composition. Some of these young men returned to produce church music that reflected a consistent degree of craftsmanship. By the end of the century there was a strong grass-roots movement in composition. Composers who had a flair for easy melody and comfortable chord relationships produced a large amount of anthem material aimed at the untrained volunteer choir. It is to these widely separated styles—the skillfully contrived pieces for professional quartets with or without supporting chorus, and the completely obvious, simple pieces for amateur groups—that we must give our attention, noting at the same time the continuance of the collections that had been so important in the first half of the century.

Music does not appear without some reason; publishers do not produce countless anthems without recognizing some market that will pay a profitable return. These new directions in anthem material were tied directly to a traceable cause, the proliferation of churches and church choirs.

Although smaller population centers lacked the numbers and variety of churches that can be found in New York by the middle of the century, the picture there is typical of some elements that could be found in any city, large or small. The groups that developed most rapidly and widely were the Methodist, Presbyterian, Episcopal, and Baptist,[1] exactly those that could be expected to find a regular place for the anthem and the set piece in a regular religious service. There was no consistent pattern in the use of choirs among those churches; their placement, constitution, and organization varied.

> In some churches the choir was clustered near the clerk's desk; in others it sang from the gallery over the narthex; in still others the choir occupied the space across the front of the church. Vested choirs were unknown in New York, since they were usually out of sight. They were usually composed of voluntary singers, although some churches had introduced professional singers and quartets as early as 1825.[2]

These professional singers served in two ways: either to bolster and support the existing volunteer choir or to substitute for it. Their existence, as we shall see, brought about a change in the published music for churches, with some effects that have outlasted the popularity of the groups that caused them. Various reasons have been advanced for the rise of quartet choirs, among them the ease with which music could be prepared, the lack of necessity for recruiting a volunteer group, the greater satisfaction of skilled performance—and the attendant evils of egoism in the choir loft—as well as the one that follows:

> It is not clear how early in the century the quartet choir became fashionable. It is hardly likely that it was as common in the thirties and forties as it was in the eighties and nineties. In the case of the Broadway Tabernacle, for instance, the structure of the organ gallery in its second church building prevented the participation of a chorus choir. It may be that the architecture of the churches built after 1840 conspired with the rising tide of fashion to give the quartet choir the pre-eminent position it enjoyed at the end of the nineteenth century.[3]

While the use of quartet choirs was only one of many matters that had to be considered by musicians and clergy, it assumed a position of considerable prominence for a time. At the 1845 meeting of the American Musical Convention, seventeen questions pertaining to the betterment of church music were distributed to the members for discussion. The ninth question was "What are the advantages derivable from Quartette Choirs?"[4] and its answer, presented a day later, after discussions and committee meetings, was "*Resolved*, That all the advantages derivable from Quartette Choirs in Churches can be combined in larger choirs, and that when larger choirs can be obtained it is not advisable to limit the number to four persons."[5] That the subject

---

[1] [Anton] Paul Allwardt, "Sacred Music in New York City, 1800–1850" (unpublished D.Sac.Mus. dissertation, Union Theological Seminary, 1950), 9.

[2] *Ibid.*, 20.   [3] *Ibid.*, 64.

[4] *Proceedings of the American Musical Convention: Held in The Broadway Tabernacle, on the 8th, 9th, and 10th of October, 1845, with the Addresses* (New York: Saxton & Miles, 1845), 5.

[5] *Ibid.*, 7.

should have come up for general discussion gives some idea of its importance. But it is only when another matter—that of congregational singing—is viewed along with it that it assumes perspective. The Reverend Raymond Seely (dates unknown), one of several speakers at the Convention, indicated that in many cases the only music to be found in a church was that supplied by the choir. He suggested that "*Congregational Singing should be revived.* In many or most of the churches this good old custom is obsolete."[6] It need not be assumed that he exaggerated, or that his views represented a limited part of the American scene. His remarks were not challenged by Thomas Hastings, Nathaniel D. Gould, Solomon Warriner, or any other of the notables in the audience. Nor should we think that Seely reflected only the practice in sophisticated congregations of the larger cities, for he held a pastorate in Bristol, Connecticut, and his problems were doubtless held in common with other pastors from country and small-city churches. Speaking apparently from experience, he continued:

> Another evil resulting from the custom of regarding the choir as performers for, rather than leaders in the worship of the people, is felt more especially in the country churches; where the congregation becomes so entirely dependent on the choir, that it rests with a few leading singers to decide whether the church shall have any music at all in its services. In this way some churches have, at times, been forced to omit this part of public worship altogether.[7]

What Seely describes here is similar to what happened in England's West Gallery practice.

Congregational singing would not need to concern us at all, except that its absence raises another question about the function of a choir. Was it, during this period, the only vocal participant in the music of certain churches? Apparently it was. Five years after Seely's advertisement of the problem, another writer describes a typical American Sunday service:

> Go into our churches on Sunday throughout the land. The music is going on. Observe the attitude and appearance of the congregations assembled. Do they appear like persons engaged in a solemn act of devotion? In some individual case, perhaps; but applied to the great mass of worshippers? For let us ask again, is listening to music, devotion? Is hearing a choir sing, worship? Is a *passive* state of *any* kind, worship?
>
> . . .
>
> It is *difficult* for a congregation in the sitting posture, with the open eye, the open book and the undevotional attitude, *difficult*, thus, to listen to music, with the thoughts on the performers, and to be devotional at the same time. It is *difficult* to be, what congregations naturally wish, and expect to be, artistically impressed, or musically gratified, and to be worshipping God at the same moment. It is *difficult* for the *mind* to follow consecutively the devotional thought of the hymn, with the unwandering attention of heart-worship, at the *slow pace* with which musical articulation must necessarily proceed, unless the tongue *be itself uttering the words of devotion*, and thereby *nailing the mind* to the devotional thought.[8]

---

[6] *Ibid.*, 61.   [7] *Ibid.*, 63.
[8] R. Storrs Willis, *Church Chorals and Choir Studies* (New York: Clark, Austin, & Smith, 1850), 9–10.

The reason for the decline of congregational singing cannot be traced with certainty, but there may be some point in considering its possible connection with printed books. The collections that followed the earliest instructive manuals tended more and more to favor the trained singers who had learned some musical skills in the singing-schools. As these singers became better equipped than their untrained counterparts, they not only sought each other out, but proceeded to more complex music than could be sung by the average worshiper. Add to this the natural reluctance of many people to raise their voices in song, and the deterioration of congregational singing becomes a hard fact. We have noted that the collections devoted more and more space to anthems, set pieces, motets, and harmonized chants as they moved into the nineteenth century. The plight of the parishioner who had no skill, no book of music, and no desire to sing is firmly established.

Hymn collections without music had been widely used in America since the last decade of the eighteenth century, when the Methodists and Baptists led the way in printing their own.[9] We need retrace such activity no farther than the end of the era of tuneless hymnbooks to see what a great change was wrought by the printing of tune-books designed specifically for the congregation. In 1843 the American Baptist Publications and Sunday School Society authorized the printing of a hymnal that would, in their opinion, best suit the needs of their denomination. *The Psalmist*[10]

> marked a decided advance in the worship by Baptists. It delivered them from the era of the "Psalms and Hymns" compromise, from "Watts entire," and from the low level of some of the spiritual songs. It also added some of the better writers of the growing Evangelical hymnody.[11]

One thing the collection could not do; that was, to limit the selection of tunes to those appropriate for the texts, or to expand the number of tunes that a congregation might use without depending on the older multipurpose collections. An early solution was found in printing a volume that contained, on facing pages, all the texts that could be sung to a single tune. In its first edition the volume had no denominational limitations; the publishers hoped to capture a segment of the total market.[12] Two years after the date of the original introduction, the substance of a new Preface indicates acceptance of the book, with suitable modification and expansion, by "a large number of. . . Baptist Churches."[13]

No single publication of this type can be given credit for the eventual change that occurred in American churches. The idea of providing a limited amount of text with

[9] Julian, *A Dictionary of Hymnology*, I, 57–58.

[10] Baron Stow and S. F. Smith, *The Psalmist: A New Collection of Hymns for the Use of the Baptist Churches* (Boston: Gould and Lincoln, 1843).

[11] John M. Lilley, "A History of Baptist Hymnody in America (1639–1844)" (unpublished Master's thesis, Baylor University, 1964), 86.

[12] *The Baptist Hymn and Tune Book: Being "The Plymouth Collection" Enlarged, and Adapted to the Use of Baptist Churches* (New York: Sheldon, Blakeman & Co., 1858). This "authorized" version contains the original Introduction, dated 1855.

[13] *Ibid.*, [iii].

Example 97.   *Sweetly come those strains melodius*, George F. Root (*The Diapason*, 338).

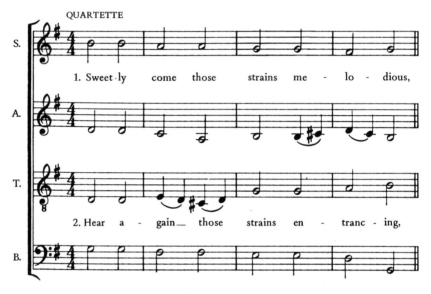

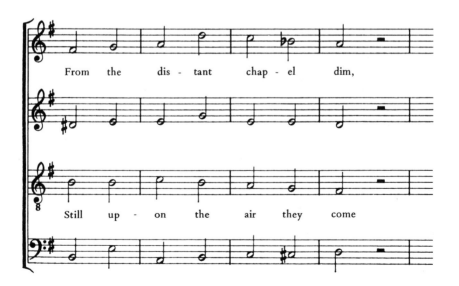

CHORUS (Let this represent a distant Chorus — mouths shut.)

Hm

1. Those swell - ing strains,

2. A - gain those strains,

suitable music, in a form that could be placed in every parishioner's hands, separated again the functions of choir and congregation. Choirs were destined to devote their efforts to singing to the congregation, rather than in its place. The doctrinal propriety of this emphasis on the concert aspect of church music has been much debated. No single answer has emerged, and pursuit of its merits or unseemly aspects will serve no purpose here.

When the choir was set apart as a group that prepared special music for the service, a number of new possibilities emerged. The membership of choirs tended to become more specialized. Churches that were dissatisfied with volunteer chorus choirs, as they were called, and which could afford to pay for their music, employed quartets of professional singers, removing the process of musical worship farther than ever from the church members. Composers, seeing the arrival of proficient performers on a generally static level of quality, began to write music that displayed the skills of these singers. On the other hand, in churches where taste or financial limitations did not encourage the quartet, volunteer choirs flourished. Church records are probably available to support this view, but they are not necessary. Ample evidence may be found, as we shall see, in the proliferation of printed music, in magazine form or in octavo single copies.

When we last considered American publications, the overwhelming bulk of printed material was being borrowed, transformed, and lifted out of context, from European works, some of them of greater size and different function from their destined use in American churches as anthems, set pieces, or hymns. The situation in the last third of the nineteenth century is one in which American composition is again sought out, prized, and promoted.

Two types of composer appeared on the American scene: the one who went to Europe—usually Germany—to be trained in the traditions of the masters, and the one who learned at home, usually less skillfully and in less depth than the one who spent his years abroad. The foreign student returned home as a student of composition, prepared to try works in the larger forms, both vocal and instrumental; the American product was more likely to limit his attempts to keyboard works, solo songs, or short pieces for the church. In any case, he was less likely to be heard in places where criticism of his skills would be public. Unfortunately for our study, many of the latter appeared on the scene, sensible that their music would not be derided simply because it was for the church and, therefore, it must be above reproach because of its intentions rather than because of its level of composition or performance. Raymond Seely touched on this matter in his lecture to the American Musical Convention in 1845, scoring church members for their lack of interest or critical attitude "when they, in some instances, rest contented with, or allow of music in the house of God which would be hissed at a public concert, hooted at the evening serenade, and secretly laughed at in the parlor."[14] He did not name either composers or pieces, but our

---

[14] *Ibid.*, 56.

Example 98. *All nations whom thou hast made*, L. O. Emerson (*Jubilate*, 231).

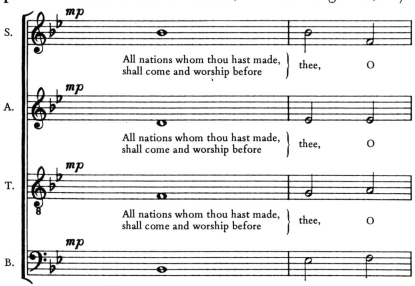

examination of materials in print just prior to the date of his lecture gives little choice in pointing the finger of scorn toward some of the books that were discussed in Chapter 6. Neither his criticism nor the efforts of publishers and choir leaders could stem the tide of mediocrity. An interest in singing had been developed, an interest without a corresponding discriminatory taste—as had also been the case in England through the development of choral societies—by the singing-school movement. Publishers, composers, and modifiers of music all moved quickly into the vacuum, righteously proclaiming their service to the cause of music while bringing it to the lowest level of taste seen in America.

The publication of collections styled in the manner of those by Lowell Mason, William Bradbury, and others continued unabated in the latter half of the nineteenth century. Reflecting a popular taste in religious choral music, many of these volumes were compiled and contributed to by men also associated with the gospel-song movement.

In 1860, George F. Root (1820–1895) edited *The Diapason*,[15] a collection intended for choirs, singing-schools, musical conventions, and social gatherings. The traditional section on music notation was the work of Lowell Mason, to whom Root acknowledged a grateful indebtedness in his Preface:

> Attention is respectfully called, first, to the "Singing School Department," which is believed to be unusually full and complete. In this department will be found a new and admirable presentation of "Music and its Notation," by Dr. Lowell Mason, who is eminently the great philosopher and teacher of this subject, and who has done more than any other man living to render logical and perspicuous the subject, nomenclature, and arrangement of the principles of vocal music.[16]

Many of the anthems and extended pieces are Root's own compositions. One of particular interest, *Sweetly come those strains melodious*, employs a solo quartet accompanied by a chorus humming the traditional Doxology tune (Example 97).

Another successful composer and compiler was Luther Orlando Emerson (1820–1915). His several collections, spanning the years 1853–1866, met with considerable public favor. *The Jubilate* (1866) is typical.[17] The anthems, or anthemlike pieces, are the work either of Emerson or composers undistinguished in their own time. Two features in this style (which we will assume, for the sake of convenient reference, to be Emerson's) are somewhat unusual. The first is an occasional use of *parlando* or chant style to introduce an anthem (Example 98). The second is the extensive use of solo passages with elaborate pianistic accompaniments. Example 99 is a case in point. Here, in the opening measures, chromatic harmonies ride over a tonic pedal point. The piece is also characterized by repeated chords in eighth-note patterns, lending an expansive-

---

[15] George F. Root, *The Diapason: A Collection of Church Music* (New York: Mason Brothers, 1860).

[16] *Ibid.*, [2].

[17] Luther Orlando Emerson, *The Jubilate: A Collection of Sacred Music, for Choirs, Singing Schools, Musical Conventions, &c.* (Boston: Oliver Ditson and Company, 1866).

ness to the lush melodic line. The effect is similar to that in much of Charles Gounod's religious music.

The volume contains very little imported music; the extensive borrowing from European sources that marked Lowell Mason's collections is absent here. There is, however, an interesting piece entitled *Blessed be Jehovah, God of Israel*, bearing the name "Bartinansky," which proves to be the well-known *Cherubic Hymn No. 7* of Dimitri Bortniansky (1751–1825).[18] Just when or where this piece was first introduced to American choirs is not known, but this is certainly an early appearance of the work, and it may well mark the entry of Russian liturgical pieces for chorus into the mainstream of American anthem repertory. His *Vesper Hymn*, noted more than three decades earlier, is essentially a hymn. It may have developed the taste that led to the appearance of this later piece.

In 1874, with the publication of *The Leader*, another name comes to the fore, that of Horatio R. Palmer (1834–1907).[19] Following the Civil War, Palmer settled in Chicago, and in 1873 became director of the New Church Choral Union which sometimes gave concerts with as many as four thousand singers. With such a ready-made market, it is easy to see why a new collection compiled by Parker with the assistance of Emerson would be profitable to both men.

The materials in *The Leader* are quite similar to those found in Emerson's *Jubilate*; that is, it contains a theoretical section, some secular pieces, and a preponderance of religious music. There are also several set pieces by Clara H. Scott (1841–1897). Women as composers have not been involved in our study of the anthem to this point, and while it is not certain that Mrs. Scott was the first to come on the scene, she certainly must be considered a trailblazer whose example would be emulated by many others.

With the help of R. P. Wright, Palmer issued yet another volume in 1881, *The Song of Triumph*.[20] In addition to a number of compositions by the compilers, the collection includes adaptations from Continental sources, and anthems by Joseph Barnby and Arthur Sullivan.

In the same year, John R. Sweney (1837–1899) and William J. Kirkpatrick (1838–1921) produced a volume entitled *Anthems and Voluntaries for the Church Choir*.[21] Both men were prominent gospel-song writers whose compositions were enormously popular. A unique feature of the volume was the use of Hood's notational system which was designed as an aid to sight-reading.[22] The compilers contributed much of

---

[18] *Ibid.*, 310–11.

[19] H. R. Palmer and L. O. Emerson, *The Leader: A Collection of Sacred and Secular Music, for Choirs, Conventions, Singing Schools, Normal Musical Academies and the Home Circle* (Boston: Oliver Ditson & Co., 1874).

[20] A. H. Palmer and R. P. Wright, *The Song of Triumph, A New Collection of Sacred and Secular Music* (Boston: Arthur P. Schmidt & Co., 1881).

[21] John R. Sweney and William J. Kirkpatrick, *Anthems and Voluntaries for the Church Choir* (Philadelphia: John J. Hood, 1881).

[22] For a complete explanation of this system, see *CMC*, 352–53.

Example 99. *Guide me, O Thou great Jehovah*, L. O. Emerson (*Jubilate*, 277).

ho - vah!   Pil - - grim   through   this   bar - - - ren   land:

their own music to the collection, but again there is quite an assortment of Continental and English composers. Adaptations from the works of Franz Abt (1819–1885), Vincenzo Bellini (1801–1835), and Gioacchino Rossini (1792–1868) are to be found, and the liberal representation of English compositions includes Thomas Attwood's *Turn thy face from my sins*, two anthems by Joseph Barnby, one by Sir George Elvey, and the well-known *God is a spirit* from William Sterndale Bennett's (1816–1875) oratorio *The Woman of Samaria*. Also the anthem *Lord, for thy tender mercies' sake* reappears, again attributed to Farrant.

Turning to the compositional work of the compilers, it is at once apparent that features characteristic of the gospel song also mark many of their extended pieces. This style is clearly evident in Sweney's eighty-three-measure anthem, *Wake the song of jubilee*, where dotted rhythms, and tonic-dominant harmonies prevail (Example 100). On the other hand, a work such as Kirkpatrick's *Out of the depths*,[23] a setting for solo

[23] Sweney and Kirkpatrick, *op. cit.*, 86–87.

Example 100. *Wake the song of jubilee,* John R. Sweney (*Anthems and Voluntaries,* 124).

voices and quartet, is quite similar to much of the anthem writing of the period.

There is no way of knowing just how successful such a collection may have been, but it is evident that the editors felt they were meeting a popular demand, for they stated in their Preface that "Many years' experience as leaders of music in the sanctuary has enabled the compilers to know what kind of pieces are most wanted; their ideas in this respect are embodied in the present volume."[24] No doubt the easy and comfortable idiom of the majority of the pieces, together with a judicious sprinkling of the most popular imports, made the collection very desirable for the less sophisticated churches.

Another gospel-song writer to turn his attention to music for the choir was E. O. Excell (1851–1921), whose two-volume work entitled *Excell's Anthems for the Choir*

---

[24] *Ibid.*, [2].

appeared in 1888.[25] The contents are aimed at the popular taste, as is the case with many others of the same period. Almost entirely made up of pieces by Excell and his contemporaries, the first volume draws twice on foreign materials; a short piece by Gounod is included in an arrangement by George F. Root, and Himmel's *Incline thine ear* is printed in exactly the arrangement that Novello had earlier supplied *The Musical Times* (see p. 255). There are, however, innovations that reflect the changing times. Rather than using the oblong shape customary for collections of this type, Excell produced his in octavo size.[26] Another feature not usually seen in earlier collections is either an independent organ accompaniment so indicated, or a two-stave reduction of the choral parts. Gone also are the theoretical introduction and the customary references to singing-schools. Thus, at least in format and text sections, Excell's work marks the decline of an old era, and a step into the future.

When hymnals commonly began to be supplied for congregations, there was no longer a need to print books that contained both hymnic and choral materials. And as choirs mastered the set pieces to their satisfaction, or to the limit of their abilities, an appetite for more anthems developed. This appetite could be satisfied in one of two ways: by the purchase of single anthems in octavo form, or by subscription to magazines devoted to supplying music regularly, and at a lower price than that of single copies. Leonard Ellinwood names 1874 as the first year that such a serial publication was available, citing a four-page magazine called *The Parish Choir*.[27] It continued publication until 1919, but its significance cannot be determined without circulation figures. By its thirteenth year it had become a weekly publication, so its popularity must have been considerable. Generally, however, monthly magazines were to become the common type. The first one of importance was the *Choir Herald*, founded in 1892 by the Chicago organist John P. Vance (1867–1897). He wrote much of his own material, and by the time he died at age twenty-nine he had built a solid position for his small company.

Three years before Vance's death there appeared the first of the magazines issued by Edmund S. Lorenz (1854–1942). *The Choir Leader* contained five anthems in its first issue, two of them for Easter, and the other three general in nature. Lorenz's editorial stated, in part:

> As the music in this number and the list of authors indicate, the "Choir Leader" will furnish music of a simple or only moderately difficult character. Our purpose is to help the mass of voluntary choirs, who desire music none the less valuable for being easy and unpretentious.[28]

---

[25] E. O. Excell, *Excell's Anthems for the Choir* (2 vols., Chicago: E. O. Excell, 1888).

[26] Other works had been given a form other than the oblong, but the convenience of oblong books seemed to persist as sufficient reason for their continuance. *Musica Sacra* was published in both quarto and oblong shape in some editions after its fifth, and the first regularly published anthem magazine, *The Parish Choir*, was printed in octavo size after its first few years.

[27] Ellinwood, *op. cit.*, 70–71.

[28] *The Choir Leader* I/1 (March, 1894), [1].

Such an undertaking could be greeted only with enthusiasm by singers who found the thick, oblong collections too limited, or filled with many items that were of no use to their choir or service. Another interesting innovation was the inclusion of hints on performance that Lorenz printed with each issue. To the volunteer choir, especially that with no professional leader, such technical and aesthetic assistance was unparalleled. The magazine's success was assured from the outset.

The May, 1897, issue contained an announcement that Lorenz had purchased the moribund *Choir Herald* and was merging it with his magazine, thereby increasing his subscription list to 11,000. This meant that every month saw that many copies of the now six new pieces in the hands of amateur singers, a circulation undoubtedly never before achieved in the history of music publishing.

That merger was only the beginning of a publishing venture that flourished vigorously, and created new markets as it grew. In September, 1897, *The Choir Leader* contained an announcement that was to stir even more interest, especially in the less skilled among its subscribers. It stated that

> owing to the high grade of music furnished in the CHOIR LEADER, many choirs whose facilities for practice are not all that could be desired, or whose members cannot all read fluently, have not been able to make use of it. Anxious to serve all who are interested in the service of sacred music, we have decided to revive the CHOIR HERALD, and through its pages furnish the easier music needed by many choirs.[29]

The decision to reestablish *The Choir Herald* as a separate publication was, at the very least, a stroke of good business. Lorenz advertising from 1902 carries a claim that the combined circulation was more than 30,000 copies, the *Herald* being promoted as "just the thing for a half-trained choir," and the *Leader* as the journal that "contains high grade music for chorus choirs and quartets. Not extremely difficult, but strong, churchly, and practical."

It was evident after some few more years that a further market existed, or that one could be created, and Lorenz accordingly announced another publication in 1913:

> Beginning with October we publish a new magazine, "The Volunteer Choir." Each issue will contain five or more very easy anthems. The music will be much easier than the music in THE CHOIR HERALD. There will be an attractive corps of contributors; E. S. Lorenz, editor; Ira B. Wilson, Frederick Jerome, H. W. Petrie, Marie M. Hine, Mrs. C. W. Morris, Wm. J. Kirkpatrick and others.
>
>   .   .   .
>
> Some of the choirs subscribing to THE CHOIR HERALD who find it somewhat too difficult, will probably ask to transfer their subscription to the new magazine, but we do not expect that number to be large.[30]

It appears that the general tendency was to seek out the large market at the lower level of skill, and to give less attention to encouraging choirs to develop better taste or

---

[29] *Ibid.*, VI/7 (May, 1897), 1.   [30] *Ibid.*, XX/7 (September, 1913), 145.

FIGURE 7. *The cover page of an issue of Lorenz's* The Choir Leader, *one of the most influential and popular choir magazines in America's history.*

the ability to perform more difficult music. Still, in March, 1941, *The Choir Leader* began to add one more difficult number to each issue, perhaps a sign that competence was increasing and that the editors saw the desirability of providing greater variety to the subscribers.

In recent years two more magazines have come from the Lorenz house, *The Quarterly Anthem Folio*, "For Professionally Directed Chorus Choirs," and *The Younger Choirs*, a monthly issued from September through April, containing in its advertising the challenge, "Give the kids music they like to sing." This appeal to enthusiasm and satisfaction has been the hallmark of all the Lorenz music periodicals. Many of the pieces they contained had the direct approach of gospel songs, the immediate appeal of rhythmically active, syllabic settings of text that attract worshipers in churches that stress a personal, emotional involvement in the religious act. Their acceptance has been far less in those choirs and congregations that developed any degree of sophisticated musical taste through training or exposure to concert repertoire, although *The Quarterly* regularly dredged that stream for all it was worth.

We shall examine the musical approach of these magazines briefly, omitting *The Younger Choirs* because of its obviously different purpose. Since *The Quarterly Anthem Folio* is no longer published, a brief review of its approach is all that will be needed. At the time of its heyday, it was the peak of Lorenz quality. The contents and advertising of the September, 1943, issue (Number 28 of the series) will serve as our model. Of its ten anthems, two were borrowed from instrumental works of the masters. *He slumbers not* was arranged from the well-known Andante Cantabile of Tchaikovsky's D-major string quartet, calling for an alto *obbligato* against choral accompaniment, as well as sections for quartet that are then repeated by the full choir. The outward appearance of the sophisticated church with paid solo quartet could be simulated by the church that had only a volunteer chorus choir with a few singers courageous enough to sing alone or as a quartet. The other arrangement was *Praise ye the Father*, taken from Gounod's *Marche Romaine*. Such borrowing from instrumental literature was common; the problems it raised were not easily solved, and the Tchaikovsky piece, while successful with string quartet, was clumsy and unvocal in its arrangement. Obviously it was good enough for the editorial staff, for the advertising pages promised pieces arranged from Schumann's piano concerto and Beethoven's Ninth Symphony. Tchaikovsky's vocal literature was raided for *contrafacta* on *Only the sad of heart* and *The Nightingale*. Vocal composers represented in issues for 1943 and 1944 included J. A. Parks, Van Denman Thompson, E. L. Ashford, J. H. Maunder, Ellen Jane Lorenz, Lee Rogers, Catherine A. Christie, Harry Rowe Shelley; from the European tradition, Mendelssohn, Purcell, and Franck; and finally, in keeping with the new taste for Russian choral music, Glinka and Kalinnikov. The choral parts were usually syllabic and, when not lifted from instrumental sources, were cast in a predictable and often hackneyed vocal idiom. Solos and quartets were features of the more pretentious pieces. The earlier publications were less complex, and they made less appeal to an

Example 101. *When the King comes in,* Charles H. Gabriel (*The Volunteer Choir,* II/3 [December, 1914], 34).

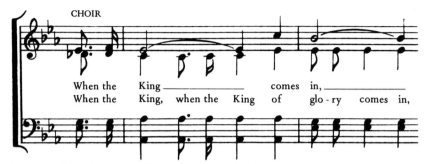

When the   King _____   comes   in, _____
When the   King,   when the   King   of   glo - ry   comes   in,

Copyright, 1914, The Lorenz Publishing Company. Used by permission.

audience to whom the names of European composers and their important compositions would have meaning.

The *Volunteer Choir* was, and still is, the simplest of the group. Its music is presented in closed score, an important feature for singers whose acquaintance with music
may otherwise be limited to hymnbooks where the same format exists. The pieces are
short, direct, simple, and either lyrical or forceful. The music is adaptable to several
voice arrangements, and the absence of one part or another will be felt less than in
more complex pieces. *When the King comes in*, by Charles H. Gabriel (1856–1932), is
representative of the style found in early issues (Example 101).

Next in difficulty, advertised as "Easy to Medium" by the publisher, is *The Choir
Herald*, the most long-lived periodical of this type in America. It contains a greater
variety of material than its simpler counterpart, and the pieces are usually longer as
well as more complex. Short solo sections abound, keyboard introductions and interludes break up many of the pieces, and greater length is regularly achieved by repetition of each text phrase. Early issues printed the vocal parts in open score, but more
recently the use of closed score was adopted, possibly for considerations of both space
and ease of reading. It is obvious, of course, that no music of great complexity can be
presented in this fashion. The style of early pieces can be seen in the opening measures
of E. G. Buchanan's *We have thought of thy loving kindness* (Example 102). The piece
proceeds in note-against-note fashion throughout, except for two measures in which
alto and bass move in unison, and one measure in which the lower voices move during
a held note in the soprano.

The quality products of the firm appeared in *The Choir Leader*. Open score was
the rule except in short settings such as responses and invocations; incidental solos and
solo ensembles could be expected in most of its longer anthems; and occasional brief
melismas occurred. Generally, however, the music did not make great demands upon
the volunteer choir, and it could be worked up to a satisfactory level of performance in
a few rehearsals. Subscribers to any of the Lorenz magazines could develop a skill commensurate with the demands of the music without great difficulty, for the keynote of
each was consistency. By careful planning, use of formulas, and controlled levels of
vocal difficulty, the staff that supplied most of the material gave the choirs a repertory
that never created problems. In 1902 the editor of *The Choir Leader* was E. S. Lorenz,

and E. L. Ashford and P. A. Schnecker were associate editors. What this meant musically was that the bulk of composition was supplied by this trio. Scarcely a month passed without a new anthem or two by each, and the remainder were usually supplied by other regular contributors such as L. O. Emerson, J. A. Parks, or Charles H. Gabriel. The amount of music those people put to paper staggers the imagination. Still, quantity did not go hand in hand with variety. The use of formulas is evident from examination of only a few issues, and considering their public, formulas were probably the best insurance for continued subscriptions to the Lorenz journals. The sale of a familiar idiom was a proven success; there was no reason to change. Lorenz and Mrs.

Example 102.   *We have thought of thy loving kindness*, E. G. Buchanan (*Choir Herald*, III/1 [October, 1899], 18).

Ashford[31] appeared to write more than the rest of the group, producing for other voice arrangements than the usual SATB combination on numerous occasions (but J. A. Parks seems to have been the most prolific writer for male quartet), serving up suitable fare for solo voices, male and female quartets, seasonal services (i.e., cantatas), and so on. They furnished their materials to other idioms as well, for Mrs. Ashford was editor of *The Organist*, a bimonthly venture in which she was assisted by Lorenz, and together they supplied the original pieces in a volume for church orchestra that was advertised with the eye-catching admonition, "Don't play dance music in church, no matter how slowly."

A common criticism of these works is their reliance on clichés and devices that are the most predictable in the musical vocabulary—repetition, sequence, reiterated short rhythmic patterns, and the rising melodic sixth. To seek examples of each is to over-emphasize the value of these pieces. The reliance on an unvaried pattern can be seen in the several examples of Mrs. Ashford's setting of the text fragment "praise ye the Lord," from several anthems (Example 103). The lyric passages of most pieces from this group are likewise simple, direct expressions of the text. Whether they should be classified as saccharine, maudlin, or simply naïve must depend on the sympathies and attitudes of today's observers (Example 104). It is possible that we have lost touch with the idiom of café and salon music of that period, for the similarities are considerable, whether the sources be vocal or instrumental. Some of these obvious devices were probably as common as handlebar mustaches, boater straws, and parlor organs. Unfortunately, when the popular idiom changed, the popular religious idiom of Lorenz's anthem factory marched bravely ahead, boldly ignoring the changing taste of the time. The Lorenz composers had found a convenient parallel to the popular ballad and the characteristic piece for piano by using formulas that were familiar to the public, providing them with words that had a familiar, comfortable, and religious sound, and never disappointing a public that had grown accustomed to the diet.

Something can be said about the positive contributions of the Lorenz dynasty, for a public was being served liberally if not well. The choirs of small churches, urban or rural, under the leadership of well-meaning, poorly trained, uninformed musicians were probably totally dependent upon monthly magazines for their musical material. Many directors had no idea of where and how to select music, how to build a library of usable anthems and short occasional pieces, how to conduct a rehearsal, or where to turn for help. The choir magazines supplied all those wants, gave helpful hints about performance, short essays on tone production, choir organization, religion and morals, and any number of other subjects. Often there were question-and-answer columns in which were solved vexing problems of choir attendance, discipline, or procedure, and which made it possible for some obscure director to get his name before the public by writing a letter of appreciation or complaint to the editor. At some

---

[31] Mrs. Ashford continued in the path already set by Clara H. Scott. In the first quarter of the twentieth century, many other women composers appeared on the scene, many of whom were strongly associated with the gospel-song publications.

Example 103.   Several settings of the text, "praise ye the Lord," by Mrs. E. L. Ashford.

(a) in *Praise to God* (*The Choir Leader*, IV/8 [October, 1897], 156).

(b) in *Universal Praise* (*The Choir Leader*, IX/4 [June, 1902], 84).

(c) in *Sing unto the Lord* (*The Choir Leader*, IX/8 [October, 1902], 180).

Example 104.   Representative lyrical passages from *The Choir Leader*.

(a) Closing solo from *Only in thee abiding*, by Mrs. Ashford, IX/5 (July, 1902), 105.

(b) Opening solo from *Jesus, these eyes have never seen*, by P. A. Schnecker, IX/7 (September, 1902), 147.

point which cannot be determined from copies at hand, it also became usual for the picture of some choir to be published in each issue, another great attraction to some subscribing groups.

Criticism there must have been, even in the early years of the publications, for Lorenz took advantage of his position as editor to defend his kind of music in at least one instance. In a short essay entitled "Pharisaism," he included the following comments:

> Idealism is a good thing; the world cannot progress without it; but it can be quite as blind and bigoted as the other extreme of practicalness ever dares to be. In no line of culture is this fanaticism more apparent than in music. The very lack of intellectual power which characterizes so many people, who are musicians and nothing more, makes this narrowness of insight more striking and unfortunate. Devotion to a high standard of music takes the place of religion and morality with some of these people, and they fall afoul of a Sunday-school ditty in dotted eighths and sixteenths with more indignation than they expend on Wagner's theft of the wife of his bosom friend and disciple, Von Bülow. Recently we have had a diatribe against American church music which has had extensive notice characterized by this narrow pharisaism and lack of broad insight. It is sheer folly to scold a people who have made progress during this critic's own life-time from the singing of doggerel spiritual songs to the use and enjoyment of Dyke's "Lead, Kindly Light," or "Nicea." It is rank injustice to demand that a new people, with no state church or public support for its religious life, shall be equal to an old people whose land is filled with endowed cathedrals, where the organization for musical service is the growth of a thousand years, and where the state supports a church whose liturgical forms inevitably demand and foster a dignified and imposing music. This ignorance of differing conditions vitiates this criticism and makes it valueless, even if it were kindly. We believe in idealism; it sweetens and refines all life; but when it ferments and sours in the narrow confinement of small minds, it has lost its virtue.[32]

We have noted that the first of these American periodicals appeared in 1874, a date that indicates some influence would well have been felt from the success of Novello's *Musical Times*. The difference in format and content, in musical quality and purpose, can be attributed to the differences in religious practice, for Novello sought to serve the Anglican tradition in England with his publications, while reaping the benefits of Nonconformist sales at the same time. American liturgical churches were amply served by older sources and the new octavo materials, and probably accounted for an extremely limited fraction of the Lorenz circulation. Among the other periodicals that sprang up, however, was one that was a direct imitation of *The Musical Times* and sought to serve a similar public in America. *The Choir Journal*, a semimonthly publication of the B. F. Wood Music Company, of Boston, provided its subscribers with one or two numbers per issue, the pieces being anthems, canticles, or responses. It appeared first in 1899, its pieces including some by Tours, Greene, Protheroe, Nevin, Smart, and lesser figures. Its indebtedness to *The Musical Times* is strengthened by the presence of professional cards advertising the services of teachers and performers, news

---

[32] *The Choir Leader*, IX/6 (August, 1902), 1.

items about choirs, usually Episcopal or Presbyterian, and the usual essays and news items. The contents of *The Choir Journal* could not supply all the needs of any choir, and this sets its place sharply apart from the others discussed here. It was of use to choirs that had some ability to begin with, a library sufficient to see them through the usual work of a church season, and a taste that was in tune with the English cathedral tradition of the period. What was not provided by such a journal was available to its subscribers in octavo form from the publishing houses that were becoming established in America and that were importing materials from England.

It was inevitable that composers should appear who sought to emulate the cathedral practice to the extent that their own churches and the American public in general could support it. Leonard Ellinwood's discussion of the Oxford Movement in America provides the best information about the establishment of choirs of boys and men, and it brings into focus the extent to which cathedral practice was possible in this country.[33] The effect of the movement was restricted to metropolitan centers; quartet choirs and mixed chorus choirs still predominated, and the return to liturgical ceremonies did not in the least affect churches other than the Episcopal at that time. We may consider Henry Stephen Cutler (1824–1902) a leader in the movement, for he firmly established the choir of boys and men at two different churches, and he left a collection of pieces that can be examined with profit. While serving as organist-choirmaster at Trinity Church, New York, he composed a volume of Services and anthems that illustrates the extent of his allegiance to older practices.[34] *The Trinity Anthems*—the title is misleading, for the volume contains four Morning Services, an Evening Service, a Burial Service, and a fragment from another in addition to its thirteen anthems—calls for *decani-cantoris* alternation in the Services, but avoids any such complexity in the anthems. In the Services and anthems alike, the organ parts are written out, but except for introductions and accompaniments of solo sections, they duplicate the voices in *colla parte* fashion.

The anthems are on texts specifically suited to the Sundays in Lent, Advent, and for Christmas Day and Epiphany. Cutler's terminology is borrowed from the English tradition, but his use of it differs from common practice. Full anthems deviate from the norm of unrelieved choral singing, and organ interludes are inserted. *The night is far spent*[35] opens with tenors and basses in unison, the full chorus repeating the melodic material in harmonized fashion immediately thereafter. The piece is extended to twice its basic length by this repetition and the subsequent repetition of the contrasting choral section that follows. What Cutler calls verse anthems are actually full anthems with verse, and he designates as solo anthems those that are properly verse anthems.

Melodically the pieces are rather dull. The opening phrase of each anthem outlines the tonic triad in one of the simpler ways available, the rising pattern finding the greatest use (Example 105). Rhythmic variety is lacking. The text accentuation is

---

[33] Ellinwood, *op. cit.*, 76–86.
[34] Henry Stephen Cutler, *The Trinity Anthems* (New York: Wm. A. Pond & Co., 1865).
[35] *Ibid.*, 59–62.

Example 105. *The Lord is my shepherd*, Henry Stephen Cutler (*Trinity Anthems*, 94).

Example 106. *Lord, who shall dwell in thy tabernacle,* Henry Stephen Cutler (*Trinity Anthems,* 71).

pedestrian, although Cutler's interest in his work is apparent from the meter changes and changes of texture that he attempts. Perhaps the most varied treatment in the group can be found in the anthem for the Fourth Sunday in Advent, *Lord, who shall dwell in thy tabernacle.*[36] The opening verse is sung in recitative style by a solo bass, the second verse is set for solo quartet, and the recitative is repeated before each of the next two verses, they being modified repetitions of the second. The seventh verse—Cutler omits the fifth and sixth—is set for full chorus. The part writing is utilitarian and on a par with the melodic and harmonic level of the pieces (Example 106). Significant as Cutler may have been to the life of the individual churches in which he worked, it is easy to see that he could not have won a share of the emerging octavo publication market. There his competition would have been the composers who served the anthem magazines, and who are the group we shall consider next.

This last group of composers consists of men whose musical education was not limited to church pieces, but who learned all the musical skills that went with a full education in the art. They were men who could compose, with varying degrees of success, operas, symphonies, cantatas, concertos, and who could play an instrument well, could conduct with some success, and who belonged to an emerging tradition that usually handed down the Germanic line of music learning from one generation to the next. It is to them that the continuing development of high-quality choral music for the American church has been indebted.

The quartet for which Cutler wrote was undoubtedly the principal singers, boys and men, of his choir. Those for which many anthems were printed by commercial publishers were the paid groups that served in place of, more often than along with, chorus choirs. By the end of the nineteenth century we find evidence that quartets and choirs were common partners, but there is positive evidence from Dudley Buck, who wrote much of his church music for quartet choir, that this was not the case in the 1870s.

> Quartet singing *alone* narrows down the scope of much good music composed for the church service, and excludes the possibility of much contrast in musical effect. It suffers especially from being incapable of those large, dignified effects which are within the scope of even a moderate-sized chorus. We do not propose, however, to argue the much-discussed topic of Quartet *versus* Chorus Choirs. We have simply to deal with the fact that the former exist, and whatever the signs of the future may be, they unfortunately form at present the majority.[37]

Although he deplored their existence, Buck thought it wise to deal extensively with the problems they presented, and he devoted an entire chapter of his volume on accompaniment to them. He recognized that the quartet could be expected to sing a more demanding, if not better quality, kind of anthem material than the chorus choir.

---

[36] *Ibid.*, 68–71.

[37] Dudley Buck, *Illustrations in Choir Accompaniment with Hints on Registration* (New York: G. Schirmer, 1877), 29.

It is useless to attempt to draw the exact line which shall divide tunes suited to Quartet from those adapted to Chorus Choirs. It will depend largely upon the training and natural voices of a given Chorus Choir as to how far its repertory may encroach upon that of the Quartet. In general, however, the *character* of the tune may be said to govern this quite as much as the relative difficulty.[38]

In the course of the following pages, we shall have opportunity to examine a few typical quartet sections. They may then be compared with the choral writing of the same period.

Buck's concern for the differing characteristics of quartet and choral music did not extend to the published anthem literature. We find that many of his pieces, although specified as mixed quartets, were being sold as anthems that were equally useful for chorus choir. No publisher or composer can be imagined who would exclude larger groups from purchasing his music in preference to a smaller one. The prevalence of quartet choirs is evident also from the prominent part that solo voices play in many anthems of the late nineteenth century. The pattern of the full anthem with verses and the verse anthem take on an important place that has fallen into a more satisfactory proportion only in recent decades. Buck's *Rock of Ages*, Op. 65, No. 3,[39] is a hymn anthem that illustrates a number of his style features. The text is T. Cotterill's rearrangement of Toplady's poem[40] with one minor change in the second stanza. The commonly used tune by Hastings is put aside, and an entirely original setting is provided. An introduction preimitates the opening choral (quartet) statement which is only lightly accompanied. The texture of the choral section remains constant thereafter, but the organ part has varying densities ranging from a simple bass to full chords. The second stanza is principally for solo soprano, ending quietly for all voices. The final stanza begins pianissimo for unaccompanied voices, adding volume to the last two lines of text, where a dramatic change of volume and unexpected rhythmic shift close the piece. Example 107 shows the opening and closing sections of the anthem.

Sing, Alleluia forth, Op. 65, No. 1,[41] has many of the same features in a piece of jubilant character. A high degree of chromaticism, change of texture in the organ part, a wide dynamic range, and solo sections for bass, tenor, and soprano, along with specific organ registrations, are features of the piece. A full anthem, *Thou wilt keep him in perfect peace*,[42] is more modest in nature, but this may be attributed to its text. Instead of solo sections, a short imitative section serves as the contrasting part of the ABA form.

Buck's anthems show a greater understanding of musical materials than do those of any earlier men we have considered from America. Cursory comparison with some

---

[38] *Ibid.*, 38.

[39] The use of opus numbers is not simply an affectation of greatness. Several composers who worked in the larger forms made use of this form of identification for songs and anthems as well. The piece was published by Oliver Ditson as octavo No. 462.

[40] Julian, *op. cit.*, II, 970–71.

[41] Ditson 462.   [42] Ditson 1337.

Example 107. *Rock of Ages*, Dudley Buck (Ditson 462, mm. 5–8, 46–50).

Example 108.   *Fear not, O Israel,* Max Spicker (G. Schirmer 4004, mm. 68–84).

mourn - est thou in night - ly watch - es?

CHORUS

Soprani

p *molto cresc.* - - -

I have re - deem - ed thee,____

Alti

p *molto cresc.* - - -

I have re - deem - ed thee____

Tenor

f

I____ have____ re -

Bass

f

I____

mf *cresc.*

of his larger pieces shows that he knew the limited capacities of church musicians. His compositional skill was not exhausted by what the anthems display. What he wrote for the quartet choir and the chorus choir is a deliberate compromise, one that falls between what he could do and what he felt the taste of the church audience would stand for. That he could do this and still improve the level of anthem production at the same time must stand as a tribute to him after his anthems have fallen completely from the repertory.

Somewhere in this same period there appeared the considerable output of P. A. Schnecker (d. 1903). Little is known about him except that he was born and educated in Germany, was for nearly three decades the organist of West Presbyterian Church in New York where he had one of the finest quartet choirs in the country, was an associate editor of Lorenz's *Choir Leader* for some years at the end of his life, and lived a double life in supplying the taste of that magazine's subscribers while trying to compose a more sophisticated kind of music that circulated among the purchasers of single octavo copies. His list of compositions, labeled "first series," on the cover of his *My faith looks up to thee*[43] is in alphabetical order, numbering forty-nine pieces in the first half of the alphabet.[44] The anthem named here is a pretentious expansion of the hymn text for SAB solos, mixed voices, and violin *obbligato*. While a fair amount of variety is achieved, it is within the area of familiar clichés, the soloists enjoying many upward leaps of a fourth, fifth, or sixth, everyone having the opportunity to breathe at the end of every second measure, and the violin moving through predictable figurations of salon music of that day. The same plodding regularity limits *The King of love my Shepherd is*,[45] an anthem varied only by the assignment of sections to tenor solo, alto-bass duet, and SATB chorus or quartet.

The interest in choral singing that gave rise to anthem magazines also made possible the development of the present mode of printing choral music, the publication in score form of complete pieces in octavo size. This was initiated, as we saw in the previous chapter, by Novello in England. The American agent for the Novello firm was Oliver Ditson & Company, and it was through that firm that the first English octavo pieces reached the American public as early as 1869. Publication of anthems by American composers was begun in 1876 when the numbered series of octavo pieces began to be printed,[46] and the practice spread rapidly to other houses until it became the most common and economical method of producing such music.

The rapid development of a new means of distributing individual anthems inexpensively brought many new composers to the scene, many of them quite skilled and others with a firm grasp on convenient musical formulas. It is possible to select examples from this point forward that will support several reasonable arguments about the course of anthem literature—at least until the third decade of the present century, where the experience of a current generation can support childhood memories. It appears, nevertheless, from surviving advertising of the turn of the century, and from copies that have not been discarded from choir libraries, that a continuation of the Dudley Buck style was general, while some attempts to inject new ideas are also apparent. A sample of the latter can be seen in *Fear not, O Israel*, Op. 50, by Max Spicker (1858–1912).[47] A dramatic piece that ranges through most of the gamut of emotions, it gives the quartet of soloists opportunity to declaim, question, and reassure, all in the course of eight pages, to suitable formula accompaniment patterns and choral passages. The result, which seems highly artificial to most listeners now, may well have represented the highest level of church concert material to accompany the fashionable Sunday service in 1900 when it was printed. The solo lines are illustrated in Example 108, along with an unusual division of voices. The latter idea, along

---

43 Ditson 10322.
44 These pieces, and apparently another group of some size, were published by Ditson.
45 Ditson 10323.
46 This information comes from Fisher, *op. cit.*, 60 *et passim*.   47 G. Schirmer 4004.

Example 109. *Some blessed day*, George B. Nevin (Ditson 11423, mm. 6–10).

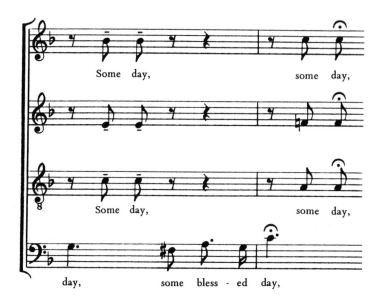

with more convincing harmonic support, was to become a regular feature of American choral music after the wider acquaintance with Russian liturgical materials had demonstrated the satisfying possibilities of full-textured chords to composers, but the present segment appears to be nothing more than an isolated exploratory venture.

Another prolific composer whose roots are obviously in the gospel-song tradition, even though he has numerous works in the catalogues of octavo publishers, was George B. Nevin (1859–1933). His hymn-anthems often smack of the Gay Nineties ballad in their use of a short solo verse and an equally short chorus, as in *Jesus, my Saviour! look on me*,[48] which has each solo section accompanied, but has the following chorus indicated for *a cappella* performance. *Some blessed day*[49] lacks the solo features, but employs the gospel-song responsive device with *fermata* (Example 109) that had caught the popular fancy. Probably Nevin's style underwent considerable change toward a higher level of composition during his many years of writing, but even such a late work as *Into the woods my Master went*,[50] published in 1926, clings to two-measure phrases and predictable patterns. The melodic outlines are those of the ballad-like gospel song; the piece has the sophisticated touches of humming accompaniment with a four-measure alto-section solo, and it has "accompaniment ad lib," meaning "sing *a cappella* if your choir is able."

The great appeal that Dudley Buck's style held for the churchgoing public seems to have been inherited, in large measure, by his pupils, of whom Harry Rowe Shelley (1858–1947), Raymond H. Woodman (1861–1943), and William H. Neidlinger (1863–1924) were the most important.

After study in composition with both Buck and Dvořák, Shelley served in several churches as organist—the Fifth Avenue Baptist Church, New York, and the Central Congregational Church, Brooklyn, being his most important posts. His anthems were immensely popular, and it is doubtful that any other composer of the era, with the possible exception of Buck, enjoyed a success in this field equal to his. There is in Shelley's anthems a certain familiar tuneful quality with which churchgoers in the late nineteenth and early twentieth centuries identified readily; in fact, many choir libraries still contain the best known of his works. This easy tuneful quality is nowhere more evident than in the opening alto solo of *The King of love my shepherd is*,[51] or the baritone solo of *Saviour, when night involves the skies*.[52] Such obvious melodic invention is frequently further enhanced by a second solo voice running in parallel thirds or sixths (Example 110).

Many of Shelley's anthems open with either a solo or a duet, and almost all of them contain solo passages. Some of the opening solos are relatively brief, as in *The King of love*, while others are extended to a point of importance outweighing the choral sections. This is certainly the case in *Hark, hark, my soul!*[53] Here in a total of 162 measures, only 24 measures are given exclusively to the choir, while the choir is cast in the role of supporting accompaniment to soloists in 45 measures.

---

[48] G. Schirmer 4027.   [49] Ditson 11423.   [50] Ditson 332-13935.
[51] G. Schirmer 3125.   [52] G. Schirmer 3256.   [53] G. Schirmer 3209.

Example 110. *The King of love my Shepherd is,* Harry Rowe Shelley (G. Schirmer 3125, mm. 24–28).

Shelley preferred flat keys, frequently employing four- and five-flat signatures. Unison choral passages are also a prominent feature of his style, especially evident in *The God of Abraham praise*,[54] where the composer wished to underscore strong, heroic melodic lines. His composition is marked by a harmonic-melodic feature common enough in this period, yet used so frequently in his works as to constitute a virtual

Example 111. *Hark, hark my soul,* Harry Rowe Shelley (G. Schirmer 3209, mm. 113–16).

signature. It is the use of degree inflection in a rising melodic passage. This can be seen in Example 111, where the underlying harmonic structure is a doubly augmented six-four-three chord resolving to a tonic six-four in E flat.

A similar harmonic style is to be found in the anthem writing of Neidlinger, who, among Buck's students, ranked second only to Shelley. Again, degree inflection of the same type used by Shelley is to be found; indeed, it appears that both of these composers had acquired this stylistic trait from their teacher, for the device is abundantly present in Buck's anthems. In his well-known *Festival Te Deum*,[55] sometimes still

---

54 G. Schirmer 5346.   55 Ditson 455.

used as a festival anthem, the rising chromatic line of the tenor solo is supported by an F-sharp diminished-seventh chord (Example 112). This short passage is typical of an overripe chromaticism characteristic of the anthem writing of the century's end, which has continued until well into our own time.

The list of other composers of the period who wrote in much the same style is lengthy; it will suffice here to name such writers as Alfred Wooler (1867–1937), Paul Ambrose (1868–1941), and F. Flaxington Harker (1876–1936) as representative of those whose works were in common use in choir libraries across the country.

Example 112.   *Festival Te Deum*, Dudley Buck (Ditson 455, mm. 170–73).

The outstanding American composer of church music in this era was undoubtedly Horatio William Parker (1863–1919). After musical study in America and Germany, he served as organist-choirmaster, first at St. Andrew's, New York, and then at the Church of the Holy Trinity, Boston. In 1894 he was appointed to the chair in music at Yale University, which post he held until his death. Parker gained fame both at home and abroad, was awarded an honorary M.A. degree by Yale in 1894, and an honorary Mus.D. by Cambridge in 1902.

Parker's anthem composition was on a par with the best church music produced in England and on the Continent during this period. No doubt his study with George W. Chadwick (1854–1931), himself a composer of church music, and further work in Munich greatly influenced him and developed his style, but there can be little doubt that he was endowed with an unusual measure of creative ability. The publication by Novello of his Christmas anthem, *Before the heavens were spread abroad* (1893),[56] as well as other titles, indicates an appreciation of his works by the English. One especially appealing feature may have been this anthem's similarities to what we have seen in

[56] H. W. Gray, C.M.R. 1472.

TABLE 12

Form of Horatio Parker's Anthem *The Lord is my light*

Organ introduction			4 measures	C major	4/4 time
SATB choir	A	a	16 measures	C major	4/4 time
		b	16 measures	E minor	4/4 time
		a′	16 measures	C major	4/4 time
Organ interlude			4 measures	A minor	6/8 time
Verse or Semichorus	B	c	24 measures	A minor	6/8 time
		c′	22 measures	A major	6/8 time
Choral transition (full choir)			5 measures	Modulatory	4/4 time
SATB choir	A	a	16 measures	C major	4/4 time
		b	16 measures	E minor	4/4 time
		a′	16 measures	C major	4/4 time
Coda (full choir)	Motivic material from theme a		27 measures	C major	4/4 time

works by Charles Villiers Stanford: strong unison passages, vigorous organ accompaniment, and bold melodic contours.

Certainly one of Parker's most effective anthems is *The Lord is my light*.[57] Here a breadth of concept and a grasp of compositional technique are evident to an extent not

Example 113.   *The Lord is my light*, Horatio W. Parker (G. Schirmer 3552, mm. 57–60).

VERSE, OR SEMI-CHORUS

S.

Heark - en un - to my voice, O Lord,

when _ I cry un - to thee; _____

[57] G. Schirmer 3552.

previously encountered in the anthems of native Americans. The formal design, a carefully developed three-part form, is unusually elaborate. Table 12 will give the reader some idea of the scope and development of the work. Parker's melodic invention is skillful and interesting. It is, to be sure, romantic, but he escaped the precious sentimentality that marked the work of most of his contemporaries. At its best it is forthright and vigorous; at its worst it suffers from the ills that afflicted most compound-meter tunes of the time (Example 113).

While the anthem is predominantly chordal, there is a considerable amount of contrapuntal writing in the B section, and stretto is used to good effect at one point. Chromaticism is fairly extensively used throughout, and altered chords are abundant,

Example 114. *The Lord is my light,* Horatio W. Parker (G. Schirmer 3552, mm. 138–41).

but Parker is more apt to use them to build tension to a climactic point rather than for mere coloristic effect. Example 114 shows his use of a German sixth chord in repetition, resolving to a tonic six-four chord in C. The effect created here is massive, acting as a springboard for a return to the main thematic material.

Naturally, Parker's style seems dated and somewhat obvious to us, but his fine craftsmanship cannot be doubted, and his work is the more remarkable when compared with the maudlin sentimentality so typical of anthem writing in this period. His anthems set a new standard for church music in this country; however, another direction was to be followed by composers of the next generation.

CHAPTER NINE

England in the Twentieth Century— The Emergence of Canadian Anthems

A composer of genuine stature in the world of music both at home and abroad, Ralph Vaughan Williams (1872–1958) stands out as the single major twentieth-century composer to write extensively for the church. In addition to that significant body of material, a number of his larger choral works with orchestral accompaniment are on religious texts. Vaughan Williams' musical study was traditional and firmly rooted in the past; he studied composition with Charles Wood at Cambridge, and at the Royal College he worked under C. Hubert H. Parry and Charles Villiers Stanford. Although both Wood and Parry appear quite progressive when measured against the prevailing Victorian musical standard, it remained for Vaughan Williams to develop a compositional style that marked a major break with the immediate past and to set the course English music would follow in the first decades of the twentieth century. The principal ingredients of the new styles are easily seen and readily understood: They are modality and folksong, elements closely related in that the former is frequently found in the latter.

The first decades of Vaughan Williams' compositional activity yielded little in the way of anthem production. His first effort in this form, *I heard a voice from heaven*, appears to have been written at the Royal College of Music in the summer term of 1891.[1] His first published anthem, *O praise the Lord of heaven*,[2] an unaccompanied

---

[1] Michael Kennedy, *The Works of Ralph Vaughan Williams* (London: Oxford University Press, 1964), 397.　　[2] Stainer and Bell 1713.

work for two full choirs and semichorus, was first performed at the Annual Festival of the London Church Choir Association, November 13, 1913.[3]

In 1920, Vaughan Williams wrote one of his most spectacular and successful anthems, *O clap your hands*.[4] An unusual feature is the use of instruments in addition to the organ (three trumpets, three trombones, tuba, timpani, and cymbals). There is, of course, nothing basically new here; the Restoration anthem was frequently augmented by instruments, but the tradition died out toward the end of the eighteenth century and lay dormant for over a century. Vaughan Williams did more, however, than

Example 115. *O, clap your hands*, Ralph Vaughan Williams (Stainer & Bell 222, mm. 4–11).

Used with permission of Stainer & Bell Ltd., Reigate, Surrey.

merely revive an old tradition; his use of brass and percussion with organ provided a new and exciting visceral sound. Gone were the polite and frequently dull utterances of the cathedral tradition, or, on the other hand, the overripe expression of Victorian composition. Quite in contrast to these, Vaughan Williams opens this anthem with a bold melodic statement that at once arrests the attention of the listener (Example 115). The theme derives much of its interest from both its rhythmic drive and the unexpected introduction of the A flat, which here suggests the Mixolydian mode.

Another feature found in *O clap your hands* is the use of massive chords expanding and contracting around a harmonic center (Example 116). Here the basic A-flat-major tonality is embellished with a G-flat-major seventh chord that revolves around the tonal center by means of two sets of parallel triads moving in contrary motion. The resultant fanfare effect is heightened by the closed position of the six-part choral structure, providing an impact and sense of excitement heretofore unknown in anthem literature.

[3] Kennedy, *op. cit.*, 461.
[4] Stainer and Bell, Church Choir Library No. 222.

Parallel triads in root position are used in abundance throughout the piece and may be considered a prominent feature of Vaughan Williams' choral style. The device no doubt had a certain shock value when first heard by congregations thoroughly accustomed to the well-behaved conduct of traditional nineteenth-century harmony.

A curious problem concerning terms arises in connection with Vaughan Williams' anthems. He used the designation *motet* for the majority of his church choral pieces, and only seldom the term *anthem*. No clear-cut delineation of type or style, either textual or musical, seems to be involved here. Most of the pieces titled *motet* are unaccompanied, but even this distinction breaks down in the case of O *clap your hands*, which is so designated and yet carries full accompaniment. The arranged hymn tunes are given neither designation. It then appears that the composer did not attach any specific meaning to those terms. We have noticed earlier, of course, that a certain

Example 116. *O, clap your hands*, Ralph Vaughan Williams (Stainer & Bell 222, mm. 30–37).

Used with permission of Stainer & Bell, Ltd., Reigate, Surrey.

freedom of terminology was in effect, but much of that freedom was in the new publications of the Americans rather than in England.

Another of Vaughan Williams' anthems, *Lord, Thou hast been our refuge*,[5] was
composed and published in 1921, close on the heels of *O clap your hands*. Again, the
composer built into the piece some highly unusual features. The unifying element of
the work is a conflation that combines Psalm 91 as found in the *Book of Common Prayer*
with Isaac Watts's versification of the same psalm, "O God our help in ages past." The
musical treatment of the two texts, however, provides striking contrast; a semichorus
is assigned the prose text in a unison melodic setting while the full chorus sings the

[5] G. Schirmer 9720.

Example 117. *Lord, Thou hast been our refuge*, Ralph Vaughan Williams (G. Schirmer 9720, mm. 1–16).

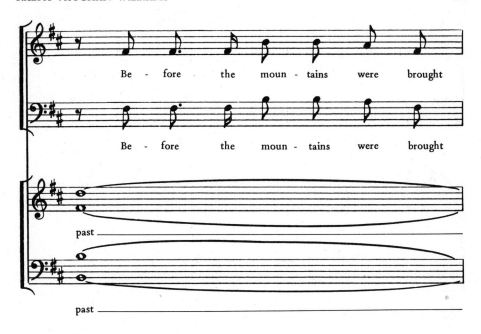

Be - fore the moun - tains were brought

Be - fore the moun - tains were brought

past

past

forth, or ev - er the earth and the world were made, Thou art

forth, or ev - er the earth and the world were made, Thou art

Our

Our

By permission of J. Curwen & Sons Ltd., 29 Maiden Lane, London, W.C.2, England.

underlying hymn to the traditional tune "St. Anne," in four-part harmony (Example 117). Several interesting features are contained in the first measures. The opening A, sounded first by the organ and then by the voices, implies a certain ambiguity as to key and mode. The melodic line in measures three through five then establishes the key of D minor, only to shift abruptly to D major with the entry of the full chorus in measure six. The tension is heightened in measures fifteen and sixteen when the semichorus reverts again to D minor while the full chorus remains in D major, thus creating a momentary bimodality. Vaughan Williams may have given, at that point, purposeful musical underscoring to the textual dichotomy apparent in the phrases "Thou turnest man to destruction" and the reference to God as "Our hope for years to come." There is significance, too, in the composer's dynamics markings which create in the hymn a mood of sustained, quiet confidence against the plaintive cry of the psalm.

The second major section of the piece exhibits a kind of word-painting not found in the anthem prior to this time. The psalm refers to a thousand years in God's sight as

Example 118. *Lord, Thou hast been our refuge,* Ralph Vaughan Williams (G. Schirmer 9720, mm. 29–32).

By permission of J. Curwen & Sons Ltd., 29 Maiden Lane, London, W.C.2, England.

a mere watch in the night, and on the words "They are even as a sleep and fade away suddenly like the grass," Vaughan Williams used an extremely thick, low-range harmonic texture, employing at the same time a descending parallel harmonic structure (Example 118). Here the major seventh chords add much to the total effect. The degree of dissonance employed here (Example 119), while not at all severe by contemporary standards of secular music, was none the less still novel in early twentieth-century church music, at least in England and America.

Example 119. *Lord, Thou hast been our refuge,* Ralph Vaughan Williams (G. Schirmer 9720, mm. 36–39).

By permission of J. Curwen & Sons Ltd., 29 Maiden Lane, London, W.C.2, England.

The composer's use of accompaniment is unusual in that he provides the option of orchestra or organ; the orchestration calls for pairs of flutes, oboes, clarinets, and bassoons, four horns, two trumpets, three trombones, tuba, timpani, organ, and strings; or simply strings and organ. This is certainly an extravagant instrumental force for a relatively simple anthem, especially in the light of the fact that the accompaniment, aside from the opening note which serves to establish pitch, is present only in the last third of the piece. It is always risky business to bring an accompaniment in after an extended *a cappella* passage lest the choir be found wanting in pitch accuracy, but in this case, after nine pages of such singing involving several key changes, the likelihood of a church choir being on pitch is remote indeed. Evidently Vaughan Williams was

well aware of the problem and solved it by opening the extensive organ interlude
with an F-sharp pedal point, quite far removed from the E-flat-major cadence on
which the choral section ended, thus obviating any pitch discrepancies. The third
major section of the anthem is much like the opening, the whole ending in a contrapuntal section which borrows fragments from the "St. Anne" theme. In all, it is a well-
crafted work that can be extremely effective if carefully performed. The question of
such a sizable orchestra as the composer specifies, and of its relatively limited use in a
piece apparently intended for normal church use, must be taken either as a sign of his
relative inexperience in the genre at its writing, or as an indication that he intended it
as much for choral societies as for church groups, for his later works called for extra
instruments only when a special occasion had been the reason for their composition,
and even then a simple organ part was supplied for ordinary performance circumstances.

Probably one of Vaughan Williams' best-known and most frequently performed
anthems is O how amiable,[6] which was originally written for a pageant in 1934. The
reasons for the popularity of the piece are not difficult to discover: The melodic line is
pleasing to both performer and listener, the choir sings in unison most of the time, and
the musical complexities that give interest and substance to the work are assigned to
the organ accompaniment. Hence, a modest but adequate choir, if accompanied by a
capable organist on a good instrument, can create with this anthem a larger-than-life
sound that will have a moving effect upon the congregation.

In 1938 Vaughan Williams wrote an extensive arrangement of the hymn All hail
the power of Jesus' name, on the well-known tune "Miles Lane,"[7] which was first performed at the Worcester Festival.[8] The festive nature of the piece is clearly evident,
not only in the music itself but in the orchestration as well; the scoring is for paired
flutes, oboes, clarinets, bassoons, double bassoon, four horns, three trumpets, three
trombones, tuba, timpani, percussion, organ, and strings. There are some optional
reductions, and an organ arrangement may be used when an orchestra is not available.

A new dimension was added to the festival-type anthem in this work—namely,
that of congregational participation. Here Vaughan Williams involves the congregation in unison singing of the hymn tune in five of the seven stanzas. This in itself offers
no particular complication, since the tune is well known in both England and America.
In this case, however, the composer has altered time values, or rather has given exact
time values to those notes in the hymn tune traditionally marked with a fermata. No
doubt some congregations would easily follow these alterations, but a safer method
might be to print the melodic line on a leaflet with the text.

Each stanza is given a different treatment, resulting in a type of hymn-variation,
and Vaughan Williams shows himself every inch the master arranger in bringing out
the full heroic quality of "Miles Lane." Consider the scalar sweep to the strong succession of chords that introduce the second stanza (Example 120a), or the tremendous

[6] Oxford A.94.   [7] Oxford 42.230.   [8] Grove's, VIII, 702.

Example 120. *All hail the power*, Ralph Vaughan Williams (Oxford 42.230, mm. 32–36, 95–99).

(b)

Used with permission of Oxford University Press.

thrust of repeated chordal patterns that leads into stanza five (Example 120 b). Given the proper setting, with large choral and orchestral forces, the effect of this anthem would be electrifying, and credit is due the composer for turning the more or less second-rate traditional hymn-anthem into a composition of substance and quality.

A very different side of Vaughan Williams' choral writing for the church is seen in *The Souls of the righteous*,[9] a motet written for the Dedication Service of the Battle

Example 121. *O taste and see*, Ralph Vaughan Williams (Oxford, unnumbered, mm. 4–12).

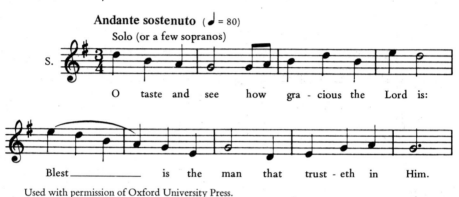

Used with permission of Oxford University Press.

of Britain Chapel in Westminster Abbey, July 10, 1947. The text, taken from The Wisdom of Solomon, III, 1–5, seems especially appropriate to the occasion, and the more so with this effective, yet unusual setting. The introductory treble solo in free recitative and the unaccompanied choral passages with varying textures that lead into remote harmonic areas combine to enhance the essential mystical quality of the text.

Two of Vaughan Williams' pieces that have been performed widely, *O taste and see*[10] and *The old hundredth psalm tune*,[11] were first heard at the Coronation of Queen Elizabeth II in Westminster Abbey, June 2, 1953. The former, which had been composed late in 1952, was sung during the Queen's Communion, where the verse from Psalm 34 has obvious relevance. The melodic line, first sung as a soprano solo, is built on the pentatonic scale (Example 121). A short piece of only thirty-five measures, it must be carefully prepared and performed with a high degree of musical sensitivity if it is to be effective.

Erik Routley has pointed out Vaughan Williams' rather unorthodox cadential formulas;[12] while he is by no means always unorthodox in this matter, the closing cadences of *O taste and see* and *The souls of the righteous* do indicate the composer's

---

[9] Oxford (unnumbered).
[10] *TECM*, V, 37–38.   [11] Oxford 42 P 953.
[12] Erik Routley, *Twentieth Century Church Music* (New York: Oxford University Press, 1964), 25.

penchant for an unusual ending, especially where there is a tendency toward modality (Example 122).

The old hundredth psalm tune follows essentially the same format as the earlier *All hail the power of Jesus' name*: It employs variation technique, congregational participation is indicated, and the instrumentation calls for full orchestra. Actually, the work is pieced together from several preexistent compositions: The instrumental introduction is adapted from the composer's cantata, *The hundredth psalm*, the harmonization of stanza two is taken from *Songs of Praise*, and stanza four is the setting by John Dowland that appeared in the Ravenscroft Psalter of 1621. It seems appropriate that these anthems were performed at his funeral.

It is difficult to assess the total influence of Vaughan Williams upon church music, but by almost any standard of measurement it is significant. His anthems, while small

Example 122. Final cadences of *O taste and see*, Ralph Vaughan Williams (Oxford, mm. 33–35), and *The souls of the righteous*, Ralph Vaughan Williams (Oxford, unnumbered, mm. 38–39).

Used with permission of Oxford University Press.

Example 123. *Let all mortal flesh keep silence,* Gustav Holst (Stainer & Bell 2309, mm. 72–78).

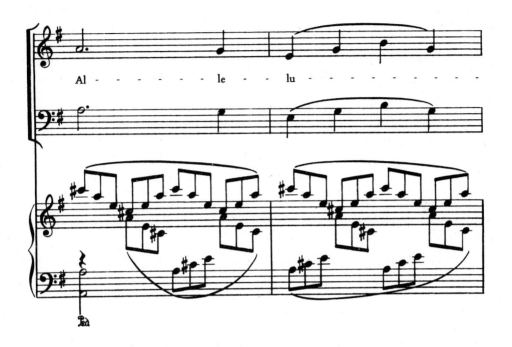

Used with permission of Stainer & Bell Ltd., Reigate, Surrey.

in number, have exercised an influence of considerable proportion upon the subsequent development of that form in both England and America; and perhaps more
than any other single composer, he ushered church music into the twentieth century.

At least one other composer was in the vanguard of those who brought about the
changes we have observed in Vaughan Williams' music—that person was Gustav Holst
(1874–1934). The close friendship that existed between these men dated back to their
student days at the Royal College of Music, and continued over the years until Holst's
death. Michael Kennedy writes of the unusual extent to which each was involved in
the work of the other.

> It was in 1895 that Holst and Vaughan Williams met. . . . Almost at once they began to
> give each other composition lessons. They played the earliest sketches of their works and
> would criticize them, with complete candour, and re-write passages together. Often they
> disagreed and would find their own way to solution of the problem either because of, or in
> spite of, the criticism. These sessions they called their 'Field Days'. They continued for
> nearly forty years, until Holst's death.[13]

Holst did not attain Vaughan Williams' degree of eminence or fame; even so, he
is a composer of major importance who contributed significantly to the many areas of
musical composition, and like Vaughan Williams he produced an abundance of choral
works, many with orchestral accompaniment.

Again, it is difficult to separate Holst's short religious pieces. Two are definitely
listed as anthems, three are styled as festival choruses with orchestra, and still others,
drawn from medieval sources, are indicated as carols, yet they are all now commonly
used as anthem material.

The set of Three Festival Choruses with orchestra was written in 1916, a year in
which Holst devoted much of his effort to choral music. Two of the pieces, *Turn back,
O man*[14] and *Let all mortal flesh keep silence*,[15] provide a study of contrast in style. One
notable feature of the former is the use of an ostinato bass throughout much of the
anthem. The basis for the piece is the melody "Old 124th," originally from the
Genevan Psalter of 1551. The first and last stanzas of the text, a fine hymn by Clifford
Bax, are set in rather straightforward fashion; the middle stanza, however, has a fair
amount of imitation, and amidst this counterpoint, remote keys are entered and left
with uncommon abruptness, producing an effect of grandeur that complements both
text and tune. The second piece, *Let all mortal flesh keep silence*, is quite different. As
Holst captured the heroic spirit of text and tune in *Turn back, O man*, so he sensed the
profound mysticism that surrounds the text from the Liturgy of St. James. The old
French melody that has traditionally accompanied the English translation, and which
fits the text so beautifully, is paid the highest respect by Holst—he simply sustains one
note in the accompaniment throughout the first stanza, except for a few notes of two-
part harmony close to the end, thus allowing the tune to be heard without distraction.

[13] Kennedy, *op. cit.*, 21.   [14] Stainer & Bell 2152.   [15] Stainer & Bell 2309.

He changes the color of successive stanzas first by means of a baritone solo with sparse chordal accompaniment, then by an *a cappella* SSAT section, and finally by full orchestral support of a unison melody. The arpeggiated chords that accompany the "Alleluya," no doubt extremely effective with orchestra, also come off well on the organ (Example 123).

In the same year, 1916, Holst also composed three carols for unaccompanied chorus, two of which were on religious texts. These pieces, *Lullay my liking*[16] and *Of one that is so bright and fair*,[17] share common features: Both texts are drawn from medieval sources; both are polymetric, allowing for proper text accentuation; and both alternate solo and chorus throughout. *Lullay my liking* displays a modal ambivalence, alternating between Aeolian and Dorian, while *Of one that is so bright and fair* is bilingual, alternating between English and Latin. These are effective pieces, and because of the refrainlike nature of the chorus sections, they are not difficult, but the unaccompanied solos require sensitive singers with a high degree of vocal control.

The two works by Holst bearing the designation *anthem* were written in 1927. *Man born to toil*[18] is a fairly extensive piece on a text by the English poet Robert Bridges (1844–1930). The first half of the anthem is somewhat involved and rather ungrateful for singers; thus, an abridged version consisting only of the second half of the original was published under the title *Gird on thy sword*.[19] In this form the anthem is an uncomplicated four-stanza setting based on the tune "Chilswell." Holst's fondness for ostinato patterns is again evident in the last stanza (Example 124), but here the ostinato repetition becomes a restatement of the entire accompaniment, and the effect may be further heightened by the optional use of bells.

The second anthem, a setting of Bridges' *Eternal Father*, opens much as *Gird on thy sword* closed, a full-organ ostinato with optional bells supporting the unison choral line (Example 125*a*). One is reminded here of the opening measures of Purcell's famous "Bell Anthem," *Rejoice in the Lord alway*. The second stanza employs the same hymnlike melody as the first in a four-part unaccompanied setting. A sparsely accompanied soprano solo follows, after which the ground bass resumes. In the closing measures the initial stanza is sung in unison and two-part harmony by the male voices while a light and graceful "alleluia" is sung by the treble voices on a repeated four-note pattern. The whole is supported by the bells and organ pedal, which sound the ground bass in augmented values (Example 125*b*).

Holst certainly cannot be considered a major contributor to the anthem in terms of quantity, but there can be little doubt that his style left an imprint on twentieth-century English church music.

The brave beginnings made by Vaughan Williams and Holst marked a period of change in English anthem writing only so far as their influence was felt by later composers, for there still were men who had been trained in the cathedral traditions and

[16] J. Curwen 1312.   [17] J. Curwen 1546.
[18] G. Schirmer 8509.   [19] G. Schirmer 8669.

who had not taken upon themselves anything that was modern or unusual. Many of these less adventurous composers were limited by not being trained for, or interested in, anything other than choral music; craftsmanship and talent could be seen, but they followed the limitations of choral practice in most cases, rarely exhibiting the freedoms explored by composers who had been practicing in the larger forms. Among

Example 124.   *Gird on thy sword*, Gustav Holst (G. Schirmer 8669, mm. 28–32).

By permission of J. Curwen & Sons Ltd., 29 Maiden Lane, London, W.C.2, England.

these traditionalists was Edward Bairstow (1874–1946), who became known to subscribers to *The Musical Times* at the turn of the century, held some important church
positions, became a professor at Durham University where he had received his Mus.B.
degree, was one of the numerous musicians knighted by King George V, and was also
known for his books on counterpoint and musical form. His traditional outlook is
obvious from the titles and text sources of representative anthems, as well as from their

Example 125. *Eternal Father*, Gustav Holst (G. Schirmer 8510, mm. 1–8, 41–42).

(b)

By permission of J. Curwen & Sons Ltd., 29 Maiden Lane, London, W.C.2, England.

Example 126. Sequential treatment in *Let all mortal flesh keep silence*, Edward C. Bairstow (mm. 30–34).

phim, _____

phim, _____

phim, _____

phim,   who   veil   their   fa - ces,

Used with permission of Stainer & Bell Ltd., Reigate, Surrey.

musical content. *Save us, O Lord*[20] is an expanded statement of a short text—an antiphon from Compline—that is first stated in unison by the men, repeated in harmonized form, given fugato treatment for one phrase, and concludes with a soprano section solo followed by a short coda. The organ is given significant material throughout. A fine prose setting of the popular text from the Liturgy of St. James, *Let all mortal flesh keep silence*,[21] opens with men in unison, proceeds to SSAA, and continues through varied vocal groupings with excellent effect. Especially notable are an imaginative treatment of sequence (Example 126) and the closing SATB "Alleluia" over which solo tenor and bass restate the opening melody.

A single stanza of text serves *Jesu, the very thought of Thee*,[22] an unaccompanied SATB piece that employs text fragments in a manner similar to the points of imitation used by earlier composers. Here the imitation treatment does not extend to all the voices; Bairstow's modification of the "points" provides both rhythmic variety and a continuous texture through the overlapping of parts at cadences. What might have been a plodding series of short phrases becomes a web of sound equal to the fine flow of some Renaissance pieces.

The Easter hymn "Aurora lucis rutilat"[23] provides text for a more extended piece, *The day draws on with golden light*.[24] The melody is borrowed from a French

[20] H. W. Gray, C.M.R. 740.
[21] *TECM*, V, 39–44; published in octavo form by Stainer and Bell, Ltd.
[22] Davies and Ley, *op. cit.*, 223–24.
[23] *Hymns Ancient and Modern* (Historical Edition) (London: William Clowes and Sons, Limited, 1909), 198–99. The translation used by Bairstow is not that given in this source, and only three verses are selected from the thirteen in the Latin original.   [24] Davies and Ley, *op. cit.*, 405–9.

source that is not specifically identified in the score examined here; the tune is sturdy and well suited to the hymn-anthem treatment that is adopted. Recomposed as a strophic piece that develops a few easily identified figures featuring various groups from the choir in unison or in parts against an accompaniment, it presents still another side of Bairstow's many talents.

Erik Routley has stressed a debt owed to the Germans, especially to Brahms, by Bairstow and others of his generation,[25] but the evidence of that indebtedness is not clear. It is equally, and probably more, possible to trace the sources of this music through the English traditions we have examined in earlier pages. Brahms was popular in England, but the influence of Mendelssohn, Spohr, and Gounod, in the first place, and the taste brought back to England by men who had been trained in German conservatories, in the second, were greater by far. Solidity of style, skill in craftsmanship, emphasis on rhythmic variety achieved through interesting inner parts and delayed accents are not the sole legacy of a Brahmsian tradition, and England's choral composers were more likely to be influenced by men whose choral works were regularly heard in England than by Brahms, who produced comparatively little they could use as a model. We do not minimize Bairstow's importance by giving him his place in a longer, continuous line of development rather than as a purveyor of Germanic tradition. Compared with Vaughan Williams and Holst, Bairstow was a conservative, but he was not a neoclassicist.

Hugh S. Roberton (1874–1952), one of the few Scottish musicians to make a mark in choral music, was not a composer whose principal interests lay in church music. His main activities involved promoting the reputation of the Glasgow Orpheus Choir, which he organized in 1906, brought to a peak of perfection, and conducted for many years to international acclaim. As a specialist in vocal music his interest lay in choral sound and not in the furtherance of dogma or the protection of liturgical propriety. His *All in the April evening*,[26] on a secular text that makes oblique reference to the Crucifixion, has found great favor in and out of religious precincts, whatever its appropriateness to a church service may be. Its popularity lies principally in its sonorities; its melodic passages are less appealing than the comfortable predictabilities and occasional surprises of its chordal relationships and delicious modulations. It is obvious that the two outstanding characteristics of his own choir, "the invariable beauty of tone and the unremitting pursuit of purity of enunciation,"[27] were uppermost in his mind as a composer also.

His strophic SSATB piece, *I see His blood upon the rose*,[28] affects a primitive style of consecutive fifths and octaves between the men's parts, parallel movement of the upper parts—the two sometimes expanding and returning in weak imitation of Vaughan Williams—and a simple three-part form. Its ingenuous qualities show planning rather than ineptness. What appears to be deliberate simplicity could be mistaken

---

[25] Routley, *Twentieth Century Church Music*, 32–37.
[26] G. Schirmer 8100.
[27] *Grove's*, VII, 188.   [28] G. Schirmer 8597.

Example 127. *Fanfare for Christmas Day*, Martin Shaw (G. Schirmer 8745, mm. 1–6).

By permission of J. Curwen & Sons Ltd., 29 Maiden Lane, London, W.C.2, England.

for lack of skill at the hands of another composer. The piece does lose effectiveness at the close of each section, where it is forced from passages principally modal into cadences in G major.

Roberton apparently left no students to follow his pattern, but the influence of his choir and his many compositions may have been of some consequence. His was not the only choir of high quality by this time. Others throughout Great Britain and the United States were pursuing a course of excellence in performance; in many cases their directors also reflected their ideals in compositions as well as public performances.

Two other prominent English anthem composers were born in the decade of the 1870s, the brothers Martin Shaw (1875–1958) and Geoffrey Shaw (1879–1943). Geoffrey held the post of inspector of music to the Board of Education, among other things promoting teacher training and music festivals, while Martin devoted more time to composition and editing, working with Ralph Vaughan Williams and Percy Dearmer in the publication of *Songs of Praise* and the *Oxford Book of Carols*. Both were church organists, and together they received the Lambeth degree of Doctor of Music from the Archbishop of Canterbury in 1932.

Geoffrey is known primarily for *Worship*,[29] an anthem setting of John Greenleaf Whittier's hymn, "O brother man, fold to thy heart thy brother." It is a tuneful piece with effective organ interludes, and a unison arrangement (*The Musical Times*, No. 967) places it well within the capabilities of choirs lacking the vocal resources to perform the regular four-part version, supplying at the same time another of those emergency pieces for Sundays when absenteeism strikes the choir loft. A Christmas anthem, *How far is it to Bethlehem*,[30] carries a Dorian melody in a simple but interesting manner.

Martin's list of published anthems is substantial, and several of them are widely sung. *Fanfare for Christmas Day*[31] is one of these. Here the composer has provided the option of singing it with or without the organ, and if the accompaniment is used, a further option of two trumpets may be elected. A short piece of just twenty-five measures in 2/2 time, it is concluded with surprising abruptness. A performance note indicates, however, that it may be sung through once pianissimo unaccompanied and then repeated fortissimo with accompaniment. Either way, it is an extraordinarily effective choral fanfare. The text consists entirely of the Latin phrase "Gloria in excelsis Deo," and seems to be intensified by Shaw's skillful mixture of block chords and short points of imitation. Another point of interest is the use of a bass ostinato in the opening measures (Example 127), very similar to Holst's use of this device seven years earlier in *Turn back, O man*.

The following year, 1923, Martin Shaw wrote his most popular anthem, *With a voice of singing*.[32] Composed as a festival number, it was provided with orchestral accompaniment. Again, ostinato patterns are prominent, contributing substantially to

[29] Novello Anth. 1147.   [30] Novello Sh. Anth. 245.
[31] J. Curwen 8745.   [32] J. Curwen 8103.

Example 128. *With a voice of singing*, Martin Shaw (G. Schirmer 8103, mm. 21–25).

By permission of J. Curwen & Sons Ltd., 29 Maiden Lane, London, W.C.2, England.

the air of excitement the piece can generate. Also, a similarity to *Turn back, O man* is seen in sudden shifts to distant keys. Example 128 shows an abrupt departure from a C-major tonality to A major, creating an unexpected burst of tonal color. A few measures later there is an equally sudden return to C major, and yet another shift to E major before the final return to the home key. There can be little doubt that much of the effectiveness of this anthem is due to those stylistic features also seen in the earlier work by Holst, by whom Shaw appears to have been influenced.

Benediction anthems are not numerous in the total repertory, and Martin Shaw's piece titled *A blessing*,[33] published in 1927, admirably suits this function. The opening words, "Go forth into the world in peace," set a mood of tranquility and, throughout, the text is brought to life by changing dynamics, melodic invention, and harmonic interest. Example 129 illustrates Shaw's use of chord alteration at a cadence point; in a C-major tonality, the E-major chord lends a brilliance to the progression, especially with the chordal expansion by contrary motion employed in the organ part. It is notable, too, that a choral unison is followed by octaves on the word *honour*, thus removing from the singers the responsibility of the altered chord, often an acute problem where degree inflection is involved.

Another of Martin Shaw's especially fine anthems is *O clap your hands together, all ye people*,[34] a setting of selected verses from Psalm 47. Verse 5 of the psalm, "God is gone up with a merry noise; and the Lord with the sound of a trump," has inspired word-painting in anthem composers from the time of William Byrd, and Shaw is no exception. The parallel thirds and horn fifths on triads suggest the merry noise of the trump, and the rising melodic figures on the words "is gone up" (Example 130) is obvious. The effect is further heightened by the successive statements of text and music at higher pitch levels, through a series of transient modulations.

His most elaborate anthem, *The greater Light*,[35] was published posthumously. The text, taken from T. S. Eliot's *The Rock*, is mystical in nature; and Shaw, not given to extravagant scorings for his anthems, here calls for tenor solo, double choir, and organ. Throughout the piece, a number of different keys and meters are explored, and the two equal choirs are used more in the Venetian style than in the English *decani-cantoris* tradition. Again, abrupt key changes are employed and ostinato patterns are plentiful, both in the choral and instrumental parts. Example 131 will give the reader some idea of the massive proportions of this work, a triumphant ending which serves as an appropriate finish to a productive life.

William H. Harris (1883–), while more closely allied with the church as a center for his musical activities than was Hugh Roberton, but less than were either of the Shaws, was also known as a choral conductor. His interest there, however, lay in large-scale works where the orchestra often shared the limelight. Perhaps for this reason the organ plays a significant part in his anthems. The choral parts of some, on the other hand, are relatively simple, as can be seen in the fact that a number of his works fit the

---

[33] J. Curwen 8668.   [34] Novello Anth. 1237.   [35] G. Schirmer 11473.

Example 129. *A blessing,* Martin Shaw (G. Schirmer 8668, mm. 12–15).

By permission of J. Curwen & Sons Ltd., 29 Maiden Lane, London, W.C.2, England.

four voices easily on two staves. Considerable skill in modulation and full use of romantic harmonies are his strongest effects; homophony is his usual product; unison passages, occasional unaccompanied sections, and brief imitative sections may be found, but these appear to be glib utterances of a man who knows his craft well. The foregoing comments hold true if we are to judge him by his Harvest anthem, *Fear not, O Lord,*[36] or his brief psalm setting, *The eyes of all wait upon thee, O Lord,*[37] An entirely

[36] Oxford E73.   [37] Oxford A142.

different picture is presented in his extended anthem, *O what their joy and their glory must be*,[38] Neale's translation of Abelard's "O quanta qualia." The piece is multisectional, employing a variety of keys, meters, vocal textures—several effective passages occur in which the men or women divide *a 3*, and they combine *a 5* without the organ in another—and several excellent unaccompanied sections that show his taste for full sonorities.

Several of the foregoing have been men whose work confined them to the church or to choral conducting. Composers who attempted all genres of musical expression have been rare since Vaughan Williams and Holst. One who achieved considerable reputation as a composer of opera, symphony, and especially of works for chamber groups was Cecil Armstrong Gibbs (1889–1960). He is variously credited with Romantic tendencies, the absorption of folk music as a style feature, and being an adherent of some ideas of Holst and Vaughan Williams. It may simply be that his connections with the Royal College of Music, first as a student and later as a teacher, show in this way. He is not to be categorized in simple fashion. As a composer of substance, he had command over a variety of skills, and they appear in different guises in his anthems. As a man of practical outlook, he composed easy pieces such as *Lord, thou hast been a refuge sure*,[39] a unison anthem with descant, and *Most glorious Lord of lyfe!*,[40] an uncomplicated but interesting unaccompanied SATB piece. For a higher level of performance he produced such works as his *Psalm CXXII* ("I was glad when they said unto me")[41] and *Easter*,[42] a setting of Edmund Spenser's sonnet. Touches of Vaughan Williams, Holst, and Martin Shaw may be found here, especially in the former, in the guise of enriched chords, sudden movements to enharmonic keys and chords, or keys a third away from the point of stability. The boldest of his works intended for nonprofessional use may well be his Harvest anthem, *Bless the Lord, O my soul*,[43] most effective in its SATB arrangement. Much of its effect comes from the impact of parallel triads in vigorous rhythmic accompaniment against chordal settings for the voices, although the contrasting middle section is effective in its quietly alternating vocal textures. Gibbs's bold style is well illustrated in Example 132, where the closing passages of this piece firmly move toward C major in the voices while the organ boldly resists until the final chord.

Three more men may be chosen to illustrate the strong attachment to the past that was felt by some composers of this period. It must be clear, however, that any small selection of anthems is not representative of a composer's life's work. The isolation of reactionary tendencies in these works, therefore, should not mislead us into believing that all the compositions of these men are of this same nature. George

[38] Davies and Ley, *op. cit.*, 367–82.
[39] Oxford T10.
[40] Davies and Ley, *op. cit.*, 296–99.   [41] Oxford A168.   [42] Oxford A3.

[43] Oxford E14, composed 1934, was for SB with optional tenor and alto, the tenors to sing with sopranos if all parts were used, thus making it an SAB work in effect. Oxford A129 is Gibbs's 1951 arrangement of the earlier version.

Example 130. *O clap your hands together, all ye people,* Martin Shaw (Novello Anth. 1237, mm, 39–41).

Copyright by Novello & Co., Ltd. Used by permission.

Example 131. *The greater Light*, Martin Shaw (G. Schirmer 11473, last 9 mm.).

By permission of J. Curwen & Sons Ltd., 29 Maiden Lane, London, W.C.2, England.

Oldroyd (1886–1951) has a setting of the *Prayer to Jesus*[44] by Richard Rolle, the four-teenth-century English mystic and hermit.[45] The barring of the piece is irregular, giving full freedom of melodic treatment to the expressively simple text. Its form consists of a short organ introduction—the only instrumental material provided for the entire piece—a treble solo repeated in harmonized form, a contrasting solo in baritone range, and a harmonized repetition that is slightly extended, the whole suitably set in Phrygian mode. The same alternation of solo and choral sections, also employing choral repetition of solo parts, is found in his Lenten anthem, *An heart that's broken and contrite*.[46] In this case the piece is underlaid with a carefully written organ part that exploits the sustaining qualities of the instrument. Joyously different is his setting of the carol *There is no rose of such virtue*.[47] The mixture of English and Latin texts is admirably set off by a change in musical material for each.

Henry G. Ley (1891–), in common with Oldroyd, enjoys giving his pieces an antiquarian touch by making the half-note the basic value. It may have been his continued acquaintance with old melodies—for he arranged a number of them for *The Church Anthem Book*—that imprinted his style with the diatonic pattern that appears at various pitches and rhythms with considerable regularity at the opening of his pieces. The archaistic appearance of the pages notwithstanding, his settings are often harmonically alive, as in his *Anthem for a harvest festival*,[48] or rhythmically vital as in his Advent anthem, *Come, Thou long expected Jesus*.[49]

Apparently of the same type is W. K. Stanton's (1891–) *When I survey the wondrous cross*.[50] Beginning with a quiet organ introduction, the piece moves through the four well-known stanzas of Watts's hymn, the third of which is unaccompanied for the first two lines. The choir is given its best opportunities at harmonically enriched chords during this brief passage. The final stanza holds a surprise; instead of proceeding with Stanton's original material, the familiar tune "Rockingham" is sung by the lower voices in augmentation while the sopranos provide a strong descant, the whole building to a grandiose fortissimo.

There is a body of anthem literature that comes in increasing quantity from Canada. The English can rightly claim to have set its patterns; the Americans properly derive satisfaction from having adopted a few of its composers' works; both are guilty of knowing too little about it. An excellent article in *MGG* fills the gap left by the total disregard for all things Canadian by *Grove's*; the Canadian Music Centre and the Canadian Broadcasting Corporation have worked toward supplying information

[44] Oxford A73.

[45] *The Oxford Dictionary of the Christian Church*, 1173, briefly discusses Rolle's life and significance as an author.

[46] Oxford A127.

[47] Oxford A127.

[48] Oxford E46.

[49] Oxford E24.

[50] Oxford A147.

Example 132. *Bless the Lord, O my soul*, C. Armstrong Gibbs (Oxford A129, last 8 mm.).

Used with permission of Oxford University Press.

about Canada's contributions;[51] and the short-lived *Canadian Music Journal* (1956–1962) supplied important data during its existence, but all have given little attention to anthems because of their small place in the total musical picture.

The beginnings of the Canadian anthem are directly traceable to England; in fact, they are essentially transplants of one line of English practice. The proximity of Canadian cities to American centers of publication appears to have had small effect except to provide, in some cases, convenient access to the works of Canadian composers by those publishers. The strong ties between the Dominion and Great Britain, and the emphasis on Anglican practices as the principal non-Latin religious outlet, may be credited with this connection. It is only recently that Americans have moved to Canada to practice the music profession, and their insignificant numbers have not caused any great stir there in the kind of music we are examining; conversely, some talented Canadians have moved southward to university and professional connections, robbing the Dominion of some of its important musical resources. It is difficult to identify Canadians easily; some who are listed as resident at some date may have left their home country by the time their works appear for consideration.

The two leading figures in religious choral music both came to their adopted land in the second decade of the twentieth century. It is to them that most of our attention must be devoted. Healey Willan (1880–1968) and Alfred Ernest Whitehead (1887–   ) influenced their own generation and the next as organists, composers, and teachers. To them must be credited a considerable amount of the energetic choral activity that has sprung up, for they worked in a relatively primitive situation despite the late date at which they began.

Healey Willan has been the more prolific by far. Of 253 short sacred choral works (other than carols) by 58 composers listed in the *Catalogue of Canadian Choral Music*, he produced 81. Alfred Whitehead has a total of 29, and other composers and arrangers have smaller numbers by far, their output ranging from a single piece in a few cases to 13 in that of Keith Bissell. Bare statistics are not to be taken as evidence of either high quality or its antithesis, but the overwhelming majority of pieces by Willan and the substantial number of works by Whitehead demand that we consider their place in this kind of music, especially since their publication by American firms has spread their music far beyond their immediate spheres of influence as local church musicians and teachers.

Willan's choral works vary from the four liturgical processions bearing the common title *Hail thee, festival day!*[52] to sets of unaccompanied motets, full anthems,

---

[51] Especially important to the study of anthem literature is the *Catalogue of Canadian Choral Music Available for Perusal from the Library of the Canadian Music Centre* (Toronto: Canadian Music Centre, [1966]), a mimeographed volume prepared by Keith MacMillan, Executive Secretary of the Centre. While this is represented as an interim catalogue only, it lists nearly 750 items, a significant number for a country so long ignored and so late to begin in the field. Church music receives some discussion in Helmut Kallmann, *A History of Music in Canada, 1534–1914* (Toronto: University of Toronto Press, 1960), but the late beginnings of the anthem production of Canadian composers can be seen in the relative absence of its discussion here.

verse anthems, and hymn-anthems. The complex anthems and motets are earlier than the other types; a trend toward simplicity and the needs of volunteer choirs can be seen in his later pieces. Coming from a childhood background that exposed him to the esoteric results of the Tractarian Reform—the restoration of plainsong in favor of Anglican chant—and that saw him trained in a choir school of some distinction in Eastbourne, it is not surprising that the results should still be visible in his early compositions. Even in Canada, he moved from a position of dignity and substance as organist-choirmaster at St. Paul's Church in Toronto to the Church of St. Mary Magdalene because he preferred to be in a High Church atmosphere.[53] It is entirely possible that the simplicity of Willan's later pieces can be attributed to his composition for a wider public than the High Church practice he favored.

One of his early pieces, *There were shepherds abiding in the field*,[54] more elaborate in its structure than most of his later works, presages at least one feature that was to become common in the anthems of his later decades. Opening with a quietly reflective passage for sopranos, and building up to full four-part texture, the text is divided by recitative passages. The Gospel story according to Luke stops with the words "good will towards men," and the anthem closes with a contrasting setting—a fugal exposition followed by a homophonic chorus, both in a new meter and tempo—of two verses from Hymn 56 of *Hymns Ancient and Modern*.[55] Only the text is used, Willan using an original setting that completely alters the character of the piece commonly known by its first line, "Let all mortal flesh keep silence." Harmonically the piece is not so advanced as were those of Stanford, Wood, or Noble, all of whom were born at least a decade earlier. Whether Willan's apparent lesser contacts with the core of musical activity can be credited with this reactionary approach, or whether it was inherent in his nature, a certain lack of inventiveness was to mark his works throughout his entire career, this apparently not doing great damage to his popularity in Canada and the United States, for at least one of his anthems has risen to the ranks of religious best-sellers and his name alone continues to stimulate sales.

Hail, true Body,[56] published in 1909, was also written before Willan left his positions in England; it shows a greater simplicity than the previous anthem and has some textual indebtedness to the Oxford Movement. It is a tenor solo with organ accompaniment, supported during its concluding third by the chorus singing reflective

[52] Intended for processional use at Easter Day, Ascension Day, Whit-Sunday, and a Dedication Festival, they employ proper texts to be sung in unison with organ, and lead to the Collect after a verse and response. H. W. Gray, C.M.R. 789, 790, 791, 792.

[53] The foregoing, and further information on Willan's career, may be found in greater detail in Godfrey Ridout, "Healey Willan," *The Canadian Music Journal*, III/3 (Spring, 1959), 4–14. A condensed list of his compositions, unfortunately not listing short works by title, appears in Giles Bryant, "The Music of Healey Willan," *Musicanada* (March, 1968), No. 9, 5–7.

[54] Novello Octavo Anthems 871. The piece dates from 1906, and obviously reflects Willan's experience with a tradition that demanded and supplied skilled soloists and a competent chorus.

[55] The numbering is that of the so-called Old Edition, 1889. In the Historical Edition it is Hymn 58.

[56] Novello Octavo Anthems 945.

phrases in alternation with the soloist. The melodic outlines are principally diatonic, the harmony is convincing but unprepossessing, and the choral parts are gratifying to all, not a dull phrase being found in their generally uncomplicated material. These features mark the output of this most prominent of Canadian anthem composers after his appearance in his new surroundings, as well. His music is appealing, relatively simple, and it communicates easily to singers and to congregations alike. It is generally true of the liturgical pieces mentioned above, and it remains true of the quantity of anthems produced about midcentury.

One piece that explores a dramatic vein he left otherwise untapped is his Christmas piece, *The Three Kings*,[57] covering a wide dynamic range and using SSA and TBB groups first as contrasting textures before combining them as a doubled three-part texture. A male chorus version, using TBB solo voices with TTBB chorus has recently been arranged.[58] Willan possibly thought this work unsuited to church use—a fact borne out by Oxford's including it under its Choral Songs series rather than one of the anthem series—for his choice of rehearsal instrument is piano rather than organ.

More consistent with the norm is his popular Thanksgiving anthem, *Sing to the Lord of harvest*,[59] which employs a stanza of unaccompanied and accompanied materials, another in which accompanied women's voices alternate with accompanied men's, each moving mainly in comfortably satisfying thirds, and a closing unison section that blossoms into full four-part texture as its finale. The acceptance of his style by such a large public does not indicate a low level of taste on the part of either the composer or the chorister. The music has substance, and it has appeal without sacrificing quality; it simply has no part in the harmonic developments that are evident in the works of many leading composers beginning with his generation. One clue to the reason for the durability of his anthems lies in their sturdy melodic material. *Sing to the Lord of harvest*, for instance, is based on the tune "Wie lieblich ist der Maien," and the vigorous harmonization Willan has provided gives it an infectious energy (Example 133). Hymn-anthems abound in his output, among them such favorites as the *Hymn-Anthem on the tune "O Quanta Qualia"*[60] and *Father of heaven, whose love profound*,[61] the latter employing the tune "Angelus." There are also a number of useful settings of psalm verses and some festival pieces. His pupil, Godfrey Ridout, in evaluating Willan's success, wrote: "No one is going to ask a century from now whether or not Willan's music was 'representative of the time,' but rather, Is it good music? I think it is, and will always be."[62] Whatever the decision of time will be, it is evident that Willan has been the first to bring Canadian music to the attention of choristers, and his compositions, while failing to reflect the changes that overtook the English anthem in its own country, were serviceable, generally dignified, and gave Canadian composers a firm footing from which to continue building a tradition.

[57] Oxford 43 P 214 (OCS 718).   [58] Oxford 41 023.
[59] Concordia 98-2013.   [60] Edition Peters 6066.
[61] Concordia 98-2005.   [62] Ridout, *op. cit.*, 14.

Example 133. *Sing to the Lord of harvest*, Healey Willan (Concordia 98–2013, mm. 5–9).

Reprinted by permission of Concordia Publishing House, copyright 1954.

Alfred Whitehead was born in 1887 in Peterborough, England, was trained in the cathedral there, and took a position as organist-choirmaster at a Congregational church in that city.[63] He went to Nova Scotia in 1912, moved on to New Brunswick the following year, and returned to the Anglican precincts after 1915, first in Sherbrooke, Quebec, and later in Montreal, where he took over the mixed "cock and hen" choir of Christ Church Cathedral in 1922, a group that he placed in the gallery while his male choir sang plainsong from the front of the church.[64]

Whitehead's anthems began to appear in print in the 1930s, although there are some carols from a few years earlier. The distinction among anthem, motet, and carol becomes increasingly tenuous by this time, depending more upon the character of text, the presence of contrapuntal lines, or the absence of accompaniment than upon historic antecedents for the several types of pieces. In his 1931 publication *Jesu, the very thought of Thee*,[65] Whitehead abandoned time signatures and provided thereby a free flow of quarter-note beats varying from two to six per measure. The text comes from *Hymns Ancient and Modern*,[66] employing four of five stanzas in through-composed fashion, but with sectional pauses at the end of each stanza. The harmonies venture beyond the ordinary sturdy chord relationships so common in Willan's anthems, using a few seventh chords in nondominant functions, but the effect is one of remote religiosity rather than daring innovation. In later years of the same decade, Whitehead drew on German tune sources for his Easter pieces *Christ the Lord is risen*[67] and *Come, ye faithful, raise the strain*,[68] on a text by Watts and a translation by Neale, respectively. These pieces show a forthright treatment, vigorous and robust. The first is accompanied by organ; the second is unaccompanied with variable triple and quadruple meter. The harmonizations are less adventurous than in his earlier free-meter piece. A similar situation prevails in his *Come, Thou Almighty King*,[69] based on the tune "Serug." The composer appears to be seeking a wider market at the expense of original ideas, and it is at this point that Canadian music turns away from its first opportunity to adopt the more vital style that had begun to appear in England just prior to the generation of Vaughan Williams.

Outright arrangements of instrumental pieces also appear. From William Byrd's *Pavane for the Earl of Salisbury*, originally a piece for virginal, he arranged a short but appealing motet, *I have longed for thy saving health*.[70] From the F-minor organ sonata of Mendelssohn he adapted *Praise him, ye that fear him*,[71] a busy piece for solo quartet, chorus, and organ. Only in the Lorenz publications have we seen this kind of treatment. Although Whitehead's greater skill is evident in the result, it seems odd that a man of his capacities should devote time to such activities instead of applying his own

---

[63] Ellinwood, *op. cit.*, 238.

[64] C. F. MacRae, "Alfred Whitehead," *The Canadian Music Journal*, V/2 (Winter, 1961), 14–20.

[65] H. W. Gray, C.M.R. 1105.

[66] *Hymns Ancient and Modern* (Historical Edition), 624–25. See Julian, *op. cit.*, I, 588, concerning the original text and its translation.

[67] H. W. Gray, C.M.R. 1129.   [68] H. W. Gray, C.M.R. 1200.   [69] C. Fischer, CM 602.
[70] H. W. Gray, C.M.R. 1679.   [71] H. W. Gray, C.M.R. 1440.

creative powers to setting the same texts. That he could write fine original material is evident from *Jesu, the very thought of Thee* and the later Easter anthem, *If ye then be risen with Christ*.[72] This last is for mixed chorus and soprano and baritone solos, accompanied throughout. The organ part for the concluding sections is carefully written out for manuals and pedal on three staves. Changes of key and meter are used to good advantage in setting off the several sections of this verse anthem, and the pairing of voices at the beginning of phrases that blossom to full four parts becomes an effective device (Example 134*a*). The closing section is built on a melody that is choralelike, but does not appear to be borrowed (Example 134*b*). The final verse of text comes from the translation of the Easter hymn *Aurora lucis rutilat*;[73] the penultimate verse is from some other source not traceable here.

We have not been able to devote space for comprehensive study of Willan's and Whitehead's works, but this overview shows the course upon which Canadian anthem composition was first set. The younger composers, especially any who can be identified as students of the two older men, will be responsible for any continuation and modification of their practices, and still others may provide some new directions.

Graham George (1912–   ), born in England but removed to Canada in his youth, was Whitehead's student from 1932 to 1936, and he studied composition with Paul Hindemith as well. He became a university professor and organist-choirmaster,[74] and it may be that some of his freedom from the tyranny of regular meter stems from his study with Whitehead. His *Lord of all power and might*[75] and *Ride on! ride on!*[76] are unhampered by meter signatures, their measure lengths varying according to the demands of their texts, but his *O worship the King*[77] holds sternly to triple meter throughout. Simplicity vies with complexity in that respect, for his treatment of material does not provide a key to the decade in which the piece was published. *In God's commands*,[78] his latest work at hand, exploits metrical freedom and seems highly chromatic at first sight. The latter feature, however, is primarily a clutter on the page caused by the avoidance of a key signature, and by the repeated printing of flats that are not often enough canceled to warrant the device of indicating every alteration within the melodic lines. George is not to be dismissed lightly. His music has a touch of the harmonic inventiveness that we saw among the later English composers; unfortunately it is often hampered by a plodding sameness of rhythm, for all that he worked at freedom from metrical uniformity. The occasional touches of quartal harmony, parallel motion of seventh chords, and other like breaks with the past provide more promise than fulfillment.

The difference among promising, adequate, good, and outstanding choral material is not something that is easily agreed upon. Differences of opinion vary as greatly as do the assorted experiences and needs of those who examine the pieces. There can be no

[72] H. W. Gray, C.M.R. 1418.

[73] *Hymns Ancient and Modern* (Historical Edition), 199.

[74] Ellinwood, *op. cit.*, 213.   [75] H. W. Gray, C.M.R. 1653.   [76] H. W. Gray, C.M.R. 1765.

[77] H. W. Gray, C.M.R. 2037.   [78] H. W. Gray, C.M.R. 2873.

Example 134. *If ye then be risen with Christ*, Alfred Whitehead (H. W. Gray, C.M.R. 1418, mm. 24–31, 90–109).

(a)

(b)

Copyright by The H. W. Gray Co. Used by permission.

question, however, that the Canadian works thus far produced have not reached the level of Wood, Bairstow, Vaughan Williams, and other leading English composers. The younger men in Canada may provide a figure of leadership in the choral field, but when he emerges his success must be demonstrated in more works than we can examine here. A few of the several promising figures deserve our attention; since examples of their work are not numerous, it will be unfair to make extensive comments on their qualities.

William E. France (1912–   ) takes his text for *Bread of the world*[79] from Bishop Heber, and for *O Trinity of blessed light*[80] from John Mason Neale. Both works are

[79] H. W. Gray, C.M.R. 2220.   [80] H. W. Gray, C.M.R. 1944.

unaccompanied, restrained pieces that have interesting part writing, an economy of text usage in their nonrepetitive, direct expression, and solidly interesting harmonies. It may be that his other pieces, published by Canadian firms, are equally interesting. A similar situation may prevail with George Fox, whose *Come, Holy Dove*[81] is a piece that shows some skill in contrapuntal writing along with sensitive treatment of text. His *Jesu, Thou wast born to us*[82] shows his familiarity with well-known pieces by Bach and Berlioz, although the apparent contamination by *Jesu, joy of man's desiring* and "The shepherds' farewell" from *L'Enfance du Christ* may be unconscious.

Keith Bissell (1912–   ) was born in Canada and studied composition at the University of Toronto with Leo Smith (1881–   ), who had come from England in 1910, thus being numbered among the considerable group that preceded both Whitehead and Willan. Bissell has not confined his compositional activities to church music, having a number of instrumental works in print and being widely known in Canadian music education. His *Christ, being raised from the dead*[83] and *Hear Thou my prayer, O Lord*[84] are accompanied SATB pieces that carry on the practice of polymetric writing to suit textual needs, employ nondominant seventh chords in consistent fashion, and the former closes with the fanfarelike use of triads moving freely from step to step. In quieter mood is his unaccompanied *Christ, whose glory fills the skies*,[85] in which the vocal parts, generally in closed position, achieve a quiet contrast by spreading occasionally through contrary motion. His anthems are solidly practical, showing a command of romantic harmonies, an understanding of the possibilities of impressionism, and always a careful consideration of what can be accomplished by the nonprofessional choral group.

The relative dearth of Canadian materials may be attributed to two factors, neither of which indicates a lack of interest in music on the part of the Dominion's population, but both of which appear to be in direct relationship to the slow development of an essentially urban practice in a country of great size, and one that is largely underpopulated. In comparing the financial returns from church music of Americans and Canadians, Charles Peaker wrote that in the United States "organists are better paid, and I do believe their social standing is better than ours, but the less said about Great Britain the better, since 'wages' there are such that the music of the church is largely in the hands of those amateurs who can *afford* to play."[86] That young people lack the incentive to study for careers in church music, and the opportunity as well, is indicated where he wrote, "in Canada, unlike most other countries (and especially unlike the United States) church music is the Cinderella of the arts since no university in the land is offering a reasonable course in the subject or acknowledging the need of that most consistent patron of music the world has ever known, to wit, the church."[87]

[81] H. W. Gray, C.M.R. 2468.   [82] H. W. Gray, C.M.R. 2591.
[83] Gordon V. Thompson G 537.   [84] Gordon V. Thompson G 544.
[85] Gordon V. Thompson G 556.
[86] Charles Peaker, "Help Wanted, Male or Female," *The Canadian Music Journal*, III/3 (Spring, 1959), 39.
[87] *Ibid.*, 38.

Canada is still coming to grips with the need to appear among the cultural nations of the world in the more sophisticated musical spheres of concert hall and opera house. The production of church music, except for a few cases, is confined to composers whose capacities are too meager for them to contribute meaningfully at other levels, or whose involvement in the more complex types of composition prohibits their devoting much attention to anthems, which all too often, if they are to win favor, must meet a relatively low standard of quality and must contribute to continuing mediocrity.

In the United States, by contrast, sheer bulk of production goes hand in hand with variety. This, as we shall see later, is not necessarily to the advantage of musical quality, although the winnowing process is theoretically easier as the harvest is plentiful. The problem is, how to dispose of the chaff.

The situation with recent and living English composers is no more simple than with the Canadians. Since the establishment of *The Musical Times*, the growth of the Novello firm, the emergence of other significant British publishers, and the development of a larger market for choral music, it has not been easy to note whether a particular composer was descended from the cathedral tradition, the parish church, or the Royal College of Music; and it has not mattered to any great extent, since most were trying to meet the taste of the singing public without losing their own sense of dignity. The few outstanding composers who dominated changing taste had done so because they were men of superior talent and training; the others who were successful became so because of an increasing need for music and because of sufficient skill as composers to warrant publication. The works of Eric H. Thiman (1900–) are sufficiently different from most others in the century to warrant a special place. Thiman is obviously of the Free Church line. His emphasis on unison singing, his penchant for forcefully melodic material, and his vigorous organ support of free-flowing melody, all stem from his life-long work in the Congregationalist denomination. His anthem melodies are the stuff one would wish hymns were made of; that his own congregation at Park Chapel Congregational Church has developed unusual skills in singing[88] may be one of the reasons his anthems bear such a firm stamp of vigorous melody rather than sophisticated harmony.

Any number of Thiman's anthems may be selected to illustrate this vigorous character; some of them, in fact, are simply unison pieces with accompaniment, and in some cases, a descant. More typical, however, is his *Grant us light*,[89] beginning with two measures for organ, continuing through a four-phrase unison stanza with organ, another two-measure link, and a harmonized second stanza with optional accompaniment. A longer organ passage leads into the closing unison section with descant, and the piece concludes with a harmonized "Amen." This successful pattern is followed in other anthems with slight variety of the length of linking phrases or, as in *A thanksgiving hymn*,[90] by the addition of a stanza for sopranos between the harmonized stanza

<hr/>

[88] *Grove's*, VIII, 421.   [89] G. Schirmer 10288.   [90] Mills Music 376.

and the usual closing one for unison voices with descant. Another variant treatment is found in *Christ the Lord is risen again*,[91] in which simple imitative entries are made on the "alleluia" sections, and a more complex accompaniment is added to the final unison section in place of the usual descant. That Thiman's approach to these pieces has been widely imitated—and often with less success than he had—should not be used as a critical weapon against him. The approach was fresh when he undertook it, and he has produced many a singable melody that will continue for years in choral libraries.

A man familiar with both the cathedral and the parish church was Percy W. Whitlock (1903–1946). He was best known in the area of organ playing and composition, but he has left anthems representative of his work as organist-choirmaster. His *Three Introits*[92] and the anthem *Sing praise to God who reigns above*[93] reflect his connection with Rochester Cathedral, where he was assistant organist. *He is risen*[94] and *Come, let us join our cheerful songs*[95] more probably stem from his parish church association where simplicity and direct musical communication were the order of the day. Whitlock's pieces are well worth exploring for practical use. His introits are excellent works of a reserved nature. The second, *Here, O my Lord, I see Thee face to face*, and the third, *Be still, my soul*, are given interesting passages that alternate and combine the singers and organ, and both show an increasing consciousness for vocal sonorities over many pieces previously examined. At cadence points Whitlock expands a normally four-part texture to five or six parts, the spacing of the voices being as important as their number (Example 135), for the effect is stunning in comparison with many earlier works that used more parts. The use of parts *divisi* for moments of intense expression has been noted before, but Whitlock adds the fullness of varied sonorities to other points in his compositions as well. The easy anthems follow the paths so well traveled by the Shaws and Thiman, but they appear less formula-ridden than the pieces of those more popular composers.

It is one of the misfortunes of our age that the most highly esteemed and best prepared composers have usually found it inconvenient and unchallenging to write short works for church use except as special favors to friends or to commemorate a special occasion. William Walton (1902–), Lennox Berkeley (1903–), and Benjamin Britten (1913–) serve as outstanding examples of our plight; a few other names also come readily to mind. It is the good fortune of the musical world generally (and the ill fortune of church music specifically) that Henry Ley recognized Walton's special abilities when the boy was a chorister at Oxford's Christ Church Cathedral Choir School. What he has given to us as useful music for the church is extremely limited, and our appetites are only whetted by examining any of it. His simple carol *What cheer?*[96] never deviates from SATB arrangement, and its direct expression clothed in interestingly varied harmonic phrases shows how even the slightest materials may be illumi-

[91] *The Musical Times* 1032. [92] Oxford A41, A42, A43.
[93] Oxford A18. [94] Oxford E10. [95] Oxford E42.
[96] *Carols for Choirs*, ed. and arr. by Reginald Jacques and David Willcocks (London: Oxford University Press, 1961), 162–64.

Example 135. *Here, O my Lord, I see Thee face to face*, Percy W. Whitlock (Oxford A42, mm. 22–30).

Used with permission of Oxford University Press.

nated in skilled hands. His anthem *Set me as a seal upon thine heart*[97] appears to be a simple alternation piece between tenor soloist and chorus at the outset, but its harmonic turns, parallel intervals, and ambiguities of harmonic center that never quite lose their orientation give it a touch of style that is new to the scene. Unfortunately, it has not been sufficiently profitable or interesting to Walton to supply a quantity of works suitable for church choirs.

Lennox Berkeley likewise has been a producer of only a few examples. His approach lies outside the traditions that nourished most English composers, bringing a taste of the French style—he was a student of Nadia Boulanger from 1926 to 1932—and showing some influences of Stravinsky's impact on his generation. *Lord, when the sense of thy sweet grace*,[98] one of a pair of anthems published in the mid-forties, opens an entirely new vista of harmonic richness. Berkeley's sense of what is practical writing for chorus is evident in his careful assignment of his harmonic peculiarities to the organ and his retention of characteristic choral textures and sonorities for the singers. Benjamin Britten is another of whom too little has been heard in churches. His longer compositions have been given attention by capable choral organizations, but pieces of anthem length and function are apparently not his choice, and the sections that can be extracted from his cantata-length works are unfortunately also limited.

Several composers born in the last decade of the nineteenth century contributed substantially to the more progressive anthem repertory. Of those under consideration here—Ernest Bullock (1890–), Herbert Howells (1892–), Alec Rowley (1892–1958), and Gordon Jacob (1895–)—Howells is the most widely recognized, with a substantial list of published works that includes a variety of instrumental as well as choral music. Although his list of church music is sizable, Howells wrote only a few anthems. One of a set of three carol anthems, *A spotless rose*,[99] was published in 1919, thus dating back to the same time as the early contributions of Vaughan Williams and Holst. It is a particularly beautiful and effective setting of a fourteenth-century Christmas text, involving frequent meter changes and parallel-motion triads, and seventh chords in a variety of inversions. Howells here seems to share Vaughan Williams' affinity for unusual cadences; the closing cadence, both extended and involved, effectively captures the feeling of the text (Example 136).

We have heard with our ears,[100] the second of a set of four anthems for chorus and organ published in 1943, also is characterized by changing meters. The piece is essentially tonal, alternating between D minor and D major, but the combined use of dissonant chords and nonharmonic tones in the accompaniment, and the angular quality of the melodic line give a truly modern air to the work. The difficulties for the choir, however, are minimized through the extensive use of unison singing, while the relatively few measures of part writing create no real problems for the singers. In this

[97] *TECM*, V, 128–32.
[98] *Ibid.*, 133–42. The editors provide an excellent analysis of the anthem on pp. 210–11.
[99] Stainer and Bell 2185.
[100] Oxford A108.

Example 136. *A Spotless Rose*, Herbert Howells (Stainer & Bell 220, last 5 mm.).

Used with permission of Stainer & Bell Ltd., Reigate, Surrey.

way the composer is able to write fresh, interesting music without removing it from the repertory of the amateur choir.

Likewise, the anthems of Ernest Bullock show a high degree of compositional skill and creative talent. In *Christ, the fair glory of the holy Angels*,[101] the composer fashions a chantlike melody, basically in the Dorian mode, setting a translation of a ninth-century text by Archbishop Rabanus Maurus (Example 137). Word-painting is used to portray the line "steps up to heaven," and shifting meters, especially 5/4 and 7/4 measures, avert the rhythmic monotony that so frequently besets anthems. The skillful use of organ accompaniment and the splendid part-writing reveal a composer of unusual ability.

Example 137.   *Christ, the fair glory of the holy Angels*, Ernest Bullock (Oxford A8, mm. 11–14).

Used with permission of Oxford University Press.

A less ambitious piece, *Drop, drop, slow tears*,[102] is based on Orlando Gibbons' beautiful Song 46. Here the restrained musical setting allows the significant lines of Fletcher's poetry to speak without hindrance.

While Bullock is mainly a church composer, Alec Rowley was not. His range of composition extended from chamber music to such unusual works as a piano concerto with military band accompaniment, and a wordless vocal suite. Rowley's anthem production, nevertheless, is fairly sizable when measured against some of his contemporaries. Although his works in this form do not rise to the level of those by Howells and Bullock, they are, for the most part, serviceable. *Praise*,[103] an earlier work, and no doubt one of his best, has been a mainstay in many church choir libraries. It has a vital rhythmic drive, and the solid melodic line and good voice-leading produce few, if any, problems for volunteer singers. Along this same line, a unison Easter anthem, *Christ the Lord is risen today*,[104] has a strong melodic line and a rousing organ accompaniment, providing an effective festal piece for choirs with limited vocal resources. A later

---

[101] Oxford A8.   [102] Oxford A45.
[103] Oxford A24.   [104] Novello, M.T. 1210.

Example 138. *The twenty-third psalm*, Gordon Jacob (Oxford E59, mm. 18–29).

Used with permission of Oxford University Press.

anthem, *Let all the world in every corner sing*,[105] likewise is possessed of an impelling rhythmic force, but here, unlike Howell's skillful handling of *We have heard with our ears*, Rowley holds the choir responsible for many of the changes in chord color and shifts in tonality, and while the piece by no means presents an insurmountable performance problem, one wonders if it is really worth the effort.

Although Gordon Jacob is best known in church circles for his anthem *Brother James's air*,[106] a perennial favorite with choirs, his major contribution has been to the field of instrumental music, for which he has written extensively and well. *Brother James's air* is a simple but effective arrangement of James Leith Macbeth Bain's tune, "Marosa," one of the fine melodies for the old Scottish Psalter version of Psalm 23. Although *a cappella* performance is the norm, string parts are available on rental. Some eighteen years after its publication, Jacob published another entirely original setting of the same text. *The twenty-third psalm*[107] shows the composer in a different light. The anthem opens with a simple melody in F major, which quickly shifts to remote keys on the words "He restoreth my soul" (Example 138). Short segments of accompaniment, sometimes only a measure long, are repeated in ostinato fashion, giving the piece a stability that is even more evident when the accompaniment figures are transferred to the vocal lines.

A more ambitious piece, however, is *O Lord, I will praise thee*,[108] where the opening unison melody invests the anthem with unusual strength and vitality (Example 139). The contrasting harmonized middle section is punctuated by massive fanfare chords in the organ accompaniment, and the piece returns to the forceful opening statement with simple harmonization at the end.

Younger British composers have begun to contribute to the repertory of church music, and they provide new directions. The situation is somewhat parallel to that we saw with the young Canadians who broke away from the pattern of their older teachers. Among the young British group are Donald Cashmore (1926–), John Joubert (1927–), and Malcolm Williamson (1931–), and it is significant that two of these men were born outside England.

The work of Cashmore may be seen in two anthems, *Give unto the Lord, O ye mighty*[109] and *God is ascended up on high*.[110] Definitely in a contemporary idiom, these pieces are characterized by melodic and harmonic inventiveness, but are faulted by excessive repetition of musical materials and by cadences that seem forced and unnatural. There is a rugged strength to his melodies, and a feeling of vitality pervades the rhythmic structure through sometimes unorthodox accentuation of text. It should be noted that Cashmore is a consistent contributor to the Novello catalogue, and examination of other works must be undertaken as well to get a true picture of his importance as an emerging figure on the choral scene.

John Joubert was born in Cape Town, South Africa, and received his early musical education there, moving to England in 1946 after having studied at the South

---

[105] Oxford A130.   [106] Oxford 763.   [107] Oxford E59.   [108] Oxford E62.
[109] Novello, M.T. 1400.   [110] Novello Anth. 1403.

Example 139. *O Lord, I will praise thee,* Gordon Jacob (Oxford E62, mm. 5–13).

Used with permission of Oxford University Press.

African College of Music. The scholarship that enabled him to attend the Royal
Academy of Music for two years was extended beyond its original term, and Joubert
took up residence in England. He is an experienced composer for all media of performance; consequently his choral music may not attract the attention given that of
n.:n who produce greater quantities, but the unusual features of style found in his few
anthems mark him as a truly significant contributor. His *Torches*[111] is a melodically

[111] *Carols for Choirs*, 150–53.

Example 140.   *Great Lord of lords*, John Joubert (Novello Anth. 1329, mm. 1–9).

su - preme___ im - mor - - - tal King, ___

su - preme___ im - mor - - - tal King, ___

su - preme___ im - mor - - - tal King, ___

su - preme___ im - mor - - - tal King, ___

Copyright by Novello & Co., Ltd. Used by permission.

strong piece, opening with a unison stanza and continuing in treble-dominated har-monization. The interval of a fourth—as well as its inversion—is prominent in melody and accompaniment alike, the latter conveying suggestions of parallel organum. The rhythmic vitality is due largely to regularly spaced chords in the accompaniment and to strong leaps and dotted figures in the melody. The composition is within the grasp of any capable volunteer choir.

Far more complex is his *Great Lord of lords*,[112] a long anthem for SATB, moving

[112] Novello Anth. 1329.

into double-chorus writing for a time. Its melodic contours are formidable, and their relationship to each other creates problems beyond the capacities of most choral organizations that meet only once weekly. Leaps of fifths, in themselves not a challenge to any group that deserves to sing together, become extremely difficult when taken as successive jumps in the same direction; when they occur in two parts, one of which must achieve stability a minor second away from the other, their only justification, from the director's viewpoint, lies in the great sense of excitement and strength that is imparted to the composition. The anthem is filled with difficulties, among the least of which are the large skips and avoidance of consonant stability (Example 140). None but the skilled and adventurous should attempt this piece; it is probably not the kind of fare that will please congregations, but it marks a brave new direction and bears investigation as a new means of communicating religious text.

Another foreign-born composer is Malcolm Williamson, whose early study was with Eugene Goosens at the Sydney Conservatory. He left Australia in 1950, studied in London, and subsequently became a church organist, a composer of instrumental and vocal pieces both secular and religious, and has sampled serial techniques and the "pop" idiom alike. His anthem output is apparently limited, but one piece is available for examination. *Let them give thanks*[113] presents no formidable problems to the choir, for he approaches dissonances in stepwise fashion, and his difficult melodic leaps and complex chord structures are confined to the organ. The congregation is expected to participate on a strong melody in simple note values, first in unison with the choir and with organ accompaniment, finally in a version wherein the choir supplies simple harmony and melodic support at the same time. This single piece is probably no more representative of his style than the examples by Cashmore and Joubert should be considered as the limits of their capabilities.

Most significant here is the fact that men of their generation have arrived on the scene and are experimenting with materials for the choir. The injection of a spirit from outside England may serve to regenerate what was a dying effort since the years between the two World Wars. The men to whom we looked with hope—Walton, Berkeley, Britten, and their generation—were not moved to supply materials that could be put to use in the choir. Those who continued to write often had nothing new to say, or took refuge in patterns that soon became commonplace. It is to men of the talent and varied skill of this youngest generation that we must turn if we are to find a new and vital kind of music to assume the position that was vacated when the excitement of Vaughan Williams and Holst subsided. We have waited in vain for a strong English-born leader to take up the cause of the religious set piece. Perhaps the new force will come, if it comes at all, from outside England.

[113] *TECM*, V, 191–95.

CHAPTER TEN

Twentieth-Century America— A Melting Pot of Tastes

A number of forces have worked toward making the American anthem different from its English and Canadian counterparts. The very size, density of population, and variety of religious practices in American Free Church groups, as well as the adoption of anthems by liturgically founded denominations—the Lutherans, for example, even though they often call their pieces motets or employ other euphemisms —and the large number of publishing houses that vie for this immense market, these are only some of the forces that have stimulated the production of a variety of choral materials. At the same time, a number of these forces have been significant deterrents to the establishment of a consistently high level of music. In churches where the term *anthem* is shunned as a dangerous remnant of liturgical practice, and where the incidental choral or solo music is called the *special*, an almost incredible lack of taste is often evident, but it is readily accepted by benumbed captive audiences because of the spirit in which they believe it should be received. There is no place in the United States that can provide such large numbers of listeners to music on a regular basis, and in which such bad performances are regularly accepted, as the churches. Unfortunately, in addition to serious, competent composers who write for this market, there are some who grasp the opportunity to cater to the lowest level of taste.

It has been apparent throughout our study that adherence to tradition is not the only answer to musical development. Traditions have been followed, modified, and

FIGURE 8. *The assembled choirs of Hollywood First Presbyterian Church. Dr. Charles C. Hirt is Minister of Music, and Lucy A. Hirt is director of the children's choirs.*

sometimes rejected; each path has brought us to significant changes in anthem composition. At no time in the course of the several centuries during which we have observed the changing anthem, however, has the opportunity for commercial gain been so great; at no time have so many composers, good, bad, and indifferent, attempted to capture the profitable top of this market. This is not the place to deplore at length the state of American church music, but it must be noted, with emphasis, that the wide acceptance of low-quality musical materials has given a bad reputation to church music in general—even those who write about it are suspect, as if to mention its deficiencies is to subscribe to them—and serious composers who could do the most for anthem composition, who could, by imaginative employment of their superior skills, improve its lot or change its direction, avoid it for fear of becoming contaminated by its reputation, or they write compositions that are so far beyond the grasp and taste of its most enlightened performers and listeners that their products are rejected as unsingable, unappealing, and unreligious. This is the state of the anthem by the last third of our century. When we try to examine what happened since the days of Neidlinger and Shelley, a period during which serious American composers were already avoiding the idiom, we shall find no one of the stature of Vaughan Williams giving serious thought to anthem writing.

While taste and talent have played their part in the establishment of current American practices, certain matters of technology have also been brought to bear. It may have been the growth of competition that caused American publishers to use better quality paper, more appealing formats (except for some few companies), and eye-catching advertising and covers. Continuing with a small number of well-established publishing houses, Britain held to a small variety of musical styles, often publishing in unimaginative editions because near-monopoly requires no deviation from acceptability.[1] American houses flourished not because of unorthodox practices, but because of the variety of their markets, and the rise of the several denominational presses and small new firms continues to give strength to this claim.

American churches can boast in only a few cases of a chapel style or tradition. Much of what is done is under the guidance of interested amateurs, more willing than able, or ill-trained professionals who may be variously known as song leaders, choir directors, or ministers of music; or rarely there may be competent professionals who serve as overseers of complex "cradle to the grave" choral programs. Most people who serve this public are part-time workers, and excellent artists are to be found among them. It does not necessarily follow that the most complicated choral program is the best, for some small choirs have achieved an excellence that is lacking in the larger programs of other churches.

Such a large variety of practitioners indicates a large variety of tastes, and an equally large series of levels for publishers to serve. Add to this a market that is virtually unknown outside this country, the public school choral organizations. Beginning with choirs in the upper grade levels of elementary school, continuing through the junior high schools, and culminating not only in high school choruses of various degrees of accomplishment, but in choral groups in many of our colleges and universities, there is a market in the educational field that absorbs as much religious music as it does secular. While spoken prayer has been outlawed in public schools, its sung counterpart coupled with praise in song has flourished and is eagerly sought because, much as we have complained about the low musical level it presents, it is often more interesting than its secular counterpart, and its directors can dip into arrangements from earlier non-English works as part of their regular fare. All in all, the American

---

[1] Not all of Britain's problems in publishing can be laid at the door of bad taste or publishers' inertia. The long fight by the Novello firm, especially under J. Alfred Novello, to put aside certain restrictive laws directed against knowledge by the taxation of paper, advertisements, and newspapers sent through the mails can be read in detail in *A Short History of Cheap Music*.

scene has found a world of publishing and marketing that would have staggered the imagination of the most successful composer-arranger of a century earlier. For this varied market the composers have written, not what is the best setting they can make of a text, but what will be useful at a certain level of learning or proficiency, what will be appealing to the director, the singers, and the judges of the spring festival or contest, what will satisfy the congregations of churches where anthems are sung as concert pieces or as fillers during the collection of the morning offering rather than as evocative settings of religious texts seasonally, liturgically, or dogmatically suitable. Unless a composer chooses to direct his efforts to one of these many markets, he may ignore them or he must attempt to satisfy them all, a virtually impossible task unless he lowers his artistic standards. We have, then, a wide variety of types of composers: competent, dedicated men and women who write a few meaningful pieces; good craftsmen who write considerable quantities with taste and skill; hack writers who work according to a formula that sells regularly; and outright charlatans who cater to the taste that developed with the foot-tapping tunes of the last century. Our pursuit of these will be limited to composers who claim to write for the church; the development of the educational market is another story entirely which, although it deserves telling, does not belong here.

So many people have entered the field of anthem composition, arranging, editing, and compiling in this century that it would be impossible to treat them equally or comprehensively. Such has not been the case in earlier chapters of this book, nor will it be in the present one. The names that are selected for consideration here are not necessarily those that reflect the greatest number of anthems in print, the highest in quality, nor the most unusual in character. Rather, two groups of composers are represented: first, those who established new practices, either related to English counterparts or along new paths; and, second, those who have pursued an acceptable level of conventionality, and who, while doing so, were able to produce anthems of unusual popularity. A few individuals who fit neither group must also be mentioned. Before considering their contributions, however, it is necessary to examine a strong current that entered the mainstream of American choral style, and which, directly or indirectly, influenced a number of native composers.

If any outside force can be said to have changed the course of American anthem composition from its patterns of imported practices and the unique developments of its early beginnings on this continent, it would be the taste for Russian liturgical music. Faint beginnings of this imported material were seen in the nineteenth century, when Bortniansky's *Vesper Hymn* made its appearance in *Templi Carmina* and in Gould's *Social Harmony*, and when that same composer's *Cherubic Hymn No. 7* (there entitled *Blessed be Jehovah, God of Israel*) first appeared in a collection of L. O. Emerson's (see p. 309). The latter composition, more truly an anthem in dimension than the former, had been one of the most popular of the Russian intrusions, appearing in numerous editions with minor changes of text or voice arrangement. Comparison of its earliest version from Emerson's *Jubilate* with an octavo setting as it was arranged by Tchaikovsky[2] (Example 141) is sufficient to illustrate its basic appeal and the relatively small amount of change it underwent from edition to edition. Scarcely a major choral publisher in this country has failed to produce a version of the work.

Russian pieces began to appear in octavo form in the early years of the second decade, the first ones adaptations by N. Lindsay Norden (1887–1956). His efforts were soon followed by those of A. M. Henderson. Later, a host of others, including Noble Cain, Max T. Krone, and Peter Tkach, joined the list of those who explored the new hunting ground for arrangers: The reception by the American public of this body of choral music was entirely on musical grounds; political sympathy played no part in its acceptance or eventual retention, since Russia was at that time engaged in international disputes of somewhat unsavory character. The musical appeal, strong enough to overcome any barriers of national difference, was essentially that of sonorities and vigorous harmonic relationships, not all features of which were truly representative of Russian liturgical practice. Fascination with the Eastern Orthodox ritual may have been involved, but the pieces caught the public's ear through the skill of their arrangers as much as through their own qualities. It is to the credit of Norden, Henderson, and their later imitators that they brought a new spirit to the American choral scene when one was sorely needed. Native composers, as we shall see, were not yet prepared to take over the market on their own merits.

The popularity of this music was greatly increased when, after the Revolution, singers experienced in the choral style of the Russian Imperial Chapel and other church groups became expatriated and formed groups that capitalized on their unusual musical qualities, costumes, and showmanship. The best-known organization was the Don Cossack Chorus under the direction of Sergey Jarov (1896–   ), an extremely popular conveyer of both the religious and secular unaccompanied literature. To the audiences, singers, and directors who came under their influence and other groups of like character, as well as under that of the printed editions that consistently claimed to be based directly on the Russian liturgy, a picture of that musical practice, at least partially accurate, developed in the minds of singers.

This is not the place to undertake a history of Russian choral music, but it must be made clear that what arrived on the American scene was not typical of the entire range of composers whose works were being adapted to English texts. Russian choral music went through several phases—an early tradition of chant under Italian leadership, a later period of German influence, and finally a revival of interest in composition with *cantus firmi* based on the traditional chants before its development was brought to a halt by the events of 1917.

The traditions of the Russian Orthodox Church permitted no instrumental music. The absence of organs in the churches placed the entire musical responsibility upon the choir. A typical sonority developed, first in the early part-songs of the later seven-

---

[2] Transliteration from the Russian varies so greatly that the forms used by Nicolas Slonimsky in *Baker's Biographical Dictionary of Musicians* will be used whenever possible; his patterns will be imitated as faithfully as the authors understand them when *Baker's* does not list the composer.

Example 141. Comparison of *Blessed be Jehovah, God of Israel*, Bortniansky (*Jubilate*, 310), and *Cherubim Song No. 7*, Bortniansky/Tchaikovsky (John Church 35357, mm. 1–6).

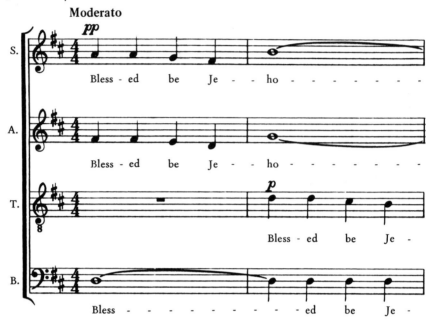

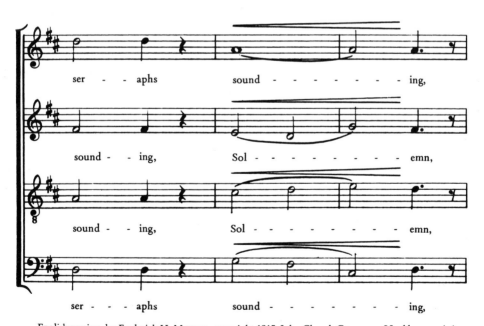

English version, by Frederick H. Martens, copyright 1915, John Church Company. Used by permission.

Example 142. *Cherubim Song*, Sergei Rachmaninoff (Boston 1067, mm. 1–8, 48–51).

(b)

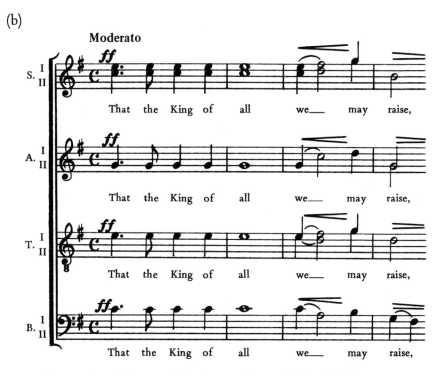

Used by permission of the Boston Music Company, Boston, MA Copyright Owners.

teenth century,[3] and it continued to develop within the court chapel which was organ-ized with a choir by 1667.[4] From within the Imperial Chapel there came a continuing influence on church practice, especially through its leaders' power as censor of all relig-ious music, a power that was absolute until the Revolution.[5] Charles Hirt's numerous transcriptions indicate that four-part writing was the norm until the end of the nine-teenth century. Parts that show basses singing in the doubled octaves that came to be associated with the style do not appear until the beginning of the present century.

Some generalizations may be made, however, for it is not what happened in Russia that affected American taste; it was what the American public sang and enjoyed, what it bought from its publishing houses, that set its image of what Russian music must have been. What we see in these editions is a sonority unlike the trans-parent one of the Renaissance Roman school. It is full, resonant, often moderately paced, with emphasis on vertical structures. Counterpoint is almost entirely absent,

[3] Charles C. Hirt, "Graeco-Slavonic Chant Traditions Evident in the Part-Writing of the Russian Orthodox Church" (unpublished Ph.D. dissertation, University of Southern California, 1946), 188.

[4] *Ibid.*, 194.

[5] Bortniansky was the first of these censors. His style was considered saccharine and unsuitable by many later men who held that post.

hinted at rather than supplied; and the fullness supplied by the doubling of parts—not always with the basses in octaves, but sometimes with tenors doubling sopranos or, in a few cases, the basses doubling the sopranos—provided the first hint that the choir could be handled with variable sounds in the manner of a vocal orchestra. Rich sonorities are evident in every page of some later pieces in the literature; Rachmaninoff's *Cherubim Song*[6] shows this in a number of places, including its quiet opening section (Example 142*a*) and its majestic middle part (Example 142*b*). The movement of the *divisi* treatment from one voice part to another provided a variety of colors that no other music had brought to the American choir loft. Whatever the voice arrangements were originally, it soon became customary to arrange them as SATB, often divided, for the American market, providing alternate versions for women's voices in some instances as well. The text adaptations were carefully adjusted to suit the nonliturgical needs of American churches which, while differing greatly from the Russian in practice, were able to assimilate general references to Cherubim, the Trinity, pieces commemorating the Holy Communion, invocations, and so on. Protestant church groups, collegiate and advanced high-school choirs, and community choruses had now a new, exciting addition to the repertory of unaccompanied music.

While most of what we see in octavo form appears to be for a chorus of mixed voices, it cannot have been so in the original in every case. Mixed choirs in Russian churches first appeared around 1880, when Alexander Archangelsky (1846–1924) introduced them into use,[7] yet the works of such earlier composers as Bortniansky and Alexey Lvov (1798–1870), among others, appear in a form that implies mixed-voice arrangements existed all along. We know, however, that choirs of boys and men were the norm until Archangelsky's reform. Arrangements have always been common in borrowed anthem materials, but it has usually been easy to trace their course; in the case of Russian liturgical materials, we are hampered by a lack of information in general, and by the abrupt elimination of a tradition by political upheaval, leaving no accurate modern counterpart for comparison. That the monastery practice called for men's groups while nunneries used women's, and that general church choirs were made up of men and boys, is generally accepted. Obviously, the music earlier than the period of Archangelsky's innovation had to be subjected to alterations in order to serve the American public.

Some confusion surrounds the alleged practice of the Russian basses in doubling the written part at the lower octave. Norden's editions often supply an editor's note, as in G. V. Lvovsky's (1830–1894) *Lord, our God, have mercy* (*Hospodi Pomilui*),[8] stating "it is customary, in Russian church music, for the octavo-bass to double the written bass, when harmonically possible. This is, perhaps, the chief element in rendering this music, and should be given the necessary preparation." Whether such knowledge was general—or accurate—is doubtful. The leading expert on Russian chant, Alfred Swan (1890–   ), was not yet in the United States and had not published any of his studies on

---

[6] Boston Music Co. 1067.

[7] *MGG*, XI, 1143.

[8] J. Fischer & Bro. 4124. Some later editions give the composer's name as S. V. Lvovsky.

the subject. The first book on Russian music by M. Montagu-Nathan (1877–1958) had not yet appeared. Yet it is these two who have supplied the most widely read material on the subject.[9] The chronological problem notwithstanding, it appears that the early choirs of boys and men were first influenced by Italians: Francesco Araja (1700–1767); Baldassare Galuppi (1706–1785), a teacher of Bortniansky; and Giuseppe Sarti (1729–1802). Nothing in their backgrounds or in the existing choral practice they knew points to the doubling of the bass part.[10] The involvement of the court chapel choir with Italian music extended to its appearing in Araja's first opera composed in Russia (1737), at which time the choir members were costumed and used as the opera chorus.[11] The period of Italian influence was followed by a German one in the nineteenth century. It was during that time that the codification of material into a daily round of services took place, bringing the chants into arrangements of vertical chords, with the doublings to which Swan referred. It is not until the end of that century that the thick texture makes its appearance in transcriptions as they are shown by Hirt, where the doubling of the bass part in the lower octave is found principally in the works of twentieth-century composers.[12]

Montagu-Nathan reported that both Schumann and Liszt, on visiting St. Petersburg, "expressed the greatest enthusiasm, especially for the Ukrainian basses."[13] Schumann's visit took place in 1840, and Liszt's before the end of 1847. It is unfortunate that we are uncertain whether their enthusiasm was for the range, resonance, or timbre of those bass voices. Recordings of Jarov's Don Cossack Chorus, and memories of their early tours, provide evidence of such doublings, but it is difficult to separate showmanship from liturgical performance practice. It may be that too much has been made of this feature of Russian style, if indeed it is a truly consistent feature, and that it has overshadowed the unusual method of choral attack that is heard on those and later recordings, where the opening chords of phrases are approached from below with a perceptible increase in volume after the attack is made. Obviously, it would be more difficult to assimilate this feature of performance practice into American life than was the adoption of bass doublings, but one without the other is not truly representative, and neither may be valid for the entire period of study. The gliding attack may well be a tradition of longer standing than the doubled bass. We have accustomed ourselves to hearing these heavy sounds of the later composers—Pavel Tchesnokov (1877–1944), Alexander Gretchaninov (1864–1956), Alexander Kastalsky (1856–1926), Sergey Rachmaninoff (1873–1943), and others—and we are probably too free in applying the same principles to the earlier compositions of Bortniansky, Lvov, and their compatriots of the preceding generations.[14]

Several composers born between 1870 and 1890 did much to shape church choral

[9] Succinctly condensed in their articles in *Grove's*, VII, 333–36, and 336–37.

[10] Swan refers to a "barbarous doubling in the basses" in the 1860s, *Grove's*, VII, 335. Whether he is referring to this practice or the doubling of the soprano line by the basses is not clear.

[11] Hirt, *op. cit.*, 200.   [12] *Ibid.*   [13] *Grove's*, VII, 337.

[14] A useful collection of representative Russian pieces is *Twenty-five Anthems from the Russian Liturgy*, J. Fischer & Bro. 9757. It contains arrangements by Norden, Henderson, and some new versions by Howard D. McKinney (1890–   ), who appears to be responsible for the selection of materials in the volume.

music in America. The first of these was William C. Macfarlane (1870–1945), who, like T. Tertius Noble, was born in England. The parallel ends there, however, for unlike Noble, who grew to maturity in England, Macfarlane came to America at the age of four. He held several positions as organist and choral conductor, and has to his credit several large works as well as numerous anthems and organ pieces. Of his anthems, the well-known *Ho, everyone that thirsteth*,[15] published in 1906, is in the Harry Rowe Shelley tradition, although somewhat more boisterous in character. The introductory organ accompaniment, with its detached octave-leap chords that alternate between Great and Swell, provides a massive preparation for the opening declamatory solo line (Example 143). Here the tenor solo plays a major role, with the chorus repeating much of the material already stated by the soloist. Likewise, *My spirit on thy care*,[16] published seven years later, relies heavily on a soloist, but there several of the choral passages are unaccompanied, suggesting a departure from the established custom of continuous and fairly elaborate organ accompaniment. A definite stylistic change is apparent in *Open our eyes* (1928).[17] A performance note suggests that the anthem should be sung without accompaniment, and the organ part provided is simply a reduction of the choral parts. Thus, the piece depends entirely on choral sonority for effect. This is achieved by the division of parts, especially at cadence points, and a fairly wide range for all voices. It appears that Macfarlane was following a path already blazed by such contemporaries as F. Melius Christiansen and Clarence Dickinson, whose works we shall next consider.

One of the first Americans to arrange and edit church music for chorus extensively was F. Melius Christiansen (1871–1955). He also wrote a number of original anthems. Born in Eidsvold, Norway, he came to the United States in 1888, and after studying at Northwestern Conservatory of Music and taking further work in Leipzig, he became director of the School of Music, St. Olaf's College, where he developed a choir of international reputation.

Of his original works, *Lullaby on Christmas Eve* (1933)[18] is a charming cradle song. The text is assigned to a soprano soloist, while the choir, for the most part, provides a humming background. It was, however, in his skillful choral arrangements of Lutheran hymns that Christiansen excelled. His *Beautiful Savior* (1919)[19] and *Lost in the night* (1929)[20] are well known to church choirs. The latter is based on a Finnish folk melody. *Lamb of God* (1933),[21] one of his finest pieces, is based on a sixteenth-century German chorale of rare beauty. Christiansen employs a limited amount of imitation, creating in each vocal line a melodic and textual independence that enhances the meaning of the words. A short piece of only three pages, it is a delicate jewel, similar in style to many sixteenth-century motets, requiring careful preparation and subtle interpretation. *O sacred Head* (1957)[22] is in much the same style, while the Advent

---

[15] G. Schirmer 4808.   [16] John Church 35401.   [17] G. Schirmer 7278.

[18] Augsburg 136.   [19] Augsburg 51.   [20] Augsburg 119.

[21] Augsburg 133.

[22] Augsburg 75. The late date is due to the work's appearing in an edition by Olaf C. Christiansen.

Example 143. *Ho, every one that thirsteth*, Will C. Macfarlane (G. Schirmer 4808, mm. 1–10).

Example 144. *Wake, awake, for night is flying,* F. Melius Christiansen (Augsburg 102, mm. 76–80).

Copyright Augsburg Publishing House, Minneapolis. Used by permission.

anthem *Wake, awake, for night is flying* (1925)[23] reflects the joy of Philipp Nicolai's chorale. The melody is assigned to various voices, and the piece is characterized by changing textures, alternating short SSAA and TTBB passages, and by phrase extension. One is reminded here of Bach's extended chorale treatment, especially in the closing section, which combines melismatic "hallelujah's" with the text (Example 144).

Very few of Christiansen's choral pieces have independent accompaniments; they are intended for *a cappella* singing, and they will still yield beautiful results in the hands of sensitive directors.

Another person who had a prominent part in molding American church music was Clarence Dickinson (1873–1969). Like Christiansen, he was a music educator as well as a composer, serving as professor and director of the School of Sacred Music, Union Theological Seminary, for many years.

Dickinson's long list of published anthems includes both original and arranged pieces. One of his original works, *The shepherds story* (1913),[24] has long been a favorite. The brilliant fanfarelike opening, with its full triads that double in both male and female sections, produces an overwhelming effect when sung by a large, well-trained

---

[23] Augsburg 102.   [24] H. W. Gray, S.C. 30.

Example 145. *The shepherds story*, Clarence Dickinson (H. W. Gray, S.C. 30, mm. 1–8).

Holp - en are all folk on earth,

Holp - en are all folk on earth,

Holp - en are all folk on earth,

Holp - en are all folk on earth,

Copyright by The H. W. Gray Co. Used by permission.

choir (Example 145). It is meant for *a cappella* performance. Even the solo passages lack instrumental support, and contrasts are produced entirely by vocal rather than instrumental means. A festival anthem, *Great and glorious is the name of the Lord* (1924),[25] appears to be patterned after the work of Ralph Vaughan Williams in that trumpets and trombones are used with the organ as in the latter's *O clap your hands*, and the hymn "O God our help in ages past" is used simultaneously by Dickinson with another melodic line, as in Vaughan Williams' *Lord, Thou hast been our refuge* (see pp. 349–353). It is a large and effective piece of more than average length. That Dickinson had a penchant for the unusual in his choral pieces may be seen in *The shofar is sounded* (1937),[26] a Hebrew call to worship which is mainly for bass solo and organ, employing the choir in only five measures, and his *Hussite battle hymn* (1957),[27] arranged for choir, organ, and optional brass. Both are short, spectacular pieces based on old traditional melodies; the latter is based on a harmonization by Smetana, the former is not readily adaptable to Christian worship because of its text.

Notwithstanding the high quality of his original anthem composition, Dickinson, much like Christiansen, seemed to excel in arranging traditional tunes, but unlike Christiansen, he did not limit himself to German and Scandinavian chorales. A cradle song from Haiti is the basis for *Jesu! thou dear Babe divine* (1913),[28] in which Dickinson augments the simple beauty of the melody with an ostinato bass (Example 146). In *What a wonder* (1920),[29] the composer adds violin, violoncello, and harp to the usual

[25] H. W. Gray, C.M.R. 215.   [26] H. W. Gray, C.M.R. 197.   [27] H. W. Gray, C.M.R. 271.
[28] H. W. Gray, S.C. 45.   [29] H. W. Gray, C.M.R. 87.

organ accompaniment to enhance a charming Lithuanian folk song. Much of the
credit for the effectiveness of these pieces must go to Helen A. Dickinson, the composer's wife, who collaborated with him in his work, but it remains that he had an
unusual ability to get out of the way of a good melody by providing a simple, yet
appropriate arrangement of it.

Example 146. *Jesu! thou dear Babe divine*, Clarence Dickinson (H. W. Gray,
S.C. 45, mm. 1–8).

Copyright by The H. W. Gray Co. Used by permission.

Of anthem writers born in the 1880s, H. Everett Titcomb (1884–1968) and David
McK. Williams (1887–   ) must be mentioned. Williams was born in Wales, but was
brought to the United States before his first birthday. Among several responsible positions he held over the years, his long tenure as organist-choirmaster at St. Bartholomew's Church, New York, was outstanding. An especially noteworthy anthem of his
is *In the year that king Uzziah died* (1935).[30] The famous passage from Isaiah 6 is set

[30] H. W. Gray, C.M.R. 1356.

without deletion through verse eight. Unison writing is employed extensively, thus minimizing the difficulties for the singers; even so, the dissonant nature of the accompaniment at times challenges the vocalists. An exciting and dramatic high point is achieved in the thrice holy, where massive organ chords support the voices, all in high tessitura, as the holiness of the Lord is declared. At that point, Williams makes effective use of sequence and dynamics changes (Example 147). Throughout the composition, he is more concerned with creating and conveying an overall mood and effect than with melodic invention, imparting to both performer and listener a distinct impression that there is something fresh and different here.

No doubt one of the most productive and popular anthem writers in America is Everett Titcomb. Although his works have been largely identified with the catalogues of two publishing houses, he has written in styles sufficiently varied that a number of publishers have accepted his anthems. His *Eight Short Motets* (1934),[31] intended for the greater festivals of the church, are unaccompanied pieces essentially in Renaissance style. They are effective if carefully sung by a well-balanced choir. In a more spectacular vein, *Behold now, praise the Lord* (1938)[32] creates an infectious mood of excitement. The opening unison theme, which sounds strangely akin to the advertising jingles heard on radio and television, gives the piece an impelling force that is not dissipated until the mood is abruptly changed on the words "Ye that by night stand in the house of the Lord." In the closing section of the anthem, Titcomb proves himself to be a master of thematic expansion. His skillful repetition of the last six notes of the theme creates an expansiveness not frequently found in anthem literature. The closing measures of the piece, again employing thematic material in augmentation, combine organ and voices in a powerful finale. Along the same line, *Victory Te Deum* (1944),[33] dedicated to the musicians then serving in the armed forces, carries an even greater sense of heroic breadth. The *Te Deum* text is not particularly easy to set, especially in its English translation, but Titcomb seems to surmount the problems with ease, providing interesting melodic material and resourceful organ accompaniment throughout, yet keeping it well within the capabilities of a good church choir.

While many of Titcomb's anthems are settings of Scripture, hymn texts are also frequently used. His anthem on Henry W. Milman's famous hymn, *Ride on, ride on in majesty* (1949),[34] also carries a feeling of breadth and grandeur so characteristic of his work (Example 148). A setting of William Walsham How's *Jesus! Name of wondrous love* (1947)[35] is invested with romantic, almost saccharine melody, yet the quiet introspective simplicity of the setting makes it appropriately suited to the text. That his hymn settings run the full gamut of style and complexity is seen in a comparison of *The Lord's my shepherd* (1963)[36] with *Eternal praise* (1949).[37] The former, based on the Scottish tune "Crimond," is a simple, unobtrusive setting that allows the paraphrase full expression; the latter, based on John Ellerton's translation of an early Latin hymn,

[31] Carl Fischer 436–443.
[32] B. F. Wood 457.   [33] B. F. Wood 637.   [34] Carl Fischer 6468.
[35] B. F. Wood 44–669.   [36] H. W. Gray, C.M.R. 2809.   [37] B. F. Wood 689.

Example 147. *In the year that king Uzziah died*, David McK. Williams (H. W. Gray, C.M.R. 1356, mm. 51–63).

Ho - - - - - - - - - ly___ is the Lord

Copyright by The H. W. Gray Co. Used by permission.

Example 148. *Ride on, ride on in majesty*, Everett Titcomb (Carl Fischer CM6468, mm. 4–12).

Copyright 1949 by Carl Fischer, Inc. Reprinted by permission.

is a full-blown anthem employing a wide range of choral effects and impressive organ accompaniment.

Few, if any, American anthem composers have displayed the skill in thematic development so evident in Titcomb's writing, a skill that has resulted not in mere clever "paper music," but in unified compositions that have a wide appeal to choirs and congregations alike.

The man to whom the regeneration of the American anthem should have been an easy responsibility was Philip James (1890–   ), the first completely trained serious musician since Horatio Parker to deal with the anthem extensively. He was taught by capable people, his experience was wide in both instrumental and vocal fields, he was recognized as a conductor, composer, and educator; in short, he was the kind of man the anthem needed if it was to emerge at the hands of a first-rate composer. Several matters prevented the needful from becoming reality: James was mainly preoccupied with concert and chamber works during the best years of his career; his recognition in the concert world brought him to a position of eminence in the educational field as chairman of an active university music department, a calling with responsibilities known to deplete creative powers; his concern for church composition was necessarily secondary to other activities;[38] and—the most hampering feature of all—his eclectic approach caused him to adopt stylistic features at odds with each other and with the period in which he lived.

A relatively early work that displays his affectionate espousal of the tools of lush romanticism and impressionism is *By the waters of Babylon* (1920).[39] Although the piece is listed in at least one source as a cantata,[40] probably because it has orchestral parts available, it is an anthem in every respect. Its 106 measures are packed to the limit with enriched chords, rhythmic complications—two against three and three against four, most of which are restricted to the accompaniment, but are quite superfluous—cascading diminished-seventh chords, flamboyant fanfares, and inevitable echoes of *Tristan* and *Daphnis et Chloé*. The solo and choral parts are not beyond the capacities of today's capable volunteer choir, but the organ part is a challenge to all but the outstanding church performer, and the saturated harmonies tie the piece firmly to a generation that otherwise bypassed the church's repertoire.

Of another character is *O be joyful in the Lord* (1944),[41] in which the organ has preliminary fanfares with horn fifths that appear again as interludes. The choral parts are direct, often in unison, and the piece moves along forcefully. At about the midpoint, however, James's exuberance again bursts forth in the organ part, laying difficulties in the way of the performer and overpowering the vocal forces (Example 149). A number of his works are still in print and used in churches where the performers

---

[38] James's prominence on the musical scene is evident in the space he is given in the principal dictionaries and encyclopedias. The best list of his works, with dates, is found in *MGG*, VI, 1677–79.

[39] H. W. Gray, C.M.R. 636.

[40] *Grove's*, IV, 577.

[41] Galaxy 1904. This is the *Jubilate Deo* listed in *MGG* as a composition of 1912.

Example 149. *O be joyful in the Lord,* Philip James (Galaxy 1904, mm. 33–37).

Quoted by permission of the publisher, Galaxy Music Corporation, New York, N.Y.

have sufficient numbers and skill to undertake them. His *Psalm 149* (1960)[42] calls for three trumpets and two trombones in addition to the organ. A comparison with similar works by English composers is inevitable. In most respects, the English come off better.

The musical vocabulary that James adopted in the early decades of this century belonged to a dying language. The Impressionist composers were already on the wane when he accepted their idiom as one of his own tongues. The post-Romantic fullness that he coupled with Impressionism was a remnant of an even more remote age. While the ingredients had a certain vogue in American concert life, their place in church music was limited to sophisticated circles that absorbed them as an antidote to the thin gruel of less skilled composers; it was right for those who found Neidlinger, Shelley, and Nevin too tame and sweet. English composers such as Vaughan Williams, Holst, the Shaws, and Thiman, on the other hand, brought to their public a sturdy interest in the folk idiom, modality, surprising chordal relationships, and beloved hymns in new arrangements, but none of their materials were borrowed from outside a basic stock of British ideas. What was new of theirs had come from within their own culture; what was new with James was of foreign origin, and it lost power as did the parent forms of his expression.

Joseph W. Clokey (1890–1960) was a product of the American educational system, under no direct influence of English tradition except as such may have been handed on to him by his teachers at Miami University or the Cincinnati Conservatory of Music. Although he finished his education in the early years of World War I, he appears to have escaped military duty. Still, his works are not on the musical scene much earlier than others of his generation except for the short operas and other works he composed for school use.[43] A relatively early anthem is *He that dwelleth in the secret place* (1931),[44] SSATBB with an organ part that supports the vocal lines without duplicating them. It shows no clear lineage from English sources, and its varied lyrical, dramatic, and imitative segments indicate that Clokey had a command of materials that found too lavish a use for such a short composition. Later examples show that he learned lessons of structural economy and textural simplicity, for they are generally built of fewer contrasting sections and tend toward SATB texture with few *divisi* segments.

A few years later his doubling of voices took the form of duplication between the upper and lower, although that treatment does not appear consistently in the pieces of his last productive years, it being dropped in favor of the practical arrangement usually found in the choir loft. His *Two kings* (1936)[45] for chorus with trumpets and trombones effectively alternates instrumental and vocal parts in forceful passages (Example

---

[42] H. W. Gray, C.M.R. 2676.

[43] Edward Ellsworth Hipsher, *American Opera and its Composers* (Philadelphia: Theodore Presser Co., 1934), 122, states that he wrote choral music as early as 1913. No titles from that period are identified, however.

[44] J. Fischer & Bro. 8821. Oddly enough, although the words are from Psalm 91, they are ascribed to Anna Temple.

[45] J. Fischer & Bro. 7211. A version for organ (8639) will be more practical for directors who have no brass players available.

150). While it is on a Christmas text found in a sixteenth-century Christ Church manuscript, it appears better suited to the concert hall than the church service. It may be used with great effect on the Christmas week concert-type program that is found in some churches, and should still find favor with school groups.

Generally, Clokey's later pieces placed a greater emphasis on the organ and less on the voices, at least so far as the number of parts was concerned. Pedal point becomes a prominent feature in *Treasures in heaven* (1941)[46] and *The Lord is my shepherd* (SATB version, 1945),[47] the former with variable measure-lengths and no signature; the latter, a dynamic setting with sharp contrasts in volume and character. His hymn-anthem *I sing as I arise today* (1954)[48] indicates his capitulation to the practical needs of the church. It is a piece adaptable to any combination of voices from unison to combined choirs. The organ, of course, must remain busy during the entire course of such a piece. An unusual series of anthems, published in three sets of four each, appeared in 1955.[49] The titles are too numerous to list here; the groups are identified as *Short Anthems*, Sets One, Two, and Three. The texts are Clokey's own paraphrases from various Eastern liturgies—Syrian, Persian, Armenian, and the Liturgies of Malabar, St. Chrysostom, and St. Mark. The pieces are adaptable to both liturgical and non-liturgical use. Technical difficulties are avoided, and the organ supports the voices, usually without duplication, at all times.

The more prolific composers of this decade have produced anthems in such quantity that a simple recounting of their types and character would require undue space. Van Denman Thompson (1890–1969) was one of these regular contributors to the literature. His works may be found in a number of publishers' catalogues; the contrast is perhaps the sharpest between those published by Lorenz and by H. W. Gray. A long-time contributor to the Lorenz magazine and octavo series, he is among their most popular composers.[50] When one recalls the success of that publishing house, the impact of one of its leading contributors cannot be ignored, and it is necessary to recognize here a man who could write in a number—although only a small number—of different styles at will. The commercial value of the long-accepted, widely used periodical material is beyond dispute. Thompson's skill in filling the needs of its public is evident in *Master, speak* (1943),[51] *Go forth to life, O child of earth* (1946),[52] and *Go ye and teach all nations* (1966),[53] the first and third of which are largely note-against-note settings, and the second a unison arrangement of an earlier piece. Almost without exception the phrases in pieces of this type are as regularly spaced as slices in a loaf of

[46] C. C. Birchard 2010.   [47] H. W. Gray, C.M.R. 1960.
[48] Concordia 98-2017.   [49] H. T. FitzSimons 2126, 2127, 2128.

[50] The Lorenz catalogue of September 1, 1953, listed the fifty best sellers of the previous year; among them were five of Thompson's anthems, two of which were in the top ten, of which it was stated, "a million copies of these 10 octavos have been sold." The continuing influence of that publishing house is obvious. Their establishment of a new division, The Sacred Music Press, featuring a higher quality anthem than had been common to their catalogue, is a recent development of importance. A few composers who were not represented in their earlier lists may be found in the new series.

[51] Lorenz 9628.   [52] Lorenz 5703.   [53] Lorenz 9951.

Example 150. *Two kings*, Joseph W. Clokey (J. Fischer 7211, mm. 13–17).

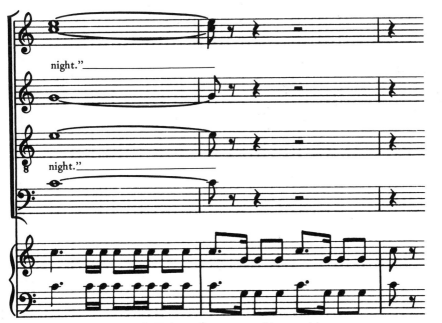

Reprinted by permission of J. Fischer & Bro., owners of the copyright.

bread. The fault is not entirely Thompson's, but may be laid partly to the requirements of the publisher's public. When he offered works to other publishers, the situation changed to some extent. The pieces published by H. W. Gray show a touch of sophistication that is lacking in those previously mentioned. Phrases are extended, cadences are masked, and there are places where independent voice-leading occurs briefly. The greatest change, however, is in the harmonic texture. Where the Lorenz pieces are almost painfully correct in their simple voice movement, and the whole is carefully supported by organ, some of the Gray publications are adventurous in their use of the various seventh chords and chords of the added sixth, the choral group is expected to be self-sufficient, a *colla parte* keyboard part is supplied "for rehearsal only," and the texts are chosen from a more imaginative group of poets. Among these works are several worth considering as comparisons with his much more popular productions—*Father, in Thy mysterious presence, kneeling* (1936),[54] *God is in His holy temple* (1955),[55] and *I only know* (1936),[56] from which Example 151 illustrates his interest in chords that would have been unsuitable to his other market. Recognition of the seventh chord is not a startling concept in American anthem writing. Other composers, at least as early as T. Tertius Noble, had developed a greater skill in it. What is significant is that Thompson is one of the first of a new group who tried to write to suit the demands of different levels of choral and religious sophistication, changing styles to suit the needs of various kinds of church choirs and those of the publishers who served them, and being consistent, so far as their capacities permitted, within each of the styles.

In the same two-year period that Noble moved from England to New York, and Willan and Whitehead to Canada, T. Frederick H. Candlyn (1892–1964) appeared in New York after early experience, study, and the receipt of a music degree in England. He held church positions and taught at New York University until 1943, when he succeeded Noble at St. Thomas' Church. A tendency toward simple style after less modest beginnings is also evident in his compositions, as it was in the others who shared his English background. The nibbling away at the highest level of taste and skill that was evident in works by others who began by jousting courageously with the philistinism of American choral groups soon began to deteriorate Candlyn's work. His early *Thee we adore* (1937),[57] based on the Communion hymn "Adoro Te devote" by St. Thomas Aquinas,[58] is still uncontaminated by the demands of the marketplace. Freely barred with two to six quarter-notes per measure, its melody has a freedom rarely encountered. Based on a plainsong, it still appears to be free from restraint through its varied use of men's, women's, and mixed voices, unaccompanied segments, imaginative interludes, and the use of the head-motif of the melody in mirror form as preliminary, interlude, and closing material. His setting of Wesley's text, *Christ, Whose glory fills*

---

[54] H. W. Gray, C.M.R. 1367.   [55] H. W. Gray, C.M.R. 2370.
[56] H. W. Gray, C.M.R. 1391.   [57] Carl Fischer 492.

[58] Using one of the several variant readings of the translation by Bishop J. R. Woodford. See Julian, *op. cit.*, I, 22–23.

the skies (1942),[59] is more regular in its construction, but retains enough freedom that a middle section alternating unison phrases with harmonized ones, all accompanied by an organ part that keeps rhythmic drive constant as the choir closes its phrases on held tones, seems fresh and vital throughout. A number of carol settings appeared in print, among them *What Child is this* (1950)[60] and *Ding dong, merrily on high* (1951),[61] the latter having its refrain varied for the last stanza. Borrowing text from George Herbert (1593–1632), he composed *King of glory* (1952)[62] with traces of the earlier style, using the form of a full anthem with verse; but despite its varied measure lengths it lacks the flow of the first pieces. Later works make obvious his search for the wider market of unskilled choirs, their comparative simplicity being evident in their appearing on two staves, having long sections for men alternating with some for women, and closing with simple harmonization or unison sections supported by organ.

It may seem that we expect too much of these composers and that our disappointment in their defection to commercial music is too pointed. It is with them that the hope of a strong continuation of the Anglican tradition lay. Candlyn, Noble (who also lowered his sights in *When I survey the wondrous cross* (1947), dedicated to the director and choir of a Fundamentalist institution),[63] Willan, and Whitehead—they were the bearers of English cathedral practice as it emerged from the Oxford Movement. What they relinquished has been grasped again by native Americans only through artificial means, although in some cases with more than a little success. How they dealt with the problems of composing for church choirs will concern us for the next pages.

Rarely does a piece written for the church become a hit that catches the fancy of the general public. Such popularity has been approached by one setting of the Lord's Prayer, an *Ave Maria*, a Palm Sunday piece of flamboyant nature, and a dramatic, bombastic solo that has unfortunately found its way into some modern hymnals, but none has found the wide acceptance that came to the *Carol of the Drum* (1941)[64] by Katherine K. Davis (1892–). More than two decades after it first appeared, this simple and folklike choral setting became the most popular Christmas piece for several seasons, being heard in schools, on radio, and on home phonographs with the same regularity as the outstanding tunes from Broadway musical shows. It had been quite widely known before its sudden rise to general popularity; its new position was largely attributable to its recorded performance by a professional choral group. It was no accident that such fame should suddenly accrue to its composer. She was well grounded in the craft of composition, having studied with Nadia Boulanger among others, and having produced a steady flow of arrangements and compositions before the meteoric popularity of that piece. Strophic settings with variation treatment are her consistent strong feature, even though she uses texts of various characters. She often demonstrates the fact that profound utterances, impressive though they may be, fail to

---

[59] Carl Fischer 622.   [60] Carl Fischer 6566.   [61] Carl Fischer 6565.
[62] H. W. Gray, C.M.R. 2234.   [63] J. Fischer & Bro. 8288.   [64] B. F. Wood 568.

Example 151. *I only know*, Van Denman Thompson (H. W. Gray, C.M.R. 1391, mm. 13–18).

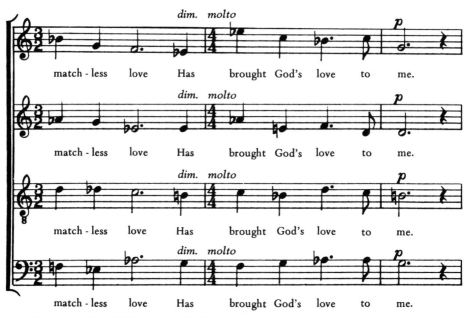

Copyright by The H. W. Gray Co. Used by permission.

reach audiences although they fascinate sophisticated listeners. Pieces that convey simplicity, directness, and uncontrived ideas are likely to achieve wider acceptance, as did this carol which still receives annual attention, particularly outside the church. Her simple setting of two verses from Psalm 51, *Renew a right spirit within me* (1938),[65] in which the chorus repeats the opening quiet statement of a solo tenor (Example 152), is an example of her direct treatment of a penitential text.

Certainly one of the most prolific American anthem composers is Carl F. Mueller (1892–   ). One measure of his popularity is evident in that three prominent publishers —G. Schirmer, Harold Flammer, and Carl Fischer—have brought out series of his works. It is doubtful that any other anthem writer has exceeded or even equaled him in total sales. What are the elements that have contributed to his success? Simplicity and variety are certainly two of them. Mueller avoids the use of a predictable formula for his pieces, for although he may write more than one anthem of a certain type, he soon lays the model aside, at least for a time. This contrast of types may be seen in such titles as *Create in me a clean heart, O God* (1941),[66] *A mighty fortress is our God* (1937),[67] and *Worship Christ, the newborn King* (1965).[68]

No doubt one of the most widely performed anthems is the first-mentioned title. In the opening section, Mueller assigns unison phrases alternately to female and male voices; the second section combines all the voices in unison; the third employs harmony and a key change to the relative major; and the fourth section continues the harmony, but in the parallel major. A final four-measure phrase restates the opening thematic material in reflective fashion, fully harmonized but unaccompanied. In six pages, the listener has been taken through several contrasting sections that reflect the changing mood of the psalm, yet the piece has unity because of its stylistic consistency, and it is capable of being well performed by the average choir since it offers no real difficulties.

In *A mighty fortress is our God*, Mueller employs the same scheme of organization that he had applied to *Now thank we all our God* (1934)[69] a few years earlier. After an opening statement of the traditional hymn tune, the second stanza is set in spirited fugal fashion, the subject stated successively in all voices. A pyramidal adding of voices on the words "A mighty fortress, a bulwark never failing, is our God" brings the piece to an impressive close with an eight-part texture (Example 153).

A more modest approach is used in *Worship Christ, the newborn King*. The piece is a combination of James Montgomery's hymn "Angels from the realms of glory" and the traditional tune "Regent Square." To this basic material Mueller adds an impressive organ and choral introduction, writes an eighth-note running figure in the accompaniment, sets the third stanza to a new melody, and, after a return to the original tune on the fourth stanza, closes with an exact restatement of the choral introduction. Thus, there is a constant unfolding of new material, saving both performer and listener from the kind of boredom so frequently encountered in hymn-anthems.

---

[65] G. Schirmer 11016.   [66] G. Schirmer 8682.   [67] G. Schirmer 8179.
[68] Carl Fischer 7496.   [69] G. Schirmer 7745.

Example 152. *Renew a right spirit within me,* Katherine K. Davis (G. Schirmer 11016, mm. 5–8).

Used by permission of G. Schirmer, Inc.

Of the long list of recognized serious composers on the American scene, none has been as concerned with church music as Leo Sowerby (1895–1968). In addition to his substantial list of secular compositions in a variety of forms, he has been a major contributor to the organ and choral repertory of the church. A teacher and practicing organist-choirmaster over a period of many years, it is likely that much of Sowerby's outstanding success as an anthem composer has been due to his intimate knowledge of choirs and the role of the organ in supporting them.

One of his early anthems, *I will lift up mine eyes* (1920),[70] an uncomplicated setting of Psalm 121, assigns to an alto soloist a warm and moving melodic line which opens and closes the piece. A middle section is quite heavily chromatic, but difficulties for the singers are minimized by the use of degree inflection (Example 154). Another piece written in this period is *Psalm CXXXIV* (1923),[71] an eight-part *a cappella* setting of the text "Behold, bless ye the Lord, all ye His servants."

Sowerby's Christmas anthems are especially effective. *Love came down at Christmas* (1935)[72] is a warm, romantic setting of Christina Rossetti's eloquent poem. As the poet seems here to capture the very essence of the Incarnation, so the composer amplifies the beauty of her theme. Never does the music obtrude; rather, the relatively simple block-chord setting serves as a nearly perfect vehicle for the text, bringing out the nuances of the delicate lines. Again, chromaticism is a prominent feature, especially in the center section. Here a dramatic key shift takes place; in the organ interlude, Sowerby appears to be traveling from the home key of E-flat major to F major, poising on a C dominant-seventh chord, but the surprising resolution as the choir reenters is a G-major tonic-six-four chord (Example 155). Such an abrupt modulation might well seem contrived in the hands of a less skilled composer; with Sowerby's sure technique, the result is a sense of tonal lift, giving significance to the text, "Worship we the Godhead, Love incarnate, Love divine."

Two other Christmas anthems, *The snow lay on the ground* (1952)[73] and *Cradle hymn* (1957),[74] are arrangements of old tunes. In fact, Sowerby originally harmonized them for the Episcopal Hymnal (1941 and 1940, respectively) and later expanded them for choir use. The former is a lilting melody in 6/8 time, based on the original harmonization, the major differences being an abandonment of the hymnic unison in favor of part-singing, and the addition of a descant in the last stanza. It is a piece that sings well, and is almost certain to draw an enthusiastic response from both choir and congregation. His *Cradle hymn* also draws from the hymnic version in the opening stanza, and becomes progressively more chromatic in the three succeeding statements, adding variety and color to a piece that, while initially interesting, might otherwise tend to become monotonous.

Sowerby's arrangements were not limited to Christmas pieces; by way of contrast may be mentioned *All hail, adored Trinity* (1960)[75] and *I sing a song of the Saints of*

---

[70] Boston Music Co. 1385.   [71] Boston Music Co. 1486.   [72] H. T. FitzSimons 2054.
[73] H. W. Gray, C.M.R. 2240.   [74] H. W. Gray, C.M.R. 2492.   [75] Oxford A165.

Example 153.   *A mighty fortress is our God*, Carl F. Mueller (G. Schirmer 8179, last 10 mm.).

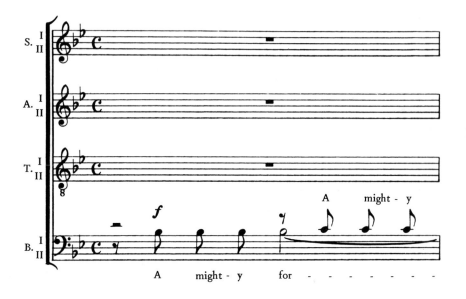

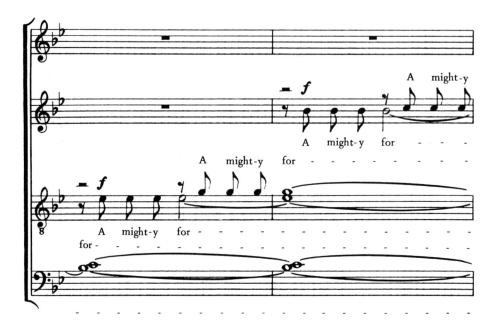

Used by permission of G. Schirmer, Inc.

Example 154. *I will lift up mine eyes*, Leo Sowerby (Boston 1385, mm. 25–30).

shade_____ up - on   thy   right - - hand._____

shade_____ up - on   thy   right - - hand._____

shade_____ up - on   thy   right - - hand._____

shade_____ up - on___ thy   right - - hand._____

Used by permission of the Boston Music Company, Boston, MA Copyright Owners.

Example 155. *Love came down at Christmas*, Leo Sowerby (H. T. FitzSimons 2054, mm. 12–18).

From the Aeolian Choral Series no. 2054. Used by permission of the copyright owners, H. T. FitzSimons Company, Inc., Chicago, Illinois.

God (1959).[76] The former is a rather austere setting, appropriate to the old chant melody on which it is based; the latter is a straightforward arrangement of Lesbia Scott's charming children's hymn and John Henry Hopkins' irresistible tune, "Grand Isle."

Example 156.   *Seeing we also*, Leo Sowerby (H. T. FitzSimons 2159, mm. 76–78).

From the Aeolian Choral Series no. 2159. Used by permission of the copyright owners, H. T. FitzSimons Company, Inc., Chicago, Illinois.

Of recent works larger in scope, there is an interesting setting of Hebrews 12:1–2, *Seeing we also* (1958).[77] Descriptive writing is the keynote here; an opening section in 3/8 time expresses, through recurring dissonant patterns, the text "let us lay aside every weight." A fugal subject, heard successively in all voices, sets the text "and let us run with patience the race that is set before us" (Example 156). The sense of motion created by the rhythm and the alternating 5/4 and 4/4 meters gives this section of the piece an appropriate and contrasting interpretation of the texts.

In his selection of anthem texts, it is apparent that Sowerby, a devoted musical servant of the Episcopal Church, has been careful to observe a rubric from *The Book of Common Prayer* (American) which states that "Hymns set forth and allowed by the

[76] H. W. Gray, C.M.R. 2608.   [77] H. T. FitzSimons 2159.

FIGURE 9 (overleaf). *Choirboys of Washington Cathedral's Choir of Men and Boys processing past the Canterbury Pulpit. The High Altar is in the background. (Photo courtesy of Washington Cathedral.)*

authority of this Church, and Anthems in the words of Holy Scripture or of the Book of Common Prayer, may be sung before and after any Office in this Book, and also before and after Sermons."[78] Hence, with few exceptions his anthem texts have been drawn from authorized sources.

It is readily seen that many of Sowerby's more ambitious anthems will prove too difficult for all but the best church choirs, but it is obvious that, through the years, he has also attempted to write for churches with more limited choral resources than those with which he was associated.

Some names occur with the regularity of the calendar in publishers' lists. Their continuous outpourings are often simple, utilitarian products such as we found in the Lorenz magazines; in other cases, however, they show a variety of styles that can be dignified in the name of composition. A consistent group of producers, all belonging to the latter type and all of whom were born in 1896, includes Noble Cain, Don Malin, W. Glen Darst, Jean Pasquet, and Will James. They represent several types of composition. That they receive less discussion than some of their contemporaries does not indicate that they are less important, but that features of their style have already been recognized in other composers' works.

One of the most influential figures on the American choral scene of the years between two World Wars was Noble Cain. He has been active in educational and community choral circles, achieved popularity as an adjudicator and clinician, wrote a book that was widely used as a basic text,[79] and composed, arranged, or edited many choral pieces, both secular and religious. His recent work has been largely in the practical vein of four-part mixed chorus music, and he has recognized, with others of this same period and later, the growing interest in male, female, and SAB choruses, thus producing works especially for them or providing parallel arrangements along with the original four-part versions. Many of his practical four-voice pieces are currently available in a number of catalogues, but his best moments are found in pieces that were composed in the years when he was active as a conductor, especially of the Chicago A Cappella Choir, which rose to eminence under his leadership. The influence of the massive Russian style, of which he demonstrated his command in his arrangement of Tchesnokov's *Let Thy Holy Presence* (1940),[80] permeates other of his pieces such as *In the night, Christ came walking* (1936),[81] although the heavy eight-part writing is more often found in his secular pieces. The massive style of doubled choirs was not uniquely Cain's, nor was it confined to composers who had worked with Russian materials, for we saw it with such earlier men as Clarence Dickinson, and we shall see it also in works by Will James and others of the period.

Cain can also be included among the arrangers who helped popularize Negro spirituals, some of which have been found useful for church. A study of the differences between the original materials from which those spirituals came, and the arrange-

---

[78] *The Book of Common Prayer* (New York: The Church Pension Fund, 1945), viii.

[79] Noble Cain, *Choral Music and its Practice* (New York: M. Witmark & Sons, 1932).

[80] Summy-Birchard B-12.   [81] G. Schirmer 7967.

ments that were passed on to the general public is sorely needed, for the notated materials probably differed from actual practice as much as did the Russian literature that we examined earlier in this chapter.

Don Malin, although associated with the music publishing trade for most of his life, and in a position to assess the commercial values of various types of church compositions, has nevertheless restricted his work to a limited range of styles. Some of his anthems are entirely original, while others are based on earlier melodies, as are *O God, O Spirit* (1958),[82] which takes its melody from Orlando Gibbons' Song 24, and *O Christ, our true and only light* (1960),[83] based on a seventeenth-century German tune. A number of his anthems employ the variation technique in which verses are separated by brief organ interludes; the treatment is carried a step beyond that of Thiman, however, in that Malin's phrases are also often separated by interludes. The voice ranges are comfortable; the harmonies are simple, often modal in flavor; and he favors minor melodies in his strongest pieces.

Another consistent producer of anthems whose work has been invariably craftsmanlike and dependably singable is W. Glen Darst. The Christmas anthem *Christ, the Lord, to us is born* (1958)[84] has a spirited melody sung initially by all voices in unison. After an alternation of male and female parts in the second stanza, and the employment of four-part harmony in the third, Darst writes the final unison stanza to be sung to a strong organ accompaniment. In *Variants on "A mighty fortress"* (1962),[85] Darst employs extended chorale treatment reminiscent of that found in the Baroque era, especially in the works of J. S. Bach. The accompaniment, with its numerous triplet figures, when played on an adequate instrument or augmented with the optional trumpets, has an irresistible driving force that strengthens the already powerful hymn tune.

The compositions of Jean Pasquet are, with few exceptions, short and simple settings of Scripture, although he has chosen texts occasionally from the Sarum Breviary and the Liturgy of St. Mark, as in *Two Short Anthems* (1967);[86] from the fifth-century Liturgy of Malabar, *Glory to Thy Holy Name* (1966);[87] and from the Dead Sea Scrolls, *Hymn of the initiants* (1965).[88] Of an entirely different nature is his Christmas suite for voices and organ, *The birth of Christ* (1952).[89] He has written a successive *quodlibet* that uses "O come, O come, Emmanuel," "A Virgin most pure,"[90] and "In excelsis gloria."[91] The sections are bound together by short recitatives in the fashion of a simple cantata. Its 116 measures are concluded rapidly enough for the piece to be used as a Christmas-season choral piece within the service, although its text provides a narrative that covers both Advent and Christmas within its short space. Pasquet's music is

[82] B. F. Wood 743. [83] B. F. Wood 783.
[84] B. F. Wood 739. [85] H. W. Gray, C.M.R. 2746. [86] H. W. Gray, C.M.R. 2980.
[87] G. Schirmer 11407. [88] G. Schirmer 11229. [89] H. W. Gray, C.M.R. 2258.
[90] Percy Dearmer, R. Vaughan Williams, and Martin Shaw, *The Oxford Book of Carols* (London: Oxford University Press, 1928), 8–9.
[91] The text is a modified version of those found in *ibid.*, 378–81, but the tune is not one of the two printed there.

utilitarian, within easy reach of the amateur choir, and it can be handled by the average capable organist as well. His studies with men of stature, including T. Tertius Noble, have not closed his eyes to the practical needs of church services, nor has he found it of interest to progress beyond fundamental chord relationships in most cases. In his case simplicity need not be confused with poor taste, however. His music does not have the obvious lack of refinement and propriety that marks some other large producers' output.

One of the most widely sung anthem composers over the past three decades has been Will James. His anthems, written primarily in block-chord style, are tuneful and easily mastered, even by choirs of limited ability. One of his earlier anthems, *Hear my prayer* (1933),[92] is a sectional work that relies on changing moods and dynamic contrasts for effectiveness. *Come, ye disconsolate* (1936)[93] is an unabashed piece of romanticism in the Harry Rowe Shelley tradition, which, with its emotion-laden solo for alto or baritone and its comfortable choral sections, will still elicit hearty praise from the vast majority of the churchgoing population across the country.

Almighty God of our fathers (1941)[94] is representative of a style discussed earlier in this chapter (see pp. 411–412) which is found frequently in his works. Massive block

[92] G. Schirmer 7739.   [93] H. T. FitzSimons 2056.
[94] B. F. Wood 569.

Example 157a.   *Bow my head, O Lord*, Sven Lekberg (G. Schirmer 11499, mm. 3–7).

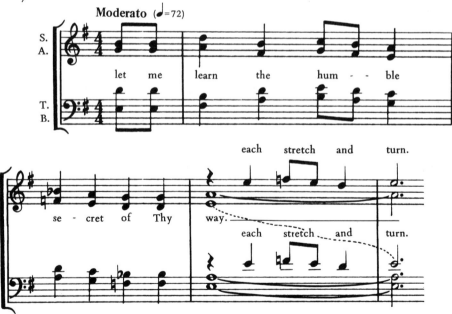

© Copyright 1967 by G. Schirmer, Inc. Used by permission.

Example 157b. *God with me lying down*, Sven Lekberg (G. Schirmer 11401, mm. 5–9).

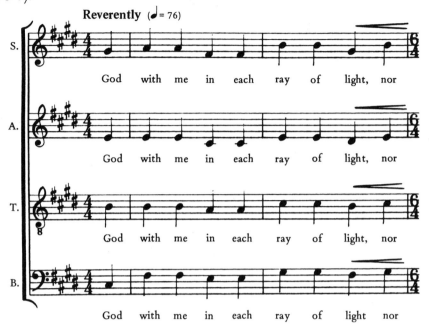

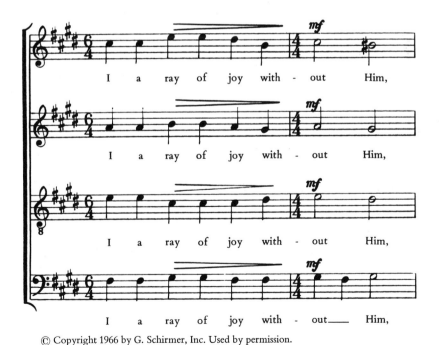

© Copyright 1966 by G. Schirmer, Inc. Used by permission.

chords are the dominant feature, with a duplication of parts between women's and men's voices, the coupling resulting in an opulent choral sonority. A contrasting center section sets the Lord's Prayer for SSA, with male voices joining on the words "For Thine is the kingdom" with great effectiveness. While his anthems are certainly not profound utterances, it nevertheless remains to his credit that James coupled an easy melodic style with colorful sonority in a way that has made his pieces especially appealing.

It has been evident that the spirit of experimentation has been lacking among composers born in the last decade of the nineteenth century. Clokey occasionally went beyond the generally bland harmonies of the preceding generation, and a freedom of barring was seen in Candlyn's work. Sowerby, however, was the only man who had a daring that was both original and timely. One other man, Sven Lekberg (1899–), has gone outside the pale perimeter of common-practice harmonization, and it is probably his mildly daring use of materials that sets him apart and, at the same time, keeps him from being better known. His few available anthems indicate that he has moved away from common harmonic practice about as far as the taste and capacities of the volunteer choir will permit. His use of seventh chords goes beyond those previously noted in that he favors parallel series of them in third inversion, as in *Bow my head, O Lord* (1967),[95] (Example 157*a*). Another device—and these illustrated here by no means exhaust his vocabulary—is the use of chords built of superimposed fourths, which he handles without losing a sense of tonality, as in *God with me lying down* (1966),[96] (Example 157*b*).

The rather wide range of styles undertaken by composers of this last period brings us to the major question of our time: What is the place of a modern idiom or a contemporary style in church music? We must omit from our consideration anything composed for the organ, since the performer is, in every case, a trained musician who willingly undertakes the performance of material that is excused from conveying text and exact meaning to the listener. The problem lies in two areas—that of the choir and that of the listening congregation.

Regardless of the fact that there are excellent choirs of trained singers that regularly produce works of taste and quality, the majority of the church choirs of America are made up of willing but poorly trained and tradition-bound groups of volunteers who meet once weekly to prepare music for Sunday services. The musical tastes of these members are as varied as their regular occupations: Some few favor symphonic fare; some listen with pleasure to the show tunes and slick arrangements that make up the programs of small FM radio stations; others follow the latest kinds of popular music avidly; and a few of them enjoy country and western music. Yet, when they gather for the singing of religious choral music, we expect that they will magically rise to a high level of taste, embracing alike the traditional works of the past and the experimental styles of the present. Nothing is farther from fact. Their ideas of suitable church

---

[95] G. Schirmer 11499.   [96] G. Schirmer 11401.

music run a small range, somewhat controlled by the normal taste levels of their denomination, from Renaissance polyphony to gospel-song settings, with the hymn-anthem acting as a mutual meeting ground.

In view of this disparity, it is difficult to say when a living composer of church music is evading a responsibility of bringing the taste of his times to his craft. He may be skilled in serial composition, steeped in the chromatic or quartal practices of a past generation, or brimming with avant-garde ideas, but these are not for the church congregation or its choir. This composer's audience lies in the public halls where the music is the only thing that brings performers and listeners together. The composer soon learns that his religious music will sell only if it does not exceed the limits of his public's tastes—and the Sunday morning public, outside of an extremely few establishments, is not ready for experiment or even contemporary idioms.

The choir of any but the most musically blessed church is in a position similar to that of the marching band at the Saturday football game. It fills a gap in the day's principal activity, remaining always secondary to the purpose for which the multitude has gathered. If its repertoire extends beyond certain commonly accepted limits—entertainment on the one hand, and the delivery of edifying text in relatively clear and pleasant fashion on the other—it is either ignored or criticized. The audience, and the congregation, is a motley crowd of varied tastes, and those tastes are not quickly changed by an incidental performance, no matter how skilled or fascinating it may be.

Despite this lack of discrimination in congregations—and let us be realistic in assuming that congregations for centuries have been such mixed and varied groups—the quality and characteristics of church music have changed. What was common in the seventeenth century lagged behind contemporary taste outside the church, especially in the ingrown practices of the English Chapel Royal; what was heard in eighteenth- and nineteenth-century American churches was not the same diet as was found in the public concerts of the time. The same kind of time-lag still exists in this century when we must point out as unusual the mild experiments with diatonic material that set apart the music of Philip James, Leo Sowerby, and Sven Lekberg, music that would not cause a ripple of excitement in the concert hall, even though there the standard fare is still that of past generations. The public does not take offense at the devices of these composers, although it recognizes something outside the normal religious-music vocabulary, because that vocabulary has permeated the already out-of-date popular music that brings fond memories to the middle-aged; it has the ingredients that the older members knew as daring innovations in the concert hall—although they were even then insulated from the experiments of Stravinsky, Schoenberg, Bartok, and were probably unaware that Debussy was dead—and it has been left far behind by the youth who are responsive, how briefly we cannot say, to strong, unrelenting rhythmic impulses and static chordal patterns in their popular fare.

There is no need to deplore this state of affairs. It has been so before, and will probably be so again. The theory advanced by Leonard Meyer that we have reached a point in time that is characterized by "the coexistence of a number of alternative styles in a kind of 'dynamic steady-state',"[97] and in which "the largest audience will no doubt continue to be that which supports and attends concerts devoted to the standard repertory of eighteenth- and nineteenth-century music,"[98] certainly finds support in the present-day church situation, whether we view it from the congregation, the choir loft, or the publishers' sales records. It certainly applies to anthem literature, which plods along behind concert-hall taste because of the peculiar nature of its audiences and performing groups.

Composers have not stopped in their attempts to break away, but as we saw with the British younger generation, experiment and acceptance do not go hand in hand. Nor do success in the concert hall and the church. American composers of wide acceptance in art music have generally rejected the church, or they have refused to make the necessary concessions to their audiences and performers in it. Samuel Barber (1910–) has made few gestures in this direction. His *Lamb of God* (1967)[99] is an unfortunate attempt to capitalize on a piece that was widely known to concert audiences and that catapulted into the general public ear by association with a national catastrophe. The success of this transcription of his *Adagio for Strings* is sadly reminiscent of the convenient *contrafacta* that were common early in the century, for the text is underlaid with little sense for its meaning or that of the music. His *Easter chorale* (1965)[100] is square, syllabic, and disappointing in its choral lines, although the added brass and timpani can give it life in proper surroundings.

The problem of setting religious text in a modern idiom is approached seriously by such men as Alan Hovhaness (1911–), Daniel Pinkham (1923–), Ned Rorem (1923–), and Samuel Adler (1928–), for they write more regularly in that genre than do Barber and others who have met with more consistent success in the concert field. Their works are sometimes florid, astringent, or complex to a degree that taxes choral groups, but there are pieces—Hovhaness' *From the end of the earth* (1961),[101] Pinkham's *Thou hast loved righteousness* (1964),[102] Rorem's *Sing my soul, His wondrous love* (1962),[103] and Adler's *Psalm 96* (1967),[104] among others—that are singable, even though they generally present some new challenge to choirs. It is to their continued efforts to expand the idiom that religious music must look for its slow development, since acceptance of features that now seem abrasive or unvocal cannot be ruled out of our future simply because they are not now widely acclaimed. Some of the challenge is being accepted by university and high school groups, and the effect of pieces first known there will eventually be felt in church choirs. The men named here are not primarily composers of church music, nor of choral music for that matter. Composers whose output is not principally vocal may hold the key to the next great change in this

---

[97] Leonard B. Meyer, *Music, the Arts, and Ideas* (Chicago: The University of Chicago Press, 1967), vii.
[98] *Ibid.*, 175.
[99] G. Schirmer 11495. It also appears with Latin text as an *Agnus Dei*, G. Schirmer 11486.
[100] G. Schirmer 11265.
[101] Edition Peters 6255.   [102] Edition Peters 6841.
[103] Edition Peters 6386.   [104] G. Schirmer 11491.

field, for they are not bound by tradition or by the limitations that grip men who have lived only in a world of choral music.

Some men in every recent period, as we have noted before, would merit mention for the sheer bulk of their output if for no other reason. A number have become notable for the quantity of their works in this century. Mention of two will suffice here, as their compositions differ in a number of respects. L. Stanley Glarum (1908–   ) has produced much and regularly since the late 1940s, each piece sufficiently different from the others that a trademark cannot be ascribed to him—unless insistent vertical sonorities can be so identified in an age when they are relatively common—but often there is reliance on a single forceful idea that is of more interest to singers than to an audience. His *We give thanks to thee* (1965)[105] is deeply indebted in its repetitious features to the popular *Hospodi Pomilui* (see p. 412), providing as its main appeal a few shifts out of its basic 5/4 meter. Many of his other pieces exhaust short sections of text through the use of repeated or slightly modified materials. Perhaps these very features of familiarity make the pieces widely used, for their consistency of pattern, except for a few passages with shifting meters, is easily grasped by any alert choir.

Another composer of apparently unflagging energy is Jean Berger (1909–   ), whose choral works have appeared in such numbers that he has established his own press to present their variety to his public.[106] He shares with Glarum a general tendency to exhaust text fragments and musical segments, and he varies the metrical divisions of his material in an effort to avoid the boredom of direct repetition. Parallel motion in abundance, often in parallel thirds, however, is a hallmark of much of his music. He is probably most widely known for his *Alleluia from "Brazilian Psalm"* (1941);[107] and *The eyes of all wait upon thee* (1959)[108] has become a favorite in both school and church groups. His setting of Psalm 117, *O praise the Lord, all ye nations* (1966),[109] uses English, Latin, French, German, Spanish, and Hebrew texts, along with plainsong and other musical fragments in an interesting fashion with tambourine, castanets, and optional handbells. Its structure provides an opportunity to demonstrate the ecumenical basis of musical praise, but its introduction to most churches would produce more consternation than acceptance.

Nearly every attempt to expand the stylistic boundaries of the anthem has been at the expense of some established feature. Several of the people we have just mentioned have deprived their listeners of either comfortable melodies or satisfying cadences in favor of rhythmic variety, new sonorities, or reiterative treatment. Until the next period of drastic change comes along, the appeal of anthems will remain strongly with those that provide the listener with tunes he can identify on later hearing, written in such a fashion that he can recognize phrase structure. Our few remaining words must, then, be directed to some typical examples of anthems that have

---

[105] G. Schirmer 11294.

[106] The John Sheppard Music Press is apparently devoted to publishing only Berger's own works that cannot be absorbed by longer-established publishers.

[107] G. Schirmer 9992.   [108] Augsburg 1264.   [109] John Sheppard Music Press 1005.

Example 158. *I will give thanks unto the Lord*, Thomas Matthews (H. T. FitzSimons 2212, mm. 29–36).

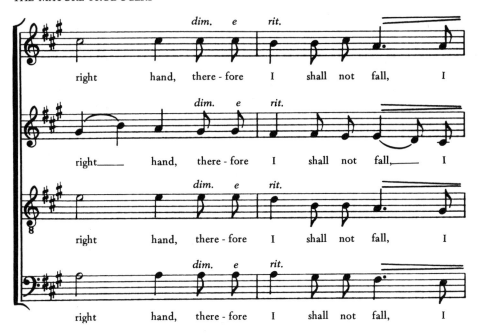

From the Aeolian Choral Series no. 2212. Used by permission of the copyright owners, H. T. FitzSimons Company, Inc., Chicago, Illinois.

continued to provide these still desirable ingredients while they have not become immersed in the mold of mediocrity.

Two composers who have written squarely in the center of current church music taste are David H. Williams (1919–) and Gordon Young (1919–). Both men are well established as prolific contributors whose numerous anthems are listed in the catalogues of several leading publishers. Although Williams draws texts from a variety of sources, he favors hymns which he endows with entirely original musical settings. Three of this type which belong to the Lenten-Easter season are especially effective: *Draw nigh to Jerusalem* (1956),[110] a Palm Sunday anthem on a text by Jeremy Taylor, makes much use of unison choral passages with a massive organ accompaniment at the end; *O come and mourn with me* (1954)[111] is a sympathetic setting of Frederick W. Faber's beautiful poem on the Crucifixion, in which a haunting minor melody is used with various voice combinations; and a stirring Easter anthem on Charles Wesley's *Christ the Lord is risen today* (1953)[112] alternates organ with unaccompanied choral sections, effectively bringing out the strong melodic, rhythmic, and harmonic drive of the music.

Gordon Young's anthems tend to place the major responsibility on the organist, assigning a less hazardous role to the choir. Illustrative of this is *From all that dwell below the skies* (1960),[113] which limits the choir to unison singing except for a few measures of two-part writing near the end. The organ part, on the other hand, is ambitious, compensating for the simplicity of the choral material by the use of mildly dissonant chords in a strong rhythmic framework. *O come let us sing unto the Lord* (1965)[114] again relies heavily on unison choral lines supported by dissonant accompaniment. A contrasting middle section is set for SSATB with open fifths and octaves after the manner of organum.

The anthems of Thomas Matthews (1915–) are characterized by a strong sense of rhythmic drive and a somewhat astringent harmonic vocabulary. *O praise God in his sanctuary* (1954)[115] makes much use of consecutive fifths, and church choirs will undoubtedly find some degree of challenge in the parallel major-seventh chords, the rhythmic variety, and the partial use of the Mixolydian mode, especially if the composer's intention of *a cappella* performance is realized. In the same joyful and vigorous vein, Matthews draws on portions of two psalms of contrasting character for *I will give thanks unto the Lord* (1964),[116] the second section of text supplying the basis for a beautifully lyrical center section (Example 158).

Matthews' sensitivity to the mood of a text is apparent in *The Lord is my shepherd* (1956).[117] The overworked and frequently mishandled psalm receives an interpretation at his hand that accentuates the finest shades of text meaning, thus making the music a vehicle for worship rather than an end in itself.

Somewhat different approaches to the development of unusual or specialized

---

[110] H. W. Gray, C.M.R. 2410.   [111] H. W. Gray, C.M.R. 2323.
[112] H. W. Gray, C.M.R. 2275.   [113] Galaxy 2186.   [114] H. W. Gray, C.M.R. 2913.
[115] H. T. FitzSimons 2124.   [116] H. T. FitzSimons 2212.   [117] H. T. FitzSimons 2137.

treatment of material may be found in anthems by Mary E. Caldwell (1909–), who either writes or translates most of the texts she sets to music, thus achieving a consistency of style that is further evident in her apparent preference for seasonal texts, especially those for Christmas; and by M. Thomas Cousins (1914–), best known for his brilliant *Glorious everlasting* (1950),[118] in which the use of a chromatic bass line in descending form is balanced by an ascending whole-tone scale, the two separated by a strongly chordal utterance for eight-part choir. Cousins does not defer to the small choir, but writes in such a fashion that demands both skill and numbers in the performing body. Lloyd Pfautsch (1921–) is no more bound to a single type of composition than other composers, but he has produced an unusual work in his *Reconciliation* (1964)[119] for mixed voices and trumpet. Not only is the piece intended to be performed with only that instrument, but the middle part is written for speech chorus. The notation for the spoken part is not to be used for exact pitch levels, but "to suggest the contour of syllabic nuance."[120] Rhythmically, at least, the speech chorus is canonic; the notation employed is the letter "x" with traditional stems and flags on the staff. Certain effects of pitch must inevitably result in its performance unless they are carefully excised in rehearsal.

There are few church libraries that are without some pieces by Jane M. Marshall (1924–) and Austin C. Lovelace (1919–). The popularity of their music may be attributed to the variety, unfailing musical interest, and the suitability of their settings to the modern church service. Congregations are able to appreciate the essentially melodic nature of their writing, which seems often to enhance text in an unusual way.

Marshall's *Blessed is the man* (1960)[121] shows some of the interesting variety so frequently found in her works. After a rather solemn D-minor opening in which a melody of quiet strength is sung by the men against a monotone repetition of the first four words by the women, the music suddenly blazes forth in D major on the words "but his delight is in the law of the Lord." The closing section, a model of melodic and harmonic beauty, captures the idealistic vision of the psalmist in rhapsodic contours (Example 159).

In much the same manner Lovelace creates a mood of quiet supplication in *The beauty of the Lord* (1956).[122] Molding the piece in an ABA form, he divides each of the A sections into an incipient three-part form. The B section consists of sharply contrasting material. But technicalities aside, the strength of this anthem lies in the elusive, ethereal quality that pervades the principal thematic section (Example 160), giving full meaning to the text.

We have observed the development of the anthem from its early stages as a captive form in a national church, during which time it underwent a series of changes with increasing importance being given to solo voices. The rise of Nonconformist and

[118] Brodt Music Company 504.   [119] Abingdon Press 345.   [120] *Ibid.*, [3].
[121] Abingdon Press 106.
[122] J. Fischer & Bro. 8921.

Example 159. *Blessed is the man*, Jane M. Marshall (Abingdon APM–106, concluding 12 mm.).

Excerpted from the anthem *Blessed is the man* by Jane M. Marshall. Copyright © 1960 by Abingdon Press.

Example 160. *The beauty of the Lord,* Austin C. Lovelace (J. Fischer 8921, last 5 mm.).

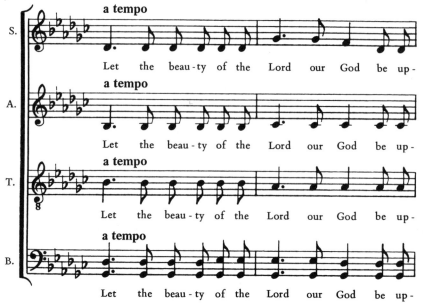

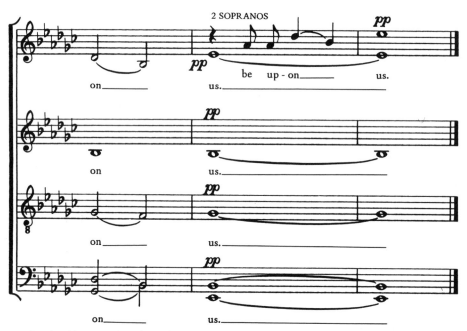

Reprinted by permission of J. Fischer & Bro., owners of the copyright.

parish church choirs occasioned further changes and brought the music into direct contact with the congregations while it placed members of those congregations— usually middle-class and not trainees to the music profession—into the choirs.

The American anthem, conversely, began outside an established church as a direct outgrowth of the Nonconformist and parish church development in England. Since that time it has developed an increasingly broader base of styles, most of which have been influenced by the art music of the preceding generation. At any time when the popular idiom has influenced its style, that popular material was either swept aside by the next generation, or it has remained as the favorite music of churches that cling to the gospel song as a common form of congregational expression.

The changes in four centuries have been numerous and varied. It is inevitable that they will continue, probably at a faster rate than before. What they will be is not in our province to predict, but so long as the choir sings for the congregation as a regular feature of worship, it will be the taste of that congregation and the sophistication of the choir that will establish what is to be sung and who the important composers will be. In the light of the past we can look to the future with hope.

Bibliography

Single octavo editions mentioned in the text are not listed in the bibliography. Collections, sets, historical editions, and volumes containing the anthems of more than one composer are listed, especially if they are not currently in print.

ADGATE, ANDREW. *Philadelphia Harmony*. Philadelphia: John M'Culloch, 1789.

——. *Philadelphia Harmony, or A Collection of Psalm Tunes, Hymns, and Anthems*. Philadelphia: Mathew Cared, [1801].

AIMWELL, ABSALOM [Andrew Adgate]. *The Philadelphia Songster*. Philadelphia: John M'Culloch, 1789.

ALCOCK, JOHN. *A Morning and Evening Service, . . .* London: Printed for the Author and Jno. Johnson, 1752.

ALLWARDT, [ANTON] PAUL. "Sacred Music in New York City, 1800–1850." Unpublished D. Sac. Mus. dissertation, Union Theological Seminary, 1950.

Anthems, Hymns, &c. usually sung at the Catholick Church in Boston. Boston: Manning & Loring, 1800.

ARNOLD, JOHN. *The Compleat Psalmodist*. 3rd edition. London: Robert Brown, 1753.

ARNOLD, SAMUEL, editor. *Cathedral Music*. 4 vols. London: For the editor, 1790.

——, and CALLCOTT, W. J. *The Psalms of David for the Use of Parish Churches*. London: Printed for John Stockdale and G. Goulding, 1791.

The ASCAP Biographical Dictionary of Composers, Authors and Publishers. Compiled and edited by The Lynn Farnol Group, Inc. New York: The American Society of Composers, Authors and Publishers, 1966.

ATTWOOD, THOMAS. *Attwood's Cathedral Music, . . . Edited, and the Organ Accompaniment, arranged, by Thomas Attwood Walmisley*. London: Ewer and Co., [ca. 1853].

ATWILL, THOMAS H. *The New York Collection of Sacred Harmony*. Lansingburgh: Abner Reed, 1802.

BAILEY, ALBERT EDWARD. *The Gospel in Hymns*. New York: Charles Scribner's Sons, 1950.

Baker's Biographical Dictionary of Musicians. Edited by Nicolas Slonimsky. 5th edition. New York: G. Schirmer, 1958. Supplement, 1965.

BAPTIE, DAVID. *A Handbook of Musical Biography*. London: W. Morley & Co., [1883].

The Baptist Hymn and Tune Book: Being "The Plymouth Collection" Enlarged, and Adapted to the Use of Baptist Churches. New York: Sheldon, Blakeman & Co., 1858.

BARBOUR, J. MURRAY. *The Church Music of William Billings*. East Lansing: Michigan State University Press, 1960.

BARNARD, JOHN. *The First Book of Selected Church Musick, consisting of Services and Anthems, such as are now used in the Cathedrall, and Collegiat Churches of this Kingdome*. 1641.

BAYLEY, DANIEL. *The New Universal Harmony or, A compendium of Church-Music containing, A Variety of Favorite Anthems, Hymn-Tunes, and Carols, Composed by the greatest Masters*. Newbury-Port: Printed and Sold by the Author. 1773.

BEXFIELD, W. R. *Church Anthems*. London: J. Alfred Novello, 1848.

BILLINGS, WILLIAM. *The Continental Harmony, containing, A Number of Anthems, Fuges, and Chorusses, in several Parts*. Boston: Isaiah Thomas and Ebenezer T. Andrews, 1794; reprint edited by Hans Nathan, Cambridge: The Belknap Press of Harvard University Press, 1961.

———. *The Psalm-Singer's Amusement*. Boston: Billings, 1781.

———. *The Singing-Master's Assistant*. Boston: Draper & Folsom, 1778.

———. *The Suffolk Harmony*. Boston: The Author, 1786.

BLAIR, SAMUEL. *A Discourse on Psalmody*. Philadelphia: John M'Culloch, 1789.

BLAKE, G. E. *Vocal Harmony, Being a Collection of Psalms, Hymns, Anthems & Chants, Compiled from the Compositions of the most Approved Authors*. Philadelphia: G. E. Blake, 1805.

The Book of Common Prayer. New York: The Church Pension Fund, 1945.

The Book of Common Prayer. . . . According to the Use of the Church of England. . . . London: Society for Promoting Christian Knowledge, n.d.

The Boston Academy's Collection of Church Music: Consisting of the Most Popular Psalm and Hymn Tunes, Anthems, Sentences, Chants, &c. Old and New; . . . 4th edition. Boston: J. H. Wilkins and R. B. Carter, 1836.

The Boston Handel and Haydn Society Collection of Sacred Music, Consisting of Songs, Duetts, Trios, Chorusses, Anthems, &c. Selected from the Works of the Most Celebrated Authors. Arranged for the Organ or Piano Forte. By the Handel and Haydn Society. Vol. I. Boston: The Handel and Haydn Society, Thomas Badger, Jr., Printer, 1821.

BOYCE, WILLIAM. *Blessed is he that considereth the Poor*. London: For Mr. Ashley by Bland and Wellers, 1802.

———. *Cathedral Music*. 3 vols. London: By the editor, 1760–1778.

———. *A Collection of Anthems, . . . For 1, 2, 3, 4, 5, and 8 Voices*. London: Printed for the Author's Widow, 1790.

———. *Fifteen Anthems, together with a Te Deum and Jubilate, in score for 1, 2, 3, 4, and 5 Voices, Composed for the Royal Chapels*. London: Printed for the Author's Widow and Family, 1780.

———. *Lord, thou hast been our refuge*. London: For Mr. Ashley by Bland & Wellers, 1802.

BRITTON, ALLEN P. and LOWENS, IRVING. "Unlocated Titles in Early Sacred American Music." *Music Library Association NOTES*, XI/1 (December, 1953), 33–48.

BRYANT, GILES. "The Music of Healey Willan," *Musicanada* (March, 1968), No. 9, 5–7.

BUCK, DUDLEY. *Illustrations in Choir Accompaniment with Hints on Registration*. New York: G. Schirmer, 1877.

BUCK, P. C. *et al.*, editors. *Tudor Church Music*. 10 vols. London: Oxford University Press, 1922–1929.

BUCKLEY, ANNIE. *History of the Providence Baptist Chapel, Lumb*. Rawtenstall: A. Riley, "Free Press" Office, 1928.

BUKOFZER, MANFRED F. *Music in the Baroque Era*. New York: W. W. Norton and Company, Inc., 1947.

BUMPUS, JOHN S. *A History of English Cathedral Music*. 2 vols. London: T. Werner Laurie, 1908.

BURNEY, CHARLES. *A General History of Music*. 2 vols. New York: Dover Publications, 1957.

CAIN, NOBLE. *Choral Music and its Practice*. New York: M. Witmark & Sons, 1932.

Carols for Choirs. Edited and arranged by Reginald Jacques and David Willcocks. London: Oxford University Press, 1961.

CARR, BENJAMIN. *Masses, Vespers, Litanies, Hymns & Psalms, Anthems & Motets Composed, Selected and Arranged for the Use of the Catholic Churches in the United States of America.* Baltimore: J. Carr, 1805.

Ye Centennial. A Quire Booke for Folke Old and Younge. Made by ye Compiler. Boston: Oliver Ditson & Co., 1875.

A Century and a Half in Soho: A Short History of the Firm of Novello. London: Novello and Company Limited, 1961.

CHAPPLE, SAMUEL. *A Second Sett of Six Anthems, In Score, Figured for the Organ & Piano Forte.* London: Goulding, D'Almaine, Potter & Co., [ca. 1820].

CHASE, GILBERT. *America's Music: From the Pilgrims to the Present.* 2nd edition, revised. New York: McGraw-Hill Book Company, 1966.

CHAUCER, GEOFFREY. *The Complete Works of Geoffrey Chaucer.* Edited by Walter A. Skeat. 6 vols. 2nd edition. Oxford: At the Clarendon Press, 1894–1900.

CHETHAM, JOHN. *A Book of Psalmody.* 6th edition, corrected. Wakefield: Joseph Lord, 1741.

CLARKE, HENRY LELAND. "John Blow, 1649–1708, Last Composer of an Era." Unpublished Ph.D. thesis, Harvard University, 1947.

CLARKE-WHITFELD, JOHN. *The Services and Anthems, in vocal score.* 4 vols. London: J. Alfred Novello, [1805].

CLIFFORD, JAMES. *The Divine Services and Anthems usually Sung in His Majesties Chappell and in all Cathedrals and Collegiate Choires in England and Ireland.* 2nd edition. London: W. G., 1664.

The Collection of Psalm and Hymn Tunes Sung at the Chapel of the Lock Hospital (from the last London Edition). Boston: Published by West & Blake; and Manning & Loring, [1809].

COX, J. C., and FORD, C. B. *Parish Churches.* Revised by Bryan Little. London: B. T. Batsford, 1961.

COX, JOHN EDMUND, editor. *Miscellaneous Writings and Letters of Thomas Cranmer.* 2 vols. Cambridge: The University Press, 1946.

CROFT, WILLIAM. *Musica Sacra: or, Select Anthems in Score. . . .* 2 vols. London: J. Walsh, [1724].

CROTCH, WILLIAM. *Ten Anthems.* Cambridge: W. Dixon, 1798.

CUTLER, HENRY STEPHEN. *The Trinity Anthems.* New York: Wm. A. Pond & Co., 1865.

DANIEL, REV. R. B. *Chapters on Church Music.* London: Elliot Stock, 1894.

DANIEL, RALPH T. *The Anthem in New England before 1800.* Evanston, Illinois: Northwestern University Press, 1966.

DAVEY, HENRY. *History of English Music.* 2nd edition, revised and rewritten with appendix to 1921. London: J. Curwen & Sons, Ltd., [1895?].

DAVIES, WALFORD, and LEY, HENRY G. *The Church Anthem Book.* London: Oxford University Press, 1933.

DAVISON, ARCHIBALD. *Protestant Church Music in America.* Boston: E. C. Schirmer Music Co., 1933.

———, and APEL, WILLI, editors. *Historical Anthology of Music.* 2 vols. Cambridge: Harvard University Press, 1959.

DEARMER, PERCY, VAUGHAN WILLIAMS, R., and SHAW, MARTIN. *The Oxford Book of Carols.* London: Oxford University Press, 1928.

DE LAFONTAINE, HENRY CART. *The King's Musick.* London: Novello and Company, 1909.

The Dictionary of National Biography. 22 vols. and 6 supplements. London: Oxford University Press, 1885–1901; supplements from 1927 to 1959.

DOOLEY, JAMES EDWARD. "Thomas Hastings: American Church Musician." Unpublished Ph.D. dissertation, The Florida State University, 1963.

DOUGLAS, WINFRED. *Church Music in History and Practice.* New York: Charles Scribner's Sons, 1937. Revised edition with additional material by Leonard Ellinwood, 1962.

DURANT, WILL, and DURANT, ARIEL. *The Story of Civilization*, Vol. VIII: *The Age of Louis XIV*. New York: Simon and Schuster, 1963.

Early English Church Music. Edited by Frank Ll. Harrison *et al*. London: Stainer and Bell, for The British Academy. 7 vols. to 1968.

ELLINWOOD, LEONARD. *The History of American Church Music*. New York: Morehouse-Gorham Co., 1953.

EMERSON, LUTHER ORLANDO. *The Jubilate: A Collection of Sacred Music, for Choirs, Singing Schools, Musical Conventions, &c*. Boston: Oliver Ditson and Company, 1866.

The Essex Harmony, Part II, Consisting of Original Pieces by Kimball, Holyoke, and others. . . . Salem: Cushing & Appleton, 1802.

ETHERINGTON, CHARLES L. *Protestant Worship Music*. New York: Holt, Rinehart and Winston, 1962.

EVANS, CHARLES. *American Bibliography, 1639–1820 A.D.* 14 vols. New York: Peter Smith, 1941–1959.

EVELYN, JOHN. *The Diary of John Evelyn*. Edited by E. S. de Beer. 6 vols. Oxford: Clarendon Press, 1955.

EXCELL, E. O. *Excell's Anthems for the Choir*. 2 vols. Chicago: E. O. Excell, 1888.

FELLOWES, EDMUND H., editor. *The Collected Works of William Byrd*. 20 vols. London: Stainer & Bell Ltd., 1937–1950.

——. *English Cathedral Music: From Edward VI to Edward VII*. 4th edition. London: Methuen & Co. Ltd., 1948.

——. *Orlando Gibbons and His Family*. London: Oxford University Press, 1951.

——. *William Byrd*. 2nd edition. London: Oxford University Press, 1948.

FISHER, WILLIAM ARMS. *One Hundred and Fifty Years of Music Publishing in the United States*. Boston: Oliver Ditson Company, Inc., 1933.

The Fitzwilliam Virginal Book. Edited by J. A. Fuller-Maitland and W. Barclay Squire. Leipzig: Breitkopf & Härtel, 1899.

FLAGG, JOSIAH. *A Collection of All Tans'ur's and a Number of Other Anthems from Williams, Knapp, Ashworth, and Stephenson*. Boston: J. Flagg, [1766].

——. *A Collection of the best Psalm Tunes, in two, three, and four Parts. . . to which are added some Hymns and Anthems the Greater part of them never before Printed in America*. Boston: Paul Revere and Josiah Flagg, 1764.

FOSTER, MYLES BIRKET. *Anthems and Anthem Composers*. London: Novello and Company, 1901.

GAWTHORN, NATHANIEL. *Harmonia Perfecta: A Compleat Collection of Psalm Tunes, in Four Parts*. London: William Pearson, 1730.

GENUCHI, MARVIN CHARLES. "The Life and Music of Jacob French (1754–1817), Colonial American Composer." Unpublished Ph.D. dissertation, State University of Iowa, 1964.

GEORGE, M. DOROTHY. *London Life in the Eighteenth Century*. New York: Harper Torchbooks, Harper and Row, 1965.

GLEASON, HAROLD, editor. *Examples of Music before 1400*. New York: Appleton-Century-Crofts, Inc., 1942.

GOULD, NATHANIEL D. *Church Music in America*. Boston: A. N. Johnson, 1853.

——. *Social Harmony, or A Compilation of Airs, Duetts and Trios. Calculated for Private Devotion: Most of which are Fitted for the Organ, or Piano Forte; Also, A number of Anthems and Chorusses, Suitable for Churches and Singing Societies. The Whole Selected from the Most Approved Authors.* Boston: Printed by Thomas Badger, Jr., 1823.

GREEN, JAMES. *A Book of Psalmody*. 8th edition, corrected and enlarged. London: W. Pearson, 1734.

GREENE, MAURICE. *A New and correct Edition of Forty Select Anthems in Score, Composed for One, Two, Three, Four, Five, Six, Seven and Eight Voices*. 2 vols. London: R. Birchall, 1795.

———. *Six Full Anthems, for Five Voices*. Westminster: Richard Clark, 1812.

Grove's Dictionary of Music and Musicians. Edited by Eric Blom. 5th edition. 9 vols. New York: St. Martin's Press, 1954. Vol. X, 1961.

HAMMETT, JOHN. *Promiscuous Singing*. [Boston]: 1739.

HANDEL, G. F. *Georg Friedrich Händels Werke*. Edited by F. Chrysander. 96 vols. and 6 supplements. Leipzig: Breitkopf & Härtel, 1858–1894, 1902.

HARRISON, FRANK LL. *Music in Medieval Britain* (*Studies in the History of Music*, ed. Egon Wellesz). 2nd edition. London: Routledge and Kegan Paul, 1963.

HASTINGS, THOMAS. *Dissertation on Musical Taste*. New York: Mason Brothers, 1853.

———, and BRADBURY, WILLIAM B. *The Mendelssohn Collection, or Hastings and Bradbury's Third Book of Psalmody*. New York: Mark H. Newman & Co., [1849].

———. *The Psalmodist*. 20th edition. New York: Mark H. Newman & Co., [1844].

HASTINGS, THOMAS, and WARRINER, SOLOMON. *Musica Sacra; or Springfield and Utica Collections United*. 3rd revised edition. Utica: William Williams, 1822.

HAWKINS, SIR JOHN. *A General History of the Science and Practice of Music*. 2 vols. New York: Dover Publications, Inc., 1963.

HAYES, WILLIAM. "Rules necessary to be observed by all Cathedral-Singers in this Kingdom," *The Gentleman's Magazine, and Historical Chronicle*, XXXV (May, 1765), 213–14.

HEARD, PRISCILLA S. "*An Annotated Bibliography of Music and References to Music Published in the United States Before 1801.*" Unpublished Master's thesis, Baylor University, 1969.

HIPSHER, EDWARD ELLSWORTH. *American Opera and its Composers*. Philadelphia: Theodore Presser Co., 1934.

HIRT, CHARLES C. "Graeco-Slavonic Chant Traditions Evident in the Part-Writing of the Russian Orthodox Church." Unpublished Ph.D. dissertation, University of Southern California, 1946.

HOLDEN, OLIVER. *The American Harmony*. Boston: Isaiah Thomas and Ebenezer T. Andrews, 1792.

———. *The Union Harmony, or Universal Collection of Sacred Music*. Boston: Isaiah Thomas and Ebenezer T. Andrews, 1793.

HOLST, IMOGEN. *The Music of Gustav Holst*. London: Geoffrey Cumberlege, Oxford University Press, 1951.

HOLYOKE, SAMUEL. *The Christian Harmonist. . . designed for the Use of the Baptist Churches in the United States*. Salem: Joshua Cushing, 1804.

HOPKINS, JOHN LARKIN. *A Collection of Anthems, Composed, and dedicated to . . . the Dean & Chapter of Rochester*. London: Surman, [ca. 1850].

HOPKINSON, FRANCIS. *A Collection of Psalm Tunes with a few Anthems and Hymns[,] Some of Them Entirely New for the Use of the United Churches of Christ Church and St. Peter's Church in Philadelphia*, 1763.

HUBBARD, JOHN. *A Volume of Sacred Music, containing Thirty Anthems, selected from the works of Handel, Croft, and other eminent European authors*. Newburyport: E. Little & Co., 1814.

HUTCHINGS, ARTHUR. *Church Music in the Nineteenth Century* (*Studies in Church Music*, ed. Erik Routley). New York: Oxford University Press, 1967.

The Hymnal of the Protestant Episcopal Church in the United States of America. New York: The Church Pension Fund, 1940.

Hymns Ancient and Modern (Historical Edition). London: William Clowes and Sons, Limited, 1909.

JACKSON, WILLIAM. *Anthems and Church Services*. Edited by James Paddon. Exeter: Printed for the Author [Paddon], [ca. 1820].

————. *Sacred Music*. Edited by James Paddon. London: Goulding and D'Almaine, [ca. 1825].

————. *Two Anthems and a Complete Church Service*. Edited by James Paddon. Exeter: Printed for the Author [Paddon], [ca. 1820].

JACOBS, ARTHUR, editor. *Choral Music*. Baltimore: Penguin Books, 1963.

JORDAN, HENRY BRYCE. "The Music of Pelham Humfrey." Unpublished Ph.D. dissertation, University of North Carolina, 1956.

JULIAN, JOHN. *A Dictionary of Hymnology*. 2 vols. 2nd revised edition. London: John Murray, 1907. Dover reprint edition, 1957.

KALLMANN, HELMUT. *A History of Music in Canada, 1534–1914*. Toronto: University of Toronto Press, 1960.

KENNEDY, MICHAEL. *The Works of Ralph Vaughan Williams*. London: Oxford University Press, 1964.

KENT, JAMES. *A Morning & Evening Service with Eight Anthems*. Revised and arranged by Joseph Corfe. [London]: Printed for the Editor, [ca. 1780].

————. *Twelve Anthems*. London: Printed for the Author by William Randall, 1773.

KERR, PHIL. *Music in Evangelism*. 4th edition. Glendale, California: Gospel Music Publishers, 1954.

KEY, JOSEPH. *Eight Anthems on Various Occasions*. 2nd edition. Nuneaton, Warwickshire: Printed for, & Sold by the Author, [ca. 1792].

————. *Eleven Anthems on General and Particular Occasions, Interspersed with Symphonies and Thorough Basses, For Two Hautboys and a Bassoon; Being particularly design'd for the Use of Parochial Choirs.* Nuneaton, Warwickshire: Printed for & Sold by the Author, [ca. 1794].

————. *Five Anthems, Four Collects, Twenty Psalm Tunes, Three Carols, A Magnificat & Nunc Dimittis*. London: Printed for Mrs. Eliz. Key, [ca. 1795].

————. *Five Anthems and Four Hymns, on General & Particular Occasions; Ten Psalm Tunes, Seven Carols &c.* London: Printed for Messers Thompsons, [ca. 1800].

KINKELDEY, OTTO. "Beginnings of Beethoven in America," *The Musical Quarterly*, XIII/2 (April, 1927), 217–48.

KNAPP, WILLIAM. *A Set of New Psalms and Anthems in Four Parts: On Various Occasions*. 5th edition. London: Printed by Robert Brown, 1752.

LANGDON, CHAUNCEY. *Beauties of Psalmody*. New Haven: D. Bowen, 1786.

Laus Deo! The Worcester Collection of Sacred Harmony... The Sixth Edition, Altered, Corrected and Revised with Additions, by Oliver Holden. Boston: Isaiah Thomas and Ebenezer T. Andrews, 1797.

LAW, ANDREW. *The Musical Magazine Containing a Variety of Favorite Pieces, Number Second*. Cheshire, Connecticut: William Law, 1793.

————. *Select Harmony, Containing in a plain and concise manner, the Rules of Singing: Together with a Collection of Psalm-Tunes, Hymns and Anth[ems]*. New Haven: T. and S. Green, 1778.

LE HURAY, PETER. "The English Anthem, 1580–1640," *Proceedings of the Royal Musical Association*, LXXXVI (1959–1960), 1–13.

————. *Music and the Reformation in England, 1549–1660*. (*Studies in Church Music*, edited by Erik Routley). New York: Oxford University Press, 1967.

————. "Towards a Definitive Study of Pre-Restoration Anglican Service Music," *Musica Disciplina*, XIV (1960), 167–95.

LIGHTWOOD, JAMES T. *Hymn-Tunes and Their Story*. Revised edition. London: The Epworth Press, 1923.

LILLEY, JOHN M. "A History of Baptist Hymnody in America (1639–1844)." Unpublished Master's thesis, Baylor University, 1964.

LITTLE, WILLIAM, and SMITH, WILLIAM. *The Easy Instructor; or, A New Method of Teaching Sacred Harmony.* Albany: Printed for Websters & Skinners and Daniel Steele, [1798].

LOCKE, MATTHEW. *Four Suites made from Consort Music.* Edited by Sydney Beck. New York: The New York Public Library, 1947.

———. *Music for His Majesty's Sackbuts and Cornetts (1661).* Transcribed by Anthony Baines. London: Oxford University Press, 1951.

L[OWE], E[DWARD]. *A Short Direction for the Performance of Cathedrall Service.* Oxford: William Hall, 1661.

LOWENS, IRVING. *Music and Musicians in Early America.* New York: W. W. Norton & Company, Inc., 1964.

LYON, JAMES. *Urania or a choice Collection of Psalm-Tunes, Anthems and Hymns From the most approv'd Authors, with some Entirely New . . .* [Philadelphia: 1761].

MCCORKLE, DONALD M. "The Moravian Contribution to American Music," *Music Library Association NOTES,* XIII (September, 1956), 597–606.

———. "Moravian Music in Salem: A German-American Heritage." Unpublished Ph.D. dissertation, Indiana University, 1958.

MCCORMICK, DAVID WILFERD. "Oliver Holden, Composer and Anthologist." Unpublished S.M.D. dissertation, Union Theological Seminary, 1963.

MACE, THOMAS. *Musick's Monument.* London: For the Author, 1676; reprint, Paris: Éditions du centre national de la recherche scientifique, 1958.

MACDERMOTT, K. H. *The Old Church Gallery Minstrels.* London: SPCK, 1948.

[MACMILLAN, KEITH]. *Catalogue of Canadian Choral Music Available for Perusal from the Library of the Canadian Music Centre.* Toronto: Canadian Music Centre, [1966]. Mimeographed.

MACRAE, C. F. "Alfred Whitehead," *The Canadian Music Journal,* V/2 (Winter, 1961), 14–20.

MADAN, MARTIN. *The Collection of Psalm and Hymn Tunes sung at the Chapel of the Lock Hospital.* (From the last London edition). Boston: West & Blake, and Manning & Loring, 1809.

MANN, ELIAS. *The Northampton Collection of Sacred Harmony.* Northampton: Daniel Wright, 1802.

MARROCCO, W. THOMAS, and GLEASON, HAROLD. *Music in America: An Anthology from the Landing of the Pilgrims to the Close of the Civil War, 1620–1865.* New York: W. W. Norton & Company, Inc., 1964.

MASON, LOWELL. *Address on Church Music.* Boston: Hilliard, Gray, Little, and Wilkins, 1827.

[———]. *The Boston Handel and Haydn Society Collection of Church Music; being a Selection of the Most Approved Psalm and Hymn Tunes; together with many Beautiful Extracts from the Works of Haydn, Mozart, Beethoven, and other Eminent Modern Composers.* 5th edition. [Boston]: Richardson and Lord, 1827.

———. *Carmina Sacra: or Boston Collection of Church Music.* Boston: J. H. Wilkins & R. B. Carter, 1842.

———. *Musical Letters from Abroad.* New York: Mason Brothers, 1854; reprinted, New York: Da Capo Press, 1967.

———, and MASON, WILLIAM. *Asaph, or The Choir Book.* New York: Mason Brothers, 1861.

MASON, LOWELL, and WEBB, GEORGE JAMES. *The Psaltery.* Boston: Wilkins, Carter, & Co., 1845.

MEES, ARTHUR. *Choirs and Choral Music.* New York: Charles Scribner's Sons, 1924.

METCALF, FRANK J. *American Writers and Compilers of Sacred Music.* New York: The Abingdon Press, 1925.

MEYER, LEONARD B. *Music, the Arts, and Ideas.* Chicago: The University of Chicago Press, 1967.

MINNIEAR, JOHN MOHR. "An Annotated Catalogue of the Rare Music Collection in the Baylor University Library." Unpublished Master's thesis, Baylor University, 1963.

The Modern Collection of Sacred Music. Boston: Isaiah Thomas and Ebenezer T. Andrews, 1800.

MORLEY, THOMAS. *A Plaine and Easie Introduction to Practicall Musicke*. London: Peter Short, 1597; reprinted and edited by R. Alec Harman. New York: W. W. Norton & Company, Inc., [1952?].

Musica Britannica. London: Stainer and Bell Ltd. (for The Royal Musical Association). 1951– . 24 vols. to January, 1969.

The Musical Times. London: 1844– .

Die Musik in Geschichte und Gegenwart. Edited by Friedrich Blume. 14 vols. Kassel: Bärenreiter Verlag, 1949–1968.

NARES, JAMES. *Twenty Anthems in Score for 1, 2, 3, 4, and 5 Voices*. London: Printed for the Author, 1778.

The New Oxford History of Music. [Various editors.] London: Oxford University Press, 1954– . 4 vols. to 1969.

NEWTON, JAMES WILLIAMS. *Psalmody Improved: In a Collection of Psalm Tunes and Anthems*. Ipswich: Printed for the Author, and sold by John Shave, 1775.

NICHOLSON, SYDNEY H. *Church Music: A Practical Handbook*. London: The Faith Press, 1927.

OLMSTEAD, CLIFTON E. *History of Religion in the United States*. Englewood Cliffs, N.J.: Prentice-Hall, Inc., 1960.

OUSELEY, FREDERICK A. G. *Cathedral Music, Services & Anthems*. London: J. Alfred Novello, [ca. 1862].

The Oxford Dictionary of the Christian Religion. Edited by F. L. Cross. London: Oxford University Press, 1966.

The Oxford English Dictionary. Edited by James A. H. Murray *et al*. 13 vols. Oxford: At the Clarendon Press, 1933.

PAGE, JOHN. *Harmonia Sacra*. 3 vols. London: Printed and published for the Editor, 1800.

PALMER, A. H., and WRIGHT, R. P. *The Song of Triumph, A New Collection of Sacred and Secular Music*. Boston: Arthur P. Schmidt & Co., 1881.

PALMER, H. R., AND EMERSON, L. O. *The Leader: A Collection of Sacred and Secular Music, for Choirs, Conventions, Singing Schools, Normal Musical Academies and the Home Circle*. Boston: Oliver Ditson & Co., 1874.

PALMER, WILLIAM. "Gibbons's Verse Anthems," *Music & Letters* XXXV/2 (April, 1954), 107–13.

PEAKER, CHARLES. "Help Wanted, Male or Female," *The Canadian Music Journal*, III/3 (Spring, 1959), 36–40.

PEPYS, SAMUEL. *The Diary of Samuel Pepys*. Edited by Henry B. Wheatley. London: G. Bell and Sons, 1893; reprinted in 2 vols., New York: Random House, n.d.

PETTET, ALFRED. *Original Sacred Music, consisting of Psalms, Hymns, and Anthems*. [London]: Chappell & Co., and others, n.d.

PHILLIPS, C. HENRY. *The Singing Church*. London: Faber and Faber, Ltd., 1945.

PLAYFORD, HENRY. *The Divine Companion; or, David's Harp New Tun'd*. 4th edition. London: Printed by W. Pearson, 1722.

PLAYFORD, JOHN, *The Whole Book of Psalms: with the Usual Hymns and Spiritual Songs*. 17th edition, corrected and amended; London: Printed by W. Pearson, 1724.

PRICE, IRA MAURICE. *The Ancestry of Our English Bible*. 2nd edition, revised, William A. Irving and Allen P. Wikgren. New York: Harper and Brothers, 1907.

Proceedings of the American Musical Convention: Held in the Broadway Tabernacle, on the 8th, 9th, and 10th of October, 1845, with the Addresses. New York: Saxton & Miles, 1845.

PROCTER, FRANCIS, AND FRERE, WALTER HOWARD. *A New History of The Book of Common Prayer.* London: Macmillan and Co., 1951.

Psalms, Hymns, and Anthems Used in the Chapel of the Hospital for the Maintenance and Education of Exposed and Deserted Young Children. London: 1774.

PURCELL, HENRY. *The Works of Henry Purcell.* London: Novello and Co., 1878– . 32 vols. to 1969.

RATLIFF, ALBERTEEN. "Second Supplement to '*An Annotated Catalogue of the Rare Music Collection in the Baylor University Library*'." Unpublished Master's thesis, Baylor University, 1969.

RAVENSCROFT, THOMAS. *The Whole Booke of Psalmes: with the Hymnes, Evangelicall, and Songs Spirituall*. . . Newly corrected and enlarged. London: Printed by Thomas Harper for the Company of Stationers, 1633.

READ, DANIEL. *The American Singing Book.* New Haven: D. Read, 1785.

———. *The Columbian Harmonist, No. 2.* New Haven: Printed for the Editor, [1793].

REESE, GUSTAVE. *Music in the Middle Ages.* New York: W. W. Norton and Co., 1940.

———. *Music in the Renaissance.* Revised edition. New York: W. W. Norton and Co., 1959.

RICH, ARTHUR LOWNDES. *Lowell Mason: The Father of Singing Among the Children.* Chapel Hill: The University of North Carolina Press, 1946.

RICHARDS, JAMES H. "Samuel Webbe as a Church Composer." Unpublished Master's thesis, Baylor University, 1965.

RIDOUT, GODFREY. "Healey Willan," *The Canadian Music Journal,* III/3 (Spring, 1959), 4–14.

RIMBAULT, EDWARD F., editor. *The Old Cheque-Book: or Book of Remembrance of the Chapel Royal from 1561 to 1744.* [London]: Printed for the Camden Society, 1872; reprinted, New York: Da Capo Press, 1966.

RIPPON, JOHN. *A Selection of Psalm and Hymn Tunes.* 5th edition, enlarged. London: Sold by Mr. Rippon, n.d.

ROOT, GEORGE F. *The Diapason: A Collection of Church Music.* New York: Mason Brothers, 1860.

ROSE, BERNARD. "Thomas Tomkins, 1575?–1656," *Proceedings of the Royal Musical Association,* LXXXII (1955–1956), 89–105.

ROUTLEY, ERIK. *The English Carol.* London: Herbert Jenkins, 1958.

———. *Twentieth Century Church Music.* (*Studies in Church Music,* edited by Erik Routley). New York: Oxford University Press, 1964.

RUSSELL, WILLIAM, editor. *Psalms, Hymns, and Anthems for the Foundling Hospital.* London: 1809.

Sacred Performances at the Dedication of the Baptist Meeting-House in Charlestown, May 12, 1801. Boston: Manning & Loring, [1801].

SCHOLES, PERCY A. *The Great Dr. Burney.* 2 vols. London: Oxford University Press, 1948.

———. *The Mirror of Music: 1844–1944.* 2 vols. London: Novello & Co., 1947.

———. *The Oxford Companion to Music.* 9th edition. London: Oxford University Press, 1955.

———. *The Puritans and Music in England and New England.* London: Oxford University Press, 1934.

SHAW, HAROLD WATKINS. "John Blow's Anthems," *Music and Letters,* XIX/4 (October, 1938), 429–42.

A Short History of Cheap Music. London: Novello, Ewer and Co., 1887.

Sixty Years of Cathedral Music [1898–1958]. (Church Music Occasional Paper No. 24). London: Oxford University Press, [1958?].

SMITH, JOHN STAFFORD. *Anthems, Composed for the Choir-Service of the Church of England.* London: Printed for the Author, [ca. 1800].

SONNECK, O. G. *Francis Hopkinson, the First American Poet-Composer (1737–1791), and James Lyon, Patriot, Preacher, Psalmodist (1735–1794): Two Studies in Early American Music.* Washington, D.C.: H. L. McQueen, 1905; reprint, New York: Da Capo Press, 1967.

Statutes of Lincoln Cathedral. Edited by Henry Bradshaw and Chr. Wordsworth. 2 vols. Cambridge: University Press, 1897.

STEVENS, DENIS. *Thomas Tomkins: 1572–1656.* London: Macmillan & Co., 1957.

———. *Tudor Church Music.* London: Faber & Faber, 1961.

STEVENS, R. J. S., editor. *Sacred Music for one, two, three & four Voices. . . .* 3 vols. London: Charterhouse, [ca. 1796–1802].

STEVENSON, ROBERT. *Protestant Church Music in America.* New York: W. W. Norton & Company, Inc., 1966.

STICKNEY, JOHN. *The Gentleman and Lady's Musical Companion.* Newburyport: Daniel Bayley, 1774.

STOW, BARON, and SMITH, S. F. *The Psalmist: A New Collection of Hymns for the Use of the Baptist Churches.* Boston: Gould and Lincoln, 1843.

STRONG, JOSEPH. *The Duty of Singing.* New Haven: Thomas and Samuel Green, 1773.

SWENEY, JOHN R., and KIRKPATRICK, WILLIAM J. *Anthems and Voluntaries for the Church Choir.* Philadelphia: John J. Hood, 1881.

SYMMES, THOMAS. *The Reasonableness of, Regular Singing, or, Singing by Note.* Boston: B. Green, for S. Gerrish, 1720.

TANS'UR, WILLIAM. *A Compleat Melody; or The Harmony of Sion.* 4th edition. London: Printed for Alice Pearson, 1738.

Templi Carmina. Songs of the Temple, or Bridgewater Collection of Sacred Music. 5th edition, improved and enlarged. Boston: West and Richardson, 1817.

———. 9th edition. Boston: Richardson & Lord, 1821.

———. 10th edition. Boston: Richardson & Lord, 1822.

Ten Full Anthems Collected from the works of several Eminent Composers, Published principally for the Use of Country Churches. London: J. Johnson, [ca. 1760].

TOWNSEND, GEORGE G., JR. "First Supplement to 'An Annotated Catalogue of the Rare Music Collection in the Baylor University Library'. " Unpublished Master's thesis, 1966.

TRAVERS, JOHN. *Whole Book of psalms, for one, two, three, four and five voices with a thorough bass for the harpsichord. . . .* 2 vols. London: Printed for J. Johnson, [ca. 1750].

The Treasury of English Church Music. Edited by Gerald H. Knight and William L. Reed. 5 vols. London: Blandford Press, 1965.

TUDWAY, THOMAS. "A Collection of the Most Celebrated Services and Anthems. . . ." British Museum MSS Harley 7337–7342.

TUFTS, JOHN. *Introduction to the Singing of Psalm-Tunes.* 5th edition. Boston: S. Gerrish, 1726.

Two St. Cecilia's Day Sermons (1696–1697). Introduction by James E. Phillips, Jr. (The Augustan Reprint Society, Publication Number 49). Los Angeles: William Andrews Clark Memorial Library, University of California, 1955.

VAN NICE, JOHN ROBERT. "The Larger Sacred Choral Works of William Boyce (1710–1779)." Unpublished Ph.D. dissertation, State University of Iowa, 1956.

The Village Harmony: or, New England Repository of Sacred Musick. Collected from the Works of the most Celebrated Masters. 17th edition, revised. Exeter: J. J. Williams, 1820.

VIRDUNG, SEBASTIAN. *Musica getutscht.* Basel, 1511; reprinted with commentary by Leo Schrade. Kassel: Bärenreiter Verlag, 1931.

WALTER, THOMAS. *The Grounds and Rules of Musick Explained: Or an Introduction to the Art of Singing by Note. Fitted to the meanest Capacities.* Boston: Printed by J. Franklin for S. Gerrish, 1721.

————. *The Sweet Psalmodist of Israel: A Sermon Preach'd at the Lecture held in Boston, by the Society for promoting Regular and Good Singing, and for reforming the Depravations and Debasements our Psalmody labours under, in Order to introduce the proper and true Old Way of Singing.* Boston: Printed by J. Franklin for S. Gerrish, 1722.

WEBBE, SAMUEL. *A Collection of Masses, With an Accompaniment for the Organ.* London: T. Jones, 1792.

————. *Eight Anthems in score, for the use of Cathedrals and Country Choirs.* London: Printed for the Author, [1788].

————. *Twelve Anthems Particularly Calculated for Families or Small Choral Societies.* London: R. Birchall, [1798].

[WELDON, JOHN]. *Divine Harmony.* 2 vols. [The first volume is by Weldon; the second, by several composers]. London: I. Walsh, [1716–1717].

WESLEY, SAMUEL SEBASTIAN. *A Few Words on Cathedral Music and the Musical System of the Church, with a Plan of Reform.* London: J. & J. Rivington, *et al.*, 1849; reprinted, New York: Hinrichsen Edition Ltd., 1961.

WESTRUP, J. A. *Purcell.* London: J. M. Dent and Sons, 1937.

WHITAKER, JOHN. *The Seraph, A Collection of Sacred Music, Suitable to Public or Private Devotion.* 2 vols. London: Whitaker and Company, 1818.

The Whole of the Music As performed at the Public Funeral of Field Marshal The Duke of Wellington in St. Paul's Cathedral. Edited, and in part Composed, by John Goss. London: Addison & Hollier, n.d.

WIENANDT, ELWYN A. *Choral Music of the Church.* New York: The Free Press, 1965.

WILLIS, R. STORRS. *Church Chorals and Choir Studies.* New York: Clark, Austin, & Smith, 1850.

WILSON, JOHN, editor. *Roger North on Music.* London: Novello and Company, 1959.

WOODFILL, WALTER L. *Musicians in English Society from Elizabeth to Charles I.* (*Princeton Studies in History*, Vol. 9). Princeton: Princeton University Press, 1953.

The Worcester Collection of Sacred Harmony. Worcester: I. Thomas, 1786.

YOUNG, PERCY M. *The Choral Tradition.* London: Hutchinson & Co., 1962.

YOUNG, ROBERT H. "The History of Baptist Hymnody in England from 1612 to 1800." Unpublished D.M.A. dissertation, University of Southern California, 1959.

Index

An asterisk (*) preceding an entry indicates that the anthem or composer is represented in one of the two volumes, *Fifteen Anthems from England* or *Fifteen Anthems from America*, published by J. Fischer & Bro. Many of the anthems will be available in separate octavo issues from the same publisher.

Abelard, Pierre (1079–1142), 376
Abraham, Gerald (1904–   ), 7n.
Abt, Franz (1819–1885), 311
A cappella performance; *see also* Full anthem
  in America, 331, 339, 414
  in Canada, 390
  in England, 254, 294, 299, 346–47, 354, 358, 363, 376, 398
Acquaint thyself with God, Greene, 159
Adagio for Strings, Barber, 450
Adams, Abraham, 193, 207t.
Adaptations
  by Aldrich, 68
  in American magazines, 317
  by Boyce, 112
  of operas, 168
  of oratorios, 167–68
  of symphonic works, 168
  by S. Wesley, 250
Addison, Joseph (1672–1719), 167, 177
Address on Church Music, Mason, 238n.
Adgate, Andrew, 197, 217, 217n.
Adler, Samuel (1928–   ), 450

"Adoro Te devote" hymn, 430
Agnus Dei, Barber, 450
Aimwell, Absalom [Andrew Adgate], 217n.
Ainsworth, Henry (d. 1622?), 171
Ainsworth Psalter, 127, 171
Akeroyde, Samuel, 131
Alack, when I look back, Byrd, 15
Alcock, John (1715–1806), 106n., 109n., 109–10
*Aldrich, Henry (1647–1710), 35, 65–73, 73n., 105, 125
Alessandri, Felice (1742–1798), 158
All hail, adored Trinity, Sowerby, 435
All hail the power of Jesus' name, Vaughan Williams, 355–57, 359
All in the April evening, Roberton, 370
All my heart this night rejoices, Harwood, 291
Alleluia from "Brazilian Psalm," Berger, 451
Allwardt, [Anton] Paul, 301n.
Alma redemptoris mater, antiphon, 2
Almighty God of our fathers, W. James, 446–48

Alto part displaced by octave, 179, 226; *see also* Octave displacement

Ambrose, Paul (1868–1941), 342

"Amen" endings, 18, 88, 95, 248, 253, 291, 391

American Harmony, The
  Bayley, 193, 209
  Holden, 211

American Musical Convention, 301–302, 306

American Singing Book, The, Read, 208

An earthly tree, a heavenly fruit, Byrd, 15

And I heard a great voice, Blow, 73*n.*, 84

Angelus ad Virginem, chant melody, 287–89, 290

Anglican practice, 3–5, 127
  in America, 169–70, 327
  in Canada, 383

Annivellarii, 7, 7*n.*

Antes, John (1740–1813), 229

Anthem; *see also* Cantata-anthem, Double-anthem, Full anthem, Full anthem with verse(s), Seasonal anthems, Verse anthems
  in American Catholic churches, 210, 224–25
  American use of term, nineteenth century, 235
  derivation of term, 1–4
  early use of term, 4
  English and American compared, eighteenth century, 193–96
  position of, 4
  use of term in Colonies, 174–77

Anthem for a harvest festival, Ley, 380

Anthem for Christmas, quodlibet, 224

"Anthem from the 114th Psalm, An," Hopkinson, 175

Anthem Taken From the Late Mr. Handel's Works, 159

Anthem texts
  conflations, 115, 349, 451
  sources of, 5, 14–15, 117, 124, 159, 200, 261, 269, 358, 419, 428, 441–44, 445, 455

"The Anthem That is to be Sung at St. George's Chappel," 175

Anthem titles, descriptive, 124

"Anthem to 100," 174

Anthems and Voluntaries for the Church Choir, Sweney and Kirkpatrick, 309–13

Anthems, Composed for The Choir-Service of the Church of England, Smith, 244–47

Anthems, Hymns, &c. usually sung at the Catholick Church in Boston, 210*n.*

"Anti-Regular-Singers," 171–72

Antiphons, 1–4, 369
  B.M.V., 2–3
  called *anthem* in America, 210
  Marian, 2, 4

Apocrypha, 117, 358

Araja, Francesco (1700–1767), 413

Arch form, 89

Archangelsky, Alexander (1846–1924), 412

Aria, 49, 55, 82

Arise, O Lord, into thy resting place, Tomkins, 32

Arise, shine, O Zion, Greene, 108

Arne, Thomas (1710–1778), 165, 216, 222

Arnold, John (1720–1792), 149–51, 168, 184, 193, 203, 207–208, 222

Arnold, Samuel (1740–1802)
  anthems, 93, 164–65, 224, 225
  collections, 39, 68*n.*, 97, 99*n.*, 103*n.*, 105*n.*, 108*n.*, 111*n.*, 116*n.*, 125, 165*n.*
  hymn–anthem, 157

Arrangements, 98; *see also* Adaptations; Aldrich
  of Handel, 104–106, 226–28
  of Russian liturgical music, 412

As it began to dawn, Martin, 274–79

As the hart panteth after the water brooks, Billings, 202

Asaph, or The Choir Book, L. Mason and W. Mason, 241*n.*

Ascribe unto the Lord
  Goldwin, 97
  Travers, 111

Ashford, Mrs. E. L., 317, 320, 321*n.*, 322–24

*Ashworth, Caleb (1722–1775), 152–55, 193, 207*t.*, 208, 226

*Attwood, Thomas (1765–1838), 247–50, 261, 311

Attwood's Cathedral Music, . . . Edited, and the Organ Accompaniment, arranged, by Thomas Attwood Walmisley, 247–48, 248*n.*

Atwill, Thomas H., 222*n.*

Aurora lucis rutilat, hymn, 387

Ave verum corpus, Mozart, 255

Awake, awake, put on thy strength, O Zion,
Stainer, 269–70
Aylward, Thomas (1730–1801), 105

Bach, J. S. (1685–1750), 252, 390, 417, 445
Bailey, Albert Edward, 127n.
Bain, James Leith Macbeth, 398
Baines, Anthony, 47n.
Bairstow, Edward (1874–1946), 365, 368–70, 389
Baptie, David, 244n.
Baptist Hymn and Tune Book, The, 306n., 330n.
Barber, Samuel, (1910–), 450
Barbour, J. Murray (1897–), 197n., 200, 200n.
Barnard, John (fl. 1640), 92n.
Barnby, Joseph (1838–1896), 261–62, 309
Barrett, W. A. (1834–1891), 268
"Bartinansky": *see* Bortniansky
Bartók, Béla (1881–1945), 449
Basso continuo, 65, 88, 104
Basso seguente, 31
Battishill, Jonathan (1738–1801), 122–23, 189
Bax, Clifford, 362
Bay Psalm Book, 171, 172
Bayley, Daniel (ca. 1725–1799), 193, 206n., 207
Be still, my soul, Whitlock, 392
Be strong and of good courage, Tomkins, 27
Beatitudes, The, Smith, 245–47
Beautiful Savior, Christiansen, 414
Beauties of Psalmody, Langdon, 194, 194n.
Beauty of the Lord, The, Lovelace, 455, 458
Beck, Sydney, 47n.
Beethoven, Ludwig van (1770–1827), 232, 233, 234n., 236
"Before Jehovah's awful throne"; see "Denmark"
Before the heavens were spread abroad, Parker, 342–45, 343t.
Behold, how good and joyful, Battishill, 122
Behold, I bring you glad tidings
Greene, 159
Purcell, 88–89
Tomkins, 32
Behold, I bring you good tidings, Greene, 108
Behold, I send the promise of my Father, Roberts, 280

Behold now, praise the Lord
Rogers, 125
Titcomb, 421
Turner, 77, 78t., 78–79
Behold, O God our defender, Blow, 84
Behold, the Lord is my salvation, [Wise?], 133, 134
Behold, Thou hast made my days, Gibbons, 22–23
Belcher, Supply (1751–1836), 216
Bellas, G., 237
Bellini, Vincenzo (1801–1835), 311
Bells
as accompaniment, 363
optional handbells, 451
Bennett, William Sterndale (1816–1875), 259, 311
Berger, Jean (1909–), 451
Berkeley, Lennox (1903–), 392, 394, 402
Berlioz, Hector (1803–1869), 390
Bexfield, William R. (1824–1853), 261, 261n., 274
Bible
Geneva, 14, 24
Great, 14, 24, 76–77, 87
*Billings, William (1746–1800), 196, 197–205, 208, 209, 209n., 210, 210n., 211, 213, 216, 216n., 222, 225, 236
"corrected" editions, 200
Birth of Christ, The, Pasquet, 445
Bishop, Henry Rowley (1786–1855), 235
Bissell, Keith (1912–), 382, 390
Blair, Samuel (1741–1818), 196–97, 217
Blake, G. E. (fl. 1805), 225n.
Bless the Lord, O my soul, Gibbs, 376
Blessed are the dead, Zingarelli, 241
Blessed are the dead which die in the Lord, Stanford, 287, 289
Blessed be Jehovah, God of Israel, Bortniansky, 309, 390
Blessed be the God and Father, S. S. Wesley, 258–59
Blessed be the Lord God, Nares, 116
Blessed be Thou, Lord God of Israel, Kent, 235
Blessed is he, Crotch, 253
Blessed is he that considereth the poor, Boyce, 114–15
Blessed is the man, Marshall, 455, 456–57
Blessing, A, M. Shaw, 374, 375

Block-chord style, 23, 32, 95, 116, 122, 124, 208, 258, 372, 435, 446, 451
*Blow, John (1649–1708), 32n., 35, 39, 43, 49, 58, 60, 72, 73n., 76, 82, 84–86, 91, 94, 95, 133, 189, 225, 280
Body of Psalmody, Green, 193
Bond, Capel (1730–1790), 228
Book of Psalmody, A
Chetham, 133, 133n., 136, 188t.
Green, 133, 135–36, 188t.
Book of Psalms, 25
Book of Common Prayer, 14, 15n., 25, 76, 349, 441 (American)
Booke of Psalms, The, H. Ainsworth, 171
Booke of the Common Praier, 3
Bortniansky, Dimitri S. (1751–1825), 238, 309, 406, 408, 411n., 412, 413
Boston Academy of Music, 240
Boston Handel and Haydn Society, 232, 234, 235, 237
Boston Handel and Haydn Society Collection of Church Music . . . , The, [Mason], 234n.
Boston Handel and Haydn Society Collection of Sacred Music . . . , The, 232n., 233
Boulanger, Nadia (1887–   ), 394, 431
Bow down thine ear, Clarke, 95
Bow down thine ear, O Lord, Greene, 108
Bow my head, O Lord, Lekberg, 446, 448
Bow thine ear, Byrd, 226
Boyce, William (1710–1779)
anthems, 93, 104, 111–12, 114–16, 225
arrangements and editions, 104, 105
collection, 9n., 10n., 13, 20, 22n., 39, 40, 42n., 58n., 60, 65n., 66, 68, 68n., 70, 73n., 74, 85n., 95n., 97, 104, 105, 106, 106n., 125, 280
influence of, 111
*Bradbury, William B. (1816–1868), 238–40, 238n., 240n.
Bradshaw, Henry (1831–1886), 3n., 287
Brady, Nicholas (1659–1726), 77; *see also* Psalters
Brahms, Johannes (1833–1897), 286, 370
Brass choir, 279, 419, 427, 450
Bread of the world, France, 389–90
Bridges, Robert (1844–1930), 363
Bridgewater Collection; see Templi Carmina
Brief Introduction to the Skill of Musick, J. Playford, 172n.

Britten, Benjamin (1913–   ), 392, 394, 402
Broadway Tabernacle, 301, 301n.
Brother James' Air, Jacob, 398
Brown, Bartholomew (1772–1854), 228
Brown, Henry, 207
Bryant, Giles, 383n.
Bryne, Albertus (?–1668), 37
Buchanan, E. G., 319, 320
*Buck, Dudley (1839–1909), 242, 330–33, 330n., 336, 337, 339, 341–42
Buckley, Annie, 129, 130n., 138n.
Bullock, Ernest (1890–   ), 394, 396
Bülow, Hans von (1830–1894), 326
Bumpus, John S. (1861–1913), 122n.
Burney, Charles (1726–1814), 9, 45, 45n., 158, 222
as organist, 92
Busby, Thomas (1755–1838), 235
Button and Whitaker, publishers, 165
By the rivers of Babylon, Ashworth, 152–55
By the waters of Babylon
Humfrey, 64–65
James, 425
Byrd, William (1543–1623), 9, 10–15, 27, 226, 262, 374, 386

C major symphony, Schubert, 248
Cain, Noble (1896–   ), 407, 444–45
Caldwell, Mary E. (1909–   ), 455
Call to remembrance, O Lord, Battishill, 122
Callcott, John Wall (1766–1821), 105–106, 164–66, 228, 235
Canada, anthems in, 380–91
Canadian Broadcasting Corporation, 380
Canadian Music Centre, 380
Canadian Music Journal, 382, 390n.
Candlyn, T. Frederick H. (1892–1964), 430–31, 448
Canonic writing
in England, 32, 148, 252
as speech chorus, 455
Cantata–anthem, 43, 49, 58, 84, 87, 89, 93, 95, 97–99, 111–15, 261
description, 82
Cantata, church, 271, 291, 359, 425, 445
Cantata, Italian solo, 88
Canterbury Tales, Chaucer, 1
Canticles, 326
Cantiones Sacrae, Tallis and Byrd, 9
Cantus firmus, 407

Captivity of Judah, The, Crotch, 252
Carmina Sacra, Mason, 220–21
Carol, 15, 286, 362, 363, 380, 386, 394, 431
Carol of the drum, K. K. Davis, 431
Caroline, queen of England (d.1737), 104
Carr, Benjamin (1768–1831), 224–25
Cashmore, Donald (1926–   ), 398, 402
Cast me not away from Thy presence, S. S. Wesley, 259
Castrati, 5n.
Caswall, Edward (1814–1878), 255
Cathedral Music, Services & Anthems, Ouseley, 261n.
Cathedral of Saint John the Divine, New York, 7
Cathedral service, 38, 38n., 91, 92–93, 106, 109–11
   in America, 294, 431
   Wesley's proposals concerning, 258
Cathedral style, 149, 225–26
Cathedral tradition, 244, 252, 256, 261, 327, 363, 391
Causton, Thomas (?–1569), 8
Central Congregational Church, Brooklyn, 339
Chadwick, George W. (1854–1931), 342
Chandos Anthems, Handel, 94, 103, 103n., 105, 106
Chants, Episcopal
   in America, 232, 238, 303
   style in anthems, 308
Chapel Royal, 8, 35, 37, 38, 39, 42, 43, 44, 45, 46, 47, 48, 49, 58, 59–60, 62, 76n., 82, 85, 87, 89, 91, 92, 93, 94, 95, 97, 98, 104, 105, 106, 109, 110, 247, 256, 258, 263, 279, 286, 449
Chapel, Russian Imperial; *see* Russian Imperial Chapel
Chapelle Royale, 46
Chapple, Samuel (1775–1833), 238, 241, 241n.
Charity children, 92, 155
   influence on anthem, 167
Charles I (1600–1649), king of England (1625–1649), 27, 34, 37
Charles II (1630–1685), king of England (1660–1685)
   coronation of, 37, 38, 39, 47
   reference to, 36, 42, 43–44, 45, 48, 59, 60, 76, 82, 84, 85, 89, 98

Chase, Gilbert (1906–   ), 171n., 173n., 175n., 200, 201n.
Chaucer, Geoffrey (1340?–1400), 1
Chauncey, Nathaniel, 172
Cheap music, 243
Cherubic Hymn No. 7, Bortniansky, 309, 406
Cherubim Song, Rachmaninoff, 413
Chetham, John (fl. 1718), 133, 136–37, 155, 188, 222
Chicago A Cappella Choir, 444
Child, William (1606–1697), 35, 37, 39–42, 55, 84, 95
Children of the Chapel, 59, 60, 82
Choir Herald, The, 314–15, 319, 320
Choir Journal, The, 326–27
Choir Leader, The, 314–17, 319, 322–25, 336
Choirs, American, 174, 194–97
   function of, 306
   placement of, 301
Choirs, Canadian, 384
   "cock and hen," 386
   male, 384, 386
Choirs, English
   boys', 294
   cathedral, 27n.
   at Reformation, 5–8
   male, 255
   mixed, 256
   placement of, 7, 255–56
   responsibilities, 8
Choirs, Russian, 407–13
   female, 412
   male, 412–13
   mixed, 412
Chopin, Frédéric (1810–1849), 286
Choral recitative, 53, 56–57
Choral singing, criticism of, 109–10, 165–67, 194–96, 258–60
Choral societies, 255, 308
Chorale, 55, 88, 414, 417, 445
Chorus, voice distribution
   in English cathedral, 27, 31
   by Locke, 47, 49
   in West Gallery tradition, 128–30
Christ, being raised from the dead, Bissell, 390
Christ Church Cathedral
   Montreal, 386
   Oxford, 392
Christ rising again, Byrd, 10–11, 14

Christ, the fair glory of the holy angels,
    Bullock, 396
Christ the Lord is risen, Whitehead, 386
Christ the Lord is risen again, Thiman, 392
Christ the Lord is risen today
    Rowley, 396
    D. H. Williams, 454
Christ, the Lord, to us is born, Darst, 445
Christ, whose glory fills the skies
    Bissell, 390
    Candlyn, 430–31
Christian Harmonist, The, Holyoke, 222*n.*
Christiansen, F. Melius (1871–1955), 414,
    416–17, 419
Christiansen, Olaf C. (1901–   ), 414*n.*
Christie, Catherine A., 317
Christmas, suppression of, in London, 32–33
Chromaticism
    apparent, 387
    harmonic, 269, 435
    melodic, 65, 73, 87, 455
Church Anthem Book, The, Davies and Ley,
    250*n.*, 380
Church Anthems, Bexfield, 261*n.*
Church, John (1675–1741), 131
Church Music Reformed, J. Arnold, 149, 193
Church of St. Clement, Eastcheap, 165
Church of the Holy Trinity, Boston, 342
Clark, Richard (1786–1856), 108
*Clarke, Jeremiah (ca. 1670–1707), 94–96,
    131, 207*t.*, 226, 228
Clarke-Whitfeld, John (1770–1836), 235,
    251–52
Classical style in America, 211, 214, 229
Clefs as distinguishing features of books,
    138, 183, 187–89
Clifford, James (1622–1698), 76, 76*n.*, 84, 92
Clokey, Joseph W. (1890–1960), 427–29,
    448
Club Anthem; see I will always give thanks
Clutton, Cecil, 45*n.*
Coates, William, 47*n.*
Colla parte accompaniment
    in America, 430
    in England, 46, 59, 133, 138, 280, 290,
        299, 327
*Collection of All Tans'ur's and a Number of
    Other Anthems, A*, Flagg, 192
Collection of Anthems, A, Hopkins, 261
Collection of Masses, A, Webbe, 224*n.*

*Collection of Psalm and Hymn Tunes sung at
    the Chapel of the Lock Hospital, The*,
    Madan, 157; *see also Lock Hospital
    Collection*
*Collection of Psalm Tunes with a few Anthems
    and Hymns, A*, Hopkinson, 175, 178,
    189
Collection of the best Psalm Tunes, A, Flagg,
    189–92, 207*t.*
Collection of Tunes, A, Ashworth, 155
Collections, hymn
    in America, 175–78
    in England, 155–68
Collections of anthems, commercial, 122–25
Collections, psalm
    in America, 172–73, 193
    in England, 105*n.*, 157–59, 163–67
Collects, 14–15, 18, 24, 27, 248, 261, 383*n.*
Columbian Harmonist, The, Read, 208
Come away to the skies, C. Wesley, 168
Come, Holy Dove, Fox, 390
Come, let us join our cheerful songs, Whit-
    lock, 392
Come, O Creator Spirit, come, Noble, 294
Come, Thou Almighty King, Whitehead, 386
Come, Thou long expected Jesus, Ley, 380
**Come unto me*, J. S. Smith, 247
Come, ye disconsolate, W. James, 446
Come, ye faithful, raise the strain, White-
    head, 386
Commonwealth, English, 32–35, 36, 37, 39,
    42, 126, 128
Compleat Melody, A, Tans'ur, 138–41, 188
Compleat Psalmodist, The, J. Arnold, 149–
    51, 184, 188
Concertato contrasts, 10, 99
Congregational singing, 26, 92, 164, 167,
    171, 174, 175, 177, 194, 235, 238, 259,
    260, 302–303, 306
    of anthems, 260
    with choral anthems, 355, 359, 402
    from hymnals, 314
Continental Harmony, The, Billings, 197–
    203, 209*n.*, 210*n.*
Continental style
    in America, 235, 236–37, 309, 311, 330
    in England, 35, 47, 53, 55, 72, 82, 254–55
Contrafacta, 236, 317, 450
Contrapuntal texture, 344, 362, 390, 411
    in Russian choral music, 414

Cooke, Benjamin (1734–1793), 159
Cooke, Henry (1616–1672), 35, 38, 39, 44, 46, 59–60, 62, 82, 92
Coperario, Giovanni (John Cooper) (ca. 1575–1626), 46
Corelli, Arcangelo (1653–1713), 224, 235
Corfe, Joseph (1740–1820), 232n.
Cornetts and sackbuts, 37, 43, 44, 46, 47
Coronation anthems
    Charles I, 27
    Charles II, 38
    Elizabeth II, 358
    George II, 104
    George III, 112
    James I, 27
    James II, 84
    William and Mary, 84
Cotterill, T., 331
Cousins, Thomas (1914–), 455
Cowper, William (1731–1800), 167
Cox, J. C., 93n.
Cradle hymn, Sowerby, 435
Cranmer, Thomas (1489–1556), Archbishop of Canterbury (1553–1555), 3n., 9, 9n., 10
Create in me a clean heart, O God, Mueller, 433
Creation, The, Haydn, 168, 222, 252
Creyghton, Robert (1639–1734), 58–59
*Croft, William (1678–1727), 32n., 93, 94, 97–102, 110, 131, 133
Cross, F. L., 126
*Crotch, William (1775–1847), 252–53, 262
Crucifixion, The, Stainer, 271, 291
Curwen, John (1816–1880), 244n.
*Cutler, Henry Stephen (1824–1902), 327–30

Dance music, 321
Dance rhythms, influence on anthem, 47, 50–53, 62, 235
Daniel, Ralph T., 76n., 141n., 171n., 174n., 175n., 184t., 189n., 193n., 194n., 200, 201n., 207t., 208, 208n., 209n., 214, 214n., 217, 226n.
Daphnis et Chloé, Ravel, 425
Darst, W. Glen (1896–), 444, 445
Dart, Thurston (1921–), 47n.
Davies, Henry Walford (1869–1941), 250n., 256n., 257n., 258n., 284n., 292n., 294n., 369n., 376n.
Davis, Katherine K. (1892–), 431, 433
Day draws on with golden light, The, Bairstow, 369–70
De Beer, E. S., 32
Dearmer, Percy (1867–1936), 372, 445n.
Debussy, Claude (1862–1918), 449
Decani-cantoris, 7, 9, 22, 27n., 118n., 261, 291, 327, 374
Declamatory style, 73, 257, 263, 414
"Deighn Layrocks"; *see* "Larks of Dean"
De Lafontaine, Henry Cart, 39n., 43n., 46n.
Deliver us, O Lord, Battishill, 122
Deliver us, O Lord, our God/Blessed be the Lord God, Gibbons, 23–24
Dencke, Jeremiah (1725–1795), 229
*"Denmark," Madan, 217–23, 225, 234
Descant with choir, 376, 380, 391–92, 435
Dettingen Te Deum, Handel, 226, 228
Dialogue in theoretical introductions, 142–48, 201
Diapason, The, Root, 308
Dickinson, Clarence (1873–1969), 414, 417–20
Dickinson, Helen A., 420
Ding dong, merrily on high, Candlyn, 431
Discourse on Psalmody, A, Blair, 196–97, 217
Dissenters, 90, 127, 127n.; *see also* Nonconformists
Dissertation on Musical Taste, Hastings, 238
Divine Companion, The, H. Playford, 131–33
Divine Harmony, Weldon, 48
Doddridge, Philip (1702–1751), 155
Don Cossack Chorus, 407, 413
Don Giovanni, Mozart, 168
Dooley, James Edward, 238n.
Double-anthem, 10, 20–22, 23–24
Dowland, John (1562–1626), 23, 359
Down steers the bass
    Billings, 208
    Read, 208
Draw nigh, and take the Body of the Lord, Harwood, 291
Draw nigh to Jerusalem, D. H. Williams, 454
Drop, drop, slow tears, Bullock, 396
Durant, Will and Ariel, 90
Duty of Singing, The, Strong, 194n.
Dvořák, Antonin (1841–1904), 286, 339

Dying Christian, The
    Billings, 216
    Harwood, 222, 225, 234
    Holden, 216, 222
Dying Christian's last farewell, The,
    Billings, 198–200
Dykes, John B. (1823–1876), 259, 326
Dynamics, early appearances
    in America, 205
    in England, 98
    instructions for, 247

Easter
    Gibbs, 376
    Spenser's sonnet, 376
Easter chorale, Barber, 450
Easter hymn, The, V. Novello, 254
Easter Ode, anonymous, 164
Eastern Orthodox ritual, 407
Easy Instructor, The, Little and Smith, 220–
    21
Echo effect, 76
Edson, Lewis (1748–1820), 211
Edward VI (1537–1553), king of England
    (1547–1553), 3n., 25
Eight Short Motets, Titcomb, 421
Eliot, T. S. (1888–), 374
Elizabeth I (1533–1603), queen of England
    (1558–1603), 126
Ellerton, John, 421
Ellinwood, Leonard (1905–), 171n., 175n.,
    314n., 327, 327n., 386n.
Elvey, George J. (1816–1893), 259, 311
Embassy chapels (Catholic) in England, 122
Emerson, Luther Orlando (1820–1915),
    307–309, 308n., 309n., 320, 406
Enfance du Christ, L', Berlioz, 390
English Reformation, 5
Essex Harmony, The, J. Arnold, 149
Essex Harmony, The, Part II (American),
    222, 222n.
Eternal Father, Holst, 363, 366–67
Eternal praise, Titcomb, 421
Evans, Charles (1850–1935), 175n., 189,
    189n.
Evelyn, John (1620–1706), 32–35, 36, 36n.,
    44, 44n., 59n.
Excell's Anthems for the Choir, 313, 314n.
Excell, E. O. (1851–1921), 313–14
Exeter Cathedral, 120

Expectans expectavi, Wood, 292
The eyes of all wait upon thee, Berger, 451
The eyes of all wait upon thee, O Lord, Harris,
    375

Falsobordone, 205
Fanfare for Christmas Day, M. Shaw, 372
Farrant, Richard (ca. 1530–1581), 72, 241,
    255, 311
Father, how wide thy glory shines, Giardini,
    158
Father, in Thy mysterious presence, kneeling,
    Van Denman Thompson, 430
Father of heaven, whose love profound, Willan,
    384
Fear not, O Israel, Spicker, 337
Fear not, O Lord, Harris, 375
Fellowes, Edmund H. (1870–1951), 11n.,
    14n., 15n., 105n., 111n., 122n., 256n.,
    258n., 262n., 269n., 280n.
Fermata, 355
    in gospel-song style, 338–39
    as used by Giardini, Holden, and Madan,
    213–14
Festival Te Deum, Buck, 341–42
Fierce was the wild billow, Noble, 294, 297
Fifth Avenue Baptist Church, New York,
    339
Figured bass, 43, 98, 158, 235, 237
First set of Psalms, Child, 42
Fisher, William Arms (1861–1948), 193, 337
Flagg, Josiah (1737–1794), 189–93, 206, 207,
    207t.
Folksong
    in American anthems, 414, 419–20
    in English anthems, 346, 376, 427
Ford, C. B., 93n.
Forty Select Anthems, Greene, 159–61
Foster, Myles Birket (1851–1922), 11n.,
    104n., 122n.
Foundling Hospital Chapel, 159
Foundling Hospital Collection, 160–61, 254;
    see also Psalms, Hymns, and Anthems
Foundling's Hymn, The, J. C. Smith, 159
Fox, George, 390
4th Psalm, The, Hopkinson, 177
France, William E. (1912–), 389–90
Franck, César (1822–1890), 317
French elements in English music, 45–46,
    47, 62–65, 79

French, Jacob (1754–1817), 173*n*., 208

French Overture, 79, 88

Frere, Walter Howard (1863–1938), 25

From all that dwell below the skies, G. Young, 454

"From heaven the loud angelic song began," Shirley hymn, 164

From the end of the earth, Hovhaness, 450

From Virgin pure this day did spring, Byrd, 15

From Virgin's womb, Byrd, 15

Fuging entries, 181*t*., 203, 208

Fuging tunes, 189, 197, 211, 213, 219
  Holden's evaluation of, 211

Fugue (fugato), use of
  Bairstow, 369
  Croft, 99, 102
  Goss, 257
  Greene, 108, 109
  Martin, 279
  Mueller, 433
  Sowerby, 441
  Willan, 383

Full anthem, 22, 23, 27, 42, 84, 85, 87, 97, 106, 108, 111, 122, 248, 252, 253, 280, 331, 383
  definition, 55

Full anthem with verse(s), 53, 58–59, 62–65, 68, 85, 87, 95, 97, 99, 103, 106, 108, 111, 122, 165, 208, 248, 274–75, 279, 291, 327, 331, 431
  definition, 58

Fuller–Maitland, J. A. (1856–1936), 47*n*.

Funeral music, 104, 111, 216, 222, 241, 257, 287, 290, 327

Gabriel, Charles H. (1856–1932), 318–19

Gabrieli, Giovanni (1557–1612), 43

Gallery musicians, 92*n*., 118, 118*n*., 128–29
  instrumentalists, 128–29, 138
  singers, 118, 128–29

Galuppi, Baldassare (1706–1785), 413

Gardiner, William (1770–1853), 236

Gawthorn, Nathaniel, 138, 138*n*., 188

Gentleman and Lady's Musical Companion, Stickney, 184, 189, 207

Gentlemen of the Chapel, 5, 8, 62, 82, 131

Genuchi, Marvin Charles, 173, 208

George II (1683–1760), king of England (1727–1760), 111

George III (1738–1820), king of England (1760–1820), 105, 112

George V (1865–1936), king of England (1910–1936), 365

George, Graham (1912–), 387

Giardini, Felice (1716–1796), 158, 214, 235

Gibbons, Christopher (1615–1676), 37, 38, 42

*Gibbons, Orlando (1583–1625), 18, 20–24, 32*n*., 42, 396, 445

Gibbs, Cecil Armstrong (1889–1960), 376

Gird on thy sword, Holst, 363, 364–65

Give the Lord the honor, Kent, 232*n*.

Give unto the Lord, O ye mighty, Cashmore, 398

Glarum, L. Stanley (1908–), 451

Gleason, Harold (1892–), 203*n*., 208*n*., 209*n*., 289*n*.

Glinka, Mikhail (1804–1857), 317

Gloria in excelsis Deo, Weelkes, 18, 19

Gloria patri, see Lesser Doxology

Glorious everlasting, Cousins, 455

Glory be to God, Tomkins, 32

Glory to Thy Holy Name, Pasquet, 445

Go, congregation, go! Antes, 229

Go forth to life, O child of earth, V. D. Thompson, 428

Go not far from me, O God, Zingarelli, 241

Go to dark Gethsemane, Noble, 296

Go ye and teach all nations, V. D. Thompson, 428

God hath appointed a day, Tours, 263, 270–71

God is a spirit, Bennet, 311

God is ascended up on high, Cashmore, 398

God is in His holy temple, V. D. Thompson, 430

God is our hope and strength, Aldrich, 68–69

God of Abraham praise, The, Shelley, 341

God so loved the world
  Goss, 256
  Stainer, 270

God spake sometimes in visions, Blow, 84

God with me lying down, Lekberg, 447, 448

Goldwin, John (ca. 1670–1719), 94, 95, 97

Goosens, Eugene (1893–), 402

Gordon, Adam, 165

Gospel-song
  movement, 308
  style, 263, 311, 313–14, 337, 339, 449, 459

*Goss, John (1800–1880), 256–57, 259, 261

Gostling, John (ca. 1650–1773), 87

Gould, Nathaniel D. (1781–1864), 237–38, 302, 406

Gounod, Charles (1818–1893), 262, 272, 286, 296, 309, 314, 317, 370

Gram, Hans (1754–1804), 214

Grand motet, French, 46, 46n.

Grant us light, Thiman, 391

Grant, we beseech thee, Attwood, 248

Graun, Karl Heinrich (1704–1759), 165

Great and glorious is the name of the Lord, Dickinson, 419

Great and marvellous, Tomkins, 30–31

Great Lord of lords, Joubert, 400–402

Greater light, The, M. Shaw, 374–75

Green, James (fl. 1715–1750?), 133–36, 168, 188, 193, 207

Greene, Maurice (1695–1755), 93, 106–109, 110, 159, 161, 225, 326

*Gregor, Christian Friedrich (1723–1801), 229

Gregorian plainsong, 4, 256, 383, 430, 451

Gretchaninov, Alexander (1864–1956), 413

Grieve not the Holy Spirit, Stainer, 269, 278–79

Ground bass, 76, 77, 89, 95, 97, 362, 363, 364–65, 371, 372, 374, 398, 419, 420

Grounds and Rules of Musick Explained, The, Walter, 172, 172n.

Grove, Sir George (1820–1900), 262

Hail, gladdening light, Martin, 279

Hail Judea, happy land, Handel, 228

Hail thee, festival day, Willan, 383

Hail, true Body, Willan, 383–84

Hall, John, 237

"Hallelujah" ending, 40–41, 42, 55, 58, 59, 88, 97, 108, 122, 133, 141, 165, 192, 369

  section, 247

Hallelujah to the God of Israel, Haydn, 234

Hammett, John, (d. 1773), 174

Hampton Court, 85, 90

Handel, George Friedrich (1685–1759), 76, 94, 103–106, 130, 148, 159, 164, 165, 193, 207, 208, 216, 222, 224, 225, 228, 232, 234, 237, 253

  influence on English composers, 94, 105–106, 130, 164

Happy soul, that free from harms, C. Wesley, 168

Hark, from the tombs a doleful sound, Watts, set to "Dead March" from *Saul*, 167

Hark, hark, my soul, Shelley, 339, 341

Harker, F. Flaxington (1876–1936), 342

Harmonia Perfecta, Gawthorn, 138, 188

Harmonia Sacra, Page, 243

"Harmony," French, 208

Harmony of Harmony, The, French, 208

Harris, William H. (1883–), 374–76

Harrison, Frank Ll., 2n., 3n., 7n., 22n.

Harvest Festival

  anthem, 375, 376, 380

  English, 99, 294

Harwood, Basil (1859–1949), 291

Harwood, Edward (1707–1787), 216, 222, 225, 235

Hastings, Thomas (1784–1872), 222, 238, 238n., 240, 240n., 241n., 302, 331

Hawkins, James (ca. 1660–1729), 94

Hawkins, Sir John (1719–1789), 9, 37–38, 128, 128n.

*Haydn, Franz Joseph (1732–1809), 165, 167–68, 224, 228, 234, 236, 237, 254

Hayes, Philip, 252

Hayes, William (1741–1790), 110

He is risen, Whitlock, 392

He slumbers not, Tschaikowsky, 317

He that dwelleth in the secret place, Clokey, 427

Hear my cry, O God, Holden, 213

Hear my crying, Greene, 108

Hear my prayer

  W. James, 446

  Tomkins, 23

Hear my words, ye people, Parry, 280

Hear, O heavens, Humfrey, 65

Hear Thou my prayer, O Lord, Bissell, 390

Hear our prayer, anonymous, 222

Heart that's broken and contrite, An, Oldroyd, 380

Heavens declare the glory of God, The, Clarke-Whitfeld, 252

Heber, Bishop Reginald (1783–1826), 389

Heighington, Musgrave (1679–1774), 158, 159, 164, 235

Henderson, A. M., 407, 413n.

Henry VIII (1491–1547), king of England (1509–1547), 9n., 25

Herbert, George (1593–1632), 431

Herbst, Johannes (1735–1812), 229

Here, O my Lord, I see Thee face to face,
    Whitlock, 392, 393
Hereford Cathedral, 259
Hilton, John (1599–1657), 241*n.*
Himmel, Friedrich (1765–1814), 255, 314
Hindemith, Paul (1895–1963), 387
Hine, Marie M., 315
Hipsher, Edward E., 427*n.*
Hirt, Charles C., 404, 411, 411*n.*, 413*n.*
Hirt, Lucy A., 404
Ho, everyone that thirsteth, Macfarlane, 414,
    415
Holden, Oliver (1765–1844), 210–19, 225,
    236
Hollywood First Presbyterian Church, 404
Holst, Gustav (1874–1934), 360–67, 370,
    374, 376, 394, 402, 427
Holyoke, Samuel (1762–1820), 222, 222*n.*
Hopkins, John (?–1570), 14, 127
Hopkins, John Henry, 441
Hopkins, John Larkin (1820–1873), 261,
    261*n.*
*Hopkinson, Francis (1737–1791), 175–79,
    189, 197
"The horse and his rider," 130
Hosanna, blessed is he that comes, Gregor,
    229
Hosanna to the Son of David
    O. Gibbons, 22, 24
    Weelkes, 18
Hospodi Pomilui, Lvovsky, 412, 451; *see also
    Lord, our God, have mercy*
Hovhaness, Alan (1911–   ), 450
How are the mighty fall'n, Wise, 70–73
How far is it to Bethlehem, G. Shaw, 372
How goodly are thy tents, Ouseley, 261
How long wilt thou forget me
    Battishill, 122
    Clarke, 95
How long wilt thou forget me, O Lord, C.
    Gibbons, 42
How, William Walsham (1823–1897), 421
Howells, Herbert (1892–   ), 290, 394–95
Hubbard, John (1759–1810), 226–28
Hughes, Dom Anselm (1889–   ), 7*n.*
Hullah, John Pyke (1812–1884), 244
*Humfrey, Pelham (1647–1674), 35, 39, 47,
    58, 60–65, 76, 82, 84, 94
Hundredth psalm, The, Vaughan Williams,
    358, 359

Hunnis, William, 15
Hussite battle hymn, Dickinson, 419
Hymn-anthem, 162, 291, 299, 331, 339,
    358, 370, 383, 384, 428, 433, 449
*Hymn-Anthem on the tune "O Quanta
    Qualia,"* Willan, 384
Hymn for Easter (Lyra Davidica), 161, 162
Hymn of the initiants, Pasquet, 445
Hymn tunes, 127, 148, 174, 207
    by Handel, 130
Hymnals, 108
    for congregation, 314
Hymns, 127
    and anthems compared, 130–31
    of "human composure," 127, 138, 157
    translations during Oxford Movement,
        255, 279, 386
Hymns Ancient and Modern, 255, 369*n.*, 383,
    386, 387*n.*
Hymns and Spiritual Songs, Watts, 127

I am Alpha and Omega, Stainer, 269
I am come into my garden, Billings, 200, 201
I am the Rose of Sharon, Billings, 200, 222
I call and cry to thee, Tallis, 9
I charge you, O daughters of Jerusalem, Wise,
    133
I charge you, O ye daughters of Jerusalem,
    Billings, 200
I heard a great voice
    Billings, 222
    Kimball, 216
I heard a voice from heaven
    Goss, 257
    Stanford, 289
    Vaughan Williams, 346
I love my Shepherd's voice, Watts, 168
*I love the Lord because He hath heard the voice
    of my pray'r,* Billings, 203
I only know, V. D. Thompson, 430
I see His blood upon the rose, Roberton, 370
I sing a song of the saints of God, Sowerby, 435
I sing as I arise today, Clokey, 428
I will always give thanks (Club Anthem),
    Blow, Humfrey, and Turner, 61–62,
    76
I will arise, Creyghton, 58
I will arise and go to my father, Clarke-Whit-
    feld, 252
I will bless the Lord (Urania), 180

I will exalt thee, Tye, 9
I will give thanks unto the Lord
   J. Arnold, 149, 150
   Matthews, 454
   Purcell, 88, 89
I will lift up mine eyes, Sowerby, 435, 438–39
I will love Thee, O Lord, Billings, 203
I will magnify the Lord (Urania), J. Arnold,
   184
*If we believe that Jesus died
   Boyce, 116
   **Goss, 257
If ye love me, Tallis, 9
If ye then be risen with Christ, Whitehead, 387
I'll wash my hands in innocency, Chapple, 241
Imitation; *see* Contrapuntal texture; Points
   of imitation
Impressionistic style, 390
In exitu Israel, S. Wesley, 251
In God's commands, George, 387
In Manus Tuas Domine, Tallis, 10*n.*
In the night, Christ came walking, Cain, 444
In the year that king Uzziah died, D. McK.
   Williams, 420, 422–23
Incline thine ear, Himmel, 255, 314
Instrumental accompaniments, twentieth
   century, 346, 354–55, 359, 362, 451
   optional, 354, 372, 451
Instrumental music; *see also* Brass choir
   · accompaniment to chant, 232
   in American churches, 208
   at end of anthem, 175
   introductions and interludes, 159, 208,
      241, 253
   in Methodist chapels (English), 130
   in parish churches
      Anglican, 118
      Nonconformist, 128–30
   as source of Continental style, 46–47
Intercession, The, King, 232, 237
Into the woods my Master went, Nevin, 339
Introduction to the Singing of Psalm-Tunes,
   Tufts, 173
Invocations, choral, 319
Is there not an appointed time (Urania), Knapp,
   185
Israel in Egypt, Handel, 104, 130*n.*
It is a good thing to give thanks, Purcell, 89
Italian elements in English music, 42, 43,
   46, 65, 73, 88

"Italian Hymn," Giardini, 158

Jackson, William, "of Exeter" (1730–1803),
   120–22, 235
Jackson, William, "of Masham" (1815–
   1866), 120
Jacob, Gordon (1895–), 394, 397–99
Jacques, Reginald, 392*n.*
James I (1566–1625), king of England
   (1603–1625), 27, 37, 126
James II (1633–1701), king of England
   (1685–1688), 84, 89
James, Philip (1890–), 425–27, 449
James, Will (1896–), 444, 446
Jarov, Sergey (1896–), 407, 413
Jehovah reigns, Tuckey, 184
Jenkins, John (1592–1678), 46
Jerome, Frederick, 315
Jesu, joy of man's desiring, Bach, 390
Jesu! the very thought is sweet, Wood, 292
Jesu! the very thought of Thee
   Bairstow, 369
   Whitehead, 386, 387
Jesu! thou dear Babe divine, Dickinson, 419–
   20
Jesu, Thou wast born to us, Fox, 390
Jesu, Word of God incarnate, Mozart; *see*
   Ave verum corpus
"Jesus Christ is risen today," hymn, 275
Jesus, my Saviour! look on me, Nevin, 339
Jesus! Name of wondrous love, Titcomb, 421
Johnson, John (d. ca. 1762), 125
Jommelli, Niccolo (1714–1774), 165
Jordan, Henry Bryce, 60*n.*, 62*n.*
Joubert, John (1927–), 298, 400–402
Jubilate, The, Emerson, 308, 309, 406
Jubilate Deo, P. James, 425*n.*
Judah, Gardiner, 236
Judas Maccabeus, Handel, 164, 228
Julian, John (1839–1913), 217*n.*, 279*n.*,
   303*n.*, 331*n.*, 430*n.*

Kalinnikov, Vassili (1866–1901), 317
Kallmann, Helmut (1922–), 382*n.*
Kastalsky, Alexander (1856–1926), 413
Keach, Benjamin (1640–1704), 127
Keble, John (1792–1866), 255, 279
Kelly, Michael (1762–1826), 248, 248*n.*
Kennedy, Michael, 346*n.*, 362, 362*n.*

*Kent, James (1700–1776), 110, 224, 224n., 228, 232, 232n., 235, 235n., 236, 237, 255

Key, Joseph (fl. 1790–1795), 117–19, 118n., 125, 225, 225n.

Key-change, 88–89, 111, 116, 149, 208, 374, 387

Kimball, Jacob (1761–1826), 213, 216, 222, 222n.

Kindlemarsh, Francis (fl. 1570), 15

King, Charles (1678–1748), 94, 103

King, Matthew P. (1733–1823), 232–33, 237

King, Robert, 131

King of glory, Candlyn, 431

King of love my Shepherd is, The
  Schnecker, 337
  Shelley, 339, 340

King shall rejoice, The
  Boyce, 111–12
  Turner, 77

Kinkeldey, Otto (1878–), 236, 236n.

Kirkpatrick, William J. (1838–1921), 261, 309, 309n., 311, 315

*Knapp, William (1698–1768), 141–48, 148n., 149, 155, 168, 186, 188, 192n., 193, 207, 208, 226

Koželuch, Leopold Anton (1752–1818), 235

Lamb of God
  Barber, 450
  F. M. Christiansen, 414

Langdon, Chauncey (fl. 1786), 194, 194n.

"Larks of Dean," 129–30, 138, 155

Latrobe, Christian Ignatius (1757–1836), 235

"Laudes Domini," Barnby, 261

Laus Deo! The Worcester Collection, Thomas, 214–16, 218–19, 222

Law, Andrew (1748–1821), 206–207, 209, 209n.

Lawes, Henry (1596–1662), 38, 84

Lawes, William (1602–1645), 47, 47n., 72

Le Huray, Peter, 5n., 8n., 14, 15, 24n.

Le Jeune, Claude (1528–1600), 222

Leader, The, Palmer, 309, 309n.

Leeds Parish Church, 258

Lefkowitz, Murray, 47n.

Leicestershire Harmony, The, J. Arnold, 149, 193

Lekberg, Sven (1899–), 446–47, 448, 449

Lesser Doxology, 25, 38, 77, 141, 149, 224

Let all mortal flesh keep silence
  Bairstow, 369
  Holst, 362–63

Let all the world in every corner sing, Rowley, 398

Let the shrill trumpets warlike voice (Urania), Lyon, 186–87t., 187

Let the words of my mouth, Attwood, 250

Let them give thanks, Williamson, 402

Let thy hand be strengthened, Blow, 84

Let Thy Holy Presence, Tchesnokov–Cain, 444

Let thy merciful ears, O Lord, Weelkes, 18

Lewis, Anthony (1915–), 84n.

Ley, Henry G. (1887–), 250n., 256n., 257n., 258n., 284n., 292n., 294n., 369n., 376n., 380, 392

Lichfield Cathedral, 109

Lift up your eyes, Billings, 204–205

Lightwood, James T., 130n.

Lilley, John M. (1939–), 303n.

Lining out, 171, 172, 260

Liszt, Franz (1811–1886), 286, 413

Lo! my shepherd is divine, Haydn, 234, 236

Lock Hospital, 155
  Chapel, 155
  Collection, Madan, 155–58, 211, 214, 217

Locke, Matthew (ca. 1630–1677), 43, 46–58, 60, 65, 65n.

Longman and Broderip, publishers, 244

The Lord, even the most mighty God, hath spoken, Crotch, 253

Lord, for thy tender mercies' sake, Farrant [Hilton], 241, 311

Lord, have mercy upon us, Mendelssohn, 250

Lord, how are they increased that trouble us, Kent, 235

Lord, how long wilt thou be angry, Purcell, 87

Lord of all power and might, George, 387

Lord is full of compassion, The, J. Clarke, 226

Lord is my light, The, Parker, 343–45

Lord is my shepherd, The
  Blow, 84–86
  Clokey, 428
  Greene, 159
  Kent, 235n.
  Matthews, 454
  Stanford, 290

Lord is my strength, The
  Croft, 98
  V. Novello, 254
Lord is my strength and my song, The, Greene, 108
Lord is risen indeed, The, Billings, 216, 222
Lord, let me know mine end, Locke, 65
Lord, Our God, have mercy (Hospodi Pomilui), Lvovsky, 412
Lord, thou hast been a refuge sure, Gibbs, 376
Lord, thou hast been our refuge
  Boyce, 115
  Vaughan Williams, 349–54, 419
Lord, when the sense of thy sweet grace, Berkeley, 394
Lord, who shall dwell in thy tabernacle, Cutler, 329–30
Lord's my shepherd, The, Titcomb, 421
Lord's Prayer, The, interpolated in anthem, 448
Lorenz, Edmund S. (1854–1942), 314–17, 319–21, 326
Lorenz, Ellen Jane (1907–), 317
Lost in the night, F. M. Christiansen, 414
Louis XIV (1638–1715), king of France (1643–1715), 43
Love came down at Christmas, Sowerby, 435, 440
Lovelace, Austin C. (1919–), 455, 458
Lowe, Edward (ca. 1610–1682), 37, 38
Lowens, Irving (1916–), 171n., 173n., 193, 193n., 207n.
Lullaby on Christmas Eve, F. M. Christiansen, 414
Lullay my liking, Holst, 363
Lully, Jean-Baptiste (1632–1687), 43, 62, 62n.
Lumb Chapel (Baptist), 129–30
Luther, Martin (1483–1546), 216
Lutheran
  hymn arrangements, 414
  use of term *motet*, 403
Lvov, Alexey (1798–1870), 412, 413
Lvovsky, G. V. (1830–1894), 412
*Lyon, James (1735–1794), 175, 177n., 178–87, 189, 197, 206
Lyra Davidica, 161

MacDermott, K. H., 92, 128–29
Mace, Thomas (1613–1709), 258, 258n.

Macfarlane, William C. (1870–1945), 414–15
Macfarren, George A. (1813–1887), 259
MacMillan, Keith, 382n.
MacRae, C. F., 386n.
*Madan, Martin (1726–1790), 155, 157–58, 164, 211, 212, 214, 217, 225, 228, 235
Madrigales and Ayres, Porter, 43
Magazines, music, 314–27, 428; *see also The Choir Herald, The Choir Journal, The Choir Leader, The Musical Times, The Organist, The Parish Choir, The Quarterly Anthem Folio, The Volunteer Choir, The Younger Choirs*
Mainzer, Joseph (1801–1851), 244
Mainzer's Musical Times and Singing Class Circular, 244
Malin, Don (1896–), 444, 445
Man born to toil, Holst, 363
Man that is born of a woman, Holden, 216
Mann, Elias (1750–1825), 217, 217n.
Manuscripts
  Br.Mus.Add.Ms. 30087, 22n., 23n.
  Br.Mus.Harley 6346, 27n.
  Br.Mus.Harley 7337–7342, 9n., 23, 32n., 33, 38n., 39n., 42n., 45n., 47n., 50, 53n., 54, 56, 58n., 60n., 61, 62n., 63, 64, 65n., 68n., 70, 73n., 75, 76n., 77n., 78, 80, 83, 87, 87n., 88n., 95n., 97n., 108n.
  Ch.Ch.Mus. 437, 38n.
  Ch.Ch.Mus. 1220–24, 38n.
  Library of Congress, ML 96.H83, 175n.
  Ordinale Exon. 1337, 7
Marche Romaine, Gounod, 317
Marriage Hymn, A, Lyon, 206
Marrocco, W. Thomas (1909–), 203n., 208n., 209n.
Marshall, Jane (1924–), 455–57
Martin, George C. (1844–1916), 274–79
Mary I (1516–1558), queen of England (1553–1558), 126
*Mason, Lowell (1792–1872), 168, 222, 229, 232, 234–37, 238, 238n., 240, 240n., 241, 241n., 259–60, 308, 309
Mason, William (1724–1797), 228
Mason, William (1829–1908), 241n.
Mass, Roman Catholic, 4
Masses, Vespers, Litanies, Hymns & Psalms, Carr, 224–25
Master, speak, V. D. Thompson, 428

Matthews, Thomas (1915–), 452–54
Maunder, John Henry (1858–1920), 290–91, 295, 317
May, J. G., 237
McCorkle, Donald M. (1929–), 229
McKinney, Howard D. (1890–), 413n.
Mein, John, 193
Melody, placement of, 148, 162–63, 165, 222
  by Billings, 203
Mendelssohn Collection, or Hastings and Bradbury's Third Book of Psalmody, The, 238, 238n.
Mendelssohn, Felix (1809–1847), 238, 247, 250, 272, 286, 298, 317, 370, 386
"Merrial," Barnby, 261
Messiah, Handel, 104–105, 118, 159, 208, 225, 253
Metcalf, Frank J. (1865–1945), 211n., 217, 217n., 228n., 240n.
Meter
  change of, 95, 111, 116, 149, 155, 158, 203, 216, 247, 330, 387, 394, 396, 441, 451
  free, 386, 430
  variable, 386, 387, 390
Meyer, Leonard, 449–50
Mighty fortress is our God, A, Mueller, 433, 436–37
Milman, Henry W. (1791–1868), 421
Milton, John I (1563–1647), or John II (1608–1674), 235
Mitchell, Nahum (1769–1853), 228
Modality, 346, 427
Modern Collection of Sacred Music, The, 210n.
Montagu-Nathan, M. (1877–1958), 413
Monteverdi, Claudio (1567–1643), 42–43
Montgomery, James (1771–1854), 433
Moravian music, 228, 229–31, 235
Morley, Thomas (1557–1603), 142n.
Morris, Mrs. C. W., 315
Most glorious Lord of lyfe! Gibbs, 376
Motet, 3, 4, 5, 68, 241, 284, 303, 383, 386
  adapted as anthem, 9, 10, 68, 226, 241, 292, 386
  term as used by Vaughan Williams, 348, 358
Mozart, Wolfgang Amadeus (1756–1791), 165, 168, 228, 232, 235, 236, 237, 247, 248, 250, 255

Mueller, Carl F. (1892–), 433, 436–37
Mundy, John (ca. 1529–1591), 8
Musica Deo Sacra, Tomkins, 24–25, 27
Musica getutscht, Virdung, 142n.
Musica Sacra; or Springfield and Utica Collections United, Hastings and Warriner, 238, 238n., 314n.
Musical Magazine, The, Law, 209n.
Musical Times, The, 244, 254–55, 262, 263, 287, 291, 314, 326, 365, 372, 391, 392n.
Musical Times and Singing Class Circular, The, 244
My faith looks up to thee, Schnecker, 337
*My God, my God, look upon me
  *Blow, 85
  Greene, 159
My song shall be alway, Purcell, 88
My song shall be of mercy and judgment, Kent, 224
My soul, there is a country, Parry, 284
My spirit on thy care, Macfarlane, 414

Nares, James (1715–1783), 116–17, 116n., 255, 259
Nathan, Hans, 200n., 209n.
National Singing Circular, The, Mainzer, 244
Naumann, Johann Gottlieb (1741–1801), 234
Ne irascaris, Domine, Byrd, 226
Neale, John Mason (1818–1866), 255, 291, 294, 376, 386, 389
Negro spirituals, 444–45
Neidlinger, William H. (1863–1924), 339, 341, 405, 427
Nevin, George B. (1859–1933), 323, 339, 427
Neumatic passages, 9
New American Melody, The, French, 208
New Universal Harmony, The, Bayley, 206, 206n., 207n.
New Set of Psalms, A, Knapp, 186t., 193
New York Collection of Sacred Harmony, The, 222n.
Newbigging, Thomas, 129
Newton, James Williams, 162–63, 163n.
Nicolai, Philipp (1556–1608), 417
Night is far spent, The, Cutler, 327
Nightingale, The, Tschaikowsky, 317
Niland, Austin, 45

Noble, T. Tertius (1867–1953), 290, 291,
    294–98, 383, 414, 430, 431, 446
Nonconformists, 90, 92, 126–27, 257, 326,
    459
  musical style of, 127, 258
  restrictions on, 127
Norden, N. Lindsay (1887–1956), 407, 413n.
North, Roger (ca. 1651–1734), 45, 45n.,
    46, 46n.
Northampton Collection of Sacred Harmony,
    The, Mann, 217n.
Not all the blood of beasts
  S. Arnold, 157–58
  Watts's hymn, 157–58
Novello, J. Alfred (1810–1896), 243, 344,
    260, 326, 405n.
Novello, Vincent (1781–1861), 120, 243,
    252, 262, 314
  as composer, 253–55, 262, 263
Now is Christ risen, Key, 118–19, 225
Now thank we all our God, Mueller, 433
Nuttall, John (fl. 1740), 129

O be joyful
  anonymous (Urania), 181t., 222, 224
  P. James, 425
O be joyful in the Lord, Read, 208
O be joyfull, Clarke, 95
O Christ, our true and only light, Malin, 445
O clap your hands
  Chetham, 133
  Green, 133
  Greene, 108
  Tans'ur, 141
  Vaughan Williams, 347–49, 419
O clap your hands/God is gone up, Gibbons,
    20–22
O clap your hands together
  J. Arnold, 149
  anonymous (Urania), 182
O clap your hands together, all ye people,
    M. Shaw, 374, 377
O come, all ye faithful, V. Novello, 263.
O come and mourn with me, D. H. Williams,
    454
O come let us sing unto the Lord, G. Young,
    454
O give thanks
  Humfrey, 62–63
  Purcell, 226

O give thanks unto the Lord
  Croft, 99–101
  Lowe, 38
O give thanks unto ye Lord (Urania), 185
*O give ye thanks unto the Lord, Tans'ur,
    189, 205
O God of my righteousness, Greene, 159
O God, O Spirit, Malin, 445
O God, thou art my God, Greene, 159
O God, thou hast cast us out, Weldon, 99
*O God, who by the leading of a star,
    Attwood, 248
O how amiable, Vaughan Williams, 355
O how amiable are thy dwellings, Weelkes,
    16–18
O living will, Stanford, 290
*O Lord, give thy Holy Spirit, Tallis, 9
O Lord God of hosts
  Crotch, 253
  Goldwin, 97
O Lord God of my salvation, Richardson, 125
O Lord, grant the King a long life
  Child, 40–41, 42
  Nares, 116
  Tomkins, 27
O Lord, how glorious, Goldwin, 97
O Lord, how manifold are Thy works,
    Barnby, 261
O Lord, I will praise thee, Jacob, 398–99
O Lord, look down from heaven, Battishill,
    122
O Lord, rebuke me not, Croft, 99
*O magnify the Lord, Bradbury, 239–40
O Nata Lux de Lumine, Tallis, 10n.
"O perfect Love," Barnby, 261
O praise God in his holiness
  Goldwin, 97
  Wise, 73, 75–76
O praise God in his sanctuary, Matthews, 454
O praise the Lord
  anonymous, 189
  Child, 39
O praise the Lord, all ye heathen, Tomkins, 32
O praise the Lord, all ye nations
  Berger, 451
  Selby, 226
O praise the Lord of heaven, Vaughan
    Williams, 346
O praise ye the Lord! prepare a new song,
    Whitaker, 168

O praise ye Lord of heaven (Urania), 185
O pray for the peace of Jerusalem
  Blow, 133
  King, 103
  Tomkins, 31
O sacred Head, F. M. Christiansen, 414
O sacrum convivium, Tallis, 9
O Saviour of the world, Goss, 256
O sing unto the Lord
  French, 208
  anonymous (*Urania*), 181
O taste and see, Vaughan Williams, 358, 359
O taste and see, how gracious the Lord is,
  Goss, 256
O thou to whom all creatures bow, Billings, 200
O Trinity of blessed light, France, 389–90
O what their joy and their glory must be,
  Harris, 376
O worship the King, George, 387
Obbligato instruments, 65, 76, 77, 82, 98, 99,
  337
Octave displacement of voice parts
  in American books, 179, 226
  in Russian liturgical music, 411–12
Octave-size
  anthems first printed in America, 337
  collections, 314
  journals, 244, 254–55, 314–27
  single copies in England, 244, 247, 260,
  299
Of one that is so fair and bright, Holst, 363
Old hundredth psalm tune, The, Vaughan
  Williams, 358–59
Oldroyd, George (1886–1951), 380
Olivet to Calvary, Maunder, 291
Olmstead, Clifton T., 170, 170n.
Only the sad of heart, Tschaikowsky, 317
Open our eyes, Macfarlane, 414
Opera in Russia, 413
Optional orchestra, 354
Opus numbers with anthems, 331n.
Oratorio, 232, 250, 252
  use of sections as anthems, 234, 255, 311
Orchestra; *see also* Instrumental music
  in American churches, 321
  with verse anthem, 47, 95n., 98, 103, 104,
  105, 111–12, 115
Organ
  absence in Russia, 407
  destruction of, in England, 128

  interludes, 44, 98, 158, 319, 372, 435, 445
  introductions, 274–75, 380, 414
  registration, 331
  use of, 27, 44–46, 92, 97, 103, 105, 106,
  111, 224, 263, 269, 296, 314, 383,
  387, 396, 398, 421, 425
Organist, The, 321
Order of the Psalms; *see* Psalms, ordering of
Original Sacred Music, Pettet, 250, 251n.
Ornamentation, vocal, 103, 116–17
Ostinato bass; *see* Ground bass
Our Lord is risen from the dead, S. Arnold, 224
*Ouseley, F. A. G. (1825–1889), 261, 274
Out of the depths, Kirkpatrick, 311
Overture to cantata anthem, 85
Oxford Book of Carols, 372
Oxford Movement
  in America, 327, 431
  in Canada, 383, 431
  in England, 255–56, 279, 291, 292, 294,
  296

Paddon, James (fl. 1820), 120, 120n.
Page, John (ca. 1760–1812), 42, 68, 95n.,
  97, 97n., 104–105, 106n., 108, 108n.,
  116n., 122n., 123, 243
Palestine, Crotch, 262
Palmer, Horatio R. (1834–1907), 262, 309,
  309n.
Parish Choir, The, 314
Parish church, English, 35, 92, 93, 105, 127
  compared to American, 193
  compared to cathedral, 93, 116, 261
  influence on American anthem, 203, 208,
  225, 241, 391
  music written for, 110, 118, 118n., 131–37,
  148–49
  and Nonconformist chapel, 127, 130, 226
Park Chapel Congregational Church, London, 391
Parker, Horatio William (1863–1919),
  342–45, 425
Parks, J. A., 317, 320
Parry, C. Hubert H. (1848–1918), 272, 280,
  284, 286–89, 291, 346
Pasquet, Jean (1896–), 444, 445–46
Pasticcio, 60
Pavane for the Early of Salisbury, Byrd, 386,
Peaker, Charles, 390, 390n.
Peck, James, 228

Pendulum, how to make, 210
Penitential Psalms, 14, 27
Pennicott, John, 129
Pepys, Samuel (1633–1703), 37, 37n., 39,
    39n., 44, 44n., 45, 45n., 49, 59n.,
    60, 60n., 62, 62n.
Performance practice
    American, 171–74, 193–94, 209–10
    biblical justification of singing, 173–74
    English cathedral, 258–59
    English parish church, 136, 139, 259
    Russian choral, 413
Pergolesi, Giovanni Battista (1710–1736),
    165, 235
Peter, Johann Friedrich (1746–1813), 229
Peters, Rev. Mr. Richard (fl. 1763), 175
Petits violons, Le, 43
Petrie, H. W., 315
Pettet, Alfred, 251n.
Pfautsch, Lloyd (1921–), 455
Philadelphia Harmony, Adgate, 217n.
Philadelphia Songster, The, Aimwell [Ad-
    gate], 217n.
Phillips, James E. Jr., 77n.
Pinkham, Daniel (1923–), 450
*Plaine and Easie Introduction to Practicall
    Musicke, A*, Morley, 142n.
Playford, Henry (1657–1720), 131–33, 168
Playford, John (1623–1686), 131, 172n.
Pleyel, Ignaz Joseph (1757–1831), 165, 235
Points of imitation, 22, 23, 73, 106, 122, 148,
    165, 203, 213, 369, 372
Ponder my words, Travers, 111
"Pop" idiom, 402
Porter, Walter (ca. 1595–1659), 42–43
Praise, Rowley, 396
Praise him, ye that fear him, Whitehead, 386
Praise the Lord, Porter, 42
*Praise the Lord, O Jerusalem
    **Clarke, 95
    Maunder, 291, 295
Praise the Lord, O my soul
    Creyghton, 58–59
    Greene, 108
Praise ye the Father, Gounod, 317
Prayer to Jesus, Oldroyd, 380
Preserve me, O God (Urania), 179
Prevent us, O Lord, Byrd, 14
Price, Ira Maurice, 14n.
Pring, (given name unknown), 237

Procter, Francis, 25n.
Promiscuous Singing, Hammett, 174
Protheroe, Daniel (1866–1934), 326
Psalm 96, Adler, 450
Psalm CXXII, Gibbs, 376
Psalm CXXXIV, Sowerby, 435
Psalm 149, P. James, 427
Psalm-Singer's Amusement, The, Billings,
    208n., 216n.
Psalm tune-books, 110, 110n., 175, 234n.,
    237, 260
Psalm tunes, 197, 216, 234
Psalmes, Songs, and Sonnets, Byrd, 10
Psalmist, The, Stow and Smith, 303, 303n.
Psalmist's Recreation, The, J. Arnold, 149
Psalmodist, The, Hastings and Bradbury,
    240n.
Psalmodist's Companion, The, French, 208
Psalmody Improved, Newton, 162, 163n.
Psalms as anthem texts, 24, 26–27, 106, 108
    conflations, 115
*Psalms, Hymns, and Anthems for the Found-
    ling Hospital*, Russell, 158n.
*Psalms, Hymns, and Anthems Used in the
    Chapel of the Hospital . . .*, 158
Psalms, metrical, 14, 26, 77, 92, 93, 105,
    127, 138, 171–87
Psalms of David for the Use of Parish Churches,
    Arnold and Callcott, 164
Psalms, ordering of, 25–26
    American variant, 25n.
Psalms, versified; *see* Psalms, metrical
Psalter, 25–26
    Ainsworth, 171
    Bay Psalm Book, 171, 172n.
    Genevan, 362
    John Playford, 172n.
    Ravenscroft, 138
    Sternold and Hopkins, 171, 178, 182
    Tate and Brady, 148, 165, 175, 177, 200
Psaltery, The, Mason and Webb, 241n.
**Purcell, Henry (1659–1695), 32n., 43, 49,
    58, 77, 82, 84, 85, 87–89, 91, 94, 95,
    103, 111, 133, 149, 225, 226, 235, 243,
    258, 280, 286, 317
Purcell's Sacred Music, V. Novello, 243
Puritans; *see also* Nonconformists: Dis-
    senters
    American, 170–71
    English, 36, 90, 126

Quarterly harmony, 387, 448, 449
Quarterly Anthem Folio, The, 317
Quartet, mixed solo
   in America, 240, 300, 304, 308, 315, 317,
     330, 331, 337
   in Canada, 386
   in England, 261, 263, 271, 280
   female, American, 321
   male, American, 321
Quartet choir, 300–301, 306, 313, 321, 327,
    330, 336, 337
Quodlibet, 224, 445

Rabanus Maurus, Archbishop (d. 856),
   396
Rachmaninoff, Sergey (1837–1943), 410–12,
   413
Ravenscroft Psalter, 138, 359
Read, Daniel (1757–1836), 208–209, 211,
   216
Reasonableness of Regular Singing, The,
   Symmes, 171
Recitative, 49, 76, 82, 105, 115, 232, 235,
   280, 330, 358, 383, 445
Reconciliation, Pfautsch, 455
Reese, Gustave (1899–), 289
Regular singing, 171–74
Rejoice in the Lord, Croft, 98–99
Rejoice in the Lord alway, Purcell, 363
Remember not, Lord, our offences, Purcell,
   87
Renew a right spirit within me, Davis, 433
Responses, choral, 319, 326
Restoration, of Charles II (1660), 32, 35,
    36–38, 39, 42
   period, 8, 42, 46, 53, 58, 95, 126, 128
Rich, Arthur Lowndes, 240
Richards, James H. (1933–), 124n.
Richardson, Vaughan (?–1729), 125
Ride on! ride on!, George, 387
Ride on, ride on in majesty, Titcomb, 421
Ridout, Godfrey, 383n., 384, 384n.
Rippon, John (1751–1836), 163–64, 164n.,
   216, 216n., 222, 222n.
Ritornello, 53, 62, 73, 82, 84, 85, 88, 226
   for organ alone, 89
Roberton, Hugh S. (1874–1952), 370, 372,
   374
Roberts, John Varley (1841–1920), 274,
   280, 285

Rochester Cathedral, 392
Rock, The, Eliot, 374
Rock of Ages, Buck, 331–33
Rogers, Benjamin (1614–1698), 35, 37, 42,
   42n., 125
Rogers, Lee, 317
Rolle, Richard (fourteenth century), 380
Roman school, 411
Root, George F. (1820–1895), 240, 304–305,
   308, 314
Rorem, Ned (1923–), 450
Rose, Bernard (1915–), 24n.
Rossetti, Christina (1830–1894), 435
Rossini, Gioacchino (1792–1868), 311
Routley, Erik (1917–), 15n., 24n., 358n.,
   370n.
Rowley, Alec (1892–1958), 394, 396
Royal Academy of Music, 400
Royal College of Music, 290, 292, 294, **346,**
   362, 376, 391
Royal Injunction of 1548, 3
Royal Melody Compleat, Tans'ur, 138–41,
   138n., 189–91, 193
Russell, William (1777–1813), 158n.
Russian
   influence on American anthems, 444
   liturgical pieces as anthems, 309, 339
   liturgy, 407
   music in America, 406–13
Russian Imperial Chapel, 407, 411
   choir in opera, 413
Russian Orthodox Church, 407
Ruth, Giardini, 158

Sacchini, Antonio (1730–1786), 216
Sacred Melodies, Gardiner, 236
Sadock the priest, Tomkins, 27
Saint-Saëns, Camille (1835–1921), 286
**Salvation belongeth to the Lord,* Kent, 235
Sarti, Giuseppe (1729–1802), 413
Sarum Use, 3, 4
Saul, Handel, 167
Save us, O Lord, Bairstow, 369
Saviour, when night involves the skies,
   Shelley, 339
Say, watchman, what of the night, Sullivan,
   262
Schnecker, P. A. (d. 1903), 320, 336–37
Schneider, Friedrich (1786–1853), 272
Schoenberg, Arnold (1874–1951), 449

Scholes, Percy A. (1877–1958), 42, 42n.,
    92n., 93n., 95n., 99n., 130, 130n.,
    244n., 252, 252n., 254, 254n., 256n.,
    262n., 286n., 291, 291n.
Schmidt, Bernard (Father Smith) (ca.
    1630–1708), 45
Schubert, Franz (1797–1828), 248
Schumann, Robert (1810–1856), 286
Scott, Clara H. (1841–1897), 309, 321n.
Scott, Lesbia, 441
Seasonal anthems
    Christmas, 224, 254, 262, 263, 264–68,
        290, 327, 342, 371–72, 383, 384, 394,
        427, 431, 435, 445, 455
    Easter, 116, 117, 118, 119, 216, 222, 224,
        254, 257, 269, 272–74, 274–75, 370,
        376, 383n., 386, 392, 396, 450, 454
Second Sett of Six Anthems, A, Chapple,
    241n.
Secular style distinguished from religious
    in America, nineteenth century, 321
    by Nares, 116–17
Seeing we also, Sowerby, 441
Seek ye the Lord, Roberts, 280
Seely, Raymond, 302, 306
*Selby, William (1738–1798), 207, 213, 226
Select Harmony, Law, 207, 207n.
Selection of Hymns from the Best Authors,
    Rippon, 163–64
Selection of Psalm and Hymn Tunes, A,
    Rippon, 163, 164n., 216
Sequence, melodic, 27n., 88, 229, 286, 421
Sermons; see also Singing-lectures
    about music, 173–74
    instead of sung prayers, 90
Seraph, The, Whitaker, 165, 167–68, 228
Serial techniques, 402
Service, Anglican, 4, 8, 32n., 106, 149, 259,
    260
    in America, 327
    canonic writing in, 32n.
Services and Anthems, in vocal score, The,
    Clarke-Whitfeld, 252n.
Set me as a seal upon thine heart, Walton, 394
Set pieces
    in America, 234, 240, 303
    in England, 99
Sett of New Psalms and Anthems, A, Knapp,
    141–48, 188
Shaw, Geoffrey (1879–1943), 372, 392, 427

Shaw, Harold Watkins, 84n.
Shaw, Martin (1875–1958), 371–75, 377–79,
    392, 427, 445n.
Shelley, Harry Rowe (1858–1947), 317,
    339–41, 405, 414, 427, 446
Shepherd, John (ca. 1521–1563), 8
Shepherds story, The, Dickinson, 417
Shirley, Walter (1725–1786), 164
Shofar is sounded, The, Dickinson, 419
Short Anthems, Sets One, Two, and Three,
    Clokey, 428
Sight singing, 244
    Hood's system, 309
Sims, Phillip W., 115n.
"Sine nomine," Vaughan Williams, 290
Sing, Alleluia forth, Buck, 331
Sing joyfully unto God our strength, Byrd,
    10, 13–14
Sing my soul, His wondrous love, Rorem, 450
Sing, O heavens
    Kent, 235
    Tours, 262–63
Sing praise to God who reigns above, Whitlock,
    392
Sing to the Lord of harvest, Willan, 384–85
Sing to the Lord with joyful voice, Watts,
    217; see also "Denmark"
Sing unto God, Purcell, 88
Sing unto the Lord, V. Novello, 254
Sing unto the Lord, O ye saints of his, Locke,
    47, 49–53
Sing we merrily, Chetham, 136–38
Sing we merrily unto God/Blow up the
    trumpet, Byrd, 10, 12, 14
Singing-lectures, 174, 194, 196–97
Singing-Master's Assistant, The, Billings,
    200n.
Singing pew
    in America, 197
    in England, 128, 255
Singing school, 174, 177, 189, 193, 194–97,
    216, 260, 303, 308
Singing societies, 232, 234, 238, 255; see
    also Choral societies
Skeat, Walter A., 2n.
Slonimsky, Nicolas (1894–   ), 407
Smart, Henry (1813–1879), 259, 326
Smetana, Bedřich (1824–1884), 419
Smith, John Christopher (1712–1795), 159
*Smith, John Stafford (ca. 1750–1836),

244–47
Smith, Joshua, 222
Smith, Leo (1881–), 390
Smith, Robert (ca. 1648–1675), 76
Smith, S. F., 303n.
Snow lay on the ground, The, Sowerby, 435
Social Harmony, or A Compilation of Airs, Duetts and Trios, Gould, 237, 406
Solo anthem, 88, 95, 97, 108, 111, 122, 253, 327
Some blessed day, Nevin, 339
Song of Solomon, The, 200
Song of Triumph, The, Palmer and Wright, 309, 309n.
Songs of Praise, Vaughan Williams, 359, 372
Songs of Sundrie Natures, Byrd, 10, 14, 15
Sonneck, O. G. (1873–1928), 175n., 177, 178–79, 183n., 184, 206n.
Sons of the Clergy, 95, 115
  Stewards of the, 115
Sons of Zion, come before him, Naumann, 234
Soprano voice, boys, 49, 53, 59, 65, 84, 89, 108, 115, 116, 255, 412, 413n.; *see also* Women in choirs
Souls of the righteous
  Boyce, 111
  Noble, 294–96
Souls of the righteous, The
  Nares, 117
  Vaughan Williams, 358, 359
South African College of Music, 400
Sowerby, Leo (1895–1968), 435, 438–41, 444, 448, 449
"Special" as euphemism for *anthem,* 403
Speech chorus, 455
Spenser, Edmund (ca. 1552–1599), 376
Spicker, Max (1858–1912), 337
Spohr, Louis (1784–1859), 272, 286, 296, 370
Spotless rose, A, Howells, 394–95
Squire, W. Barclay (1855–1927), 47n.
St. Anatolius (third century), 294
St. Andrew's, New York, 342
St. Bartholomew's Church, New York, 420
St. Bride's Church, London, 77n.
St. Cecilia's Day, 77, 77n.
St. George's, Windsor, 8, 39, 42, 92, 95, 105
  new organ for, 128

St. James group, 59–60, 76, 82, 89, 91, 103
St. Mary Magdalene, Church of, Toronto, 383
St. Paul, Mendelssohn, 250
St. Paul's Cathedral, 37, 77n., 82, 92, 94, 95, 106, 111, 115, 256, 259, 268
St. Paul's Church, Toronto, 383
St. Thomas Aquinas (ca. 1225–1274), 430
St. Thomas' Church, New York, 294, 430
Stainer, John (1840–1901), 262, 263, 268–80, 290, 291
Stanford, Charles V. (1852–1924), 272, 286–90, 294, 343, 346, 383
Stanley, John (1713–1786), 159, 225
Stanton, W. K. (1891–), 380
Steele, Anne (1716–1778), 167
Stephenson, Joseph, 193, 203, 207–208, 213, 216, 225, 226
Sterndale Bennett, William; *see* Bennett, William Sterndale
Stenhold, Thomas (?–1549), 14, 127
Stevens, Denis (1922–). 9n, 24n., 32n.
Stevens, R. J. S. (1757–1837), 95n., 97, 98, 98n., 106n., 108
Stevenson, Robert (1916–), 175n., 177n., 184
Stickney, John, 184, 189, 207
Stoughton Collection of Church Music, 229
Stow, Baron, 303n.
Stravinsky, Igor (1882–), 394, 449
Strong, Joseph (fl. 1773), 194, 194n.
Suffolk Harmony, The, Billings, 204, 205n.
Sullivan, Arthur (1824–1900), 261–62, 309
Summer ended, Wood, 294
Swan, Alfred (1890–), 412–13, 413n.
Swan, Timothy (1758–1842), 216
Sweet is thy mercy, Barnby, 261
Sweet Psalmist of Israel, The, Walter, 173–74, 173n.
Sweetly come those strains melodious, Root, 304–305, 308
Sweney, J. R. (1837–1899), 261, 309, 311–13
Sydney Conservatory, 402
Syllabic settings, early English, 9, 18, 23
Symmes, Thomas, 171–72
"Symphonies" in verse anthems, 44, 45, 46, 49, 50, 60, 61, 62, 65, 77, 88

*Tallis, Thomas (ca. 1505–1585), 9–10, 232, 255

*Tans'ur, William (1706–1783), 138–43, 155, 168, 188, 189–91, 193, 203, 205, 207, 209, 211

Tate, Nahum, (1652–1715), 77

Taylor, Raynor (ca. 1747–1825), 224

Tchaikovsky, Piotr Ilyitch (1840–1893), 286, 317, 406–407

Tchesnokov, Pavel (1877–1944), 413, 444

Te Deum, 228

Te Deum and Jubilate in D, Purcell, 77

Teach me, O Lord, Attwood, 248

Teach me, O Lord, the way of thy statutes, Rogers, 42

Temple, Anna, 427n.

Templi Carmina. Songs of the Temple, or Bridgewater Collection of Sacred Music, 228–31, 234, 235, 238, 406

Tempo changes, 116, 217, 247
   directions for ascertaining, 148

Tempo marks, early appearances, 98

Ten Anthems, Crotch, 252n.

"Tenor Bass" [baritone?], 108

Text-painting, 10, 23, 32, 73, 99, 115, 122, 149, 155, 208, 252, 296, 353, 374

Thanksgiving anthem, A, Thiman, 391

Thanksgiving anthems
   in Canada, 384
   in England, 98–99, 391

That I may dwell in the house of the Lord, anonymous, 234–35

Theatrical style
   in America, 217
   In England, 103, 158, 247

Thee we adore, Candlyn, 430

Then David mourned, Tomkins, 31

Theophilus, Bishop of Antioch (second century), 142

Theoretical introductions to tune-books, 133, 135–36, 138, 142–43, 148, 201, 216, 308, 309

There is a river, V. Novello, 254

There is joy in the presence of the angels of God, Sullivan, 262

There is no rose of such virtue, Oldroyd, 380

There were shepherds abiding in the fields, Willan, 383

They have taken away my Lord, Stainer, 269, 272–73

They that go down to the sea, Attwood, 250

Thiman, Eric H. (1900–), 391–92, 427

This is my commandment, Tallis, 9

This is the record of John, O. Gibbons, 23

Thomas, Isaiah, 214

Thompson, Van Denman (1890–1969), 317, 428, 430

Thou hast loved righteousness, Pinkham, 450

Thou Judge of quick and dead, S. S. Wesley, 259

Thou, O God, art praised in Sion
   Green?, 133, 135
   *S. Wesley, 251

Thou wilt keep him in perfect peace, Buck, 331

Three Introits, Whitlock, 392

Three Kings, The, Willan, 384

Thy beauty, O Israel, is slain, Aldrich adaptation of Wise's *How are the mighty fall'n*, 71–73

Thy way, O God, is holy, Goldwin, 97

Time-beating, 209

Time-values explained
   by Billings, 209, 210t.
   by Knapp, 148

Titcomb, H. Everett (1884–1968), 420–21, 424–25

To God the Lord a hymn of praise, S. Arnold, 165

Tomkins, Nathaniel (1599–1681), 24, 32

Tomkins, Thomas (1572–1656), 15, 23, 24–25, 27–33

Toplady, August M. (1740–1778), 331

Torches, Joubert, 400–401

Tours, Berthold (1837–1897), 262–68, 326

Tractarian Reform; *see* Oxford Movement

Travers, John (ca. 1703–1758), 110–11

Treasures in heaven, Clokey, 428

Trillo, 43

Tristan und Isolde, Wagner, 425

Tuckey, William (1708–1781), 175n., 184

Tudway, Thomas (1650–1726)
   activities, 45, 60, 68, 97, 106
   collection (Harley 7337–7342), 58, 60, 68, 73, 76, 85, 97, 106, 125
   compositions, 103

Tufts, John (1689–1750), 172, 173

Tune-books
   American, 236, 303, 303n.
   English, 127

Turn back, O man, Holst, 362, 372

Turn thou us, good Lord, Tomkins, 32–33

Turn thy face from my sins, Attwood, 311
Turner, James A., 174
Turner, William (1651–1740), 39, 60, 61, 76–82, 83, 84, 131
Trinity Anthems, The, Cutler, 327–30
Trinity Church, New York, 327
*23rd Psalm, The, Hopkinson, 175, 176, 177, 178–79
Twenty-third Psalm, The, Jacob, 397–98
*Two Celebrated Verses by Sternhold & Hopkins set to music (Urania), [Lyon], 182, 187
Two Kings, Clokey, 427–29
Two Short Anthems, Pasquet, 445
Tye, Christopher (ca. 1500–1573), 8–9

Unaccompanied singing by Nonconformists, 127–28; *see also A cappella*
Union Harmony, The, Holden, 211, 211*n.*, 212–14, 212*n.*, 216
Unison passages for choir, 214, 217, 263, 279, 291, 294, 341, 343, 349, 355, 363–65, 369, 384, 391, 394, 396, 398, 401, 421, 425, 431, 433, 445, 454
Universal Praise, Billings, 203–204
Universal Psalmodist, Williams, 193
Urania or a choice Collection of Psalm-Tunes, Lyon, 175, 177–89, 177*n.*, 206

Van Nice, John R., 111*n.*, 115*n.*
Vance, John P. (1867–1897), 314
Variants on "A mighty fortress," Darst, 445
Vaughan, Henry (1621–1695), 284
Vaughan Williams, Ralph (1872–1958), 290, 292, 346–62, 363, 370, 376, 386, 389, 394, 402, 405, 419, 427, 445*n.*
Venetian school, 43
  style of, 374
Vento, Mattia (1735–1776), 158
Verdi, Giuseppe (1813–1901), 286
Verse anthem, 18, 22, 23, 27, 32*n.*, 42, 43, 49*t.*, 50, 73, 76–82, 84, 85, 87, 95, 97–99, 98*t.*, 103, 106, 108, 111, 133, 248, 252, 253, 274, 327, 330, 383, 387
  definition, 58
  with instruments, 43–44, 45, 46–53, 76–79, 82, 98–99
Vesper Hymn, Bortniansky, 238, 309, 406

Vicars-choral, 5
Victory Te Deum, Titcomb, 421
Vingt-quatre violons du Roi, 43–46
Viotti, Giovanni Battista (1755–1824), 235
Virdung, Sebastian (ca. 1465–?), 142*n.*
Virginal music, 386
Vital spark of heavenly flame, Pope; *see* "The Dying Christian"
Vocal Harmony, Being a Collection, Blake, 225*n.*
Volume of Sacred Music, containing Thirty Anthems, Hubbard, 226*n.*
Volunteer Choir, The, 319
Volunteer choirs, 136–38, 291, 313
  American, 196–97, 300, 301, 306, 314–17, 425, 448–49
  Canadian, 383
  English, 216

Wagner, Richard (1813–1883), 286, 326
Wake, awake, for night is flying, F. M. Christiansen, 416–17
Wake the song of jubilee, Sweney, 311–13
Walker, Thomas (late eighteenth century), 163
Walmisley, Thomas Attwood (1814–1856), 248, 250
Walter, Thomas (1696–1725), 172–74
Walton, William (1902–), 392, 394, 402
Wanless, Thomas (d. 1721), 207, 222
Warriner, Solomon (1778–1860) 238, 302
Washington Cathedral, 441*n.*, 442–43
Watchman, tell us of the night, Mason, 240
Watts, Isaac (1674–1748), 127, 157, 167, 168, 177, 217, 222, 349, 380, 386
Ways of Zion do mourn, The, Handel, 104
We give thanks to thee, Glarum, 451
We have heard with our ears
  Aldrich, 125
  Howells, 394
We have thought of thy loving kindness, Buchanan, 319–20
We praise thee, O God, Handel, 226
We will rejoice in thy salvation, Croft, 99, 102
Webb, George J. (1803–1887), 240, 241, 241*n.*
Webbe, Samuel (1740–1816), 122, 124, 224, 262
Wedding music, 112

Weelkes, Thomas (ca. 1575–1623), 15–19

Weigh House Chapel, London, 260

Welcome, Yule, Parry, 286

Weldon, John (1676–1736), 94, 99, 131, 226

Wellesz, Egon (1885–), 2*n.*

Wesley, Charles (1707–1788), 130, 167, 168, 250, 430–31, 454

Wesley, John (1703–1791), 130

*Wesley, Samuel (1766–1837), 250–52

Wesley, Samuel Sebastian (1810–1876), 258–59, 260, 261

West, Benjamin, 207

West Gallery tradition, 138, 194, 255, 296, 302; *see also* Gallery musicians description, 118, 118*n.*, 128–29

West Presbyterian Church, New York, 336

Westminster Abbey, 37, 42, 82, 92, 94, 358

Westrup, Jack A. (1904–), 43*n.*

What a wonder, Dickinson, 419

What cheer, Walton, 392

What Child is this, Candlyn, 431

Wheatley, Henry B., 37*n.*, 60

When I survey the wondrous cross
  Noble, 431
  Stanton, 380

When the King comes in, Gabriel, 319

When the Son of man, Locke, 53, 55–57

When the Son of man shall come, Kent, 237

Wherewithall shall a young man cleanse his way, King, 103

While shepherds watched, Stanford, 290

Whitaker, John (1776–1847), 165, 167–68, 228, 229

White, Robert (ca. 1530–1574), 8

Whitehead, Alfred Ernest (1887–), 382, 386–89, 390, 430, 431

Whitlock, Percy W. (1903–1946), 392

Whittier, John Greenleaf (1807–1892), 372

Who can tell how oft he offendeth, Weldon, 103

Whole Booke of Psalmes
  J. Playford, 173
  Sternhold and Hopkins, 14

Widdub, (given name unknown), 237

Wilhem, Guillaume-Louis [*recte* Bocquillon] (1781–1842), 244

Willan, Healey (1880–1968), 382–85, 386, 387, 390, 430, 431

Willcocks, David (1919–), 392*n.*

William III and Mary II (reg. 1689–1694), 84, 85, 89, 127

Williams, Aaron (1731–1776), 193, 203, 207–208, 213, 216, 225, 226

Williams, David H. (1919–), 454

Williams, David McK. (1887–), 420–23

Williams, Roger (ca. 1604–1683), 171

Williamson, Malcolm (1931–), 398, 402

Willis, Richard Storrs (1819–1900), 302*n.*

Wilson, Ira B., 315

Wilson, John (1595–1674), 37, 38

Wilson, John (twentieth century), 45*n.*

Winchester Cathedral, 258

Winkworth, Catherine (1829–1878), 291

Wisdom of Solomon, 117, 358

Wise, Michael (ca. 1648–1687), 39, 60, 70–71, 73–76, 82, 84, 133, 134

With a voice of singing, G. Shaw, 372–74

With joyful hearts and tuneful song [Holden?], 216–17

Woman of Samaria, The, Bennett, 311

Women as composers, 309, 315, 317, 320–21

Women in choirs
  affected by Oxford Movement, 255–56, 296
  American, 196
  English rural, 196

Wood, Abraham (1752–1804), 216

Wood, Charles (1866–1926), 290, 291, 292, 294, 346, 383, 389

Woodbury, Isaac (1819–1858), 240

Woodford, Bishop J. R., 430*n.*

Woodman, Raymond H. (1861–1943), 339

Wooler, Alfred (1867–1937), 342

Worcester Cathedral, 110, 259

Worcester Collection of Sacred Harmony, The, 207

Word-painting; *see* Text-painting

Wordsworth, Christopher (1807–1885), 3*n.*

Worgan, John (1724–1790), 158, 159

Worship, G. Shaw, 372

Worship Christ, the newborn King, Mueller, 433

Worship, concept of, 302

Worship, restricted during Commonwealth, 33–35

Wranitzky, Paul, (1756–1808), 235

Wright, R. P., 262, 309

Wulstan, David, 22*n.*

Ye Centennial. A Quire Booke for Folke Old and Younge, 222
Young, Gordon (1919–), 454
Young, Robert Hexter (1923–), 127, 129
Younger Choirs, The, 317

Zadock the priest
  Handel, 104
  Lawes, 38
Zingarelli, Nicola (1752–1837), 241